The Blair Legacy

The Blair Legacy

Politics, Policy, Governance, and Foreign Affairs

Edited By

Terrence Casey
Rose-Hulman Institute of Technology, USA

First published 2009 by
PALGRAVE MACMILLAN

Palgrave Macmillan in the UK is an imprint of Macmillan Publishers Limited,
registered in England, company number 785998, of Houndmills, Basingstoke,
Hampshire RG21 6XS.

Palgrave Macmillan in the US is a division of St Martin's Press LLC,
175 Fifth Avenue, New York, NY 10010.

Palgrave Macmillan is the global academic imprint of the above companies
and has companies and representatives throughout the world.

Palgrave® and Macmillan® are registered trademarks in the United States,
the United Kingdom, Europe and other countries.

ISBN-13: 978-0-230-21661-7   hardback
ISBN-10: 0-230-21661-7   hardback
ISBN-13: 978-0-230-21662-4   paperback
ISBN-10: 0-230-21662-5   paperback

This book is printed on paper suitable for recycling and made from fully
managed and sustained forest sources. Logging, pulping and manufacturing
processes are expected to conform to the environmental regulations of the
country of origin.

A catalogue record for this book is available from the British Library.

Library of Congress Cataloging-in-Publication Data

The Blair legacy : politics, policy, governance, and foreign affairs / edited
  By Terrence Casey.
      p. cm.
  Includes bibliographical references and index.
  ISBN 978-0-230-21661-7
  1. Great Britain—Politics and government—1997–2007. 2. Blair, Tony,
    1953– I. Casey, Terrence.

JN238.B55 2009
320.95109'0511—dc22   2008041051

10 9 8 7 6 5 4 3 2 1
18 17 16 15 14 13 12 11 10 09

Printed and bound in Great Britain by
CPI Antony Rowe, Chippenham and Eastbourne

This book is dedicated to my wife, Allison, who is more wonderful than she realizes and more tolerant of me than she ought to be, and to the best three things to come out of the Blair years – Maria, Jack, and Oliver.

Contents

Tables

Figures

Preface and Acknowledgements

The genesis of *The Blair Legacy* was a conference organized by me under the auspices of the British Politics Group of the American Political Science Association. By late 2006 Tony Blair announced that he would be stepping down as prime minister, although he had yet to set the date. It seemed an opportune moment to organize a conference to assess his legacy. This germinated into a conference entitled 'Britain after Blair: The Legacy and the Future' held in Chicago in conjunction with the August 2007 meeting of APSA. This conference pulled together many of the premier scholars of British politics from the US, UK, and continental Europe. As fate would have it, Blair stepped down at the end of June 2007, just two months before we met. The programme was organized around two key questions: What has been the legacy of the Blair government, both in terms of politics and public policy? What are the likely directions for the future, either under the leadership of Gordon Brown or beyond? Many, although not all, of the chapters in this book began as presentations at that conference. Many other participants in the conference, for various reasons, did not end up contributing chapters to this volume. Nevertheless, they were an integral part of this project and deserve mention: Ray Barker, John Coakley, John Curtice, Arthur Cyr, Glen M. E. Duerr, Richard Flickinger, Jane Green, Scott Greer, William Hazelton, Holly Jarman, Grant Jordan, Caroline Kenny, Michael Macaulay, William Maloney, Jeff McCausland, James Mitchell, Richard Rose, Douglas Stuart, Donley Studlar, Paul Whiteley, John Wilson, Tom Wolf, and Joel Wolfe.

This project would have never gone from idea to fruition without the efforts of a large supporting cast. Conferences first of all require financial support, and 'Britain After Blair' was generously funded by three academic co-sponsors: the Department of Humanities and Social Sciences at the Rose-Hulman Institute of Technology, headed by Caroline Carvill; the Department of Political Science at Purdue University, chaired by Bert Rockman; and the Department of Political Science and Public Administration at Roosevelt University, under the leadership of David Hamilton. We also received support from the Palgrave journal *British Politics*, Routledge Journals, and Professor David Coates. Merry Miller at Rose-Hulman gave invaluable administrative assistance prior to the event, and Amanda Stephan and Jon Atkinson – two of my best students – travelled with me to Chicago to help run the conference itself.

Conference papers, of course, do not automatically become books. This book would not have come to be without the interest and support of Amy Lankester-Owen at Palgrave Macmillan, who was enthusiastic for the project even when the conference was still in the planning stages. Thanks also to

Gemma D'Arcy-Hughes, Alison Howson and the many other excellent folks at Palgrave Macmillan for seeing it through the production process.

I must also commend all the contributors to this volume, (almost) all of whom got their contributions in on time, on topic, within the word limit, and in the proper format. More importantly, I greatly appreciate the good-natured manner in which they accepted my numerous editorial critiques and pestering requests throughout the process. Others also went above and beyond the call in offering feedback and review. Scott Greer offered invaluable and timely assistance. Alix Howard suffered through numerous drafts of the introductory chapter and showed an amazing ability to turn my rough verbal constructions into elegant edifices. The quality of the presentation owes much to his keen eye. Jerold Waltman, Jack Moran, Jon Tonge, and Wyn Grant were also kind enough to offer advice on the introduction. My gratitude toward Wyn Grant, in fact, extends well beyond his contribution to this book. Going back to my graduate school days, when he generously offered to assist an American graduate student who emailed him out of the blue, he has provided me with support and guidance that has been invaluable in helping me grow as a scholar – and I am sure I am only one of many who would say the same. He also represents something of an ideal role model for any budding political scientist: he focuses on real politics rather than trendy theory; he eschews partisanship and ideology, tempering his analysis with a reasoned skepticism; and his research is always thorough, insightful, and – separating him from the bulk of the profession – readable. I should hope to be that good some day.

This is also the first book ever published with direct links to the British Politics Group, for which I am proud to serve as the Executive Director. The BPG is without doubt one of the most engaging and enjoyable groups of scholars to which I have had the pleasure to be affiliated. Thanks go out to all of the members of the BPG, especially those on the Executive Committee and the officers of the group at the time of the conference – Wyn Grant, Terry Royed, Joel Wolfe, and Tom Wolf. And a special thanks to Donley Studlar, whose spectacular legacy as the previous Executive Director of the BPG provided me with the opportunities to make this conference and book happen.

Lastly, an extra large thanks to my wife, Allison and my three children – Maria, Jack, and Oliver – for tolerating my long days (and some nights) at work as I struggled to pull all of this together. But it is all done, so now we can finally go to the zoo.

I end on an ironic note. By chance this manuscript was completed on 27 June 2008 – one year to the day that Tony Blair stepped down as prime minister. We shall have to see how well our collective wisdom holds up on subsequent anniversaries.

Terrence Casey

Notes on Contributors

James E. Alt is Frank G. Thomson Professor and Director of Graduate Studies in the Department of Government at Harvard University. He is author, co-author, or co-editor of *The Politics of Economic Decline* (Cambridge University Press, 1979), *Political Economics* (University of California Press, 1983), *Advances in Quantitative Methods* (Elsevier, 1980), *Cabinet Studies* (Macmillan, 1975), *Perspectives on Positive Political Economy* (Cambridge University Press, 1990), *Competition and Cooperation* (Russell Sage, 1999), and *Positive Changes in Political Science* (University of Michigan Press, 2007). He has been a Guggenheim Fellow and is a member of the American Academy of Arts and Sciences.

Tim Bale teaches British and comparative party politics at Sussex University. He is currently researching and writing two books on the Conservative Party – one on the Conservative Party from Thatcher to Cameron for Polity and a longer-term study for Oxford University Press. He is also the author of *European Politics: A Comparative Introduction* (Palgrave Macmillan, 2008) and has edited and contributed to a special edition of the *Journal of European Public Policy* on centre right parties and immigration and integration policy in Europe. This will be published as a book by Routledge in due course.

Mark Bennister is an ESRC-funded doctoral researcher, studying comparative prime ministerial leadership in Britain and Australia, in the Department of Politics and Contemporary European Studies at the University of Sussex. He has published on prime ministerial predominance in the *British Journal of Politics and International Relations* and *Parliamentary Affairs*, and has been a visiting research student at the Australian National University in Canberra. He gained an MSc in Social Research Skills (Political Science) from Sussex University and an MA in Contemporary European Studies from Loughborough University. He previously worked as an executive officer in the Political Branch of the Australian High Commission in London.

Mark Bevir is a professor in the Department of Political Science at the University of California, Berkeley. He is author of *The Logic of the History of Ideas* (1999), *New Labour: A Critique* (2005) and has co-authored with R.A.W Rhodes *Governance Stories* (2006), Interpreting British Governance (2003).

Jonathan Bradbury is the author of *Union and Devolution* (Palgrave Macmillan, forth 2009), editor of *Devolution, Regionalism and Regional Development: The UK Experience* (Routledge, 2006) and *British Regionalism and Devolution* (Routledge, 1997) as well as guest editor of special editions of *Regional and Federal Studies and Regional Studies*. He has published articles in a wide range of journals including *Political Studies, British Journal of Politics and International Relations, and Parliamentary Affairs*, and has directed or participated in ESRC-funded research projects on devolution, political parties, and representation. He is the co-convener of the UK PSA Territorial Politics Research Network and is academic convener for the UK PSA annual conference, Swansea University 2008.

Ted R. Bromund is the Margaret Thatcher Senior Research Fellow at the Heritage Foundation. He has published articles on British politics and Anglo-American relations in *Contemporary British History, Historical Research, New England Quarterly, and Parliamentary History*. He received his PhD in History in 1999 from Yale University. His thesis was awarded the Samuel H. Beer Dissertation Prize from the British Politics Group of the American Political Science Association in 2000, and he is under contract with Frank Cass for *Selling Europe: The Struggle Over European Integration in Britain, 1956–63*, a book based on his revised thesis.

Terrence Casey is an associate professor of Political Science at the Rose-Hulman Institute of Technology, where he has taught since receiving his doctorate from George Washington University in 2000. He is the executive director of the British Politics Group of the American Political Science Association. His previous publications include *The Social Context of Economic Change in Britain* (Manchester University Press, 2002) and numerous articles in such journals as *Political Studies, Social Science Quarterly, and Comparative European Studies*. His research interests include British political economy, models of capitalism, and issues of globalization.

David Coates has held the Worrell Chair of Anglo-American Studies at Wake Forest University since 1999. He was previously professor of Contemporary Political Economy at the University of Leeds, and then professor of Labour Studies at the University of Manchester, both in the UK. He has written extensively on UK labour politics, comparative political economy, and US domestic and foreign policy. Recent publications include *Models of Capitalism* (2000), *Blair's War* (with Joel Krieger, 2004), *Prolonged Labour: The Slow Birth of New Labour Britain* (2005), and *A Liberal Tool Kit: Progressive Responses to Conservative Arguments* (2007).

David Cutts is Senior Research Fellow at the Institute of Social Change at the University of Manchester. His main research interests are political behaviour and participation with particular emphasis on the importance of context and the application of quantitative methods. He has published in a number of refereed journals including the *British Journal of Political Science, Political Geography, and the Journal of Elections* and *Public Opinion*.

David Denver is professor of Politics at Lancaster University. Among other works, he is the author of *Elections and Voters in Britain*.

John Dumbrell is a graduate of Cambridge and Keele Universities. He has held appointments at Manchester Metropolitan University and at the universities of Keele, Leicester, and Durham, where he is currently professor of Government in the School of Government and International Affairs. His books include *The Making of US Foreign Policy* (1990 and 1997), *The Carter Presidency: A Reevaluation* (1995), *American Foreign Policy: Carter to Clinton* (1997), *A Special Relationship: Anglo-American Relations in the Cold War and After* (2001), *President Lyndon Johnson and Soviet Communism* (2004), and *A Special Relationship: Anglo-American Relations from the Cold War to Iraq* (2006). He has recently co-edited, with David Ryan, a book of essays entitled *Vietnam in Iraq: Tactics, Lessons, Legacies and Ghosts* (2007). He is currently researching the foreign policy of President Bill Clinton.

Stephen Benedict Dyson is an assistant professor in the Department of Political Science at the University of Connecticut. His research interests are in psychological influences on foreign policy decision-making, with particular focus on the Blair years. Recent work has appeared in *Political Psychology and Foreign Policy Analysis*. Prior to moving to the University of Connecticut, he was the Byron K. Trippet Assistant Professor of Political Science at Wabash College, in Crawfordsville, IN.

Florence Faucher-King received her BA in Politics from Bordeaux and a PhD in Comparative Politics, *mention Félicitations*, from Aix-en-Provence in 1997. She is currently an associate professor in European studies, political science, and sociology at the Max Kade Center for European and German Studies at Vanderbilt University. Previous positions included *Chargée de recherche* at CEVIPOF Sciences-Po Center for Political Research in Paris and serving as a lecturer at the University of Stirling in England. Professor Faucher-King's publications include *Tony Blair 1997-2007: Le bilan des réformes*, with Patrick Le Galès, (Paris: Presses de Sciences Po, 2007); *Changing Parties: An Anthropology of British Political Party Conferences*, (Houndsmills/New York: Palgrave Macmillan, 2005); and *Les habits verts de la politique*, (Paris: Presses de Sciences Po, 1999), winner of the 2000 Habert Prize (*Prix Habert*) for the best book on political studies by a young researcher. Her research interests include political activism, political parties, green politics, British and French politics, political anthropology, and political consumerism.

Justin Fisher is professor of Political Science at Brunel University and co-editor of the *Journal of Elections, Public Opinion & Parties*. He has published widely on many aspects of elections, campaigning, parties, and political finance.

Chris Game is an Honorary Senior Lecturer at the University of Birmingham's Institute of Local Government Studies (INLOGOV), where he has worked since 1979, writing extensively on all aspects of the politics of sub-central government. He is joint author of the leading text on *Local Government in the United Kingdom* (Palgrave Macmillan), currently in its fourth edition, and recently completed a thematic paper for the independent Councilors Commission that reported to Secretary of State Hazel Blears in December 2007.

Wyn Grant is president of the UK Political Studies Association and a member of the Executive Committee of the International Political Science Association. He has published extensively in a number of areas of political science, but his research is now with biological scientists on plant protection products, cattle diseases, and the environmental footprint of horticulture.

Alistair Howard joined Temple University's Political Science Department in 2000. He teaches political economy, comparative politics, and public policy. His research interests include the politics of capitalism in liberal market economies, chiefly Britain and the United States. His undergraduate degree is from Hertford College, Oxford, and he completed his doctorate in 2004 at George Washington University, and has published in *West European Politics*.

Scott James is a doctoral research student at the University of Manchester, and is currently in the process of completing an ESRC-funded project analysing the pervasive impact of European integration on national patterns of policymaking in the UK and Ireland since 1997. He has presented papers at international conferences in both the UK and US and has a forthcoming article on the EU policy process under Blair in *Public Administration*. Scott James graduated from the University of Liverpool in 2002 and has served as co-editor for the postgraduate journal *Political Perspectives* since October 2006.

Joel Krieger is the Norma Wilentz Hess Professor of Political Science at Wellesley College. Professor Krieger's works include, *Globalization and State Power: Who Wins When America Rules?* (Pearson Longman, 2005); with David Coates, *Blair's War* (Polity Press, 2004); *British Politics in the Global Age* (Polity Press, 1999); and *Reagan, Thatcher and the Politics of Decline* (Polity Press and Oxford University Press, 1986). Krieger also served as editor-in-chief of the *Oxford Companion to Politics of the World* (1993, 2001).

Richard Maiman is professor of Political Science at the University of Southern Maine and a visiting fellow of the Human Rights Centre at the University of Essex. He is the co-author of *American Constitutional Law: Introduction and Case Studies*, and *Divorce Lawyers at Work: Varieties of Professionalism in Practice*, which won the American Political Science Association's Pritchett Award as the 'best book on law and courts published in 2001'.

Kai Oppermann is assistant professor at the Institute for Political Science, University of Cologne, where he has been working since 2002. He has recently finished his PhD on 'Principals and Agents in Two-Level Games: The Domestic Constraints of British European Policy under the Blair Government (in German)' (VS Verlag, 2008). He has studied at the Universities of Marburg, Canterbury (UK), and Berlin. His recent publications include 'Public Opinion and the Development of the European Security and Defense Policy', in *European Foreign Affairs Review* 12 (2) 2007, 149-67 and 'Transatlantic Conflict and Cooperation: What Role for Public Opinion?' in *Journal of Transatlantic Studies*, 5 (1) 2007, 43-61 (both with Alexander Höse). He has also published several German-language articles on current British European policy.

Calum Paton has been professor at Keele University since 1993. Between 2000 and 2006 he was (non-executive) chairman of the University Hospital of North Staffordshire NHS Trust, one of the UK's largest NHS hospitals. In 2006, he published *New Labour's State of Health: Political Economy, Public Policy and the NHS* (Ashgate). In 2000, he published *World, Class, Britain: Political Economy, Political Theory and British Politics* (Macmillan). He is the author of eight other books and he is editor-in-chief of the *International Journal of Health Planning and Management* (Wiley). His main research interests are the politics of health policy and health system reform.

Nick Randall is a lecturer in British Politics at the University of Newcastle. His research on the politics of New Labour forms part of a general research interest in social democracy and British political parties and their ideologies. In addition, he holds research interests in respect of the issue of European integration in UK politics and the politics of the media, particularly in respect of political cinema.

Andrew Russell is senior lecturer in Politics at the University of Manchester. He has published extensively on party politics and all aspects of electoral behaviour and engagement. He is co-author (with Ed Fieldhouse) of *Neither Left Nor Right? The Liberal Democrats and the Electorate* published in 2005 by Manchester University Press. In 2004 he was a board member for the Electoral Commission's Review of the Minimum Age for Voting and Candidature in UK elections.

James Sloam is lecturer in politics and international relations at Royal Holloway, University of London. His research focuses on political parties and social democracy in Europe. He has published books and articles on German Social Democracy, the British Labour Party, and the Communist Successor Parties of East Central Europe. Current interests also include citizenship and political participation with respect to youth participation in democracy and political science education.

Mark Stuart is a researcher in the School of Politics at the University of Nottingham, where he helps run a long-running project on backbench voting behaviour. He is also a political biographer, having published *John Smith: A Life* (2005) and *Douglas Hurd: The Public Servant* (1998). He writes a regular political column in the *Yorkshire Post*.

Jonathan Tonge is professor of Politics in the School of Politics and Communication Studies at the University of Liverpool. His recent books include *Northern Ireland* (Polity, 2006), *The New Northern Irish Politics* (Palgrave Macmillan, 2005), and *Sinn Fein and the SDLP* (Hurst/O'Brien 2005, with Gerard Murray). He is co-editor, with Andrew Geddes, of a UK general election book series (the latest being *Britain Decides: The UK General Election*, Palgrave Macmillan, 2005). Recent articles include items in *Political Psychology, Political Studies, Electoral Studies, Party Politics*, and *Terrorism and*

Political Violence. Professor Tonge is Chair of the Political Studies Association of the UK.

Jerold Waltman holds a PhD from Indiana University. He held teaching positions at Louisiana College and the University of Southern Mississippi before moving to Baylor University. His recent publications include *Minimum Wage Policy in Great Britain and the United States* (2008), *The Case for the Living Wage* (2004), and *The Politics of the Minimum Wage* (2000) along with articles in *Policy Studies*, the *Journal of Supreme Court History*, and the *Journal of Labor Research*. Currently he is working on a project involving federalism and the free exercise of religion.

Introduction: How to Assess the Blair Legacy?

Terrence Casey

On the morning of 2 May 1997, an exhausted and victorious Tony Blair arrived at 10 Downing Street amid cheers and flag-waving supporters. After 18 years in the wilderness, Labour was back—unquestionably so, with its majority of 179. It was, of course, a rebranded party born of past defeat: not the Labour of beer and sandwiches, but "New Labour" of claret and cool Britannia. That morning, all seemed within the grasp of the new, vibrant prime minister. And the contrast to John Major could not have been starker. The Conservatives were a lackluster, exhausted government, whose final years were marked by policy drift and political sleaze. By dragging Labour back to the political center, Blair and his allies hoped not only to win the election, but also to make it once again an enduring party of government in the eyes of the electorate. In their manifesto they exclaimed that Britain deserved better. Hospitals, schools, roads—all things they said the Tories neglected—would be put right. With Blair leading the way, New Labour was going to make Britain great again. Blair told the Downing Street crowd, "Today, we are charged with the deep responsibility of government. Today, enough of talking—it is time now to do."

For the public a decade on, however, the Blair governments simply had not done enough. His 1997's approval ratings of 72 percent were replaced by active dislike of the man and gray disillusionment with his administration. The PM's approval plunged to 28 percent by April 2007 (Ipsos MORI, 2007b). Yet this is something of a paradox. By many of the objective measures of political performance—economic growth, low unemployment, and improved public services—the Blair government was a success. But the public was having none of it. This collective funk was captured in a survey published shortly before he left office: clear majorities felt the quality of life and the delivery of public services had suffered under New Labour. Only 27 percent thought the country a more successful place than in 1997; only 26 percent gave the government a positive overall rating.[1]

If domestic discontent weakened Blair's popularity, his decision to participate in the US-led invasion of Iraq in March 2003 left it mortally wounded. His party also turned against him. Despite delivering electoral riches, the

1

relationship was never strong. With no connections to the union move-ment, he was never really one of them; it was from the start a marriage of convenience. The Iraq decision was too much for them. The Chancellor of the Exchequer Gordon Brown had been the long serving heir-apparent, going back to the purported deal struck between the two at their Granita meeting in May 1994. In the wake of Iraq, a growing number of Labour backbenchers wanted that day to come sooner rather than later. Even before the 2005 general election Blair felt obliged to publicly state his intention to step down before the end of the parliament. Impatient for a date certain, a handful of junior government aides tried to force the issue by resigning in fall of 2006. The mini-coup attempt failed, but forced the prime minister to set the timetable for withdraw. In May he announced that he would step down in 27 June 2007.

On that spring morning Prime Minister Blair stepped through the famous front door of Number 10 to nothing more than the snaps of cameras, and headed for his final Question Time in the Commons. It was an uncharac-teristically mild and laudatory affair, with relatively softball questions and best wishes from the leaders of the Conservatives and Liberal Democrats. Even the often acerbic Democratic Unionist Leader Ian Paisley had nothing but kind words. To conclude, Blair simply stated, "I wish everyone, friend or foe, well. And that is that. The end." He exited to a standing ovation. After a brief meeting with the Queen, he slipped off the British political stage, no longer wanted by his party, largely unloved by his people. Brown, the media anointed "dour Scotsman," stepped before the banked journalists on Downing Street and quoted his old school motto: "I will try my utmost." The glitz and glamor of Blair's entry was nowhere to be seen. The image was one of sober dedication, the mood serious. The Blair era had come to an end.

Tony Blair was one of few British premiers to dominate their age. Yet what is his lasting importance? This volume examines the legacy of Blair and his three New Labour governments. Used here, "legacy" means the ways Labour altered—or did not alter—the structures and relationships between institu-tions, changed the terms and the limits of political debate, established an ide-ological stamp, transformed economic management, and repositioned Britain in a wider world. "Tony Blair's legacy" then encapsulates how he and New Labour fundamentally *changed* British politics, for good or ill. Of course, the record of any decade-long government is significant, and obviously no one volume can treat the subject exhaustively. The examination here is thus organ-ized around the themes of politics, policy, governance, and foreign affairs.

Assessing legacies

Should Tony Blair be considered one of the great prime ministers of modern British history? There is certainly a *prima facie* case that he should. He was the youngest premier since 1812 and had the longest tenure in office for any twentieth century premier bar Margaret Thatcher. He governed Britain through a period of political stability and economic prosperity. He led the country through multiple humanitarian interventions, not to mention major wars in Afghanistan and Iraq. Finally, he led Labour to landslide victories twice and was the party's first leader to win three consecutive general elections. But did he equal the great premiers of Britain?

It is often said that great political leaders "make the weather" rather than suffer it—they are able to set the agenda and transform politics rather than merely responding to the climate (Theakston and Gill, 2006, p. 196). During the 20th century three administrations had undoubted meteorological influence: the Liberal Government under Henry Campbell-Bannerman and Henry Herbert Asquith (1905–15); the postwar Labour Government of Clement Attlee (1945–51); and the Conservatives under Margaret Thatcher and John Major (1979–97) (The following draws on Riddell, 2006, Chapter 1; and Studlar, 2007).

The country's last Liberal government won a landslide election largely on the issue of free trade and moved on to establish the foundations of the British welfare state, changing the perception of the state's role from the passive night watchman of the Victorian era toward accepting responsibility for improving the lot of the poor through taxation and redistribution (Riddell, 2006, p. 4). The battle over, David Lloyd George's "People's Budget" led also to the showdown with the House of Lords and the permanent curtailing of the Lord's legislative powers via the 1911 Parliament Act. Finally, Asquith brought Britons into, and Lloyd George guided them through, the conflagration of the First World War.

The Attlee government transformed both the policies and the politics of the postwar period. By nationalizing the "commanding heights" of industry (rail, steel, coal, electricity, gas), the state entered into direct economic control of a significant share of the economy. They also adopted the tools of Keynesian demand management as a means of securing full employment. The universal welfare state was greatly expanded, with the National Health Service (NHS) as its flagship. Taken together, the changes in domestic policy amounted to a fundamental alteration of the boundaries between the public and private sectors, with a considerable role for the state in both providing services and managing the economy. Acceptance of the Keynesian mixed economy and the universal welfare state by the second Churchill government—and Conservative governments through the early seventies—converted this into a "postwar consensus."[2]

Yet it was the inability of these policies to stem Britain's relative economic decline that led to Margaret Thatcher's Conservative government. Thatcher changed the terms of political debate, redefining the postwar consensus as a cause rather than solution of Britain's ills. Wherever feasible, the teachings of neoliberal scholars like Friedrich Hayek and Milton Freidman were put into action, particularly via the early adoption of tight, anti-inflationary monetarist policies. Thatcher soldiered on through then resulting unemployment, refusing a U-turn *à la* Edward Heath. The Conservatives also sought to decrease the state's role by cutting taxes, reducing spending, and privatizing state holdings. Marginal tax rates were slashed and the core industries nationalized under Attlee (and a good chunk of council houses) were back in private sector hands by decade's end. The welfare state, particularly the NHS, proved a much more impenetrable redoubt; net government spending was essentially unchanged.[3] Thatcher also attacked "corporatism," meaning the privileged consultative role of interest groups, mainly unions (Studlar, 2007, p. 13), culminating in the defeat of the miners' strike of 1984–5. If the pillars of the postwar consensus were nationalization, full employment, respect for union power, and the welfare state, then three out of four pillars were demolished by the Iron Lady. Only the welfare state proved resilient.

Did three New Labour governments "change the weather" in comparable ways? The chapters that follow explore various policy domains to answer this question, with a conclusion by Jonathan Tonge providing a reflective overview. The concern here is to set out parameters for the book as a whole.

Agreeing on a conceptual framework for assessing historical importance is difficult indeed. League tables of prime ministers may make for great political sport, but their scholarly value is limited by their inherent subjectivity and murky standards of comparison. Historians and political scientists are particularly at odds (see Theakston and Gill, 2006; their results are discussed in more detail in Tonge below). Still, a structured evaluation of any leader's political legacy must build on three foundations: comprehensive scope, a long-term view, and clearly elaborated standards of comparison.

Legacies are multifaceted. Proper understanding requires a *comprehensive analysis* of policies pursued and institutions restructured—"the consequences of decisions already taken, as well as the consequences of those that have not been taken" (Gamble, 2007, p. 123). It also means surveying the political landscape, sketching new political boundaries. Distinguishing legacies across multiple areas is also necessary as achievement (or radical change) in one area may be countered by disappointment (or stasis) in another. Finally, scholars should avoid disproportionately emphasizing even the most prominent of single decisions. In Blair's case, of course, this would be the Iraq War. Labour's reputation may suffer for the Iraq adventure, but this should not distract from the broader picture. After all, each of the three "weather changing" governments discussed above saw their parties suffer long-term electoral droughts thereafter (Wilson, 2007, p. 5).

Existing scholarly evaluations of the Blair decade vary. For Vernon Bogdanor (2007), the key legacies are public service reform, constitutional amendments, and the war in Iraq—with real and lasting substantive changes in the former overwhelmed by war's political costs. Graham Wilson (2007), distinguishes policy, institutional, and political domains, and sees

New Labour's legacy as the net change overall. Policy changed only moderately compared to the previous Conservative Government; institutional power was spun off to devolved institutions, while Downing Street concentrated its grip on the central core of government. Politically, Blair returned the Labour Party to electability and secured three victories, but the foundations of his political support in the public and the party were in fact weak. Taken together, Wilson views Blair as more of a consolidating than radical leader, promoting a kinder, gentler Thatcherism (Wilson, 2007, p. 12). Finally, Donley Studlar (2007) adopts the distinction between political eras (encompassing the key issues and policies of a period) and political orders (alterations in party competition and institutional practices). In his view New Labour brought the political order of Britain into congruence (increasing transparency and accountability through, for example, devolution) with the political era of neoliberalism initiated by Thatcher.

In the concluding chapter of this volume, Jonathan Tonge takes an approach similar to Bogdanor, Wilson, and Studlar. He adopts four tests: (1) whether "Blairism" amounted to a coherent ideology; (2) whether his government produced novel and durable policies; (3) whether the "Blair settlement" was sufficient to reshape the policies of the Conservatives; and, finally, (4) whether the Labour Party emerged as a "Blairite" organization. Tonge's conclusion is supported by the book's 20 substantive chapters, each of which is focused on a specific area, but broadly falling under the headings of politics, policy, governance, and foreign affairs. Taken together, the book offers a comprehensive overview of the impact of ten years of Blair.

To assess legacies one must also transcend ephemera. It follows that scholars should do more than recount a period's key events or survey the state of play as a leader leaves the field. We want to understand the *long-term impact* on politics and government. Did the leader change the game itself, as well as winning his (or her) innings? Moreover, change matters whether it is for good or ill, well received or broadly unpopular. Prime ministers can leave just as indelible legacies through failure—witness the decades-long reputation for incompetence Labour suffered because of the Callahan government's inability to deal with the 1970s economic crisis.[4] Moreover, legacies result from inaction as well as radical reform. Without the Tories' acceptance of Keynesian macroeconomics, the welfare state, and the mixed economy in the 1950s, what mark would the Attlee government have left? Equally, issues that seem of great importance at the time often prove to be less compelling in retrospect. The politics of the "poll tax" were crucial to the downfall of Margaret Thatcher; now it is little more than a historical footnote. Moreover, opinions change; Attlee's stock, for example, rose after a series of favorable biographies starting in the 1980s (Theakston and Gill, 2006, p. 210).[5]

In short, only the wisdom of time and competitive scholarship will provide a thorough and accurate understanding of how ten years of Blair changed Britain. But it is important to begin. Despite their close historical proximity to the events, contributors to this volume were urged to focus not only on Gordon Brown's 2007 inheritance, but to reflect more generally on the long-term legacy of the Blair decade.

Finally, perhaps the most important question to grapple with regarding legacy is: compared to what? Since all are dealing with a commonly known record, the greatest variation across authors is the *standard of comparison*. Bogdanor, Wilson, and Studlar rely on history—the performance of previous governments is the yardstick against which to measure Blair's stature. Yet one can also gauge a legacy based on expectations. With the public's over-inflated expectations of Blair at the start, he was bound to disappoint in the end (Morris, 2007).[6] Peter Riddell portrays Blair as an "unfulfilled Prime Minister" because he did not use his electoral and political advantages to secure more substantial changes in policy—a regret expressed by Blair himself (Riddell, 2006, p. 196). A similar point is made by Anthony Seldon, who argues that Blair's agenda only began to crystallize as a coherent body of reform in 2006–7 (2007, p. 648). For both authors then the metric of Blair's legacy is what he could have done. Like many left-wing critics, Stuart Hall (2007) sees New Labour as apostasy, a continuation of the long march of neoliberalism and the betrayal of social democracy. That Blair, Brown, or any other signif-icant New Labour figure never suggested that they would do any such thing seems beside the point; for Hall and his ideological companions this is what they should have done and were thus found wanting. Prime ministerial expectations are equally a function of the political climate in which they operate (Theakston and Gill, 2006, p. 212). The guru of the third way, Anthony Giddens (2007), contends that, given globalization[7] and British political culture, New Labour was the only viable progressive program.

Given the wide variety of subjects covered in *The Blair Legacy*, no attempt was made to impose a uniform standard of comparison on the contributions below. Most naturally fall into comparing the Blair years with previous British experience. Others make explicit cross-national comparisons. Some focus on the context in which decisions were made while others attempt to frame the questions in terms of theoretical concerns. Despite these varia-tions, the commonality across all of the contributions (with the exception perhaps of the chapters on the Iraq War) is that they are not oriented to what could have been or should have been, but rather what did, in fact occur during the Blair years and the implication for future British politics.

In short, a valuable assessment of Blair's legacy requires a comprehensive review on the full range of public affairs with an eye on long-term implica-tions. The focus should remain broadly objective, analytical, and should avoid fanciful alternative histories or normative critiques. We hope that, given the contributions of the many talented scholars gathered here, the reader will be better able to answer the "big question": *How has Britain changed as a result of the Blair years?*

Organization of the book

The book's chapters are organized around the key themes of politics, policy, governance, and foreign affairs. Within their area of expertise, contributors were asked to address a common series of questions:

- What did New Labour face on gaining office? What were its stated aims?
- What key policies, programs, or reforms were implemented?
- How did Labour's policy, positions, or approach change over the decade?
- How far were stated goals met? What is the government's broad legacy?

Beyond these questions, authors were encouraged to interpret and structure their responses at will. Their contributions are previewed in the following paragraphs.

Part I—Politics

Certainly in terms of electoral results, Blair was triumphant. He easily managed what had eluded all previous Labour leaders—winning three straight general elections. The 1997 and 2001 elections produced landslide majorities of 179 and 167 respectively. Even as the Iraq War eroded Blair's personal approval, Labour still managed a respectable majority of 66 in 2005. Neil Kinnock and John Smith may have banished the left, but it was Blair who cemented the party in the political center. If Margaret Thatcher sought to demolish the *policies* of socialism, producing a decisive victory for the market, Tony Blair sought to destroy the *politics* of class warfare, handing a decisive victory to Middle England (See Curtice, 2007a for a more detailed discussion of Blair's appeal to the middle class). The ultimate tribute to Blair's success is how much David Cameron seems to be aping of his political style as he attempts to restore Tory electability.

In office, the opposition never seriously threatened Labour's majority and, with a few notable exceptions, the majority of Labour MPs stayed loyal, albeit grudgingly. To be sure, there were large rebellions, not least over the Iraq War (when 139 Labour MPs voted against invasion), but the government did not lose a whipped vote until the Terrorism Bill in November 2005 (see Mark Stuart below for a more detailed discussion).[8] And for all the rumor and innuendo regarding Blair's combative and dysfunctional relationship with his chancellor, neither Brown nor any other credible player directly challenged Blair's leadership. He may not have had full freedom of action and the pressures to go were increasing. Yet in the end, neither voters, nor party, nor failing health actually drove him from office. Tony Blair did something rather unique among British prime ministers: he simply walked away from power.

For David Denver and Justin Fisher (Chapter 1) it was Blair's personal popularity, as much as policy positioning or ideology, which explains New

Labour's electoral success. Even at the end the electorate preferred Blair as PM to the other party leaders. Not until the ascension of David Cameron was his lead seriously eroded. Still, his electoral magic was not infinite. Labour's share of the national vote fell with each successive contest and the party suffered defeats in many "second-order" elections. Overall, though, the party's electoral record after 1992 was remarkable, and was grounded in the ideological and organizational changes initiated both by Kinnock and Smith. Florence Faucher-King (Chapter 2) argues further that the "modernization" of Labour between 1994 and 2007 had dramatically changed the party. Its organization was more centralized, streamlined, and organized along business lines, yet it also was increasingly disconnected from the grassroots and ill-prepared financially.

Blair had an equally dramatic impact on the opposition parties. As Tim Bale chronicles in Chapter 3, after unsuccessfully attempting to maximize the appeal to base voters under William Hague, Iain Duncan Smith, and Michael Howard, Tory fortunes were renewed by Cameron's "valence" strategy, highlighting centrist policies and governing competence. David Cutts and Andrew Russell (Chapter 4) track the rather different trajectory of the Liberal Democrats, who benefited disproportionately from both anti-Conservative sentiment in the late 1990s and the unpopularity of New Labour in the 2000s, but now see their electoral prospects ebbing following turmoil in the leadership and the repositioning of the Conservatives.

Wyn Grant (Chapter 5) investigates the characteristics of the Blair government's interaction with pressure groups, observing five themes: the turn toward business, but away from business associations; a decline in the role of trade unions; the emphasis on new consultation procedures; the emergence of the regulatory state; and the growth of direct action and single issue groups. The influence of pressure groups in policymaking was central to both governance and scholarship in the seventies and eighties, but New Labour's approach was largely *ad hoc*. Grant thus calls for a renewed consideration of the proper role of these groups in the modern British polity. This section is rounded out by Nick Randall's and James Sloam's analysis of the "third way" (Chapter 6). Rather than attacking or defending it on normative terms, they look at how it was expressed in manifesto commitments, translated into public policy, and how it compares to the governance of other European social democratic parties. New Labour is found to be not only ideologically coherent, but solidly within the social democratic tradition and comparatively favorable in practice to other governing center-left parties.

Part II—Policy

Blair's policy record is a frustrating mix of great success and grave disappointment. The economy outperformed the major continental European economies on just about every macroeconomic indicator for the entire decade. The various New Deal programs were implemented to offer job training, improve skills, and tackle the problems of long-term unemployment. The National Health Service (NHS), seriously underfunded in 1997, saw a 50 percent increase in spending in real terms from 2000–7. The government successfully handled a massive terrorist attack on the London transport system in July 2005 as well as unsuccessful attacks in London and Glasgow in June 2007. Overall crime rates were down from when Labour entered office; educational attainment was up compared to other countries (see PISA). And while new arrivals may have grated at the sensibilities of nationalists, the flood of East European workers illustrated economic and social vibrancy.

In short, by most measures the three New Labour governments succeeded; people truly "never had it so good." Yet the mood of the country was distinctly uneasy when Blair stepped down ("On Hypochondria," *The Economist*, 8 April 2007).

Nothing better encapsulates the paradoxes of Blair's policy record than developments in the NHS. Fixing the NHS was a top priority and, after two years of fiscal austerity, spending was increased dramatically. The government could fairly point to tangible improvements in performance, but the net results fell well short of public expectations and reasonable return on the increased investment. Calum Paton argues in Chapter 7 that the mixed record on the NHS was a combination of Labour's policy approach, plagued by top-down direction and "initiativitis," and the structural limitations of trying to produce a high-quality taxpayer-funded healthcare system in a society with a center-right voting majority that would not tolerate vast tax increases. In social policy (Jerold Waltman, Chapter 8), New Labour's ambition was to re-engineer the welfare state around principles of work and responsibility. Their strategy was to get people into work via the New Deals and to make that work more lucrative through a minimum wage and a restructured tax and benefits system, especially the Working Families Tax Credit. These policies are well entrenched for the near term, yet Blair was not able to establish a new cross-party welfare orthodoxy (as did Attlee) that is invulnerable to the whims of a future government.

Perhaps the sharpest contrast with Labour's past came in the realm of economic management, as detailed by Terrence Casey and Alistair Howard in Chapter 9. Establishing their *bona fides* as credible economic managers through fiscal and monetary constraint was seen by Blair and Brown as the prerequisite for expanding social welfare. In parallel, growth rates would be boosted through increased investment to improve productivity. The increased tax revenue from a growing economy could then be used to expand social welfare spending. On one level this strategy was an enormous success. By nearly every measure the UK was the European economic leader during the Blair years. Still, economic inequality remained a problem and absolute productivity lagged. This raises a conundrum at the heart of what is termed by Casey and Howard the "Anglo-Social" model of political economy—can you replicate a Scandinavian-quality social welfare state in an economy that does not match American levels of productivity?

Sweeping changes were also initiated in regards to judicial reform and human rights (Mark Bevir and Richard Maiman, Chapter 10). The Blair government passed the Human Rights Act (1998), incorporating the European Convention on Human Rights into British Law. The Constitutional Reform Act (2005) restructured the office of the Lord Chancellor, reformed the process of judicial appointments, and initiated the creation of a Supreme Court. Gordon Brown even raised the issue of producing a codified "Bill of Rights and Duties." Bevir and Maiman contend that, even barring further reforms, the judiciary now enjoys an unprecedented level of independence and authority, which in turn opens questions about their appropriate role in Britain's democratic system.

Part III—Governance

Blair was at his most radical when it came to the institutions of British governance. Scotland was granted a devolved parliament, Wales got a National Assembly, and Northern Ireland gained an autonomous assembly and power-sharing executive. (Although the latter was suspended for several years, it was back in business when Blair stepped down.) London was given an assembly and directly elected mayor, and regional development agencies were established throughout England. At Westminster, hereditary peers in the House of Lords were stripped of voting rights, although ministers dithered over whether they should be replaced by elected or appointed members, or some combination thereof. Yet in rather typically British fashion, these changes were haphazard, without an underlying vision of the proper balance of power and responsibilities between institutions. Within the confines of central government, moreover, Blair pursued a very personalized style of governance, centered on a small group of advisors in 10 Downing Street who sought relentlessly to control the political agenda and media. Extensive input from either cabinet or parliament was largely eschewed. Last but not least, New Labour altered the constitutional structure by incorporating the European Convention of Human Rights into UK law and initiating the creation of a Supreme Court. In short, the institutions of government and constitutional arrangements of the UK underwent extensive tinkering during the Blair decade.

One of the criticisms of Blair, for which he was formally admonished in the Butler Report (see Mark Bennister, Chapter 11), was his penchant for centralized control, informal decision-making ("sofa government"), and bilateral relations with ministers that precluded collective decision-making through the cabinet. Even the decision to invade Iraq—arguably the most important taken during the Blair years—was only superficially vetted by the cabinet. From Blair's perspective, as Bennister reports, the ambitions of the New Labour project required centralization. He was not without constraint, especially from Gordon Brown in Number 11 (who asserted control over greater swathes of public policy than previous chancellors) and a lethargic bureaucratic structure. Nevertheless, Blair used his personal appeal to increase the power and capacities of office compared to previous incumbents. But it was a fleeting strength that faded with his approval ratings. Even after Blair executive power in Britain will continue to strengthen because, as Bennister explains, it is driven by modern government's complexity and the personalization of politics.

Contemporary observers also portrayed an overweening executive running roughshod over an increasingly supine parliament. Mark Stuart (Chapter 12) contends that, despite the government's wishes, parliament actually became slightly more responsive to a media-oriented culture; a more rebellious House of Commons emerged, alongside a more assertive House of Lords; the Commons became more representative of the country as a whole; and parliamentarians were given better resources with which to serve their constituents. Admittedly, legislative scrutiny remains less than desirable, but reports of the death of parliament were highly exaggerated.

Moves to centralize control in Westminster and Whitehall seem contradicted by Labour's quite extensive giveaway of power to sub-national governance. Commitments to devolution preceded Blair's ascension to the leadership and it is far from clear that he was ever a convinced advocate. Still, Jonathan Bradbury (Chapter 13) contends that he bought into the formulation propounded by William Gladstone that "power devolved is power retained at Westminster." Bradbury contends the ease with which devolution was implemented and finally achieving the long-sought peace in Northern Ireland showed Blair's regional policies largely to have succeeded. Alternately, Brown, as a Scot who strongly pushed for devolution, may face increasing difficulties in managing an asymmetrical system with an unresolved "English Question." At the local level, Labour also promised more decentralization to reverse, from councilors' perspective, the authoritarian centralism of the Thatcher-Major years. In practice, the Blair years were noted for only moderate reforms that were still monitored through top-down control. Chris Game (Chapter 14) argues that local government gained neither substantial administrative or financial control, nor was local democracy enhanced during the three Blair governments.

James Alt (Chapter 15) assesses the status of the British constitution post-Blair. It is easy to portray the above reforms in governance as representing a discontinuity in constitutional practice. Yet Alt contends the core elements of the constitution remain in place. It is largely still unwritten, even if more is written down than before (for example, the Human Rights Act, 1998). The system is still parliamentary, lacking separation between executive and legislative. Parliament remains sovereign and constrained by the rule of law. Devolution is a modification rather than an abandonment of unitary government, covers only a minority of the population, and is hardly unprecedented (for example, the Stormont Parliament that ruled Northern Ireland from 1921–72). A. V. Dicey argued a century prior that the rule of law was the essence of the constitution. The Blair reforms may have explicitly specified more of the rights so protected, but this fundamental principle is largely unchanged.

Part IV— Foreign Affairs

The most viscerally negative feelings are aroused by Blair's foreign policy. September 11 changed everything for the British prime minister as much as for the American president. From the very beginning Blair made clear that he backed the US in a strong, aggressive prosecution of the War on Terror. This not only drew British troops into Afghanistan, but also into Iraq—and millions of Britons turned onto the street to oppose the wars. That no weapons of mass destruction were found once Saddam Hussein's regime was decapitated only emboldened critics. Blair and colleagues were accused of "sexing up" the evidence leading Britain into war. And despite the Butler Review and Hutton Inquiry's favorable findings the public remained skeptical (hence "Tony BLiar"). The perception of him as "Bush's poodle" further undercut his support with both the public and the party, a condition that only deepened as Iraq become bogged down in sectarian violence. By the time of his departure, four years after the invasion, Iraq was still far from establishing a stable, democratic government. Mr. Blair's political career may have begun along the banks of the Thames, but his legacy will ultimately be shaped on the banks of the Tigris and Euphrates.

Would Blair's legacy be substantially different if he had not gone to war in Iraq? Perhaps, but Stephen Benedict Dyson (Chapter 16) argues that this was never likely; Blair's personality and worldview—vividly demonstrated in the pre-Iraq wars he fought—disposed him to become involved. Yet this result was not predetermined by geopolitics or the imperatives of national interest. Dyson examines the choices made by leaders facing similar crises in the past, as well the views of those who could have plausibly replaced Blair as premier, to make the case that while the broad outlines of British foreign policy from 1997–2007 might have been the same with a different prime minister, Blair's personality and leadership style made a significant difference in explaining British policy toward both Kosovo and Iraq. John Dumbrell (Chapter 19) comes to a similar conclusion in his review of the "Special Relationship" with the US. Structural factors—not only common interests and culture, but the institutionalized linkages of diplomatic and military cooperation across the Atlantic—inclined London to stand squarely behind Washington. But it was Blair's personal beliefs about international politics and the opportunities and obligations of the Special Relationship that was key. For many British observers, Blair's subsequent experience demonstrated the dangers of being too close to the US. Hence it was not surprising that Brown rhetorically distanced himself in his early days as premier. At the same time, Dumbrell notes, he showed no inclination to dismantle the structures of Anglo-American relations (for example, close defense cooperation) and the rhetoric warmed in due course. It is thus unlikely that Brown or any future prime minister will radically reconfigure relations with the US, whatever Blair's experience. Blair's mistake, in Dumbrell's view, was not in maintaining the Special Relationship; it was in deluding himself that he was an equal partner.

Given the centrality of Iraq to Blair's legacy, two additional contributions were invited specifically on the decision to go to war. David Coates and Joel Kreiger (Chapter 17) argue that Blair blundered into the Iraq War, signing on early to the Bush Doctrine, choosing to believe faulty intelligence, and justifying the invasion on that premise. Politically his strategy was to lead from the front, assuming his persuasive powers would attract followers at home and abroad. When they demurred he was caught out and backed into a war that he could have and should have avoided. For Coates and Krieger, the foray into Mesopotamia is less the result of the prime minister's unique foreign policy views as a revival of outdated imperial impulses. In contrast, Ted R. Bromund (Chapter 18) argues the invasion was a just war intended to uphold the principles of collective security. Backing the US effort was neither a sycophantic reflex nor imperialistic nostalgia; it was the logical application of a liberal interventionist strategy—clearly elaborated by Blair in a speech in Chicago in 1999—against a legitimate threat. Nor was this strategy alien to the foreign policy traditions of either the UK or US, having antecedents in both Gladstonian and Wilsonian thinking. Rather, it was the Labour left, as well as continental European leaders, who abandoned the principles they had previously supported rather than face military conflict, undercutting the *casus foederis* of the United Nations. Ironically, it was the very forces of "political modernization" that Blair sought to advance at home that undermined his foreign policy.

Ironies also abounded in European policy. Blair committed to "putting Britain at the center of Europe," yet as Scott James and Kai Oppermann (Chapter 20) show, his approach was inconsistent. The government showed leadership in some areas, such as European defense cooperation through the St. Malo agreement. In other important policy areas they either kicked the ball down the field (Economic and Monetary Union) or intentionally obfuscated their position (the Constitutional Treaty). The irony is that in doing so they negated Europe as a political issue, even though it was so corrosive to the Major government. In 1997, EU policy loomed large as potential legacy issues, particularly the question of whether to join the single currency. By 2007, through a combination of governing tactics and fortuitous events, the salience of Europe to British voters declined. This was electorally beneficial to Labour, but at a larger price. It prevented the government from formulating a coherent strategy and further reinforced the innate Euroskepticism of the populace. Paradoxically, support for the EU declined over the decade even though the integration process has actually aligned with UK preferences.

Unique features of *The Blair Legacy*

Much has already been written about the Blair years, and there will doubtless be much more. There are several scholarly biographies (Seldon, 2005 and 2008 foremost among them), insider accounts (Cook 2007; Prescott, 2008; Campbell, 2007; Blair, 2008), and journalistic appraisals (Stothard, 2003; Riddell, 2006; Coughlin, 2006). Nor is this the first or only academic anthology. There are quality volumes edited by Beech and Lee (2008) and the series under the tutelage of Anthony Seldon (2001; with Dennis Kavanagh, 2005; 2007). Why, then, another compilation, and why should readers consult this over (or at least prior to) others?

The Blair Legacy has, of course, the great benefit of being a thorough, comprehensive book by some of the premier scholars of British politics on both sides of the Atlantic. Beyond this, two other traits warrant serious attention. First, the authors have integrated theoretical insights, historical comparisons, or cross-national analysis into their chapters. Retrospective anthologies are too often mere chronologies of the events and issues of the period; several examples suggest the greater depth offered in this volume. Faucher-King, for example, applies neo-institutional analysis to elucidate the relationship between external and internal stimuli in Labour's transformation. Randall and Sloam illuminate third way ideology by comparing it to its continental cousins. And rather than merely review economic performance, Casey and Howard reflect on the ways Britain's "variety of capitalism" changed over the era. The concept of "skill in context" developed by Theakston and Gill is used by Bennister to assess Blair as prime minister. Dyson uses the tools of political psychology to understand "the Blair effect" on UK foreign policy, results of which Dumbrell interprets via the influences of structure and agency in the Anglo-American relations.

The latter examples highlight the second unique feature of this book: its encompassing view of foreign policy. Tony Blair's international legacy was just as important as his impact on UK. The book emphasizes the Iraq War, including arguments both for and against invasion, and pays special attention to the US-UK relationship. This should widen the appeal to students of international relations and British domestic politics alike.

Conclusion

In 1997, Tony Blair and his New Labour Party set out on a campaign of national renewal—a campaign no less ambitious than that launched by Margaret Thatcher two decades prior. The chapters presented here chronicle the successes, failures, and long-term implications of this project. Of course, writing political history is itself a long-term project, and what follows is a beginning rather than the end. Some of our conclusions will withstand the test of time while others, no doubt, will seem myopic or uninformed in retrospect. Nevertheless, they are an excellent first effort.

Timeline of the Blair years

12 May 1994	Labour leader John Smith dies of a heart attack at 55.
31 May 1994	Tony Blair and Gordon Brown meet at Granita restaurant and reportedly agree that Blair would lead a future government, with Brown as a powerful chancellor and only later gaining the leadership.
21 July 1994	Tony Blair beats John Prescott and Margaret Beckett to become leader of the Labour Party with 57 percent of the vote.
29 April 1995	In a crucial symbol of New Labour, Blair convinces the party to abandon Clause IV of its Constitution, which had urged "the common ownership of the means of production, distribution and exchange."
1 May 1997	After 18 years in Opposition, Labour wins the general election by a landslide of 419 seats to the Conservatives 165, a Commons majority of 179.
6 May 1997	Chancellor Gordon Brown gives the Bank of England operational independence to set interest rates.
19 June 1997	William Hague is elected Conservative leader.
31 August 1997	Tony Blair captures the nation's mood on the death of Diana Princess of Wales by dubbing her the "peoples' princess."
12 September 1997	A referendum in Scotland backs devolution; Wales follows a week later.
27 October 1997	Gordon Brown establishes five tests for adopting the euro; rules out British entry until they have been met.
11 November 1997	A £1m donation from Formula One boss Bernie Ecclestone is returned by Labour when it is revealed that ministers exempted Formula One from a proposed tobacco sponsorship ban.
10 April 1998	The Good Friday Agreement establishing a power-sharing devolved government in Northern Ireland

	is signed. Although the Northern Ireland Assembly would be suspended three times during Blair's tenure, it was finally restored in May 2007.
16 December 1998	The UK and US launch air strikes against Iraq after Saddam Hussein's failure to comply with weapons inspections.
23 December 1998	Blair confidant Peter Mandelson forced to resign over a home loan scandal.
24 March 1999	NATO air strikes begin against Serbia to halt "ethnic cleansing" in Kosovo; strikes continue for more nearly two months until Belgrade agrees to withdraw.
9 August 1999	The Liberal Democrats elect Charles Kennedy to replace Paddy Ashdown.
11 October 1999	Peter Mandelson returns to the cabinet as Northern Ireland Secretary.
4 May 2000	Ken Livingstone wins inaugural London Mayoral election.
20 May 2000	Leo Blair is born, the first child born to a sitting PM for more than 150 years.
24 January 2001	Peter Mandelson resigns (again) over allegations of improperly arranging for a passport for a wealthy Millennium Dome sponsor.
20 February 2001	Foot and mouth outbreak begins; general election is delayed for a month.
7 June 2001	Labour wins historic second term with a majority of 165.
11 September 2001	Blair cancels planned speech to TUC to express shock at the attack on America and promises to stand shoulder to shoulder with the US in tracking down the perpetrators.
13 September 2001	Iain Duncan Smith elected as Conservative leader.
1 January 2002	Euro becomes the currency for 11 EU countries.
8 November 2002	UN Security Council unanimously passes Resolution 1441, offering Iraq a "final opportunity to comply with its disarmament obligations."
December 2002– March 2003	Intensive negotiations are undertaken by Britain and America to secure a "second" UN Security Council resolution authorizing the use of force against Iraq.

They are mainly opposed by France, Germany, and Russia.

15 February, 2003	An estimated one million people protest the war against Iraq in London.
10 March 2003	In a television interview, French president Jacques Chirac says that France will veto any resolution authorizing force against Iraq "regardless of the circumstances."
17 March 2003	Leader of the House of Commons Robin Cook resigns in opposition to the invasion.
18 March 2003	139 Labour MPs vote against decision to go to war with Iraq.
20 March 2003	The invasion of Iraq begins.
12 May 2003	Clare Short resigns from the cabinet, claiming that Blair broke promises over Iraq's future.
29 May 2003	Andrew Gilligan on BBC *Today* program reports allegations that the government "sexed up" its dossier on Iraq's WMD.
9 July 2003	The Ministry of Defense names weapons expert Dr. David Kelly as source for Andrew Gilligan's report.
18 July 2003	David Kelly is found dead in the woods near his home after having committed suicide.
19 October 2003	Blair suffers an irregular heartbeat and spends a few hours in hospital, fueling speculation of his resignation.
6 November 2003	Michael Howard becomes leader of the Conservative Party, replacing the ineffective Duncan Smith.
14 December 2003	US forces capture Saddam Hussein hiding in a hole near Tikrit.
27 January 2004	Government narrowly wins vote on university top-up fees, despite rebellion by 72 Labour back-benchers.
28 January 2004	Hutton Report absolves the government of blame in death of David Kelly, criticizing instead BBC reporting.
14 July 2004	The Butler Report finds that some intelligence on Iraq's WMDs was unreliable, but Blair had acted in good faith.
30 September 2004	At Labour's annual conference, Blair announces he will run for third term but not stand for fourth.

18 November 2004	Parliament Act invoked to secure passage of Hunting Act 2004, banning fox hunting with dogs.
15 December 2004	Home Secretary David Blunkett resigns over visa row.
6 February 2005	Blair becomes longest serving Labour PM.
5 May 2005	Labour wins third term with majority reduced to 66.
29 May 2005	French voters reject EU Constitution; Dutch voters follow three days later. Plans for UK referendum on Constitution are scrapped shortly thereafter.
6 July 2005	London wins bid to host 2012 Olympic Games.
7 July 2005	Suicide bombers kill 52 people in London Underground and bus bombings.
8 July 2005	G8 summit hosted by Blair in Gleneagles, Scotland ends with an agreement to boost aid for developing countries.
21 July 2005	Second wave of attempted bombings on London transport fails.
9 November 2005	Blair suffers his first Commons defeat on the Terrorism Act, which would have allowed suspected terrorists to be held for 90 days without charge. A 28-day period is later approved.
6 December 2005	David Cameron is elected as new Conservative leader.
6 January 2006	Charles Kennedy is forced by colleagues to resign as Liberal Democrat leader after publicly admitting to a drinking problem. Menzies (Ming) Campbell is elected leader.
16 March 2006	It is revealed that the Labour Party had secretly borrowed millions of pounds, launching the "cash for honours" scandal.
6 September 2006	Tensions between Brown and Blair reach boiling point, sparking resignation of a junior minister and seven government aides, who demand a timetable for Blair's resignation.
14 December 2006	Blair interviewed by police in cash for honors affair.
10 May 2007	Tony Blair announces he will step down as prime minister on 27 June 2007.
27 June 2007	Blair appears for his final Prime Minister's Questions; Gordon Brown takes over as prime minister.

Notes

1. Blair: The Poll *The Observer*, 8 April 2007 (http://www.guardian.co.uk/politics/2007/apr/08/tonyblair. labour3). Accessed on April 3, 2008.
2. Changes in foreign affairs were equally significant. The Attlee government began the process of decolonization and dismantling the British Empire, reinforced the US-led the Western alliance by joining NATO, and initiated Britain's nuclear program.
3. Although there was a substantial shift from direct to indirect taxation.
4. Labour's travails stemmed from the collapse of its supposed special relationship with the trade unions amid the strikes and industrial unrest of the 1978–9 Winter of Discontent, a legacy as much of the Wilson as Callaghan Government.
5. The same is true for Harry Truman in the US. George W. Bush and Tony Blair may be hoping for a similar "historian's bounce."
6. Morris further makes the point that the decline in Blair's numbers occurred mostly before the Iraq War.
7. Acceptance of globalization as a "given" was one of the hallmarks of New Labour.
8. Resistance centered on the government's desire to hold suspects without charge for 90 days. In the end they got 28. Gordon Brown faced renewed resistance when he pushed to up the period to 42 days in June 2008—a vote he narrowly won.

Part I Politics

1
Blair's Electoral Record

David Denver and Justin Fisher

Introduction

Writing shortly after the 1992 general election which resulted in a fourth consecutive victory for the Conservatives, Anthony King (1993) linked the UK with Japan as examples of 'democratic one-party states' (p. 224). The main British Election Study (BES) report on the same election was entitled *Labour's Last Chance?* (Heath et al., 1994) and in the final chapter ('Can Labour Win?') the authors painted a gloomy picture of Labour's electoral prospects.

In hindsight these assessments look absurd but at the time there were good reasons for thinking that the Labour party was in terminal decline. The Conservatives had convincingly won four general elections in a row (1979, 1983, 1987 and 1992) – a feat unmatched in the twentieth century – and Labour's performance in all four was poor. The shares of UK votes obtained by the party in these elections were, respectively, 36.9 per cent, 27.6 per cent, 30.8 per cent and 34.4 per cent.

The nadir was in 1983. Following the 1979 election, the left wing of the party became more influential and internal divisions led to four senior figures breaking away to form the new Social Democratic Party (SDP), which initially had spectacular success (Crewe and King, 1995). In the 1983 election, Labour was saddled with a manifesto that was much too left wing for most voters (memorably described by Labour MP Gerald Kaufman as 'the longest suicide note in history') and a leader (Michael Foot), who was not a credible potential prime minister. After the election, under a new leader (Neil Kinnock) a start was made in changing the party's image, reviewing policies and modernising the party machine (see Shaw, 1994). Some progress was made but it was not enough to avert defeat in 1987, although in that election Labour did at least reassert its claim to be the principal opposition party. In 1992 the prospects for Labour appeared better. Margaret Thatcher was no longer prime minister, Conservative divisions over the European Union were becoming more fractious, and Britain was experiencing a deep economic recession. Yet, once again, Labour failed to win.

Although the party's vote share increased, it was still smaller than it had been in 1979. The future did indeed look bleak.

Following the 1992 election Kinnock resigned and was replaced in July of that year by the previous Shadow Chancellor, John Smith. Almost immediately Labour's ratings in the opinion polls began to show an improvement, rising to 43 per cent of voting intentions in August, and this was sustained in the months that followed.

Over the 21 months of Smith's leadership Labour averaged 46 per cent in the polls compared with 30 per cent for the Conservatives (see Figure 1.1). At the same time, Smith's personal popularity rose. At the 1992 general election Kinnock had trailed the Tory leader, John Major, in perceptions of who would make the best prime minister by 39 to 28 per cent. Within three months of taking over, however, Smith had overtaken Major and during his time as leader he was preferred as prime minister, on average, by 32 per cent of Gallup's respondents compared with 22 per cent for Major.

It would be wrong, of course, to attribute Labour's apparent revival entirely to the change in leadership. In September 1992, the Conservative

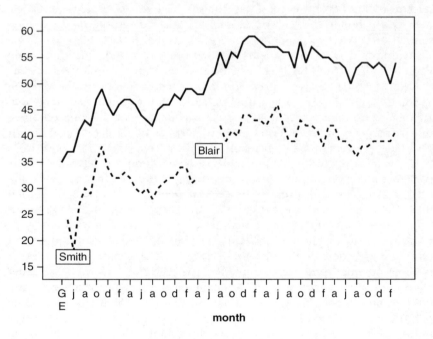

Figure 1.1   Labour's share of vote intentions and leaders' ratings as best person for prime minister, 1992–7
Note: The solid line refers to voting intentions and the broken line to the 'best Prime Minister' question.
Sources: Voting intention figures are the monthly averages of regularly published polls. Best prime minister figures are from Gallup.

government was forced to withdraw Britain from the Exchange Rate Mechanism (ERM) after failing to maintain the value of Sterling against the Deutschmark. Britain's membership of the ERM was a cornerstone of the government's economic policy and thus withdrawal was a major humiliation (Denver, 1998). At a stroke, this event destroyed the Conservatives' longstanding reputation for economic competence. Critically, Labour was now regarded as the more economically competent party – an accolade it had never previously enjoyed. In the following few months, Conservative support in opinion polls tumbled and in the space of ten weeks an average Labour lead of one point was translated into one of 17 points.

John Smith died in May 1994 and in July Tony Blair was elected Labour's youngest-ever leader. Blair was fortunate that he inherited the leadership at a time when the Conservatives were deeply unpopular. The 1994 European Parliament election was held in the interregnum between Smith's death and Blair's accession and proved a triumph for Labour, the party taking 44.2 per cent of votes across Britain and 62 (of 84) seats. The Conservatives, in contrast, won just 27.9 per cent of votes and 18 seats – at that point their smallest vote share in any national election during the twentieth century (Mortimore, 1994). There was a similar story in local elections. In 1993 the Conservatives lost almost 500 councillors in the shire counties (although the Liberal Democrats benefited to a greater extent than Labour) and the pattern of heavy Conservative losses was repeated in the 1994 local contests held while Smith was still party leader.[1]

Nonetheless, as measured by opinion polls, the impact of Blair on Labour's popularity and electoral prospects can only be described as electric. From his accession through to the 1997 general election, Labour's share of voting intentions never fell below 50 per cent and he easily outscored his rivals as the best person to be prime minister. Over the 32 months from August 1994 to March 1997 Blair was preferred on average by 41 per cent of electors compared with 19 per cent for Major. In this respect, Blair's personal ascendancy was a central fact – perhaps the central fact – of British politics from 1994 onwards.

Landslide: The 1997 general election

By any standard Labour's victory in the 1997 general election was a remarkable achievement. Having come close to being written off just five years previously, the extent of Labour's success was astonishing (see Table 1.1). The swing from the Conservatives to Labour at 10 per cent was almost double the post-war record. Labour's haul of 418 seats was the largest ever won by the party and its majority over all other parties (177), the largest for any government since 1935. On the other side, the Conservatives were completely wiped out in Scotland and Wales and the number of Conservative MPs elected was the smallest since the Liberal landslide of 1906. According to MORI, Labour outpolled the Conservatives among women, older voters and

Table 1.1   Results of general elections, 1997–2005

	Votes (%)			Seats		
	1997	2001	2005	1997	2001	2005
Con	30.7	31.7	32.4	165	166	198
Lab	43.2	40.7	35.2	418	412	355
Lib Dem	16.8	18.3	22.0	46	52	62
Others	9.3	9.4	10.3	30	29	31
Labour Majority				177	165	64
Turnout	71.4	59.4	61.4			

Note: The figures are for the UK.
Source: Rallings and Thrasher (2000, 2001, 2005)

owner-occupiers (all traditionally Conservative-inclined) and reached near parity among the solid middle classes (Worcester and Mortimore, 1999, p. 243). As Tony Blair swept into Downing Street on a sunny May 1st he did so on a national tide that had flowed like a torrent in his favour.

Nonetheless, the 1997 election was also a verdict on the incumbent Conservative government. It was not only that the forced withdrawal from the ERM continued to haunt them. In addition, the government was deeply and publicly divided over Europe and had been beset by sexual and financial sleaze. Also, the once popular policy of privatisation of publicly owned industries had run its course. The BES found that only 14 per cent of respondents wanted more privatisation and, indeed, it had come to be associated with corporate greed, overpaid managers and directors and a so-called 'revolving door' from cabinet to boardroom which allowed Tory politicians to feed at the very troughs they had created (see Denver, 1998).

Tony Blair's achievement, however, was to make Labour a safe alternative for those disillusioned with the Conservatives. In co-operation with like-minded colleagues, in just three years he had created 'New' Labour which could plausibly depict itself as a party with new leaders and new policies. Blair had removed much of the party's ideological baggage including, in 1995, replacing the historic, if largely symbolic, Clause IV of the party's constitution, which contained a commitment to public ownership, with a more anodyne statement focusing on the virtues of community. During 1996 the Conservatives ran an advertising campaign which featured Tony Blair with red Devil-like eyes and the slogan 'New Labour. New Danger'. This was spectacularly off the mark. New Labour was much more palatable to 'Middle Britain' than the old Labour party. The voters noticed that things had changed and liked what they saw (see King, 1998 , p. 197–205).

On top of an improved party image, however, Blair's youth, energy and charisma contrasted sharply with the widely held view of the Prime Minister

John Major as tired, boring and grey. As early as 1996, according to Gallup, Blair outscored Major by huge margins on being caring, tough, effective, trustworthy, competent, firmly in charge, decisive, likeable and likely to unite the country (Denver, 1998, p. 42). When it came to the general election, Blair was clearly the voters' choice for prime minister. In five MORI campaign polls he was chosen, on average, by 39 per cent of respondents compared with 25 per cent for Major. In the last of these polls before Election Day, the gap was 40 per cent to 23 per cent (Ipsos-MORI website). For the first time in four elections the Labour leader was more popular than his Conservative counterpart.

So unpopular was the Major government, however, that it seems likely that Labour would have won the 1997 election under John Smith or, indeed, practically any credible leader. Nonetheless, Blair was unusually popular. In the period between his becoming leader and the election, his approval rating, as reported by Gallup, slipped below 50 per cent only once (in September 1994) and by April 1997 stood at 70 per cent. In addition, Blair had indirect effects on Labour's popularity. Under his leadership, the party re-fashioned its policies and image and greatly improved its campaigning and media relations. Labour may have won the election without Blair but his presence ensured that it was won in a landslide.

On the crest of a wave: 1997–2001

Figure 1.2 shows monthly voting intentions for the three major parties from the 1997 general election until Blair's departure from office. The period between 1997 and 2001 is remarkable in that this was the first inter-election period since regular polling began in which the governing party never once lost its lead (on the basis of the average figures from all published polls) in a single month. The Conservatives improved their position very slowly after 1997 but the only time that they came within hailing distance of Labour was in the autumn of 2000 when there were widespread protests over petrol prices with oil tanker drivers, farmers and others causing widespread disruption to traffic and cutting off petrol supplies to filling stations. Immediately after the 1997 election Labour reached dizzy heights of popularity, hitting 60 per cent of voting intentions. After that, apart from the dip during 2000, support was usually at or above 50 per cent.

The poll ratings were reflected, to an extent, in parliamentary by-elections. The unwritten law of British by-elections in the post-war period is that the governing party loses support and – at least since the 1960s – seats. There were nine by-elections in Labour-held seats between 1997 and 2001 and the party's share of the vote did decline in almost all of them. Nonetheless, every seat was held. Blair's government became the first (excluding the short parliament of February-October 1974) to not lose a seat in a by-election since the Conservatives between 1951 and 1955.

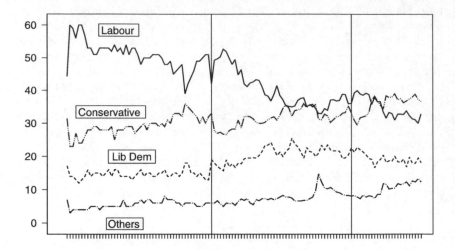

Figure 1.2   Monthly voting intentions: General election 1997–May 2007
Note: The graph shows mean percentage intending to vote for each party in all published polls in the month concerned. The starting point is the 1997 general election
and the vertical lines indicate the 2001 and 2005 elections respectively.

Although the Chancellor of the Exchequer, Gordon Brown, won plaudits
for his prudent handling of the economy after 1997, it is difficult to deny
that Tony Blair's personal popularity was a key element in maintaining support for Labour among the electorate. Figure 1.3 shows the trend in the electorate's preference for prime minister from July 1997 (i.e. after William Hague
took over as Conservative leader) to April 2001. Throughout, Blair was the
preferred prime minister by large margins. Hague's ratings improved slightly
during 2000 but never made a serious dent in Blair's huge lead. The Liberal
Democrat leaders also trailed far behind. In these terms, no prime minister
had ever had such a commanding lead over his/her rivals for so long. In addition, Blair initially achieved remarkable satisfaction ratings among the electorate (per cent satisfied with how he was doing his job as prime minister
minus per cent dissatisfied). According to MORI, he averaged +54 from the
1997 election to the end of the year and he remained well 'in the black', as
it were, until the second half of 2000. This sustained record of popularity was
unmatched by any prime minister since regular polling began.

Blair's electoral magic did not apply to the same degree in other elections
in which the government of the country or the person to be prime minister was not at stake, however. As well as losing support in by-elections, governments also usually lose support in local council elections during the
parliamentary cycle and Blair's government was no exception. In 1998

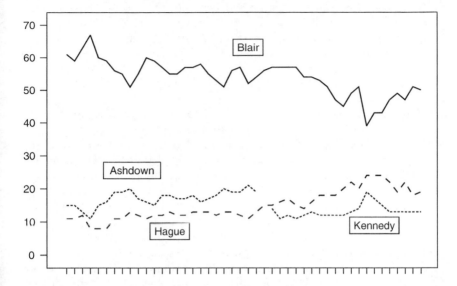

Figure 1.3 Best person for prime minister, 1997–2001
Source: Gallup.

Labour had a net loss of only 151 council seats (a trifling number) and had a clear lead in the 'national equivalent' vote share (37 per cent to 33 per cent for the Conservatives). In 1999, things seemed less rosy as the party lost 1346 seats, but this was still far from a disaster as Labour continued to lead in national equivalent vote share – 36 per cent to 34 per cent. Things were more difficult in 2000 when the Conservatives at last profited from 'mid-term blues' and were estimated to lead Labour by 38 per cent to 30 per cent in national vote shares.

In the first elections for the Scottish Parliament in 1999 Labour performed satisfactorily. The party took 38.8 per cent of the constituency votes and 53 of the 73 constituency seats. Labour was denied an overall majority in the parliament due to the operation of the additional member electoral system (AMS), but nonetheless was the dominant force in the Labour-Liberal Democrat coalition which emerged to form the first Scottish executive.

Things did not go so well in Wales, however, where Labour's campaign was blighted by the UK leadership's insistence on imposing, more or less, a Blairite leader (Alun Michael) on an unwilling Welsh Labour party. With only 37.6 per cent of the constituency votes Labour, against all expectations, failed to win a majority of seats in the Welsh Assembly (losing some previously rock-solid constituencies in the process). Eventually, as in Scotland, the party was forced to form a coalition with the Liberal Democrats.

Also in 1999, Labour was soundly defeated by the Conservatives in the European Parliament elections, now held under a party list PR system. The latter took 35.6 per cent of the votes to Labour's 28.0 per cent and 36 of the 84 British seats to Labour's 29. However, this outcome was produced on a turnout of just 23 per cent. British voters knew little and cared less about the European Parliament so that the government was easily able to shrug off this apparent setback.

Finally, in the first set of elections for the London Mayor and Assembly in 2000, the picture for Labour was again less than triumphant. In the election for Mayor, Labour's candidate (Frank Dobson) came third, well behind the winner Ken Livingstone, who stood as an Independent after losing the internal Labour selection contest. The elections for the Assembly (using AMS) were only slightly more satisfactory. Labour trailed the Conservatives in the popular vote in constituency contests (by 33.2 per cent to 31.6 per cent) and secured only nine of the 25 Assembly seats.

Overall, after four years in office Labour remained electorally dominant as another general election loomed. The party appeared invincible in national politics, and the cumulative losses at local level could in part be seen as simply restoring some equilibrium following Labour's spectacular gains in local elections in the mid-1990s. The poor results in Wales and London were more to do with miscalculations and mismanagement of internal party matters rather than dissatisfaction with the government or the prime minister. Similarly, the European result said more about the antipathy of many and the apathy of most towards the EU than about the popularity of the government.

As the campaign for the 2001 general election began, Labour under Blair were hot favourites and in terms of seats won the result showed hardly any change from 1997 (see Table 1.1). There was a small swing of votes (1.8 per cent) from Labour to the Conservatives but the latter made a net gain of only one seat while Labour had a net loss of 6. This was a triumph for Tony Blair. As he had done throughout the inter-election period, he towered above his rivals in judgements as to who was the best person for prime minister. The Gallup election poll showed that more than half of respondents chose Blair (52 per cent) compared with just 20 per cent for William Hague. Moreover, a sophisticated analysis of BES survey data concluded that even when all sorts of other factors (such as economic and other policy evaluations) were taken into account, evaluations of the party leaders remained an important determinant of party choice in 2001. Blair, rather than any kind of Blairism, was a trump card for Labour (Clarke et al., 2004, Ch. 4).

Hanging on: 2001–5

During the 2001–5 parliament, Tony Blair and the New Labour government tasted serious unpopularity for the first time (see Figure 1.2). Labour experienced the usual 'honeymoon' with the electorate after the 2001 election but then support for the party declined, although there was something of a recovery from the latter half of 2004. The Conservatives, on the other hand, held fairly steady throughout and their support was on a slow upward trend. As a result, although Labour was usually in the lead, the gap between the two main parties was relatively small from about the middle of 2003 and, indeed, the Conservatives slipped into the lead on a few occasions. The Liberal Democrats, meanwhile, also held steady and were generally at a slightly higher level of support than they had achieved in 2001. 'Other' parties – in particular United Kingdom Independence Party (UKIP) – experienced an upsurge of support at the time of the European elections in June 2004, but this faded in the following months.

The decline in the popularity of Labour reflected a decline in the popularity of the prime minister himself. Figure 1.4 shows the electorate's preferred prime minister from January 2003 (when YouGov began to ask the 'best Prime Minister' question on a regular basis) to March 2005. At the start of the period Iain Duncan Smith was the Conservative leader. He was widely regarded as out of his depth and, following a vote of no confidence by his own MPs, was succeeded in November 2003 by Michael Howard who significantly closed the gap on Blair as a potential prime minister. Although he was certainly able, Howard was not perceived by the electorate as particularly likeable. Moreover, he was seen as something of a throwback to

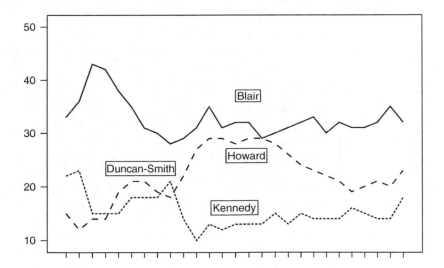

Figure 1.4 Best person for prime minister, January 2003–March 2005
Source: YouGov.

Thatcherism and fairly soon his appeal declined, leaving Blair clearly the most preferred prime minister as the 2005 election approached. Nonetheless, in this inter-election period he was undoubtedly less of an electoral asset to his party than he had been up to the 2001 election. His net satisfaction ratings (figures from MORI) for the six months after the 2001 election averaged +25 but thereafter were generally negative right up to the 2005 general election. Scores averaged –5 in 2002, –23 in 2003 and –30 in 2004. The main reason for this clear decline in satisfaction with the performance of the prime minister was almost certainly the Iraq War and its aftermath.

Britain invaded Iraq along with US forces in March 2003. At first the war had majority support among the British public. Gradually, however, as doubts grew about the intelligence reports used to make the case for war and no weapons of mass destruction were found, opinion swung against the war. From May 2004 YouGov consistently found pluralities saying that the intervention had been wrong. Well before that, voters began to lose trust in Blair. In June 2003, according to MORI, just over a third of the electorate (36 per cent) described Blair as trustworthy but this proportion continued to decline and was 32 per cent by April 2005.

The government's travails were reflected in parliamentary by-elections. In the six by-elections that took place, Labour's vote share dropped by an average of almost 20 percentage points and two seats that had previously been held were lost (Brent East and Leicester South). The beneficiaries were the Liberal Democrats campaigning on an anti-Iraq war platform. In the local elections too there were significant losses of seats and Labour trailed the Conservatives in national equivalent vote share from 2001 to 2004 – in the latter case by 26 to 37 per cent. Labour was clearly being steadily reduced from its once dominant position in local government. In the London elections of 2004, there was more bad news. Although Ken Livingstone (now an official Labour candidate) retained his position as Mayor, Labour secured only 24.7 per cent of the constituency vote (some 6.5 points behind the Conservatives) and ended up with only seven of the 25 Assembly seats.

As in 1999, the European Parliament election of 2004 produced poor results for the government. The fact that this election coincided with local elections in England and Wales meant that the turnout (38.2 per cent) was more respectable than in 1999 but, even so, Labour received only 22.6 per cent of the Great Britain vote, trailing behind the Conservatives on 26.7 per cent. Labour took just 19 of the 75 seats available.

There was further bad news in the Scottish Parliament elections in 2003. Although still easily the largest party, Labour's share of the constituency vote dropped from 38.8 per cent to 34.6 per cent and seven constituencies were lost. Nonetheless, the Labour-Liberal Democrat coalition continued in office. In Wales, on the other hand, there was something of a recovery compared with 1999. Labour's vote share increased both in the constituency (to 40 per cent) and list voting (to 36.6 per cent) and the party was able to form a Welsh administration on its own.

The 2001–5 inter-election cycle represented a return to normality in British politics in that the incumbent government ran into rough weather, electorally speaking. It was not 'normal', however, in that the official opposition did not reap most of the benefit. In the London and European elections it was UKIP (and, to a lesser extent, the Green Party); in Scotland it was the Scottish National Party (SNP), Scottish Socialists and Greens, and in the opinion polls the Liberal Democrats and others prevented the Conservatives capitalising fully on Labour's relative unpopularity. In a normal cycle, however, the government would be expected to stage a recovery as the next general election approached and so it proved.

In the general election of May 2005 there was significant decline in Labour's vote share (see Table 1.1). The main beneficiaries were the Liberal Democrats but the Conservatives inched upwards a little. The net effect was that the Conservatives gained 33 seats and the Liberal Democrats 11 while Labour lost 47.[2] The result made a serious dent in Labour's massive majority over all others in the House of Commons, but at 64 this was very secure by historical standards[3] and certainly enough to see Labour through a full term of office. In that respect, the 2005 outcome appeared disappointing for Labour only in comparison with the party's outstanding performances in 1997 and 2001.

During the election campaign, YouGov continued to monitor opinion on the party leaders and over five surveys, the proportion preferring Blair as prime minister varied between 34 per cent and 37 per cent while Michael Howard's scores were always between 23 per cent and 25 per cent. Blair's leads were much smaller than those he had recorded over Hague in the 2001 election – and that, no doubt, helps to explain Labour's weaker performance – but they were clear and sustained. The electorate had misgivings about the Labour leader and a majority were dissatisfied with his performance as prime minister, according to MORI data. Nonetheless, the voters clearly believed that he would be a better prime minster than either of his rivals and that goes a long way in explaining why Labour won. The importance of evaluations of the respective leaders in determining the election outcome was conclusively demonstrated by two separate studies highlighting the continuing importance of Blair, rather than Blairism to Labour's success. Although Clarke et al. (2006: 12–18) found that negative attitudes towards the Iraq war depressed both perceptions of party performance and the image of Tony Blair, the positive impact of Blair was still greater than policy or economic evaluations. Similarly, Evans and Andersen (2005, p. 177) found that:

appraisals of Blair, Howard and Kennedy are significantly and strongly related to vote in 2005. These results persist even after controlling for many other predictors of vote ... we also show that these leader effects are far more important than a wide range of issues, social background, and even, though to a far lesser degree, party identification. Simply put ... Blair's decline in popularity lost the Labour Party votes and seats ... [but] this was not enough to endanger ... control of Westminster.

The end of the affair: 2005–7

Despite having returned to power in a somewhat muted triumph, the last two years of Blair's premiership finally saw the end of the affair between him and the electorate. Labour's lead in monthly voting intentions had disappeared by the end of 2005 (see Figure 1.2). For most of 2006 and in the months before Blair's resignation in June 2007 the Conservatives were clearly in the lead. Such a sustained Conservative lead had not been seen since the days of Mrs. Thatcher. Not unexpectedly, local election results in 2006 and 2007 were disastrous for Labour. Rallings and Thrasher (2006) estimated the national equivalent vote in 2006 at 39 per cent for the Conservatives, 26 per cent for Labour and 25 per cent for the Liberal Democrats. Labour lost a further 350 seats. The 2007 contests, according to Rallings and Thrasher (2007, p. vii), were 'a triumph for the Conservatives' who gained about 900 seats while Labour lost around 550. The national equivalent vote shares were 40 per cent for the Conservatives, 26 per cent for Labour and 24 per cent for the Liberal Democrats.

The elections for the devolved institutions in Scotland and Wales in May 2007 were an embarrassment for Labour in two countries that were once safe areas for the party. In Scotland, Labour came second to the SNP in terms of support in both the constituency (32.1 per cent compared with 32.9 per cent) and the list votes (29.1 per cent compared with 31.0 per cent), lost nine constituencies and was ousted from control of the Scottish executive. In Wales, Labour mustered less than a third of the constituency vote (32.2 per cent), an even smaller share of list votes (29.6 per cent) and lost six constituency seats (while also gaining one).

There can be little doubt that Labour's poor electoral performance after 2005 was due to the shine coming off Tony Blair. Figure 1.5 shows that immediately after the election he was easily the public's preference for prime minister ahead of Howard and Kennedy. By March 2006 the Conservatives and Liberal Democrats had new leaders and the picture after that was very different. Menzies Campbell made little impact but David Cameron, the young, new and previously almost unknown leader of the Conservatives, was vying with Blair as the best person for prime minister in the eyes of the electorate. Further evidence of Blair's fall from grace comes from the MORI data measuring satisfaction with how he was doing his job as prime minister. During his first term his monthly net satisfaction averaged +23; in his second term the average was –14; in the short third term it was –28.

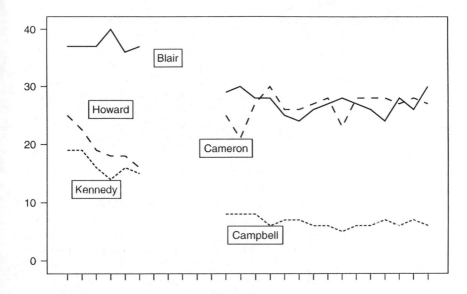

Figure 1.5 Best person for prime minister, 2005–May 2007
Note: The best PM question is not asked when any of the parties is in the process of selecting a new leader, hence the gap in the data.
Source: YouGov.

Thus Tony Blair's premiership ended on a low electoral note for his party. By the end also, his personal appeal to voters had apparently evaporated. A YouGov poll in April 2007 found clear majorities of respondents believing that Blair had not cleaned up politics (78 per cent), was not able to unite the nation (72 per cent), had lost touch with ordinary people (66 per cent), had played fast and loose with the truth (66 per cent), could not be trusted (63 per cent), was ineffective (60 per cent), was too influenced by the rich and powerful (59 per cent), was concerned only for himself and his party (57 per cent) and did not stick to principles (51 per cent). The only bright spot for Blair in this report was that 51 per cent thought that he was likeable as a person.

Of course Blair is not alone among prime ministers in experiencing a sharp decline in public estimation. As Enoch Powell (1977, p. 151) famously observed, 'all political lives ... end in failure, because that is the nature of politics and of human affairs'. It is also well established empirically that governments suffer from the 'costs of ruling'. Because they can be blamed for virtually anything that goes wrong (and don't get equivalent credit when things go well), popularity declines the longer they remain in office (see Sanders, 2005, pp. 176–7). The same dynamic applies to leaders.

To put the electorate's eventual disenchantment with Tony Blair into some context, therefore, we can compare his fall from grace with that of other recent prime ministers. During the last six months of his premiership,

Blair's average net satisfaction rating (–34) was somewhat worse than that for John Major (–27, October 1996 to March 1997) but identical to that for Margaret Thatcher (–34, June to November 1990). The difference between Thatcher and Blair was that the latter fell further in public esteem. Mrs. Thatcher had never reached anything like the levels of satisfaction achieved by Blair – even when her popularity was at its height – and so had less far to fall. So it was not Blair's unpopularity when he left office that was unusual but his earlier popularity. Other data suggest that in some respects Blair's reputation when he resigned was more positive than Mrs. Thatcher's. The latter was a much more divisive figure. In November 1990, 39 per cent of MORI respondents said that they liked her while 60 per cent said that they disliked her. The respective figures for Blair in May 2007 were 57 per cent and 37 per cent. Similarly, the 'likeability index' (per cent like minus per cent dislike) for Blair's policies was –28 compared with –43 for Mrs. Thatcher (MORI, 2007). Despite his precipitous fall from grace, Tony Blair did not leave office regarded with quite as much derision as his long-serving predecessor.

Conclusion

The story of the relationship between Tony Blair and the British electorate had, then, a rather ignominious – if not unusual – end. This should not, however, diminish or obscure his genuine electoral achievements. He transformed a party that seemed condemned to permanent opposition and led it to three successive general election victories. Given that Labour's electoral performance from 1945 to 1997 could be described as 'patchy' at best, this was no mean achievement. The long period of Labour government that he initiated in 1997 is still continuing at the time of writing (mid 2008). While *Labour's Last Chance?* had typified the mood after the 1992 general election, the last chapter of *Britain At the Polls 2005* had the title 'New Labour's Hegemony' (Crewe, 2006).

In part, of course, Blair benefitted from the state of the Conservative party. Almost any credible leader could have led Labour to victory in 1997, and the shattering Conservative defeat left the party in a state of shock from which it took a decade to emerge. They had a series of weak and/or unpopular leaders, were plagued by divisions and in the post-Thatcher vacuum appeared to have no clear ideas about policy. The latter was not helped by the fact that Labour clearly shifted to occupy the electorally fruitful centre ground and adopted some traditionally Conservative stances in areas such as law and order with relative ease.

It is also the case that Labour's electoral record was not one of unbroken success under Tony Blair – there were poor performances in European Parliament elections as well as losses at local government level. In 1996 there were 10,934 Labour councillors in Britain (47.9 per cent of the total); by 2007 there were 5485 (24.9 per cent). In addition, examination of the data in the Table 1.1 suggests that other problems were brewing. First, the Liberal Democrats steadily improved their position in general (and local) elections and became a more powerful rival to Labour on the Left of British politics. In 2005, their opposition to the Iraq war enabled them to pick up many votes from erstwhile Labour supporters (Kavanagh and Butler, 2005, p. 191). In Scotland the SNP strengthened its position in devolved elections to the extent of forming a minority Scottish administration in 2007.

Under Blair, as in some other European countries, there was also a growth in support for the extreme right. In the 2004 European elections the British National Party (BNP) received more than 760,000 votes (5.3 per cent of the total) in England as compared with just under 100,000 in 1999 (1.2 per cent). In local elections there were some spectacular results for the party. In 2004, the BNP took 4.8 per cent of the votes in the list voting for the London Assembly and was denied a seat only because there is a 5 per cent threshold for election. In the 2006 local elections the party won 32 seats across the country – by far the best ever performance by the far right. Although BNP successes were highly localised they nevertheless suggested that, in some areas at least, the white working class was being alienated from New Labour.

Perhaps the most striking electoral development under Tony Blair, however, was the decline in turnout. In the 1997 election, turnout had been a respectable 71.4 per cent – although this was the poorest turnout to date in post-war general elections. Worse followed in 2001 (59.4 per cent) and there was only a slight improvement in 2005 (61.4 per cent). Yet, it is difficult to pin the blame for the upsurge in electoral apathy on Blair and his governments. The biggest declines in turnout were in socially deprived areas and, it could be argued that since Blair took the Labour party to the centre of politics, and in some people's eyes made it indistinguishable from the Conservatives, the incentive to vote was reduced. However, if Blair had kept the Labour party where he found it he would have risked electoral suicide. It was also not Blair's fault that the principal opposition party failed to mount much of a challenge to the government and that both the 2001 and 2005 elections were widely seen as foregone conclusions.

As is almost inevitable, there are strengths and weaknesses in Tony Blair's electoral record. It is certainly true that in elections for devolved legislatures, local elections and European elections the record is not strong. These are clearly 'second-order' elections, however, and it is to be expected that incumbent governments will lose support. Losses at these levels have to be accepted as part of the price that a party pays for taking on the responsibility of government. The elections that matter are general elections.

Here one might carp about the fact that in terms of shares of votes the performance of Labour under Tony Blair was again not particularly distinguished. The share obtained in 2005 (35.2 per cent) was smaller than the party achieved in every election that it lost from 1951 to 1979 and even the 2001 vote (40.7 per cent) was not impressive in historical terms. On the other hand, the modern party system is much more complicated than it used to be. Whereas throughout the 1950s and 1960s elections were two-horse races, many more parties now contend seriously for votes in general elections. More significant, however, is the simple fact that under Tony Blair Labour won – very comfortably – three general elections in a row. In the context of Labour's electoral history that is a remarkable record. Labour's success under Blair was arguably more to do with the man himself than with ideological or policy positioning (although the two are linked). In both the 2001 and 2005 elections, Blair had a stronger positive influence on the Labour vote than the policies pursued by his government. Thus his legacy of undoubted electoral success is only likely to last if Labour is able to find leaders with similar electoral appeal.

Notes

1. Most of the local election data cited in the text are derived from the annual *Local Elections Handbook* series produced by Colin Rallings and Michael Thrasher and published by the Local Government Chronicle Elections Centre, University of Plymouth. The exception is figures for 'national equivalent' vote shares. These were supplied by Rallings and Thrasher and will appear in their forthcoming new edition of *British Electoral Facts*.
2. Following boundary changes in Scotland prior to the 2005 election, these net changes are partly based on 'notional' results for the 2001 election (see Fisher, 2006).
3. Eight of the ten elections between 1950 and 1970 produced smaller majorities than that in 2005 (the exceptions being 1959 and 1966).

2
The Party is Over: The "Modernization" of the British Labour Party

Florence Faucher-King

When Tony Blair assumed office as Labour leader in 1994, the party had lost four consecutive general elections. The last defeat was on a knife-edge and came as a surprise against an unpopular Conservative party facing a number of deep divisions over economic and European policies. When he stood down from the premiership in June 2007, Blair left the party transformed. Such changes were announced in his first conference speech in 1994: "parties that do not change die, and this party is a living movement not an historical monument ... It requires a modern constitution that says what we are in terms the public cannot misunderstand and the Tories cannot misrepresent" (Blair, 1994). In the following years, his team set out to "modernise" the organization and adapt it to the new times of economic globalization and permanent campaign. Once seen as almost unelectable (Heath et al., 2001; Jowell et al., 1994), Labour has, under the leadership of Blair, won three consecutive general elections. Such a turn around in the fortunes of the party cannot be only explained by external pressure (the succession of defeats), or the personality and the talent of Tony Blair.

Parties are "conservative" organizations but they are by no means static. A number of changes were introduced over the years by Neil Kinnock and John Smith, but neither leader presented their internal reforms as out of step with the party's history and culture. For this matter, the coalition led by Blair took a radical stance. Parties are always changing: policies are redrafted and strategies are adapted; leadership teams succeed each other, and support is sought in different strata of the electorate. However, "change does not 'just happen'" (Harmel et al., 1995, p. 2). The self-labelled modernizers felt that reforming the organization was an electoral necessity. Change was needed to convince voters that the party had become a viable governmental alternative and the leadership needed to adopt a more efficient and streamlined organization that would be more reactive to its initiatives while providing a source of democratic legitimacy and a sounding board for policy proposals. However, the content of the "modernization" project remained

vague, loosely bound up with faith in new technologies, in the superior efficacy of new management techniques and in a model of human behavior
inspired by the rational instrumental consumer of economic theories. The
positive connotations of the idea of modernization allowed Tony Blair to
denounce the forces of conservatism within his own party (those who could
not accept his policies or his organizational reforms) and within the country (those who wanted to maintain their privileges and prevent the opening
up of opportunities to the many).

"New Labour" in 1994[1] was little different from the party of Kinnock and
Smith. The dichotomization between *old* and *new* Labour that was then
deployed was primarily driven by public relation considerations. However,
an assessment of the Labour Party in 2007 reveals new processes for policymaking, a strengthened central bureaucracy and a streamlined party on-the-
ground, an ideological drift that affects many policy areas, the domination
of a coalition of self-labelled modernizers (whether Blairites or Brownites).
To understand the changes, it is necessary to take into account the design-
ing of the reform packages and how internal factors made *particular* innovations possible. This chapter analyzes change in the Labour Party from two
angles. First it tests the relative importance of external and internal stimuli.
Then it analyzes the nature of party change in light of neo-institutional
approaches highlighting the isomorphic tendencies of organizations.

The causes of party change

A number of theories have been formulated to explain the process of party
change. Harmel and Janda (1994) isolated for (analytical purposes) exogenous and endogenous stimuli while acknowledging the existence of slow
processes of adaptation. In the case of exogenous stimuli, changes are
imposed on the party by the environment, often in the shape of external
shocks such as electoral defeat. Not all stimuli coming from the environment are about electoral defeats. Although they are the most obvious, such
stimuli include changes in the legislation regulating electoral or party funding; political/historical transformations that bring the party out of step with
the dominant political culture (such as the Thatcher "cultural revolution")
or simply technological developments (such as information and communication technologies or the advent of 24-hour news channels). Although
electoral defeats are often necessary, they are not always sufficient to trigger
change (Harmel et al., 1995). Endogenous stimuli refer to the internal pressures for change such as leadership decisions and changes in the conformation of the leading coalition: shifts of alliance between internal factions.
Leadership change is an independent variable that is likely to affect change
because a new leader may be tempted to make his mark (whether he has
been chosen in order to affect change or not) and to consolidate his position (Harmel and Janda, 1994). Although decisions were usually taken on a

background of electoral preoccupations, successive Labour leaders played a determining role in effecting change (Harmel et al., 1995; Wilson, 1994).

External factors and piecemeal changes

Electoral defeats are important triggers of internal party changes: since 1979 all defeats have led to piecemeal changes (Russell, M. 2005). In the early 1980s, Michael Foot introduced organizational reforms (election of the leadership and selection/reselection of candidates) that reinforced the "unelectability" of the party as they demonstrated the growing ascendancy of the Left. The 1983 electoral manifesto (dubbed the "longest suicide note in history") included unpopular policies on unilateral nuclear disarmament and the nationalization of industries and services. The party was also seen as soft on crime and lenient on union demands. It could be caricatured as the party of high taxes and inefficient bureaucracy.

Following the electoral debacle, Neil Kinnock, a representative of the soft left, was elected leader. He initiated a policy review that moved the party away from the extreme left. He championed the introduction of new internal electoral procedures (one-member–one-vote, first rejected by conference in 1984 then introduced progressively) as a means to limit the influence of the Left. By 1990, "the highly pluralistic, deeply polarised party characterised by the institutionalised dispersal of power and weak central authority ... had been replaced by a powerful central authority exercising tight control over all aspects of organisational life" (Shaw, 2000, p. 133). A new public relation strategy was also initiated with the creation of the Shadow Communication Agency in 1986 (directed by Peter Mandelson). However, Kinnock stopped short of reforming the policymaking process and challenging the central role of the annual conference. Although the conference was not the only policymaker, its sovereignty meant that party policy was to an extent uncontrollable by party elites. Kinnock devised means of influencing the compositing process (Faucher-King, 2005, pp. 108–9) but he failed to come up with an alternative.

An active reflection on reforming policymaking developed in various sections of the party. It focused on increasing individual participation and the inclusion of minorities and was inspired by the burgeoning enthusiasm for study groups and quality management. The objective was to provide an effective and democratic policy deliberation process which the conference failed to deliver because of its cumbersome delegatory system. Not only did policy documents become contradictory or redundant from one year to the next but the arcane and often ideological debates projected the image of a divided organization whose leader was constrained, behind the scenes, by unruly delegates and unelected unionists. As the 1992 general election drained the resources of the party, further reforms were postponed. Following the surprise defeat, the new leader seized the opportunity to revise relationships with trade unions. The unions were a capstone in the Labour Party. They had founded it in 1900 to represent the working class and were still playing an essential role by the early 1990s. They provided a substantial portion of its funding, activists and organizational stability. The party culture reflected a working-class ethos in the ambivalent relationship to business practices and to its own leadership (Drucker, 1979). Concerned that their influence was an obstacle to the election of the party, the trade unions were convinced by John Smith in 1993 to give up the block vote and to reduce their weight at the annual conference from 90 per cent to 70 per cent.[2] The principle of one-member-one-vote (OMOV) was adopted and the formula for the "electoral college" was modified.

Internal factors: The "New Labour" tendency

The untimely death of John Smith provided opportunities to push for further reforms. With the exception of 1987, defeats also brought new leaders who pressed for organizational changes. Did Blair and his team introduce reforms that were of a different scale or nature from the previous reforms? Does his legacy benefit from the aura of electoral success or good publicity? It is clear that four consecutive defeats had prepared the ground but, in 1994, the leader was also for the first time elected under a new college system with greater use of OMOV. It conferred on the winner an enhanced legitimacy while its charm and dynamism gave him the popularity to press for bolder reforms.

Tony Blair articulated an attractive, if fatalistic, vision: "the issue is: do we shape [change] or does it shape us? Do we master it, or do we let it overwhelm us? That's the sole key to politics in the modern world: how to manage change. Resist it: futile; let it happen: dangerous. So – the third way – manage it" (Blair, 2000). The modernizers he brought with him were prepared to take risks and challenge the internal *status quo*. They demanded symbolic changes that his predecessors had not dared to undertake. The belief in the need to modernize was limited neither to the party nor in time, but there was no blueprint or a defined "Project. " More than a clear plan, the modernizers had a few principles and directions, such as a deep-seated suspicion of activists (a view already shared by Kinnock and Smith as illustrated in the move towards OMOV) and the will to replace the traditional representative procedures and the trade union links with a "modern," business-inspired effective campaigning organization. These were combined with great pragmatism, a willingness to use existing achievements and to build internal consensus. For this purpose, they used positive rhetoric and mantras such as *modernization, democratization* or *partnership*. These concepts were never clearly defined, leaving plenty of room for adaptation to the perceived constraints of the environment but little to skeptics. Many Labour modernizers attributed the 1992 defeat to the party's close association with unpopular trade unions. Advised by Philip Gould, the party shifted its focus away from the working class and to the aspiring middle classes; transformed by the Thatcher years but alienated by the corruption and the economic mismanagement of the Conservatives (Gould, 1998).

The first dimension of the strategy involved public relations. Labour "communicators" endeavored to prevent "destruction by a hostile press" (Campbell, 2002, p. 19). They were guided by the conviction that "communication was not something that you tagged on the end, it is part of what you do" (Campbell, 1998). Modernization is a powerful rhetorical tool. It is of course ambiguous and has been used by "New Labour" as an imperative, a plea and a description of their actions (Finlayson, 2003; Newman, 2001). Thus, the party engaged in rewriting Clause Four of the constitution and re-branded itself with a new name and copyrighted logo. "Old Labour" became charged with all the evils (incompetence, division, bureaucracy, lack of democracy) from which the party wished to distance itself. The re-branding of the party was an interesting ploy devised to convince the electorate and observers as well as party members (Lees-Marshment, 2001). The speed of the changes, the determination and repetition were devised to give the impression of a radical break from the past and of a clear strategy.

In order to increase control over the news agenda and project an image of unity and professionalism, discipline was enforced upon candidates and conference delegates (Faucher-King, 2005, pp. 165–6). The party's new public relation expertise was brought into government by "New Labour." However, "spin doctors" became increasingly unpopular and the growing distaste for such practices culminated during the Iraq war with dispute over the "dodgy dossier" and the enquiry into the death of Dr David Kelly. Despite his resignation in 2003, Alastair Campbell has carried on working for the party and played a key role during the 2005 general election campaign. If the party has taken a lighter approach to relationships with the media, public relations stayed a central concern of "New Labour" throughout Blair's premiership. Indeed, a great deal of the strategy remained focused on the leader's personality, his immense communication flair and talent.

Second, the leadership focused on bypassing the party activist base, perceived as too radical. For many years, little effort had been put in recruiting. Local activists, who were the primary recruitment agents, were suspected of restricting membership growth because fears of diluting their own influence dampened their efforts. Moreover, following May's curvilinear law of disparity (1973), it had become a fairly common assumption among the party elite that the alleged extremism of activists put off potential Labour supporters. In line with evolution in other Western democracies, activism was declining (Seyd and Whiteley, 2002). From 1994, a membership drive encouraged direct debit contributions and national rather than local affiliations. As it bore its fruit, it was followed by a program of political education, the promotion of policy forums and a critical evaluation of the traditional local party structures. Blair bolstered the legitimacy of his reforms by appealing to the widest constituency possible, appealing to party members in the name of "democratisation." Internal ballots were used in 1995 to rewrite Clause Four and in 1996 to ratify the draft electoral manifesto. "Minor" changes to the party rule in 1995 made the selection of women as conference delegates mandatory. This challenged old patterns and power strongholds, opening up opportunities to a new generation of members less involved in factional politics.

Third, the reform of the policymaking process was brought to fruition as the 1997 electoral victory produced a willingness to ensure a smooth relationship between the party and its new government. *Partnership in power* challenged the centrality of the conference in traditional decision making and created a new rolling process for policymaking designed to ensure regular updating of party positions and responsiveness to the public agenda. It was promoted as a means to foster greater levels of deliberation within the party, opening debates to local party members and supporters. In practice, it partially freed the leadership from arcane and complicated deliberation processes. The cumbersome rules of conference preparation were replaced by an "organic" system of consultation, led by powerful policy commissions and a joint policy committee largely dominated by the government. Taken together this created a sounding board for governmental initiatives, a platform from which to "educate" members and a legitimating process.

The various organizational reforms adopted during the Blair years were introduced according to a tested format that involved a phase of consultation, highlighting dissatisfaction with the existing process or rules.[3] Thus, the changes advocated by the leadership could be presented as a response to membership demands or as "dictated by circumstances." A second phase of "experimentation" then led to the naturalization of the new procedure and its institutionalization. A number of changes, from the introduction of policy forums to managerial best practices and the tentative breaking down of the General Management Committees (the constituency organizations) were progressively accepted. As Tom Sawyer, former general secretary, candidly explains, "when it's done, it's done, nobody thinks about it."[4]

The nature of party change

New institutionalism has shown how it is no longer possible to assume that "organisations function according to their formal blueprints" (Meyer and Rowan, 1977, p. 342) and how culture makes the process of deliberate change extremely difficult (March and Olsen, 1989; Powell and DiMaggio, 1991; Newman, 2001:26–7). Organizations need to justify their practices and therefore "are driven to incorporate the practices and procedures defined by prevailing rationalised concepts of organisational work and institutionalised in society" (Meyer and Rowan, 1977, p. 340). Thus, the incorporation of '*externally legitimated formal* structures' can satisfy public opinion demands, thereby increasing "the commitment of internal participants and external constituents" (1977, p. 349). Not all rules are adopted because they improve the efficiency of the organization or correspond to an internal demand for change. The main purpose is to bring legitimacy by demonstrating that the group abides by societal norms. At a time when trust in conventional politics is challenged like never before (Pharr and Putnam, 2000), parties across Europe have attempted to renew their legitimacy by adopting rules that proclaim their commitment to two societal myths (Meyer and Rowan, 1977, p. 341): the supremacy of the efficiency of business as a form of organization and the centrality of democracy in its non-representative forms.

The business model

Labour looked for models that could help build an effective organization and make them an alternative to the Conservatives. Considering the cultural atmosphere of the period, it is no surprise that many came to believe in the inherent and unquestionable superiority of the business model. There were still many signs of resistance through the 1980s, and Labour overall "clung to a 'politically correct' approach to relationships with business" (Harris and Lock, 2002, p. 138). Things started to change with the election of Tony Blair and the arrival of a team that had no intention of challenging the "cultural revolution" introduced by Margaret Thatcher. Her successful challenge to the unions' power and legitimacy was accompanied by the triumph of neoliberal policies.

The adoption of a business model was a slow process, bound up with image concerns. The promotion of "professionalism" was central for external as well as internal objectives. First, "New Labour" wanted to project the image of an efficient organization that could be trusted to manage itself and the country. Thus, efforts were devoted towards the development of an expert handling of public relations, with far reaching implications for campaigning as well as day-to-day interactions with the media. Second, Tom Sawyer, the new general secretary, encouraged the emergence of new rules of interaction within the party because he believed that cosmetic changes had to be intimately linked to cultural transformation. He developed new instruments for the motivation and control of staff and sent the National Executive Committee to a management course. From 1995, all party bodies had to submit business plans, name objectives and audit their performance (Faucher-King, 2008, p. 132). Succeeding general secretaries followed a similar path: functions were outsourced to private consultants or delocalized to services in the provinces, task forces were sent to fix problems in the regions and best practices were shared. Team-building away days were introduced to motivate staff and help them assimilate the party's new "mission statement." The old bureaucracy and its quaint habits gave way to professionals.

This evolution is not out of step with other European political parties, which have seen a rapid increase in staff numbers, particularly at the central level. Labour, however, has moved faster than others in adopting the model of a campaigning party (Farrell and Webb, 2000). "In 1964 the Labour Party had one employee for every 2786 individual members, whereas in 1998 there was one employee for every 1231 individual members, a net change of 56 per cent in staff to membership ratio. The change is even more pronounced if we narrow the focus to the real locus of staff growth, the central (extra parliamentary) party organization; in 1964 there was one central party employee for every 16602 individual members but by 1998 there was one for every 2263 members, a change of 86 per cent" (Webb and Fisher, 2003, p. 10).

Powell and Di Maggio have considered the role of professionalization as a factor of isomorphic organizational change. It involves the growth and elaboration of networks that span organizations and across which new models diffuse rapidly (Powell and Di Maggio, 1991, p. 71). In the Westminster system, there are few opportunities for consultants at the local or constituency level as the central parties dominate campaigns (Miller and Dinan, 2000) but New Labour elites contrast with previous Labour generations in their ability to move between governmental roles and the private sector. Many now conceived working for the party as an important career step: it allows them to develop specific knowledge and to build networks before moving to positions as politicians or as lobbyists (Webb and Fisher, 2003, pp. 15–16; Faucher-King and Le Galès, 2007, p. 68). Margaret McDonagh, general secretary between 1997 and 2001, is quoted by employees as insisting on autonomy and initiative, urging them to think of themselves as "'entrepreneurs' free to exercise their imaginations even at the risk of making mistakes" (Webb and Fisher, 2003:18). She set up, in 1999, programs to train central level staff. Training and recourse to consultants explains a marked rise in professional ethos.[5] Qualities such as flexibility, competence, commitment and adaptability are increasingly sought from party personnel (Webb and Fisher, 2003, p. 18).

Such changes were also made possible by a concomitant transformation in party funding. Throughout most of the twentieth century, trade unions provided Labour with most of its income, but New Labour endeavored to reduce its dependency. While the working-class party ethos (Drucker, p. 1979, p. 11) combined ambiguity towards leadership and money with a strong sense of comradeship and class solidarity, the business-oriented culture of the 1990s favored the professionalization of fundraising (Webb, 2002, p. 166). Small direct debit donations became a key source of income[6] until the appointment of Amanda Delew as a consultant to Tony Blair, in 1996, led to the creation of the High Value Donors Unit (Webb and Fisher, 2003, p. 13) and a new emphasis on large individual donations. Over the years, Labour became dependent on expensive consulting and generous donations. As Blair and Brown shared an infatuation with the world of enterprise and with economic success, businesses grew worried about the reaction of their shareholders to their close relationships with politics (Faucher-King, 2005, p. 227–33). The expensive 2005 election campaign weighed heavily on the party's financial situation, leading it to accept courtesy loans and donations. This entrepreneurial spirit contributed to marring the end of Blair's premiership in scandals concerning the connection between political donations and the award of life peerages. By 2007, the party was burdened with a debt reaching over 17 million pounds and a reputation so tarnished as to deter generous donors. In December 2007, the "donorgate" exposed how, contrary to legislation passed during the Blair years to restore confidence in politics, Labour had been receiving significant financial donations made anonymously via third parties. Having looked for legal loopholes, the Labour Party is turning back to trade unions.[7]

As the modernizers understood, written rules are important but insufficient to make change happen. They worked hard to eradicate traces of a working-class tradition: they replaced the old symbols and rituals with new ones and used the annual conference to publicize these changes to members as well as to voters. Red disappeared from the set, it was replaced by purple in most cases. The *Red Flag* was no longer sung, it was replaced by pop songs. The jargon changed (comrades became colleagues), composites disappeared and a new oratory style emphasized positive acknowledgment of the government rather than ideological disagreements. Instead of nurturing its traditional base, New Labour focused its attention on creating selective incentives that could attract new "citizen consumers." Most policies have been focused on the middle classes and have integrated the model of the rational individual. Treated like consumers, members have shown as little loyalty to their party as shoppers do to their store. The party's limited resources[8] do not provide much to reward instrumentally driven activists or to hire labor to replace those that could have worked for free as identifiers. The modernizers have not only distanced the party from the working class but also alienated the Left; and when the enthusiasm of the 1997 victory dried out, the influx of new members proved short-lived. As a consequence, Labour has faced a haemorrhage of activists, members and supporters that has seriously weakened its traditional strongholds.

"Deepening" democracy?

In the early days, Tony Blair promoted the opening up of the party base. Direct ballots were used in 1995 and 1996, and recruitment allowed the membership to rise beyond 400,000 members by 1997. However, Blair's enthusiasm waned. Direct democracy proved very expensive while low turnouts failed to bring legitimacy and limited internal support (Whiteley and Seyd, 2002, p. 147). The modernizers thus quickly turned to other forms of democracy: reforms focused on policymaking and on "partnership." Gordon Brown shared this approach: "in the past, people interested in change have joined the Labour Party largely to elect agents of change. Today they want to be agents of change themselves" (Brown, 1992). Such a vision of democratic participation had important implications for the party itself, no longer perceived as an effective conduit for political participation or for a two-way communication with the public.

Many of the innovations included in the 1997 *Partnership in Power* had been debated for years (Russell, M. 2005) by activists increasingly convinced that good policy could only emerge from discussions conducted away from TV limelight. The policy forums were seen as offering the possibility of widespread (localized) participation and of informed decision making (as experts and "stakeholders" could be invited). Advocates claimed that the new system would lead to a consensus on "good" policies, thanks to long and thorough private discussions. The policymaking process is now structured around a new National Policy Forum (NPF), whose members are elected every other year by the various sections of the party. All major political issues (economics, health, education, etc.) are discussed periodically on a two-year cycle. Policy commissions' drafts are examined in forums and at the NPF. The full reports of the NPF are then debated by the annual conference, which has retained the power to reject or refer them back.

The reforms replaced a complex and overly rule-bound process (based on the supremacy of the annual conference) with a system that is largely *ad hoc* and fluid. The practice of the NPF has shown that the informality of the new process opens the way for stricter control by the party leadership. In the first few years, that fear of negative publicity contributed to turn the NPF into a rubber-stamping institution. Repression of dissent eased out in the following years: the conference was presented with alternative NPF documents and the leadership lost a few votes. However, the government carried on undeterred with its program of public service reforms, the expansion of private finance initiatives (PFI) or the war in Iraq. The rolling process dramatically reduced the role of the conference and later changes further limited the possibility of dissent. Instrumental activists who had political ambitions could not afford to be seen to disagree (Dunleavy, 2006, p. 333), so the system bred conformism rather than support a responsive government.

NPF representatives have often complained about the difficulties involved in maintaining communication with the grassroots and tight control over NPF deliberations. Although all members are encouraged to send submissions to the NPF, there are few means to assess whether they are taken into account. The system had been presented as a two-way communication process designed to facilitate policy innovation. In practice, horizontal communication was made more difficult and party members were "educated" (Faucher-King, 2005, p. 184) in order to create consensus. In early years, such control was inspired by the conviction that the government could "guide" party members to reach the best solution. Thus, any disagreement would either require improved pedagogy or could be dismissed as ideological. Absence of decision making helped evacuate contentious questions (Faucher-King, 2005, pp. 90–100).

Organizational reforms were brought under Tony Blair to improve communication between the grassroots and the government. However, members are increasingly convinced that the leadership is not listening to them (Seyd and Whiteley, 2002). Low turnout in internal ballots shows the low level of engagement of party members, and the succession of Blair highlights caution towards direct ballots. The spiral of demobilization is combined with membership collapse. The headquarters tried to reintroduce "social events" and talked up "participation," but such efforts proved unable to reactivate some local groups. In 2007, the party had less than 200,000 members, and local and by-election results show a loss of ground in traditional working-class strongholds.

To "modernisers," democratization meant questioning social hierarchies, the introduction of new rights to information and participation and unmediated and informal style of interaction between the government and the people. Thus, Labour developed new qualitative and quantitative research tools for public opinion evaluation (Gould, 1998; Mulgan, 1994) and consultation. Multiple committees were created to foster participation. The party also expanded its use of the Internet in order to reach different target groups without necessarily improving participation. Beyond a presence online through party and government websites, Labour has developed blogs, Q&A sessions and ensured its presence on *YouTube*. To an extent, the party was, during the Blair years, deprived of many of its traditional functions. It has been reduced to a campaigning organization, aptly directed from the top by consultants, experts and politicians. The "democratization" of the party is part and parcel of New Labour's ambition to create a "partyless society" (Mair, 2000).

The leadership succession in 2007

In 1994, the leadership election was the occasion of a national media campaign and a membership ballot. Tony Blair brought a team of determined self-proclaimed modernizers who were prepared to take bold steps to bring their party back into power. Moreover, the process gave the winner an aura of democratic legitimacy that none of his predecessors could claim. This was so compelling as to lead the Conservatives to introduce leadership elections with their 1998 constitution. Interestingly, it was decided in 2007 to dispense with a proper leadership election. The smooth transition neither involved competition, nor any real change in the conformation of the dominant coalition beyond a change of personnel.

Blair first announced his retirement in 2004 but it is only in 2006 that he was pressed by an increasingly rebellious party to announce that he would resign within 12 months. After years of bitter tensions and fights with his prime minister, the chancellor presented himself as less manipulative and media savvy and announced in January his plans for "a new kind of politics." Having convinced his opponents to back away, Brown stood unopposed to the leadership and became prime minister in June 2007.[9] Many saw Brown as closer to the traditional party networks and culture, emphasizing how he had stopped talking about "new" Labour as early as 2000. However, it is important to remember how, in the early 1990s, he had argued that "the renewal of Labour [was] not a distraction from winning power. Instead the modernisation of the Labour Party is the first step to the modernisation of Britain" (Brown, 1992). Moreover, Brown had been, to a large extent, enmeshed in the architecture of "New Labour," fully benefiting from the centralization of power allowed by the organizational reforms and a keen advocate of the new professional and neo-managerial culture within the party. Fascinated by the policy instruments of new management and classical microeconomics, the architect of many of the policies of the previous ten years arrived in the leadership position with no clear agenda for change – for the party or the country. As a minister in the Blair governments, he had devised instruments to centralize controls of the executive. In the party, he had manoeuvred the deliberation processes introduced since 1997 and several times ignored their recommendation. Nevertheless he immediately engaged a consultation on "extending and renewing party democracy," insisting on developing membership participation. By autumn 2007, faith in such a renewal was fading.

Conclusion

Gordon Brown only enjoyed a short honeymoon period. International economic difficulties and unnecessary suspense over early elections brought lassitude from party supporters within six months. Within a year of Blair's resignation, Gordon Brown has faced a disastrous local election (including the loss of London), a calamitous by-election raising questions about campaign strategy and unhappy predictions by pollsters of a looming general election defeat. His efforts to "renew" party democracy are taken with skepticism by Labour supporters and the structural weakness of the grassroots organization augurs badly for the future. In a country exhausted by over ten years of change and reform for its own sake, Labour is ill prepared financially. It has lost the communication talent of Blair and seems to have run out of ideas. New Labour may be over, as Conservative leader David Cameron triumphantly proclaimed in May 2008, and the Labour Party needs to reconnect with its base and reflect on a strategy for the future.

Notes

1. The new name was first used at the 1994 conference with the slogan "new Labour new Britain." "New Labour" was thus launched without consultation or deliberation as a marketing venture. I have examined elsewhere in detail the slow process of party change (Faucher-King, 2005). See also Michel Crozier, *On ne change pas la société par décret*, Grasset, 1979.
2. It was reduced to 50 per cent when direct membership reached 300,000 in 1995.
3. This was the case for *Partnership in Power* or *21st Century Party* under Blair but also for Brown's consultation *Extending and Renewing Party Democracy*.
4. Interview with the author in May 2002. Similarly, New Labour's adoption of economic globalisation has been presented as a *fait accompli* one can only adapt to. This is an example of how an uncritical acceptance of the inevitability of "globalisation" creates its own reality (Cameron and Ronen, 2004).
5. The evolution was largely associated by the party staff I interviewed with the move to Millbank and the adoption of a "war room" office design. During the 1997 campaign, the interior architecture helped foster new modes of interactions. Additionally, 95 per cent of Millbank workers had university degrees (Webb and Fisher, 2003: 14).
6. Ninety-six per cent of its income came from trade unions in 1983. By 1997, 500,000 annual donations helped reduced this share to 40 per cent (Neill 1998: 32).
7. Labour drew in 2008 more than 90 per cent of its cash from trade unions (Hélène Mulholland, "Labour's funding crisis," *The Guardian*, 29 May 2008).
8. This is particularly the case as Labour is losing ground in local councils. The 2008 local election defeat has dire implications for party activism (see Seyd and Whiteley, 1992: 206).
9. On the contrary, the deputy leadership contest was a close race leading to the surprise election of Harriett Harman. The succession process somehow weakened Brown's legitimacy, leaving him more vulnerable to criticism by politicians and members.

3
The Conservatives: Trounced, Transfixed – and Transformed?

Tim Bale

By the time Tony Blair took over the leadership of the Labour Party in the summer of 1994, the Conservative Party was already in big trouble. Divisions over Europe, sleaze, Black Wednesday, weak leadership, and worries about the neglect of public services meant that Blair inherited a poll lead of around 25 percentage points. Although they narrowed this to 12.5 per cent on Election Day, the Tories were still left with less than 200 seats in parliament for the first time since 1945. Their performance in 2001 was just as dismal, and in 2005 it was only slightly improved. Clearly, the Conservative Party was unlucky to come up against an unusually gifted opponent who went on to run a government that presided over an unprecedentedly benign economy. Yet many of the wounds it suffered were self-inflicted. They also represented a marked contrast with the party's historical experience. The twentieth century had seen the Tories trounced before but they had, in fairly short order, picked themselves up, dusted themselves off and started all over again (see Ball and Seldon, 2005). Few, then, would have predicted that it would have taken them so long to perform the same trick after 1997.

This chapter, which is carved up chronologically, examines, first, how and why it was that the Conservative Party – once Britain's 'natural party of government' – found the Blair years so difficult and, second, whether it has at last changed to win. It also touches on, and tries to contribute to, more general debates about political party adaptation. To do this it employs a simplifying assumption, namely that what the Tories needed to do after their devastating defeat in 1997 was not rocket (let alone political) science. Like Labour after it lost office in 1979 – indeed, perhaps even more so given the UK appears to have moved into an era of 'valence' rather than 'position' politics – the Conservative Party needed to present itself as a united and competent alternative administration rather than an ideologically inspiring but potentially fissiparous crusade. And like Labour, it had to consistently and convincingly project some kind of progress back to the centre ground on which, in Britain at least, elections are generally won. Why and how it so patently failed to do this is a puzzle that demands an answer.

Standard accounts and suggestions

The Tories' failure to adapt is attested to by both narrative accounts penned by journalists (see, for instance, Wheatcroft, 2005), as well as the more explicitly analytical accounts put together by academics (see, for example, Garnett and Lynch, 2003 and Seldon and Snowden, 2005). Too long in power and supposedly unable psychologically to come to terms with the matricide of Margaret Thatcher, the party under John Major sank into sleaze and an internal row over Europe. Perhaps even more seriously, it failed not just to deliver the 'feel-good-factor' and good governance but also to see that it was driving public policy too far to the right of the electorate (see Dorey, 1999). When Major resigned after the 1997 election the row over Europe prevented the party from choosing the one leader – Kenneth Clarke – capable of steering it back towards the centre, thereby stranding it outside the electorally crucial 'zone of acquiescence' in which a plurality of largely moderate voters would be prepared to reward it with office (Norris and Lovenduski, 2004, p. 99–101). Any nascent attempts to reposition the party by the more obviously right wing and Eurosceptic leaders who followed Major – William Hague, Iain Duncan Smith and Michael Howard – were strangled at birth, each ending with what became a familiar collapse into the cul-de-sac of what came to be called, not altogether accurately (see Green, 2005), the 'core vote' strategy – an appeal based on nationalism, nativism and lower taxation that mobilised the committed but not the floating voters the party needed to lure away from Labour. Only after this strategy had been tested to destruction, runs the standard account, did the party begin to come to its senses. It elected a leader, David Cameron, who was apparently determined to drag the party into the twenty-first century and move it back into the middle ground that so many of his colleagues had previously affected to despise.

Political historians familiar with the Conservative Party's legendary ability to adapt to changing circumstances were clearly frustrated by its failure to get back in touch with the broadly centrist preferences of the electorate. Some, though, cautioned that even a return to form might fail to dislodge Labour until the latter began to fall apart of its own accord or in the face of events beyond its control (see Ball, 2003). Political scientists, however, should not have been too surprised. Of course, parties can and do change: a recent cross-national contribution finds, for instance, 'strong evidence that parties [particularly 'disadvantaged parties'] adjust their policies when public opinion clearly shifts away from them' (Adams et al., 2004, p. 606) even if (counter-intuitively perhaps) they 'show no significant tendency to adjust their policies in response to past election results' (Adams et al., 2004, p. 590). But even those who specialise in studying party change (see, for example, Harmel and Janda, 1994), stress that inertia rather than adaptation is the default setting.

In fact, party change is not only difficult; it may not even be rational. Budge (1994), for example, argues that, given the lack of expert consensus surrounding what voters think and how they make up their minds, politicians (and therefore parties) are likely to stick with what they know because they are ideological creatures. Norris and Lovenduski (2004, p. 90) list even more reasons not to expect too much of parties; 'rationally adapting to the public mood in pursuit of office' can be prevented by 'long-standing principles and symbolic traditions', the dropping of which will strain public credulity, by 'bureaucratic entrenchment', by fear of factionalism, by a grassroots membership that prioritizes principles over power, by a leadership that believes its 'central task is to persuade, rather than to follow, public opinion' or which may, because of groupthink and a tendency to recruit like-minded rather than innovative individuals, fail even to perceive that they are out of step with public opinion. Tracing the party's progress (or lack of it) after 1994 should allow us to see which of these factors was important in the Conservatives' case.

Fag end and first try – 1994–2001

The Conservative Government under John Major never really resolved how best to deal with New Labour and its new leader. Blair, as one ministerial advisor put it, 'could be a socialist wolf, red in tooth and claw but dressed in Bambi designer-chic, or he could be an opportunistic closet Tory who was stealing Tory policies. But he could not be both.' (Williams, 1998, p. 69). The Conservative leadership, preoccupied with holding things together over Europe and flummoxed by Labour's solemn promise not to raise income tax and to stick to the Government's spending plans, failed, however, to come down on one side or the other. Moreover, Major, convinced that a negative campaign was not the way to go in 1997, vetoed some of the more aggressively personalised anti-Blair material lined up by Conservative Central Office. Prime ministerial compunction also stopped the home secretary (and future leader of the party), Michael Howard, making immigration an election issue. Instead, Major (as well as key allies like Clarke and Heseltine) hoped the public would give him enough credit for putting the economy on a sound footing to enable him to restrict what was obviously going to be a Labour majority to around 30 seats.

Perhaps the most striking thing about the ins and outs of the Conservative leadership contest that followed Labour's landslide is how much discussion seemed to turn on Europe and how little it was concerned with either why the party lost and what it was going to do about Labour. This was not merely self-indulgence. It was also because many Conservatives, as they will now admit, seriously underestimated the will and the ability of Tony Blair and his colleagues to govern. So convinced were they that New Labour represented the ultimate triumph of style over substance, of PR over political reality, that they expected it swiftly to implode as hard choices exposed its pretences and contradictions. Their own priority, therefore, had to be to sort out, as quickly as possible, what they regarded as their key problems – leadership, Europe, sleaze and a party machine that had shown itself manifestly inferior to its main opponent's. And this they did. The leader apparent, Michael Portillo, having lost his seat, the party turned to William Hague – not a 'Europhile' like Ken Clarke, yet apparently more presentable than fellow sceptics, Peter Lilley, Michael Howard and John Redwood. In fairly short order, Hague moved to rule out joining the single currency in the next two parliaments and saw through structural reforms of the party. The dwindling band of Tory members were given a vote on the leadership and a bigger say in the administration of the party in return for enhanced central control over their constituency associations' conduct, information and resources. The era of division and dodgy donations was declared to be over.

Hague's emphasis on resolving matters institutional and European was not, however, just down to his background in management consultancy and the widespread belief that Blair and company would quickly fall apart under pressure. It stemmed, too, from a second comforting myth – and one that was all the more dangerous because it could less obviously be exposed as misleading. This was the idea that New Labour represented a capitulation to Conservatism – that the Tories had lost the election not because the public disliked their policy direction and distrusted their ideological instincts but because Blair had the chutzpah to steal their clothes while they were look-ing the other way. If that were true, and it was almost universally assumed to be so from the top to the bottom (and from the right to the left) of the party, then there was no need even to consider whether it had overshot in policy terms and therefore needed to signal a move back to the centre. Of course, the party needed to come up with some fresh policies, but these should not be rushed out too early lest they get stolen or create hostages to fortune. When they did emerge they should show that the Tories were ready to take Thatcherism (economically dry, socially hard-line) to the next level. So hegemonic was this conviction that few Conservatives seemed to notice that, rather than being flattered by imitation, they were being outflanked by a government savvy enough to demonstrate competence and credibility before (rather than after) going on to enact a programme of taxing, borrow-ing and welfare spending that (apart from its insistence on maintaining an Anglo-Saxon-style flexible employment market) was classically social demo-cratic. Moreover, it was undeniably popular with voters who were rewarding Blair (and Brown) with double-digit poll leads even in mid-term while the Tories 'flat-lined' at or below 30 per cent.

The myth that Labour had shifted pathetically (if slightly irritatingly) onto Conservative territory, and therefore could and should be fought not from the centre but from an even more radical position, was not the last of the illusions under which Conservatives initially laboured – especially on the right of the party. If anything, it was reinforced by a persistent tendency to attribute the Tories' defeat in 1997 to the 'fact' that over four million of their natural supporters had stayed at home or voted for the Referendum Party or UKIP. The route back to power, then, was not to worry too much about winning voters back from Labour but to mobilise this hidden Conservative support by a more robustly right wing, Eurosceptic stance. In fact, research by the Tories' own pollster (Nick Sparrow of ICM) clearly showed Tory abstention was probably no more than three quarters of a million whereas defections to Labour and the Liberal Democrats ran at something like 3.5 million. But this seemed to have no impact in the face of such deeply held instincts.

The leadership, however, did pay rather more attention to such research and, after morale-sapping cuts at Central Office freed up a little money towards the end of 1998, began at last to do a little of its own. This, and its *Listening to Britain* consultation exercise, told a sorry tale. The Conservatives were seen as out of touch and uncaring; indeed, they were seen to have changed very little since their defeat, while most voters either did not know or did not like William Hague. Where the party suffered most obviously in comparison with Labour was on its perceived attitude to public services: to large swathes of voters; the Conservatives couldn't wait to cut or privatise services in order to achieve tax cuts for the better off. To an outsider, the obvious implication from such findings was that the party would have to move to close down the gap between itself and the Government on such an important bread and butter issue. Yet even those Central Office staffers responsible for pulling together the research and suggesting a strategic response – many of whom believed the Tories could learn a lot from the New Labour playbook, Philip Gould's *Unfinished Revolution* – refused to accept its centrist logic.

Clearly, they argued, a certain amount of reassurance was needed on health, education and welfare, but this need not mean the party backing away from radical (and in some cases private sector), solutions in these areas. Yes, their position paper *Kitchen Table Conservatism* suggested, the party needed (to use a phrase they borrowed straight from Gould) to 'concede and move on'. But this simply meant drawing a line under the past, admitting they had taken their eye off the ball after 1992 and that the electorate had been right to kick them out; it most certainly did not mean (as some offended right wingers who distrusted them and their focus groups claimed) apologising or overturning anything fundamental. These young advisors might be urging Hague to signal strength and change by taking on vested interests inside the party, but if the example they gave of one of these '10,000 volt shocks' – challenging the Conservative Carlton Club to drop its opposition to full membership for women – was anything to go by, they were hardly aiming to provide a Tory equivalent to Kinnock's rounding on

Derek Hatton and abandonment of unilateral nuclear disarmament, or Smith's reduction of the unions' block vote, or Blair's rewriting of Clause IV.

Ironically enough, the only high-profile member of Hague's team who came anywhere near to doing so was one of Mrs Thatcher's original blue-eyed boys, the Deputy Leader, Peter Lilley. Just before the local elections in the spring of 1999, and just as Conservatives were celebrating the anniversary of Thatcher's moving into Downing Street 20 years previously, Lilley gave a speech in which he declared that there were 'distinct limits to applying the free-market paradigm in the public services'. He also said that the party needed to stop sending out the 'subliminal message' that it wasn't interested or wanted to privatise them – words that were pounced on by the media, not altogether accurately, as a repudiation of Thatcherism by one of its chief disciples.

If ever there was a critical juncture, this was it. The reaction inside the party, and among the right wing commentariat, was hysterical. Hague was unprepared for the row and even Lilley's limited departure from Thatcherite orthodoxy was considerably further than he himself believed the party needed to go. Had this not been the case, he might have seized the moment to tell it some painful home truths, to insist that on social and economic policy it had to be where the voters were, not the other way around, and to re-commit it (at least before it got into government) to the politics of the pragmatic centre. Instead, after a few days of trying to clarify and qualify Lilley's remarks, which were accompanied by a promise (similarly criticised by many on the right) by Shadow Chancellor Francis Maude to match Labour's spending plans on health and education, Hague basically backed off. Understandably concerned about a leadership challenge, advised by his new media team (Nick Wood and Amanda Platell) that he had to espouse some populist causes to bolster the tough-guy image they felt was essential to rescue his personal ratings, and buoyed up by the marginal improvement the party experienced as a result of its strongly sceptical campaign during the 1999 European Parliament elections, Hague gave up any attempt to fight New Labour on the territory that mattered most to most voters.

It did not take much after that for the increasingly influential policy chief Andrew Lansley and vice-chairman Tim Collins to convince Hague that the party would be better advised to talk up and campaign on the issues on which it did have an advantage over the government, namely, immigration, law and order, and (rather more dubiously) Europe. Consequently, Hague went into the long campaign and then the election proper promising (in documents like *The Common Sense Revolution* and *Believing in Britain*) to defend Britain's borders, put more police on the streets, and to 'save the pound', only to find that public support for such stances simply did not translate into anywhere near enough votes: 'Tory issues' may have risen up the agenda but never came close to displacing 'Labour issues' like health and education. Meanwhile, efforts by Michael Portillo (who had returned to parliament at the end of 1999 and then been appointed Shadow Chancellor) to tone down his colleagues' tax-cutting rhetoric proved only partially successful: despite his warnings that the public now automatically associated such reductions with spending cuts that they patently did not want, the party also promised to give billions back to the electorate by eliminating public sector waste. Given all this, and given Labour could claim to be able to competently manage the sound economy it had inherited from the Conservatives, the result of the 2001 election was hardly surprising.

Take two – 2001–5

Whatever the Tories had done in 2001, they would probably have lost, and lost badly. But at least a more self-consciously centrist campaign would have allowed them to signal a change of heart that might have put them in closer contention next time round. Instead, after four virtually wasted years, they were back at square one. Anyone thinking that things could only get better, however, was in for a disappointment. Hague's much vaunted reforms had clearly not had the positive impact on the party's capacity to match Labour's electoral machine that he had hoped for, nor had they boosted membership or made it any more representative of British society. Of the 257,000 grassroots Tories who returned their ballots, some 60 per cent voted for the candidate who, like Hague, had been endorsed by Margaret Thatcher and looked least likely to provoke internal division. Ominously, Iain Duncan Smith had failed in any of the parliamentary rounds of the contest to win the support of even a third of his fellow MPs. Some (even if they, too, saw themselves as on the right of the party) had never forgiven him for his rebellious behaviour as a Eurosceptic backbencher under John Major. Others, especially those who thought of themselves as 'modernizers' had him pegged as an old reactionary incapable of leading the more socially liberal party which they believed – probably wrongly given the narrow mindedness of the majority of voters – was the key to electoral success.

If Duncan Smith impressed few of his fellow parliamentarians, he failed just as miserably to capture the affection or the imagination of the public and the media. He was quickly written off as a stumbling throwback picked only because his supposedly superior rivals for the leadership had lost their bearings and their appetite (Michael Portillo) or were insufficiently right wing and Eurosceptic (Ken Clarke). This meant he gained little credit, inside or outside the party, for his efforts to reposition it in ways that, under another leader, might have provoked more interest. Whether those efforts went far enough, however, is another matter. Chairman Teresa May's address to the 2002 Conference set the tone, telling delegates that they were thought of by many voters as 'the nasty party', reminding them that '[t]wice we went to the country unchanged, unrepentant, just plain unattractive. And twice we got slaughtered', insisting that '[s]oldiering on to the next election without radical, fundamental change is simply not an option'. Yet the strategy proposed was not quite as radical or fundamental as some might have hoped for. Stressing the concern of 'compassionate Conservatives' to ameliorate the conditions of the most 'vulnerable' in society by encouraging civil society rather than the government to take on-the-ground action may have been laudable. But it risked coming over as a patronising way of saving the great unwashed from themselves – and saving the state some money. Trying to make the party itself look more like twenty-first century Britain by widening its base of candidates likewise addressed a real problem: only one of 38 new Conservative MPs elected in 2001 was female and none came from an ethnic minority. But, by ruling out anything than even hinted at positive discrimination, the party appeared to will the end but not the means. And, by insisting (unsuccessfully as it turned out) that its MPs vote against allowing gay adoption, the leadership demonstrated that its new-found tolerance toward minorities was far from infinite. In any case, a host of female, ethnic, or even gay candidates at the next election would make little difference if the social and economic policies on which they campaigned were still seen by most voters as some way to the right of where they considered themselves – and the Labour Government – to be.

Paradoxically, where it might have been useful for the Conservatives to have opened up some 'clear blue water' between themselves and Labour, they were unable to do so. In the wake of 9/11, they felt obliged, as convinced Atlanticists, to support the subsequent 'war on terror' and invasion of Iraq. Meanwhile, even though Duncan Smith hardened the party's position on the single currency, Europe failed to emerge as an issue since it soon became clear that Blair neither could nor would seek to persuade the country to adopt the euro. As for the economy, its continued rude health gave the lie to periodic Conservative predictions that Brown's sums would not add up, thus preventing the party getting any traction on the one issue that might have trumped Labour's continued lead on most others. By the summer of 2003, it was clear to most Conservative MPs that they stood no chance of substantially reducing Labour's lead under IDS, who also ran into trouble over accusations about the running of his private office. On their return to Westminster, backbenchers made use for the first time of the new procedure that allowed them, once they had gathered the requisite number of signatures, to trigger a vote of confidence in their own leader without a named challenger. When Duncan Smith was defeated, they conspired to avoid a protracted leadership campaign, and prevented ordinary members voting by colluding to ensure the emergence of only one candidate, the veteran right winger, Michael Howard.

Few Conservatives expected Howard to signal a change of ideological direction, and even fewer appeared to want one. What they did want, and what they got, was someone they, the media and the electorate could take seriously – an experienced politician who knew what he was doing, could hold his own against Blair and stood at least a chance of pulling the party out of its nose-dive. But any boost to party discipline and morale came at a price. To many voters, especially those who could remember the eighties and nineties, Howard turned the Conservative Party from a joke back to being a threat: no one doubted the new Tory leader could run the country; they simply did not want the country run in that way. Just as seriously, Howard's elevation to the leadership spelt an end to the (admittedly faltering) steps taken by Duncan Smith towards changing public perceptions of the party by emphasising social exclusion and broadening its base of candidates.

For a brief, slightly surreal, moment, it looked as if Howard might confound expectations on this score. In what was effectively his acceptance speech, the new leader seemed to promise a more moderate and inclusive Conservative Party: perhaps Nixon might go to China or de Gaulle let go of Algeria. But normal transmission was resumed almost immediately. Howard was neither inclined towards nor, he and his advisors knew, able credibly to sell, a more centrist stance. In the famous *I Believe* advert released to the media in January 2004, Howard made it clear that although everyone hated 'injustice', wanted 'equality of opportunity' and had a 'duty to look after those who cannot help themselves', the role of politicians was to remove the obstacles to the 'wealth, health and happiness' people naturally wanted 'for their families and themselves', not to leave the 'nannied or over-governed' by the state's 'armies of interferers'. By the time Blair called the election, this credo had been just as famously crystallised, with the help of Australian campaign guru, Lynton Crosby, into just ten words – 'school discipline, more police, cleaner hospitals, lower taxes, controlled immigration'. Few people – especially those who might otherwise have been tempted by a populist party like UKIP – would have disagreed, either in the country as a whole or in the marginals that Crosby zeroed in on. But too many mainstream voters suspected there was much more a Conservative government, especially one led by Mr Howard, would like to do. They didn't like Labour, but they didn't trust the Tories. The party was still seen as too right wing, too out-of-touch and too unrepresentative of ordinary people (see Ashcroft, 2005) – possibly good enough for the protest vote its campaign tried to whip up, but not a government-in-waiting.

At last? 2005 Onwards

One of the ironies of Michael Howard's leadership was that it was crucial in promoting the man who was not only to take over from him but also to insist that the party had to 'change to win'. David Cameron came into the Shadow Cabinet under Howard, and then benefited greatly from the delay introduced into the process of choosing his successor by Howard's ultimately unsuccessful campaign to restore the exclusive right to do so to MPs. This pause that gave Cameron, by far the youngest, least experienced candidate, time to make his mark. As the front-runner, the former minister and party chairman, David Davis, failed to inspire; Cameron – just 39 years old and an MP since only 2001 – wowed the audience at what turned out to be something of a beauty contest at the party's Blackpool Conference in the early autumn of 2005. With a BBC focus group (conducted by the controversial American consultant Frank Luntz) seeming to confirm Cameron would have the same effect on voters as Tory members, he shot into the lead, topped the parliamentary stage of the contest and eventually crushed Davis by a two-to-one margin in the ballot of ordinary members. At long last the Conservative Party had elected a leader for who he was rather than for who he wasn't – and picked someone who, even if he was Howard's protégé, was willing to talk explicitly about bringing the party back into the centre ground. It had also chosen a prodigiously talented communicator. Little wonder that people – including, it was alleged, David Cameron himself – began to talk about the Tories finally finding 'the heir to Blair'.

In fact, things were inevitably more complicated than they first appeared. Cameron was lucky enough to be facing a prime minister who had already become a lame duck. But not everything was plain sailing. Because of his (probably sensible) desire not to 'bang on about Europe' (see Bale, 2006), Cameron had to finesse his commitment – unwisely made at a time when the leadership contest was not yet sewn-up – to pull the party out of its current association in the European Parliament with the European People's Party. There was disquiet over the influence allegedly exerted over the new leader by his advisor, Steve Hilton, who some were comparing to Peter Mandelson, and who was the man behind the so-called 'brand decontamination' strategy. This aimed at downplaying 'Tory issues', like Europe, tax-cutting, crime and immigration, and at talking instead about topics the party hadn't previously concerned itself with and in a tone that suggested fresh thinking and a desire to return to the centre ground of British politics. This, allied to an insistence that Conservatives valued public services and a policy review process designed to deflect pressure to demonstrate exactly where the party stood, would gain it 'permission to be heard', after which it could begin to reintroduce more tried and tested themes.

Conservatives who worried that their core concerns might be forgotten altogether, however, were restive, even if there was little hard evidence (because there was little hard policy) that talk of a return to the centre ground was real rather than rhetorical. In particular, Cameron's plea that anti-social youngsters needed understanding rather than just punishment – tagged 'hug-a-hoodie' – attracted criticism from some sections of the party and the right wing press. They were also worried about his emphasis on environmental issues: it might go down well with middle class Liberal Democrat voters, Cameron's critics asserted, but would it play with hard-pressed tabloid readers for whom green concerns were an irrelevant luxury? Meanwhile, the creation of a 'priority list' of centrally endorsed candidates or 'A-listers' aimed at raising the numbers of women and ethnic minorities in winnable seats encountered serious opposition from constituency associations. They also reacted very badly to a speech in the spring of 2007 by the Shadow Education Secretary which confessed that not only would the party not be creating any new grammar schools but also that they would not contribute to social mobility to anything like the extent that was axiomatic among grassroots Tories.

When, in the summer of 2007, at the height of the 'Brown bounce' the party's candidate (running, note, under the label 'David Cameron's Conservatives') came third in a by-election with only 23 per cent, the new leader came under considerable pressure. In the face of that pressure and the possibility of a snap election, something of a change in tone occurred – in part facilitated by the recruitment of tabloid journalist, Andy Coulson (the new Alistair Campbell?), to beef up the Conservatives' media operation. Cameron kept his cool while many around him were panicking. But he also began to talk much more about crime and immigration – issues which seemed to grow more important to voters as their worries about health and education declined following a decade of sustained action by the government. Meanwhile, George Osborne, his key ally and Shadow Chancellor, having just committed the party to keeping to Labour's spending plans until 2011 (not quite as original a pledge as it was billed, given Maude's similar promise in 1999) used the Tory Conference to commit the party to abolish inheritance tax for estates valued under a million pounds and to use the tax and benefit system to favour married over unmarried couples. Those on the right of the party, and those who believed that there need be no contradiction between staking out new positions in some areas and returning to core Conservative (by which they meant Thatcherite) policies in others, breathed a sigh of relief. And, although, because the threat of an election telescoped the timeframe, this 're-balancing' (inevitably labelled a 'lurch to the right' by opponents) probably occurred much earlier than 'Team Cameron' had planned, voters seemed to respond positively. By the spring of 2008, the Conservatives were recording impressive local election victories and registering double-digit poll leads over Labour – leads so convincing that they provoked calls from party members and press alike that the party could now safely return to advocating tax cuts and tighter spending. This would surely be a high risk strategy: how much opinion poll leads represent a real change of heart towards the Tories on the part of the electorate, and how much they are due to economic difficulties and disillusion with the Brown government's apparent incompetence, notwithstanding its role in helping to stave off a global banking crisis, remains a moot point.

Also moot (see Bale, 2008) is the extent to which this new-found willingness among voters to turn to the Conservative Party is predicated on its leadership having achieved genuine and measurable change when it comes to personnel, organisation, policy selection and emphasis, distance from past practice and resistance to internal opposition to changes on these other dimensions. Beneath the headline leads (and the reassuring fact that the party seemed to be close to overhauling Labour's crucial lead not just on handling the economy but public services as well) polls suggest that brand perceptions of the two parties remain more than a little sticky. An examination of the Conservatives' policy offer also reveals it is less centrist than meets the eye. This does not undermine the assumption that the party's lack of competitiveness during the Blair years was largely due to its failure to move into the middle ground. But it suggest that the necessity (and the extent) of such a move varies according to how strong and economically successful a government an opposition is facing. It also suggests that such a move can be as much symbolic as substantive as long, that is, as the rhetoric of change and centrism which accompanies it is sustained over time – something the architects of New Labour, which was never quite as big a departure from Old Labour as they liked to suggest (see Bale, 1999), certainly realised (see Hindmoor, 2004).

Tories transformed?

Many in and around the Tory leadership after 1997 grudgingly admired some of the techniques that brought Tony Blair to power. Indeed, they sometimes appeared to be almost transfixed by his political genius. The upside of this fascination was that they believed they could learn from Blair. The downside was that they forgot about how much groundwork had been done by his predecessors. They also failed to fully appreciate the extent to which New Labour was not just a political conjuring trick by a master magician but also a profound, genuine, and sometimes agonizing move away from long-held positions and prejudices towards the preferences of the electorate and, where they coincided, the policies of opponents. If the Conservatives wanted to emulate (and perhaps even short-circuit) the process, they too would have to sacrifice some sacred cows, not simply nibble a little humble pie. Their failure to adapt was in no small part a stubborn refusal to do that – or, as Labour had, to find a leader or leaders who would make them do it.

A credible and comprehensive explanation of that refusal cannot be monocausal. It has to capture the interplay between interests, institutions, ideas and also individuals. It also has to recognise the importance of path dependency – the tendency of earlier decisions to constrain and even drive later ones. This chapter's thickly descriptive analytical narrative aims to do all this. It is clear, for instance, that the internal and media backlash against the poorly prepared attempt, in spring 1999, to distance the party from Thatcherism risked overwhelming a leader (Hague) who was already weak and anyway unconvinced. This led him to back-peddle and to pursue a populist course – one that (after European elections and at several key moments thereafter) suddenly looked as if it might prove capable of pulling apart a New Labour electoral coalition which, (as other chapters will show), was always more contingent than some acknowledged. After those hopes went unrealised in 2001, new rules combined with old antipathies to Europe and minorities to ensure the party picked leaders who were incapable of selecting or at least selling anything but the same sub-optimal strategy. But these particularities need not prevent us reconnecting with some of the off-the-shelf explanations for party inertia provided by other political scientists. This case study, at least, suggests that neither electoral defeat nor polling evidence that a party is out of touch with voters is enough to make it change. It also suggests that, while Budge is correct to identify ideology as a crucial factor, Norris and Lovenduski are right to include others along with it.

Leaders of parties that lose office stick to their guns because they believe that they are right – and that their opponents are wrong and will eventually come a cropper as a consequence. A related, if sometimes unrealistic, sense of efficacy, even mission, is also important: they believe voters can be made to see things their way and that this is what politics is about. Personal survival has to be considered as well: if leaders, or anyone close to them, even hint at an ideological departure, internal and media criticism follows and their position is immediately questioned. And time horizons matter a great deal too: leaders are nowadays expected to deliver by the next election, yet change will not only provoke resistance but will also take time. Finally, we cannot forget contingency: ironically, achieving change, and minimising internal resistance to it, is easiest when it coincides with an upswing in political fortunes that may have less to do with the merits and strategy of the opposition than with the perceived flaws and failings of the government. The belated revival of the British Conservative Party – one that has arguably come about without the kind of wholesale change required by Labour between 1983 and 1997 – owes much to David Cameron but also a good deal to Gordon Brown. Against a more impressive (or at least a less unlucky) prime minister, the leader of Her Majesty's opposition would almost certainly have had a lot more to do to change his party, and would probably have had a lot more trouble trying to do it.

4
The Liberal Democrats after Blair

Andrew Russell and David Cutts

Introduction

Tony Blair was good for the Liberal Democrats. Throughout his leadership of the Labour Party the fortunes of the Liberal Democrats, Britain's third party, were boosted. At the start of the Blair era the Liberal Democrats profited from anti-Conservative sentiment in constituencies where Labour could not defeat the Tories. By the end they benefited disproportionately from unpopular New Labour policies. In parliament, the Liberal Democrats tripled their numbers across Blair's three election victories and in Scotland and Wales they were able to share power in the new devolved institutions.

However at the end of Blair's premiership the outlook for the Liberal Democrats was less encouraging. As the Liberal Democrats seemed to lurch from crisis to crisis, and the Brown honeymoon period dissolved, dissatisfaction with New Labour transferred directly to the Conservatives leaving the Liberal Democrats facing – for the first time since the 1992 election – a crisis of identity, desperately fighting to establish credibility.

This chapter analyses the health of the Liberal Democrats in the post-Blair era. It analyses how the Liberal Democrats adapted to the challenge of New Labour and how the party adapted to changes in the political landscape. It investigates the nature of the Liberal Democrat vote in the 2005 general election in order to assess the challenges the party faces in retaining and recruiting supporters. Changes at the helm of the party are scrutinised in order to assess the impact of the leader on the party's fortune and prospects. Finally the future scope of Liberal Democrat strategy is assessed as the party is forced to come to terms with a new electoral battleground in the post-Blair era.

New Labour and the Liberal Democrats

The growth of the Liberal Democrats in the 1990s failed to fit the model for centre party revival as the party did not 'wander about in the middle' (Klingemann et al., 1994, p. 254) but sought new space for themselves outside the traditional spectrum. On the one hand the Liberal Democrats were keen to maintain continuity on a number of traditional liberal issues such as civil liberties and individual freedoms, for ideological stability could provide a sense of purpose to a party unlikely to gain office in the near future. On the other hand the party moved away from the halfway house of centrist politics in areas such as educational and taxation policy.

Under the leadership of Paddy Ashdown the Liberal Democrats had seemingly found common cause with Tony Blair's New Labour – indeed according to the former leader's published diaries (Ashdown, 2000 and 2001) the extent of common thinking between the two men was remarkable. By 1995, the party had officially abandoned its policy stance of 'equidistance' from both Labour and Conservative parties in the midst a Conservative government mired in allegations of 'sleaze' and incompetence (Leaman, 1998).

Although plans for formal coalition or Liberal Democrat representation in a Labour cabinet were thwarted by Labour's landslide majority, the two parties did co-operate in the new Joint Consultative Committee (JCC), and the Liberal Democrats played kingmaker to enter coalition with Labour in the new institutions in Scotland and Wales. Nevertheless, the ultimate failure of the Blair-Ashdown project – after Labour rejected Roy Jenkins' recommendation for electoral reform – put an end to the prospect of even closer relations with Labour and may have precipitated Ashdown's resignation as party leader in 1999 and his replacement by Charles Kennedy.

Despite being less authoritative than his predecessor, Kennedy oversaw the party's retreat from the JCC and the Blair-Ashdown project. Under Kennedy the Liberal Democrats amended the tone of election campaigning from 'constructive opposition' to 'effective opposition' (Russell and Fieldhouse, 2005) as disappointment and disenchantment with Labour grew within the party. Nevertheless, the coalition with Labour in Scotland was to survive until 2007 and the partnership agreement with Labour in Wales lasted to 2003.

Anxiety over the reaction to the terrorist attacks in the US on September 11 2001 seemed to crystallise Liberal Democrat unease with New Labour. Unsettled by Labour's enthusiastic support for the Bush administration, Kennedy's party offered qualified support for the war in Afghanistan but became the focal point for anti-war dissent in the run-up to the invasion of Iraq. Domestically the Liberal Democrats opposed government plans for identity cards, a range of counter-terror legislation and the imposition of student top-up fees. The crucial factor about these policy stances was not that they were hostile to the Labour in power *per se*, but that they were similar to left wing criticism of the Blair government. This enticed the Liberal Democrats to capitalise on disillusionment from Labour's heartland – and offered the party the prospect of taking votes and seats from Labour's core support. However, it also created a dangerous asymmetry as the party sought to craft policies designed to woo Labour defectors from the left while at the same time retaining support from disenchanted one-nation Conservatives in the centre. Meanwhile, other Liberal Democrat policies, such as the party's plans to introduce a new top rate of income tax for high-earners and the introduction of a Local Income Tax, were less popular with potential voters from the right than the left.

The 2005 general election and the Liberal Democrats

The 2005 general election marked a key opportunity for the Liberal Democrats. The party had grown in parliamentary terms at the expense of the Conservatives at every election since 1992, but now Labour was also a target

The Liberal Democrats had allowed talk to flourish of their 'decapitation strategy' which threatened to remove high profile Conservative MPs in marginal seats. In the event, however, all the Liberal Democrat challengers fell away in all the targeted Conservative seats. Furthermore the party discovered that their asymmetric policy appeal had repercussions in a national election campaign.

The Liberal Democrats' performance in 2005 (the party took almost a quarter of the popular vote and won 62 constituencies) was hailed as a high watermark for third party British politics. On reflection however the Liberal Democrat's performance was politically uneven and the party's 23 per cent share of the vote was worse than that achieved by the Liberal-SDP Alliance in 1987 (which was so poorly received that it precipitated the end of the Alliance) and while 2005 saw the Liberal Democrats mount a systematic challenge in Labour seats for the first time, the party was harmed by a Conservative revival elsewhere. In short the 2005 election demonstrated the fatal weakness in this asymmetrical approach since advance on the edge of Labour's northern heartlands was countered by retreat in the Conservative south. Given the level of expectations encouraged by the party before the election, the Liberal Democrat performance in 2005 was a relative disappointment.

The Liberal Democrat vote

Using 2005 British Election Study survey data, we investigated Liberal Democrat voting in the 2005 general election. We constructed two models, the first analysis (Model A) was a binomial logit where the outcome variable, a dichotomous classification (voted Liberal Democrat or not), was used to estimate model parameters. The second analysis (Model B) was a multi-level logistic model, with individuals at level 1 nested within constituencies at level 2. This allowed us to scrutinise the spatial contexts in which voters are politically socialised and electorally mobilised (Johnston and Pattie, 2006, Cutts, 2006). It also enabled us to analyse the impact of Liberal Democrat credibility through local government strength and proximity to areas of previous success (MacAllister et al., 2002). In summary, to take account of the importance of place, we simultaneously modelled both individual and aggregate data (Table 4.1).

Table 4.1   Modelling Liberal Democrat voting in 2005

Predictor Variables	Model A Estimates			ML Model B Estimates	
	(β)	SE	Odds	(β)	SE
Age (comparator = 18–25)					
Age 25–44	0.94**	(0.42)	2.53	1.06***	(0.34)
Age 45–64	1.38***	(0.42)	3.96	1.40***	(0.35)
Age 65 and over	1.30***	(0.44)	3.66	1.48***	(0.36)
Age Finished Education (vs 15 >)					
Seventeen	–	–	–	0.46**	(0.22)
Nineteen	–	–	–	0.42**	(0.19)
Region (vs Greater London)					
North	−0.72***	(0.29)	0.49	–	–
Scotland	−0.57**	(0.28)	0.57	–	–
Prior Intention to vote Lib Dem	1.62***	(0.35)	5.02	1.42***	(0.23)
Labour best on most important issue	−0.44**	(0.20)	0.63	−0.34**	(0.16)
Conservatives best on most important issue	−0.71***	(0.29)	0.48	−0.89***	(0.21)
Lib Dems best on most important issue	0.83***	(0.25)	2.22	0.83***	(0.18)
Labour party identification	−0.84***	(0.23)	0.43	−0.73***	(0.18)
Conservative party identification	−1.44***	(0.31)	0.24	−1.20***	(0.22)
Lib Dem party identification	1.58***	(0.16)	4.87	1.44***	(0.17)
Other party identification	–	–	–	−1.04***	(0.25)
Labour mobilisation index	−0.40***	(0.16)	0.67	−0.25***	(0.12)
Lib Dem mobilisation index	0.70***	(0.17)	2.01	0.52***	(0.12)
Feelings for Tony Blair	−0.12***	(0.03)	0.88	−0.13***	(0.03)
Feelings for Michael Howard	−0.08**	(0.04)	0.92	−0.09***	(0.03)
Feelings for Charles Kennedy	0.32***	(0.04)	1.38	0.35***	(0.04)
Full Time Students 2001 Census	–	–	–	0.04***	(0.02)
Labour Spending 2005				−0.01***	(0.00)
Liberal Democrat Spending 2005	–	–	–	0.01***	(0.00)
Constant	−3.66***	(0.60)	0.03	−3.94***	(0.54)

(Continued)

Table 4.1 (Continued)

Predictor Variables	Model A Estimates			ML Model B Estimates	
	(β)	SE	Odds	(β)	SE
Pseudo R²	0.40				
Log Likelihood	−1082.74				
Per Cent correctly classified	89				
Between Constituency Variation				0.088	(0.059)

*** p< 0.01; ** p<0.05.
Source: 2005 BES Pre–Post election survey
Weighted : Post election weight for GB for Binary Logistic model.Model A – Estimates calculated using STATA; Model B – Multilevel model: estimates calculated using MLwIN (PQL estimation procedure).
Model A and Model B: Insignificant variables at the individual level: Gender; Socio economic class – all (comparator = salariat); Belong to a social class – working, none (comparator = middle); Religion – all (comparator = No religion); Tenure – all (comparator = own outright); Age finished education – 16, 18, still in education; Region (comparator = Greater London); Party best on most important issue – Other parties (comparator = no party); Labour party best at managing the economy; Party ID (comparator = no party); Conservative mobilisation index; Economic voting – Retrospective evaluations national economy, Retrospective evaluations personal conditions, Prospective evaluations national economy, Prospective evaluations personal economic conditions.
Model B: Insignificant constituency level (area level) variables: Factor score 1 (Social Class); Factor score 2 (Affluence/Deprivation); Factor 3 (Retirement and Rural); % Muslims in the constituency; Labour spending 2005; Conservative Spending 2005; Liberal Democrat seats won on the council 2002–5; Liberal Democrat majority on the Council.

At the individual scale, both models account for social class and other demographic characteristics along with valence models of electoral choice. We included party identification, evaluations of economic conditions, party performance on important election issues and party leader images. We also include variables that measure the direct appeal of parties through local campaigns – mobilisation indices to reflect party activity. The inclusion of a vote intention variable from the pre-campaign survey controlled the effects of predictor variables before the actual election campaign. Model B also includes constituency level predictor variables at level 2. Here we took account of both traditional (such as age and education) and new cleavages of support (such as areas with student and Muslim populations) along with constituency level variables that are often significant influences on Liberal Democrat support (measure of contiguity, strength of Liberal Democrats in local government). We also included party campaign spending variables as surrogate measures of party activity at the constituency level.

Both models include significant variables, with Model A also including significant exponents (odds) at the 5 per cent confidence level. The majority of socio-demographic characteristics were insignificant, although those who lived in the North and the Midlands were less likely to vote Liberal Democrat than those from Greater London. Older voters were more likely to vote Liberal Democrat than those aged 24 and under, with the baby boomer group (aged 45–64) and older people being 3.96 and 3.66 times more likely to vote Liberal Democrat than the youngest group. The significance of the prior intention to vote Liberal Democrat variable suggests that indirect campaign factors influenced Liberal Democrat support. Despite having fewer partisans than the two main parties, activating Liberal Democrat identifiers – who were nearly five times more likely to vote Liberal Democrat than no party identifiers – positively affected Liberal Democrat voting, while the activation of both Conservative and Labour identifiers reduced the likelihood of supporting the Liberal Democrats. The leadership of Charles Kennedy also proved beneficial to the Liberal Democrats, although positive feelings about the other party leaders did have a negative influence. Perceptions that the party was best able to handle the most important issue was also a significant predictor, indicating that the party's reactions to important issues during the campaign increased the likelihood of voting Liberal Democrat.

Direct local campaign effects also proved important. Those who were targeted by Liberal Democrat campaigning (doorstep canvassing, party broadcasts, telephone canvassing and knocking-up) were twice as likely to vote Liberal Democrat as those who received no contact. Conversely, Labour party campaigning reduced the likelihood of voting Liberal Democrat. Model A performs well (a pseudo R^2 or Nagelkerke R^2 of 0.40); the votes of 89 per cent of respondents were correctly classified.

The multilevel analysis (Model B) confirms that at the individual level, few socio-demographic characteristics influenced Liberal Democrat voting. Once again prior vote intention was vital, suggesting that activating predispositions to vote Liberal Democrat in 2005 was a crucial part of campaign strategy. This is emphasised by the large influence of Liberal Democrat partisanship, perceptions that the party was best able to handle the most important issue and positive feelings towards Kennedy. Similarly, exposure to party campaigning increased the likelihood that an individual voter would support the Liberal Democrats.

After taking account of individual level effects, only a few predictors were significant at the constituency level. Those voters living in student areas were more likely to support the Liberal Democrats, as the party's policy on tuition fees resonated in these areas. This represents a decisive break from previous strategy where the party strengthened support in areas of existing strength. It also helps explain why local election success and contiguity variables proved to be insignificant. However, individual voters who lived in constituencies where the Liberal Democrats campaigned intensely were more likely to vote for the party, provided Labour were less active.

It is vital here to emphasise the profile of Liberal Democrat support in 2005. Typically Liberal voters tend to be similar to Conservative voters socially, but to Labour supporters attitudinally (Russell and Fieldhouse, 2005).

Analysis of 2005 might lead to the conclusion that the Liberal Democrats transformed campaigning tactics in an assault on Labour's heartland vote. Nevertheless, it is important to acknowledge that the Liberal Democrat advance urban areas were typically confined to gentrified urban areas. All nine Liberal Democrat victories from Labour were in seats that had been Conservative-held until quite recently. Perhaps the Liberal Democrats were the grateful receptacle for protest in the least working class of Labour's working class base. Elsewhere the Liberal Democrat challenge to Labour fell short of victory. A post-2005 strategy based on turning second places into victories in Labour's heartland is far from a foregone conclusion. It may be challenge enough to ensure that ground gained in 2005 is not lost.

There are several reasons for supposing that the Liberal Democrat performance in 2005 was artificially boosted by the relative unpopularity of both the incumbent Blair government (Curtice, 2007b) and the Howard opposition (Fieldhouse et al., 2006). The party was able to exploit fissures in the enduring relationship between Labour and its core voters in 2005 that might be less pertinent in the future while the Conservatives might be seen as fit to govern again by a large slice of the electorate that has deserted them since 1992. Liberal Democrat success in 'university seats' may continue but there are too few of these constituencies to represent a blueprint for substantial growth. Furthermore while the Liberal Democrats made significant in-roads into the Muslim community's vote in 2005 it is not certain that this is the basis for a durable relationship between Britain's Muslims and the Liberal Democrats. Certainly some of the issues that pulled voters to the Liberal Democrat cause in 2005 – such as the Iraq war and student top-up fees – may simply lose relevance over time. With all three main parties under new leadership the Liberal Democrats might fear that 2005 was their golden opportunity.

Dropping the pilot: Leadership changes in the Liberal Democrats

Exit 'Chat Show Charlie': The departure of Charles Kennedy

Charles Kennedy's time as leader saw the Liberal Democrats improve share of the national vote and presence at Westminster at two successive elections. His avuncular public image enabled the party to have a distinctive voice in British politics. Analysis of the rolling campaign survey of the 2005 British Election Study reveals that he was the most popular (or the least unpopular) of all three party leaders at the time of the 2005 contest (Russell, A. 2005). Although the party leader's image had proven to be a bonus for the Liberal Democrats in successive general elections (Clarke et al., 2004), there is a persuasive argument that the Liberal Democrats failed to capitalise on popular leadership.

Kennedy's time as leader was frequently characterised by speculation about his future. As the parliamentary party grew, it became an effective rallying point for opposition to his leadership style and the future direction of the party[1]. Dissatisfaction at Westminster with Kennedy's management style and the party's perceived underperformance in 2005 heaped pressure upon the leader until he was compelled to stand down as party leader in January 2006 (see Hurst, 2006). The timing of Kennedy's resignation was influenced by his personal struggle with alcohol, but in reality the parliamentary party – weary of 'lacklustre' leadership (Denham and Dorey 2007) – had flexed its muscles to affect the leader's removal. Indeed a striking feature of the 'defenestration' of Kennedy was that his popularity was seemingly undamaged outside Westminster. (Russell et al., 2007).

The shortest of dynasties: The Ming Campbell interregnum

The Liberal Democrats elected Sir Menzies (Ming) Campbell as their new leader in March 2006 after a particularly unfortunate election contest. One leadership candidate (Mark Oaten) was forced to withdraw from the contest as vivid claims about his personal life came to light. Another contender, Simon Hughes was forced to admit to having previously lied about his sexual orientation. In the end, Campbell's chief challenge came from Chris Huhne, a former MEP who had only been elected to parliament in 2005.

Signs that Campbell would not get an easy ride from the British press were evident immediately. On 3 March 2006, the day after his election as leader, the editorial in the *Sun* must have been uncomfortable reading in the new leader's office:

> Having dumped an alcoholic, shunned a rent-boy botherer and rejected a liar, they (the Liberal Democrats) settled for a man who looks ready to retire. The sad truth that emerged during the contest is: He's just not up to the job.

Campbell's public image did not improve much. Whereas the Conservatives skipped a generation in 2005, the Liberal Democrats had plumped for their most experienced figure, who did not always benefit from the comparison. Although being born in 1941 put him in the same generation as an increasingly important slice of the electorate (there are more Britons over 60 than under 16), his age was seen as a handicap. The BBC Television satire *Dead Ringers* paid Campbell the compliment of regularly impersonating him, but the ex-Olympic athlete was inevitably portrayed in a bath chair, wrapped in a blanket and offering the older person's confection of choice, *Werther's Original* toffees. Campbell's supporters may have been outraged by this treatment but his authority as leader was undermined from the start and the polls continued to be disappointing for the party.

Criticisms of Campbell's performances in the Commons were rife and much was made of the Liberal Democrats' poor ratings under Campbell while the Conservatives embarked on a steady rehabilitation.[2] By the summer of

2007 Labour's new prime minister was riding high in the polls, but Campbell had been unable to turn around Liberal Democrat fortunes. The *New Statesman* commented:

> Campbell is thought to be doing an even worse job than Cameron. ... It is often joked that Sir Ming is less popular sober than Charles Kennedy was drunk – and it's true that the heady 23% scored by the Lib Dems at the last general election seems a long way off.
>
> (Prince, 2007)

Gordon Brown's bubble was unceremoniously popped in the autumn of 2007. Clearly enjoying Conservative discomfort while Labour rode high in the polls, the prime minister encouraged speculation about the prospect of a snap general election to cement his authority as premier. The party conference season was dominated by tergiversation on the necessity for an election. However, Labour strategists failed to anticipate that the Conservatives – even in their darkest hour – would rally at their conference. Moreover, David Cameron's impressive speech from the conference dais and the announcement of a number of innovative – and populist – financial policies enabled the Conservatives to gain some momentum. A small Tory revival in the polls was enough for Labour to call off the election that never was and Gordon Brown's problems began in earnest.

At the September 2007 party conference there were only two topics of gossip, the prospect of an early election and Campbell's future as leader. Nick Clegg hardly defused speculation by admitting that he wanted to lead the party if Campbell stood down (earning him a rebuke from the leader's wife). In his closing speech to the conference, Campbell promised to lead the party into the next election. However, it was not to be. With the confirmation that there was to be no early election, Campbell surprisingly stood down as leader on 15 October 2007. His letter of resignation conceded that his age had been critical and questions about his leadership were, he claimed, 'getting in the way of further progress by the party'.

Another new beginning: Nick Clegg – calamities and changes

The rationale behind Campbell's resignation made it difficult for other senior Liberal Democrats to run for the leadership – Campbell's deputy, Vince Cable, only two years younger than Campbell, ruled himself out on this basis. Nevertheless Cable took charge of the party as a caretaker, while the party embarked on the lengthy process of a leadership election. Cable performed ably in the Commons and the party responded well to his management style. In particular, he appeared to have a masterful overview of the *Northern Rock* crisis. Moreover with the loss of half the population's data records and the ongoing scandal of Labour party funding, Cable's withering criticism of Brown's fall from grace – 'the prime minister's remarkable transformation in

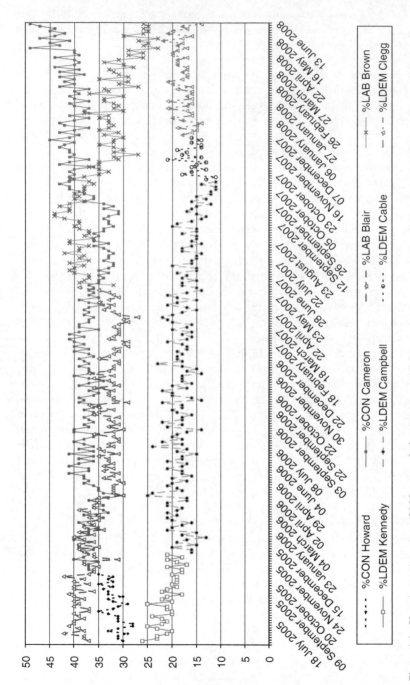

Figure 4.1 Vote intention since 2005 general election
Source: ukpollingreport.co.uk

the past few weeks – from Stalin to Mr. Bean, creating chaos out of order rather than order out of chaos' – immediately entered Westminster folklore (Hoggart, 2007). Unfortunately, Cable's impressive caretaker leadership failed to translate into a significant boost to Liberal Democrat support (see Figure 4.1).

There were only two candidates in the leadership election, Nick Clegg and Chris Huhne. There were many similarities between the two men; both were educated at Westminster School and Oxbridge, both had worked as journalists and both entered parliament in 2005 after stints as MEPs. Huhne impressed the grass roots with his leadership campaign in 2006, but Clegg's popularity with the party elite made him the ante-post favourite. In the end the contest was rather lacklustre, most notable for the narrowest of winning margins as Clegg with 20,988 votes defeated Huhne by just 511 on 18 December 2007. The official turnout (64.1 per cent) shows that the Liberal Democrats had lost around 7400 members since 2006; a potential problem since we have seen how the party relies on its foot soldiers to influence voting during campaigning.

Since Clegg's election the Liberal Democrats have improved only slightly in the polls (Figure 4.1) and still face a constant struggle for recognition and credibility. Incredibly, the most Europhile of all British parties managed to engineer a parliamentary split on the issue of Europe – as Clegg's instruction to abstain on the need for a referendum on the European Union constitution led to rebellion from a fifth of the parliamentary party, two resignations from the Liberal Democrat shadow cabinet and ridicule in the popular Tory press.[3]

Since Clegg became leader, the Liberal Democrats have been sidelined in three electoral contests. The party outperformed Labour in the 2008 local elections – although this was more a reflection of Labour's travails than Liberal Democrat triumph – but Conservative victories in the London Mayor election and, in particular, the Crewe and Nantwich by-election demonstrate that the Liberal Democrats failed to galvanise disenchantment as voters transferred directly from Labour to Conservative for the first time since the election of the New Labour government.

Adjustment and realignment? New Challenges for the Liberal Democrats

The change of all three party leaders has exacerbated the need for the Liberal Democrats to address the fault lines in their electoral strategy. David Cameron's rise to the leadership of the Conservatives has unambiguously threatened the Liberal Democrats in the south of England – and the suburban edges of affluence in northern cities. He has parked his tank on the lawn of the Liberal Democrats with environmental and educational policy, and might signal a revival of Conservative fortunes at the expense of the third party. The arrival of a new prime minister and then another change in

Liberal Democrat leadership underscored that the 2005 election had been a very different contest from the one we can expect next time.

Popular leadership has been a small but significant factor in inducing Liberal Democrat support in previous elections, but Campbell, Cable and Clegg have struggled to match the level of public recognition and popularity enjoyed by Ashdown and Kennedy. So, if a popular leader espousing popular policies had only a weak effect on Liberal Democrat support, it might be difficult to see a relatively less popular leader having a stronger impact.

Nevertheless, it should be borne in mind that the chances that the Liberal Democrats will play a pivotal role in British politics after the next election are not negligible – even if they lose some ground to the Conservatives in the south of England. This suggests that the political impact of the third party may be measured in something other than sheer parliamentary size.

Parliamentary, local and devolved elections

The Liberal Democrats' position as the primary party of protest has often resulted in spectacular by-election victories. Indeed the party managed to defeat Labour in Dunfermline and West Fife in 2006 at a time when they had no permanent leader and were the source of much public ridicule over the misfortunes of Kennedy, Oaten and Hughes. A strong showing in the Conservatives stronghold of Bromley and Chislehurst in 2006 was followed by a disappointing result in Ealing Southall in 2007 – a constituency which fitted the profile of the types of inner-city seats that the Liberal Democrats took from Labour in the last parliament (Brent East and Leicester South being obvious comparisons). Labour retained the seat with only a modest swing to the Liberal Democrats as the Conservatives vote held up. Worse was to come in May 2008, as a spectacular Conservative victory in Crewe and Nantwich was achieved through widespread defection from Labour directly to the Tories. This revived trend of British psephology will not have gone unnoticed in the headquarters of all three parties.

For the Liberal Democrats, local election success has been vital to their improvement in parliamentary representation since the 1990s. Building a strong local base has been one of the main mechanisms the party has used to bridge the electoral credibility gap. Local success gives the party organisational strength through new members and activists that often enhances grass roots campaigning and allows the local party to target resources more effectively, which in turn can heighten the intensity of future campaigns. The combination of local representation and grass roots campaigning can be particularly salient to the electoral fortunes of the Liberal Democrats (Cutts, 2006; Cutts and Shrayne, 2006).

A third party in Britain is likely to face a battle to establish credibility, for as Duverger (1954, p. 217) famously claimed 'the simple majority single ballot system favours the two party system'. Cox (1997) has asserted that third parties can breakthrough by establishing local credibility first and this seems to have been the blueprint for Liberal Democrat success in the 1990s. Indeed 18 of the party's 1997 gains had been built on the platform of success in local government, although the potency of this strategy had waned by 2001 and was marginal by 2005. The party's councillor base may also have diminished; the party's 5078 councillors and control of more than 50 local councils in 1995 representing the high watermark before the tide turned and the focus of power within the party has shifted from the councillor base towards the party's parliamentarians.

In Scotland and Wales, the Liberal Democrats seem to be in retreat. Having been involved in a partnership agreement with Labour in Cardiff from 2000–3 and in full coalition with Labour in Edinburgh from 1999 to 2007, the speculation prior to the 2007 elections was that the Liberal Democrats could again expect to play a pivotal role and hold the balance of power in both the Scottish Parliament and the National Assembly for Wales (NAW). However, the Liberal Democrats found themselves outmanoeuvred politically in both Scotland and Wales.

Returning six Assembly Members (AMs) again the Welsh Liberal Democrats could have expected to reprise their role in the Welsh Assembly Government with the largest party, Labour. However, two Liberal Democrat AMs campaigned against such an outcome and in the end, Labour preferred to forge a deal with Plaid Cymru. Some might pointedly enquire of the ultimate point of the Welsh Liberal Democrats since they remain the fourth party in the NAW and are further away from power than at any point since 1999.

In Scotland the Liberal Democrats had been the beneficiaries of coalition with Labour since 2000 (Mitchell and Bradbury, 2004) and were supposed to be kingmakers again in 2007. A continued Labour-Liberal Democrat coalition seemed probable but coalition with the SNP was a distinct possibility. In the event the SNP narrowly beat Labour into second place while the Liberal Democrats came fourth. The post-election politics proved a harsh obstacle to the Liberal Democrats. Determined not to compromise on the referendum, the Nationalists simply declared themselves the moral victors of the election and dared the Liberal Democrats to face the consequences of upholding a 'discredited' Labour regime in Scotland. In the end the Scottish Liberal Democrats found neither the desire nor the resolve to pursue a coalition with Labour and thus their bargaining power evaporated. The lesson from Wales and Scotland is that even in apparently favourable circumstances the Liberal Democrats have struggled to impose themselves since the end of the Blair era.

Conclusion and party prognosis

The problems facing the Liberal Democrats in the post-war era might seem familiar to those who study third parties elsewhere or historically in Britain. The party faces the perennial prospect of being marginalised by their more powerful counterparts who benefit from a more catch-all, or more heart-landed approach (Kirchheimer, 1966; Gudgin and Taylor, 1978). In the 1980s the Alliance might have displaced the divided and ineffective Labour Party; since 1997 Liberal Democrat strategy appeared to have the Conservatives in its sights. However, the British party system has proven remarkably resilient. Without the financial means and organisational strength of either Conservative or Labour parties the Liberal Democrats are unlikely to break the mould of politics without a sustained reversal of fortune of one of their counterparts. Labour, it should be remembered, prospered at the expense of the Liberals in the early 20th century through social and electoral change (as the trade union movement galvanised working class support enabled by a broadening electorate) and sufficient political dexterity to outmanoeuvre the Liberal Party and capitalise on public thirst for radicalism (Cook, 1989; Cyr, 1977). The prospect for Liberal Democrat growth in the contemporary climate is largely reliant on the condition of the other parties. In an environment of public hostility to the Conservatives, the Liberal Democrats prospered but failed to be seen as an alternative Opposition. In a period of Conservative revival, the challenge for the Liberal Democrats is to be seen as relevant in Britain's bi-partisan environment.

In this light it is hardly surprising that Clegg saw the political realignment of the party as one of his key priorities. While the party went into the 2005 election promising to increase taxes on the top-earners, Clegg has begun a public discourse on lowering the burden of taxation. While Campbell had a one-sided view of co-operation with other parties (he set five tests – preconditions for coalition – for Gordon Brown but did not seem to contemplate the prospect of a working partnership with the Conservatives), Clegg has been more relaxed about taking his party closer to the ground that Cameron's Conservatives now occupy.

One of the central strategic problems for the Liberal Democrats after Blair concerns the struggle to align the party politically. Whiteley et al. (2006) note the Liberal Democrats are constrained as a political party; 'waiting for Godot' while relying on the misfortunes of others in order to advance. Since the early 1990s the party has grown through its emergence as part of an anti-Conservative alliance. Voters who might term themselves one-nation Conservatives were targeted by the Liberal Democrat campaign rhetoric that suggested that the Conservative Party had surrendered to the Eurosceptic right. In recent times the Liberal Democrats have made gains from Labour, through dissatisfaction with the nature of the new Labour project – appealing to core Labour voters unhappy with New Labour's movement away from the party's ideological and social heartland. Both of these tactics were made possible by the abandonment of equidistance in the 1990s, but may seem anachronistic now. The contemporary Conservatives seem less like the bogey-men of the previous decade and prolonged disenchantment with Labour makes a close relationship with them less logical. Clegg has seemingly recognised this and in February 2008 explicitly used the term 'equidistant' to describe his party in relation to the others, effectively disinterring the principal tactic of the 1992 general election. He warned that the Conservatives needed to be more liberal on civil liberties, public service reform and the environment and seemed to rule out a full coalition without reform to the voting system, but told the *Financial Times* that he would be happy to deal with either Conservative or Labour parties, *'I don't care who produces a more liberal document for government. If it is more liberal then of course I would be interested to look at it.'*[4]

A final problem for the Liberal Democrats then is that the party's chances of success remain largely dependent on the chances of a hung parliament. However, that prospect of electoral stalemate could be self-denying if too much attention is paid to it. Certainly Clegg and the party will be under pressure to announce post-election strategy during the pre-election campaign.

Meanwhile a continued Conservative revival could dilute the chances of an electoral stalemate, and the outcome of the devolved elections in Scotland and Wales in 2007 demonstrated that even when occupying an apparently promising position the Liberal Democrats might find themselves frozen out by circumstances. The central dilemma for the Liberal Democrats in the post-Blair era remains a familiar one – the party has to fight to establish relevance and remains in danger of being chiefly defined by their opponents rather than by itself.

Notes

1. Richard Grayson, Kennedy's former speech-writer told the 2005 Conference that Kennedy was chairman rather than leader of the party, he should be 'stamping his personal authority on the strategic direction of the Liberal Democrats rather than allowing debates on key policy issues to go on around him'.
2. Julian Glover, 'Conservative Revival is Bad News for Lib Dems', The *Guardian*, 27 July 2006.
3. Edward Heathcoat-Amory, 'Calamity Clegg's Spectacular Blunder', *Daily Mail*, 6 March 2008.
4. George Parker and Alex Barker, 'Lib Dems Could Back Conservatives', *Financial Times*, 7 February 2008.

5
The Pressure Group Challenge[*]

Wyn Grant

Any proper understanding of the role of pressure groups in British politics during and after the Blair government needs to proceed from a historical analysis of their changing place in the polity. Such an analysis must necessarily draw on the work of Samuel Beer given his distinctive and path-breaking contribution to the topic. However, although we have an insightful historical understanding of the changing role of groups, this has not led to any informed or fundamental normative debate about their place in the political process, even in the context of a renewed interest in constitutional issues and the challenges to healthy democratic governance in Britain.

This chapter sets out an ideal typical model of the historical development of group politics in Britain. It then explores five themes which are taken as characteristic of the Blair government's engagement with groups: the turn towards business, but away from business associations; a corresponding decline in the role of trade unions; the emphasis on new consultation procedures; the emergence of the regulatory state and the growth of direct action and single issue pressure groups. A sixth theme might be devolution, which undoubtedly has important impacts on British pressure groups in three respects: how existing groups cope with the emergence of decision-making entities in Edinburgh and Cardiff (and, in a different sense, in Belfast); the emergence of new groupings focusing on the regional governments in Scotland and Wales; and the extent of any 'California effect' whereby new policy initiatives are pioneered elsewhere than in England, e.g., the recent decision to have a pilot cull of badgers in Wales when the UK government had failed to come to any resolution on this controversial issue. These are important developments, and there is an emergent literature on them (Keating, 2005; McGarvey and Cairney, 2008), but the situation is a fluid and developing one and it is difficult to come to authoritative judgements yet.

'Happy is the country': The historical perspective

Beer's analysis of British politics gave a central place to the role of groups as a means of understanding changing patterns and philosophies of politics. He considered that their significance increased over time. He emphasized how the tradition of consultation with organized producer groups was deeply rooted in British history. He saw a 'widespread acceptance of functional representation in British political culture' (Beer, 1969, p. 329). Under the post-war managed economy and welfare state, government required from pressure groups 'advice, acquiescence and approval' (Beer, 1969, p. 330). The analysis presented was basically a benign one of the influence on policy exerted by consumer and producer groups and the narrowing of the ideological divide between the parties. British politics is portrayed as representing a balance between 'the powerful thrust of the new politics of group interest and, on the other, the continuing dynamic of ideas' (Beer, 1969, p. 386). As Beer states in the concluding sentence of the original book: 'Happy the country in which consensus and conflict are ordered in a dialectic that makes of the political arena at once a market of interests and a forum for debate of fundamental moral concerns' (Beer, 1969, p. 390).

Beer endorsed contemporary thinking which saw an essentially corporatist future for Britain. The period of the Heath government, at least from 1972 and the Labour Government from 1974–9 saw the most sustained experiment that Britain ever experienced (or is likely to experience) with a tripartite form of government in which economic policy was formed in conjunction with the employers, represented by the Confederation of British Industry (CBI) and the trade unions represented by the Trades Union Congress (TUC). This approach is exemplified by the 1974 white paper (HM Government, 1975, Cm. 6151) which launched the Labour government's statutory incomes policy: there are 15 references in the main text to the TUC and nine to the CBI. These are not incidental references as is shown by the conclusion which refers to 'The measures the Government, the TUC and the CBI are taking' (Cmnd. 6151, p.12) with similar language used throughout. One cannot imagine such language being used by the Blair government: part of its understanding of what differentiated New Labour from Old Labour was a repudiation of corporatism.

Beer became aware of the dangers of what he termed 'the new pluralism', reflecting the fact that many analysts saw corporatism as little more than a degenerate form of pluralism. In *Britain Against Itself* the central argument was that 'the collectivist polity, that culminating success of political development in the postwar years, itself engendered the processes which converted success into failure' (Beer, 1982, p. xiv). Beer explained, 'Intrinsic to the collectivist polity was a heightened group politics. This rising pluralism so fragmented the political system as to impair its power of acting for the long-run interests of its members' (Beer, 1982, p. 4). The decline of parties relative to the rise of interest groups removed a major restraining influence: 'The fatal conjunction occurred when the new group politics ... confronted from the mid 1960s, a party regime with diminishing powers of aggregation' (Beer, 1982, p. 210).

It is possible to suggest a threefold ideal typical historical typology of the development of pressure group politics in Britain since 1945 (Grant 2008). This is a cumulative typology, so by the time the third stage is reached all three forms of group politics can be found in the polity. In the first phase, approximately from 1945 to 1979, politics is dominated by 'sectional' interest groups related to producer interests, whether they are industry or the professions, e.g., the British Medical Association. There are some promotional or cause groups but they are relatively small and tend to draw on an elite or at least professional or upper middle class membership, e.g., the Howard League for Penal Reform or the then Council for the Preservation of Rural England.

This period culminated in its most progressive or degenerate form in the 1970s with the institutionalization of the roles of the CBI and the TUC in the period of tripartism discussed earlier. However, by this time a new type of mass membership, 'other regarding' group, was developing. This happened after the revival and reinvigoration of older groups, e.g., the Abortion Law Reform Association or the formation of a new generation of groups concerned with a range of issues such as housing, child poverty, lone parents, sexual minorities, the Third World, human rights and, above all, the environment. They were generally concerned with groups inside or outside the UK that were in some sense deprived of rights or resources that would be enjoyed by the generally prosperous supporters of these groups. 'It was during [the mid-1960s] that academics, politicians and commentators began to pay attention to the casualties of modern British society: the unemployed, the mentally disabled, the sick, the elderly and so on' (Sandbrook, 1997, p. 600).

The members of the group were not themselves casualties or likely to be so: they were not, for example, agitating for a more liberal penal policy as an insurance against their own imprisonment. They were concerned with deficiencies in society which, as they saw it, could not be remedied by campaigning through political parties alone, although many of them were also party activists, if somewhat disillusioned by what they saw as the shortcomings of the Labour government of 1964–70. In particular, they had a concern with negative externalities such as pollution, leading to what has been described elsewhere as a 'politics of collective consumption' (Grant, 2000).

The third phase, which became pronounced during the lifetime of the Blair government, but had earlier origins, was the emergence of 'inner directed' single issue pressure groups. They were concerned with very particular demands, e.g., patients who wanted a drug to be paid out of public funds to treat a particular illness or motorists upset by the use of cameras to enforce speeding laws. The difficulty with such groups was that most of their demands were in a 'zero sum' form that imposed costs elsewhere, e.g., reductions in spending elsewhere in the health service or increased risks to cyclists and pedestrians. In their most extreme form, they represented a direct threat to democratic government itself. Participants in the fuel tax protests of 2000 which halted delivery of petrol and diesel from the refineries to the filling stations spoke with pride and regret that, in their view, they came close to toppling the democratically elected government: 'I was on the barricades in the fuel strike, which was a whisker away from toppling the government in 2000' (*Farmers Weekly*, 11 April 2008). Not much sign there of the civic culture which Beer had specified as a key underpinning of the collectivist polity, although by 1982 he was balancing this against the contradictions of 'the new populism' (Beer, 1982, p. 3).

The turn towards business

The Blair government was very close to business interests, particularly large corporations. This was consistent with the ambition stated by Tony Blair in a speech to American financiers in New York to make Labour 'the natural party of business'. (10 Downing Street Newsroom, 14 April 1998). Blair liked to meet with successful individual businesspersons, particularly Americans, or with groupings like the Multinational Industries Chairmen's Group. For Blair the phrase 'really successful businessman' was an accolade of high praise. 'Although concerned at the rhetorical level with the promotion of social justice ... "New Labour" is principally concerned with strengthening the power of capital ... Blair's designated image for his Labour Party is that it is a party for and of business' (Heffernan, 2001, p. 73). As Blair put it himself, 'New Labour is pro-business, pro-enterprise and we believe that there is nothing inconsistent between that and a just and decent society' (*Financial Times*, 16 December 1997).

New Labour did not perpetuate the interest of the preceding Conservative government, particularly Michael Heseltine and Richard Page (Greaves 2004) in rationalizing and modernizing the structure of business associations in Britain. The impression was given by civil servants that trade associations were seen as part of the problem rather than part of the solution. Early in the life of the government the chief executive of one major industry association was told that the government preferred to meet 'real people', i.e., the executives of companies rather than their representative intermediaries (Interview information, 16 April 2008). When the sector skill councils with their training focus were set up, it was specified that members of their governing bodies had to be actively involved in running companies, i.e., they could not be trade association officials. Reinforcing this perspective was a relative lack of interest on the part of government in manufacturing industry which was seen as something of an 'Old Labour' preoccupation. The future was seen as to be found in a service based and 'knowledge' economy with a particular emphasis on the financial services industry. As Coates notes (2008, p. 8):

> It is the service sector, not manufacturing, that now provides two-thirds of all employment in the UK with financial services alone accounting for 4.1% of all jobs and 8.5% of GDP. The manufacturing sector, by contrast, has seen its share of GDP fall from over 20% in 1997 to less than 15% today.

Nevertheless, even if it was initially reluctant to engage with trade associations, the Blair government did try to build a relationship with the CBI, headed by Digby Jones, the former chair of the CBI's West Midlands Region, later to become a minister under Gordon Brown. The CBI had emerged from the long darkness of the Thatcher and Major years, when it was seen as a corporatist hangover, as a much smaller organization in terms of staff. It entered the sunlit uplands again with the election of the Blair government. After the first two years of New Labour, the outgoing CBI president commented, 'the working relationship between the government and the CBI is probably closer than at any time in the last 25 years, certainly closer than under the Thatcher or Major governments' (*Financial Times*, 10 July 2000). Consultation was close, frequent and intense. Concessions were often given to the CBI, if less frequently publicized.

Over the lifetime of the government the relationship became more strained. There was increasing resentment over what was perceived as the increased regulatory burden on business, although much of it emanated from Brussels. Human relations legislation that gave additional protection or rights to workers as parents or employees caused particular resentment, although the government fought a determined rearguard action to prevent the extension of the rights of temporary or agency staff, a key concern for business determined to keep labour costs down. Calls for the abolition of the Department of Trade and Industry (DTI) were strongly resisted by business interests that saw it as their spokesperson within government. It survived, albeit in a new form as the Department of Business, Enterprise and Regulatory Reform. (BERR). The role of BERR was defined by John Hutton, the secretary of state, in terms of the 'Prime Minister's mission ... to be a strong voice for business at the heart of Government' (Trade Association Forum, 2008, p. 1).

Over time the relationship between government and trade associations improved. The bursting of the original dot.com bubble led to a renewed government interest in the contribution of manufacturing industry to the economy. For example, in 2008 the business minister, Shriti Vadera, ordered a review aimed at helping the UK motor industry tackle the twin challenges of low-cost competition and emerging low-carbon car technologies. The effective implementation of the Climate Change Levy was found to require the cooperation of trade associations. The Department of Environment, Food and Rural Affairs (Defra) negotiated with trade associations representing energy intensive business sector agreements on climate change known as 'umbrella agreements'. In these agreements the sector undertakes to meet an energy efficiency or carbon saving target in return for an 80 per cent discount from the levy. Ultimately, there are expected to be some 40 climate change agreements.

In 2008 BERR provided some funding for a research based review of the effectiveness of business associations by the Trade Association Forum (TAF). The decision to undertake this study was in part a response to the tenth anniversary of the TAF set up within the CBI in the summer of 1997. Although this body was established when New Labour came into office, it was really a response to initiatives taken by the Major government to stimulate good practice and benchmarking among trade associations, in particular the publication by the DTI of a *Best Practice Guide for the Model Trade Association* in February 1996 (Greaves, 2004, p. 86). It was considered that trade associations had become more effective in their internal management, particularly in terms of the way in which their staff had become more professional. What was less certain was whether this had translated into a more effective involvement in policymaking, thus prompting a return to some of the questions discussed by the Devlin Commission on Industrial Representation in its report in 1972[1] (Greaves, 2008).

The relationship between government and business remained a generally constructive one until the proposals of the Brown government on capital gains tax and the taxation of non-domiciles caused a real rift. The government eventually beat a retreat, but not after some damage had been caused to the relationship, despite the inclusion by Gordon Brown of politically unaffiliated businesspersons in his government and the creation of an International Business Advisory Council for the UK.

Trade unions

The Blair government was more receptive to trade union views than the preceding Conservative governments, but did not restore the symbiotic relationship that had characterized Old Labour. The broad position taken has been well explained by Shaw (2008, p. 121):

> The incoming Blair government promised the unions 'fairness not favours'. 'Not favours' meant, on the one hand, that the industrial relations settlement that had emerged from the Conservative years was, in its essentials, to be respected. 'Fairness', on the other hand, was defined principally in terms of affording employees protection against exploitation and arbitrary management and ending mass unemployment.

The unions did not come away empty handed from their relationship with Labour. They were given the minimum wage (which moved upwards above the rate of inflation), the EU working-time directive, new union recognition rights, flexible working and nearly 400,000 new public sector jobs. The Blair government made 'a battery of concessions at the [University of] Warwick Agreement in the run up to the 2005 general election' (Shaw, 2008, p. 134). The Blair government was perceived in the autumn of 2005 to have backed down in the face of threatened strikes over public sector retirement. It was agreed that three million workers in existing schemes could continue to retire at 60 and only new entrants would be required to retire at 65. Areas of tension remain, for example, over the clause in the Warwick Agreement that bans even partial privatization of the Royal Mail, something that particularly annoys business interests.

The Blair government stood up to new militant union leaders, Alan Johnson as trade and industry secretary mocking trade unionists who wanted a return to 'what he called "the planet Zog" days of pre-Thatcherite union rights' (*Financial Times,* 16 April 2003). Demands to allow secondary industrial action have been brushed aside and, even under the weakened Brown administration, the unions obtained limited concessions from the Warwick II agreement. In broad terms, the union movement is still characterized by the New Unionism represented by the Trades Union Congress (TUC) general secretary Brendan Barber, described as 'a creed of constructiveness, conciliation and caution' (*Financial Times,* 4 September 2007).

The role of the TUC itself has been called into question given the merger of the Transport and General Workers Union and Amicus in 2007 to form Unite, a combined union with about two million members, outstripping Unison, the largest public sector union with 1.3 million members. These two unions account for approaching half the total union membership of just over seven million, with less than 20 per cent membership in the private sector. However, the concentration of union membership in the public sector is a potential obstacle to New Labour's ambitions for public sector reform and attempts under the Brown government to hold back public sector pay.

Consultation

New Labour created a new formal framework for consultation which sought to be more inclusive, but may have had the opposite effect. It claimed that it was seeking to respond to concerns about open government and transparency when it published a code of practice on written consultation in 2000. The preface, written by Tony Blair, claimed that New Labour was consulting more than governments in the past, although that is difficult to measure. The stated intention of the code was to make written consultations more effective, opening decision-making to as wide a range of people as possible. To put the objective in academic terminology, if its objectives were to be achieved, the outsider by necessity category of interest groups should disappear, i.e., those groups that lacked the resources and skills to access the policymaking process.

The code placed considerable emphasis on the use of the Internet to make documents available and to facilitate responses to consultation. This does not, of course, eliminate all biases as Internet consultation still requires some educational skills and may work less well for the socially (and politically) excluded. Moreover, the ability to submit views electronically is no substitute for real dialogue with ministers and civil servants. However, in principle, only ideological outsiders should remain politically excluded from the consultation process, i.e. those 'Underground activist communities [who] are wary, or even hostile, about interacting with policy-makers' (Plows, 2008, p. 93).

In September 2003 a consultation was initiated on the code of practice on consultation. The view that emerged from the consultation was that the code of practice had been effective in embedding a 12-week consultation period into policymaking practice. However, users took the view that the code was quite long and was made up of a mixture of guidance and principles.

The writer has had some experience in responding to consultations, initially on higher education policy on behalf of the Political Studies Association and subsequently as a participant in two Rural Economy and Land Use (RELU) research programme projects. The way in which consultations are structured follows the government's agenda rather than what might be the different priorities of relevant stakeholders. The questions asked are often not the ones that stakeholders would like to be asked or the wording is not necessarily helpful from the point of view of those being consulted. Organizations are generally asked to respond to a highly structured questionnaire or at least to a series of specific points. Of course, in part this is necessary to make it practicable for the consulting department to summarize the points being made. This task usually falls to an 'epitomiser', a Grade 6 or Grade 7 civil servant. One can appreciate the need for government departments to be able to analyse responses systematically without undue effort, but it also makes the process somewhat mechanistic. It can be difficult for groups to emphasize the points that are important to them or at least to do so and ensure that they will be heard.

In some cases the written consultation will be supplemented by stakeholder meetings, perhaps held at different venues around the country. The writer participated in one such meeting held as part of a government proposition to merge the Pesticides Safety Directorate (PSD) into the Health and Safety Executive (HSE). The meeting was conducted in a scrupulously fair fashion and all those present were given ample opportunity to respond to the structured agenda and to make any additional points that they wanted. The written record that was produced of the meeting was a fair reflection of the concerns that were expressed. Only a small number of respondents were strongly in favour or against the proposition with most being broadly supportive, but expressing reservations about implementation and the anticipated benefits of the reorganization.

It was evident from the wording of the proposition that government had already made up its mind to merge PSD into HSE, despite a speech by the responsible government minister which declared that he had an 'open mind' on the issue. This may have been the case, but it was evident that government policy was being driven by the Hampton Review's view that the number of regulatory agencies should be reduced. In the stakeholders' meeting it was evident, as a participant observer, from non-verbal cues that responses that supported or developed the government case received a more favourable reception than those that did not. From a government perspective, the main value of the consultation appeared to be allowing HSE and PSD to gain 'a better understanding of stakeholder concerns and issues which has informed plans for implementation of this organisational change' (Department for Environmental Food and Rural Affairs, 2008, paragraph 5).

Although the consultation may therefore seem to be a rather formalistic process to show that stakeholders had been consulted rather than to change the proposition, except perhaps in particular details, it was successful in engaging a large range of relevant stakeholders (See Table 5.1). Although this may reflect the nature of the particular consultation, it is striking that 17 (34 per cent) of the responses came from quasi-governmental organizations or the devolved administrations. Seventeen (34 per cent) of the responses came from business interests, mostly trade associations, but also firms. Non-governmental organizations, consumers and trade unions were relatively weakly represented.

Table 5.1 Stakeholders responding to consultation on the future of PSD

Stakeholder category	Number of responses
Quasi-governmental bodies	15
Trade associations	11
Firms	6
Non-governmental organizations	4
Researchers	3
Individuals	3
Consumers	2
Devolved administrations	2
Local government organizations	2
Professional association	1
Trade union	1
TOTAL	50

What is evident is that the traditional distinctions between core insiders, niche insiders and peripheral insiders still have some value despite criticisms of their empirical relevance (Page 1999). The documents on consultation contain strong hints that some groups, largely core insiders, will be treated more seriously than others. It is argued that in order to avoid placing extra burden on groups with limited resources, e.g., voluntary and community organizations, 'it may be better to target consultation through umbrella bodies, including trade associations and business organisations. But it is important to speak to these bodies at an early stage' (Cabinet Office, 2000, p. 13). Similarly, it is said that analysing responses is not just a matter of counting votes, bearing in mind what are seen as the risks of single issue interest groups exerting a monopoly over debate. It is also evident that relatively few consultations are initiated by core executive bodies such as the Cabinet Office or the Treasury which tend to have close relationships with core insiders such as the CBI.

The observation of the informal rules of the game required for insider status continues to be important. In their analysis of patient and carer organizations, Baggott, Allsop and Jones found (2005, p. 235) that 'If [a group] understands and complies with the rules of the game ... and does not engage in destructive criticism of policy, its chances of inclusion are further increased'. In one case a group that caused trouble and was vociferous was excluded from policymaking, although sometimes such groups were co-opted to try and reduce their public criticism of policy. It was also found that 'groups that had insider status were more likely than outsiders to report an instance of influence' (Baggott, Allsop and Jones, 2005, p. 228). Consistent with New Labour's claims it was found that the groups studied 'had more access to government and greater opportunities to influence policy than before' (Baggott, Allsop and Jones, 2005, p. 234).

The regulatory state

The depoliticization thrust of the Blair government has seen the assignment of responsibility for a range of tasks that were formerly carried out by central government to a range of regulatory agencies that have a considerable measure of operational autonomy. This is, of course, the culmination of a longer-term trend dating back to the 1980s for the greater use of executive agencies to discharge the tasks of government. Various accounts of the resultant 'regulatory state' have offered 'a fundamentally benign view of this state, picturing it as way of standing back from, and empowering, civil society' (Moran, 2005, p. 530). In particular, 'It is now much easier to find out how decisions are made in the new regulatory state than under the system that preceded it; and knowing who is making decisions, and how they are being made, is a first condition for the exercise of democratic control'.

It is difficult to generalize about regulatory agencies because they are so varied in their objectives and methods of operation. However, as a broad generalization it is possible to discern three types of relationship between such agencies and pressure groups:

1. Agencies which would regard too close an engagement with stakeholders as incompatible with their regulatory role and hence keep their distance from stakeholders.
2. Agencies which tend to favour a particular category of stakeholders because they see that as consistent with their defined mission.
3. Agencies which have been innovative in reaching out and developing new forms of relationship with stakeholders.

No regulatory agency can entirely distance itself from stakeholders or it would be difficult to obtain all the information they need to carry out their tasks. Following the example of government consultation code, one approach they have adopted is to develop consultation principles of their own (see Ofcom, 2008). Even so, they may feel impelled to keep that relationship within certain bounds, e.g., the Financial Services Authority (FSA) which offers an example of the first category above. This would also apply to the utility and other market regulators, although once again information asymmetries may shape the relationship in practice. Héritier (2005, p. 127) found that access to rail regulators was related to the size of the firm. The formation of associations facilitated access, although not to the same extent for all types of firms; a complicating factor being the restructuring of associations when the sector was liberalized.

The Food Standards Agency (FoodSA) which was set up by the Blair government offers an example of the second category. Because of its statutory mission to protect the public's health and consumer interests in relation to food, the FoodSA felt the need to reach out to various stakeholder groups that claimed to represent their interests. It uses stakeholder forums which have an even handed structure in the sense that there are separate forums for consumer organizations, industry and enforcement authorities. Although the Food and Drink Federation (FDF) accepts that FoodSA does engage with partner organizations, its members expressed the view that the FoodSA was encouraging a labelling scheme 'that many executives feel to be non-scientific (the traffic light system); they feel that further consultation could have avoided the confusing situation where multiple front-of-pack labeling systems are on display' (Food and Drink Federation).

An example of the third category is PSD. As part of its efforts to ensure that more biologically based alternatives to chemical pesticides are available, PSD has sought to reach out to the industry through building relationships with the relevant trade association, the International Biocontrol Manufacturers Association (IBMA). This has been done through PSD staff attending IBMA meetings, but more particularly through a joint working party between PSD and IBMA. The writer was invited to observe one of these meetings and a high level of constructive engagement was evident. One can conclude that the observable variability makes it more difficult to generalize about relationships between pressure groups and regulatory agencies than with central government departments.

Single issue interest groups and direct action

Single issue interest groups and direct action are not necessarily the same thing. A single issue interest group may not engage in direct action and there are groups with broad interests that engage in direct action, e.g., Greenpeace. However, often the two go together and they have posed problems for the Blair government. Some forms of direct action are relatively innocuous and are largely designed to gain media attention. For example, in April 2008, a coalition of three pressure groups concerned about biofuels policy (Greenpeace, Oxfam and the Royal Society for the Protection of Birds) went to Parliament Square 'for a high-profile demonstration, with giant maize cobs prancing around in the shadow of [the statue of] Sir Winston Churchill' (*Farmers Weekly*, 18 April 2008). More generally, 'UK green protest is broadly non-violent but nevertheless focuses on disruptive and interventionist forms of action' (Plows, 2008, p. 99).

Greater challenges have been presented by animal rights groups that are opposed to the use of animals for experiments. In some cases their actions have involved attacks on persons and property and they have been dealt with under the criminal law. However, there has also been an extension of the ability to obtain injunctions restraining demonstrations under civil law and this has led to concerns about the erosion of the right to protest peacefully. Of course, much depends on the distinction between peaceful protest and attempts to disrupt the operations of companies or universities. Those concerned about animal protection would point out that 'the animal research community ... is a big business. Not surprisingly, these interests, with considerable capital invested in their industries are well organised, and this, in part, explains the limitations of animal welfare provision' (Garner, 2008, p. 111).

Changes in society, in particular class decomposition, provide an underlying driver for the formation of single issue interest groups. The available evidence suggests that 'more *collectivistic* forms of participation have declined and that more *individualist* forms have come to the fore' (Stoker, 2006, p. 92). This reflects a society in which social identities are no longer substantially ascribed, e.g., class membership, but are constructed or created through a process of personal choice, a process which some analysts would see as emancipating. A particular set of lifestyle choices can give rise to a pressure group, e.g., the Lesbian and Gay Christian Movement or, an even more specific example, the Evangelical Fellowship for Lesbian and Gay Christians. Thus, in the latter example, one has a movement of persons who identify themselves as (a) Christian, (b) Evangelical and (c) Lesbian or Gay. As Crouch states, 'the present time is a particularly rich one for innovation in interest and identity definition and mobilization' (Crouch, 2006a, p. 67).

Politicians occasionally engage in bouts of hand wringing about single-issue pressure groups. Riddell notes (1996, p. 5) that politicians 'are really complaining' about the proliferation of cause and single interest groups as a larger share of a growing market for political activism. Jack Straw has argued that measures to cap donations to political parties 'could lead to undue influence being wielded by single-issue pressure groups'. In the US 'the effect of campaign finance rules has been to channel money away from mainstream political parties into single-issue organisations, which are becoming increasingly powerful' ('Pressure Groups Could Exploit Party Funding Limits, Warns Straw', *The Guardian*, 5 September 2006).

The formation of such groups is, of course, consistent with a fundamental principle of democracy, that of freedom of association. Moreover, there has been a long tradition in Britain, consistent with its liberal traditions, of regarding voluntary associations as something that lie outside the remit or responsibilities of government. It might be argued that government, with all its resources, should simply face down single-issue pressure groups. For example, a civil servant in interview distinguished between 'Nimbyism' and 'genuine issues' and while admitting that the two could be mixed, made it clear that his department did not want to be seen to be giving way to 'Nimby' pressures. However, in practice, it is often hard to resist a well organized campaign that captures the media's imagination. Ministerial reputations, and even that of the government as a whole, can be damaged.

Conclusions

Constitutional reform has been a key theme of the Blair government and it looks like being one of the Brown government's as well. Yet constitutional reform usually means changes in the processes and institutions of government: devolution, reform of the House of Lords, greater transparency etc. Except in relation to electoral reform or perhaps state funding of political parties, the wider polity is much less considered in these debates. In particular, there has been very little attention to the role that interest groups should play in the political process, although it is generally agreed that they have become more important over time and political parties less so. It is interesting that a Smith Institute volume *Towards a New Constitutional Settlement* produced to accompany the transition from Blair to Brown (including a series of seminars held at No.11 Downing Street while Brown was still Chancellor) includes two chapters on political parties and even one on the establishment of the Church of England but nothing on interest groups (Bryant, 2007).

The Governance of Britain Green Paper (Ministry of Justice, 2007, Cm. 7170) issued by the Brown government shortly after taking office includes just two paragraphs on pressure groups compared with two pages on the relationship between the state and the Church of England, including such arcane matters as the Royal Peculiars (para. 66). Only one of the paragraphs on pressure groups and social movement is about them in general terms, the other considering the position of voluntary organizations that are charities. This is clearly insufficient, particularly against a background of the declining role of political parties as bodies that aggregate demands and select priorities (Political Studies Association, 2007). A broader debate is urgently needed about the role of pressure groups in the modern British polity.

Notes

* This chapter draws on research conducted as part of the Rural Economy and Land Use (RELU) research programme, grant RES-224-25-0048.

1. The Devlin Commission was set up by the CBI and the Association of British Chambers of Commerce to review the system of industrial representation with some government encouragement including the secondment of a civil servant.

6

New Labour, the Third Way and Social Democracy: An Ideological Assessment

Nick Randall and James Sloam

The Third Way (Giddens, 1998; Blair, 1998) which has provided the ideological underpinning for Labour during the Blair era has proven persistently controversial. It has been 'widely derided as vacuous' (Fielding, 2002, p. 81), characterized as thinly veiled neo-liberalism (Callinicos, 2001) and relativised as just one of several *Third Ways* in a comparative context (Merkel, 2000).

Existing analyses have often sought to defend or criticise New Labour in normative or policy terms. In this chapter, however, we adopt a different line of argument. We consider New Labour's Third Way from three distinct perspectives. Firstly, we examine its ideological structure as revealed by Labour's policy statements and manifestos. Secondly, we investigate key policy outcomes which serve as ideological markers of New Labour's impact in office. Thirdly, we place New Labour in a comparative ideological context by reference to its European social democratic sister parties. We argue that not only is New Labour a coherent ideological project, it is one which can both be credibly understood as social democratic and which stands up well in comparison to other centre-left parties in the European Union.

Social democracy

Since it is central to our argument, we need to establish our definition of social democracy at the outset. We view social democracy as a hybrid ideological tradition which draws upon both socialism and liberalism. It is pragmatic and averse to utopianism and consequently no stranger to periodic ideological reappraisal. Indeed, the Third Way represents one of a sequence of revisionist moments in social democratic history.

Nonetheless, it has maintained an evolutionary vision of social progress ever since Eduard Bernstein's (1961) reappraisal of Marxism in the late nineteenth century. It views human nature in positive terms, with individuals ultimately being virtuous, moral, fraternal and co-operative. Contemporary societies may frustrate the full realisation of such characteristics, but human nature is sufficiently malleable to submit to improvements engineered by a beneficent, social democratic state. Indeed, social democrats envisage an interplay between individuals and their social environment. This places them between classical liberalism's ontological individualism and the collectivism of Marxism (even if it has been strategically difficult for some social democratic parties to shed their Marxist rhetoric).

Social democrats also hold an egalitarian impulse, agreeing upon the need to go beyond the classical liberal juridical conception of equality. Although they disagree whether equality of outcome, opportunity or status best satisfies this demand, they all endorse, in Berlin's (1969) terms, a positive conception of liberty, which recognises that individuals require resources to enjoy the liberty to develop their lives in their own way. Coupled to their egalitarianism this leads social democrats to a normative commitment to social citizenship, charging governments with enlarging and enriching people's life chances through action to confront poverty and inequality. Moreover such social citizenship also serves to enhance social integration and stability and thereby generate fraternity and solidarity.

Such beliefs have been diversely implemented by social democrats in different national and historical contexts. Nevertheless, they have generally impelled them to economic intervention to promote growth and opportunity and to prevent unemployment and exploitation. In the context of an evolving socio-economic environment, the means to achieve these goals may have changed from Keynesianism to – in Gordon Brown's terms – 'post-neoclassical endogenous growth theory', but the principle of an active state remains constant. Social democrats' normative commitment to social citizenship leaves them dissatisfied with liberal residual welfare states. Instead they have sought welfare states funded by general taxation and organised on the basis of universal programmes with limited opportunities for exit which extend life chances, increase collective consumption and decommodify basic goods such as health, housing and education. Indeed, for social democrats education has particular significance in allowing self-advancement and generating equality of opportunity. Therefore they have regarded education as a good which must be publicly provided (or at least free at the point of delivery) and in which selection should have a minimal role. Social democratic faith in the malleability of human nature also implies a criminal justice policy which prioritises rehabilitation over retribution or deterrence.

The ideological content of New Labour's Third Way

Having established this definition of social democracy against which to measure New Labour we will first consider New Labour's ideology as expressed in policy statements and manifestos in the period since 1997.

New Labour's teleology expresses a characteristically social democratic faith in evolution and progress. For example, the 1997 manifesto promised 'a fresh start, the patient rebuilding and renewing of this country – renewal that can take root and build over time' (Labour Party, 1997, p. 3). The good society which New Labour would construct is, on the one hand, vague, aspiring to 'a country in which people get on, do well, make a success of their lives' (Labour Party, 1997, p. 4). However, as noted below, such generalities sit alongside a recognisably social democratic commitment to reducing poverty.

Similarly, that New Labour intervenes to alter individual behaviour across a swathe of social policies implies a continued social democratic faith in the malleability of human nature. Yet it has become increasingly aware of the self-regarding side of human nature, for example, attempting to tackle indolence and mendacity among social security recipients. Moreover, it seeks to promote individuals who are active and independent, rather than passive and dependent on the state. It has also been quick to assign individuals responsibility for their actions, particularly in respect of criminality and social disorder.

However, such heightened awareness of individualism and individual responsibility has not inhibited New Labour from recognising the traditional social democratic precept that individuals are profoundly shaped by their social environment. Indeed, it remains characteristically collectivist believing 'in a society where we do not simply pursue our own individual aims but where we hold many aims in common and work together to achieve them' (Labour Party, 1997, p. 4). It also maintains faith in collective solutions initiated (if not always delivered) by the state to enhance both human and social capital.

Thus, collectivities and the inequalities in resources and power they encounter persist in New Labour's analysis. Divisions associated with gender, ethnicity and sexual orientation have particularly troubled the party. It has been rather more reluctant to employ the class vocabulary traditionally utilised by social democrats (given the shrinkage of the party's traditional core electorate of manual workers). Yet while it denies fundamental antagonisms between workers and employers, New Labour is not ignorant of economic inequality, as we shall see below.

New Labour eschews vivid egalitarian rhetoric for the more nebulous vocabulary of 'social exclusion'. This might be taken to imply little more than re-integrating the marginalised into a profoundly inegalitarian society. However, the party signals a more ambitious prospectus, seeking 'to liberate people's potential, by spreading power, wealth and opportunity more widely, breaking down the barriers that hold people back' (Labour Party, 2001, p. 6). As this indicates, New Labour embraces equality of opportunity rather than equality of outcome but nevertheless recognises that the former still demands measures to address social justice and poverty.

Solidarity and community are integral to the social democratic tradition and New Labour has insisted upon promoting communal solidarity and enhancing social capital (Putnam, 2003). For New Labour such solidarity originates from the interdependence of individuals and their subscription to communal norms and obligations. It is this recognition of interdependence that leads New Labour to social capital as a fundamental organising concept. By enhancing social capital, both by assisting individuals to fulfil their potential by measures to deliver equality of opportunity and by requiring individuals to meet their obligations to the community, communal solidarity is enhanced and collective goods, not least higher economic growth, are delivered.

Such is the value of communal solidarity that New Labour willingly limits individual freedom. For example, antisocial behaviour is deemed so corrosive of community that curfews and antisocial behaviour orders are issued despite their implications for civil liberties. Yet New Labour has not shied away from extending rights to minority groups. The disabled and the elderly have gained new protection from discrimination, particularly in the workplace, while the rights of sexual minorities have also been extended, for example, via civil partnerships.

In viewing the state as holding the primary responsibility for generating positive liberty by reforming social policy on the behalf of individuals, New Labour subscribes to a characteristically social democratic view of the state. However, the relationship between New Labour's state and the market is more difficult to reconcile with the social democratic tradition. It would be unfair to suggest that New Labour offers no criticism of the market. The 2001 manifesto professed that 'we know the power and value of markets, but we also know their limits' (Labour Party, 2001, p. 5), and a proliferation of new quangos and extended powers for existing regulatory bodies since 1997 testifies to reservations about untrammelled markets and a desire to protect consumers. Similarly, while the fundamentals of Conservative industrial relations law remain, New Labour has extended workers rights through the social chapter, new rights to union recognition and more extensive maternity and paternity rights. It has also modified the rewards generated by the market by introducing a national minimum wage.

Yet, New Labour has prioritised preserving the rights above extending the responsibilities of capital. It has striven to assuage business fears, securing credibility through operational independence for the Bank of England and a fiscal policy organised around the 'golden rule' which permits borrowing only to fund investment. It has diminished the public sector, albeit at its margins, through part and wholesale privatisation, compelled emulation of private sector disciplines in the belief that 'a "spirit of enterprise" should apply as much to public service as to business' (Labour Party, 2001, p. 17) and generated an extensive web of Private Finance Initiative (PFI) deals.

New Labour's approach to economic globalisation is similarly revealing. It discerns a new epoch of hyperactive and dynamic capital, placing new, non-negotiable exogenous constraints upon nation states. New Labour does not ignore the negative externalities of globalisation nor suggests that states are powerless. For example, its 2005 manifesto promised fairer trade and ending the conditionality of aid upon liberalisation and privatisation. Indeed, it believes that the constraints of the global economy can be navigated in a manner which will permit the extension of equality of opportunity for its citizens and has taken to international institutions, particularly the European Union, an anxiety that they adapt quickly to secure the full fruits of globalisation.

New Labour offers no pretence that it will displace the primacy of the market or significantly modify the dynamics of the capitalist economy. It offers instead a pragmatic managerialism which seeks to support 'enterprise and wealth creation by making Britain the best place to do business' (Labour Party, 2005, p. 15). The principal goal since 1997 has accordingly been 'stable, low-inflation conditions for long-term growth' (Labour Party, 1997, p. 11). This has sidelined much of the traditional repertoire of social democratic political economy. Nationalisation is eschewed except to resolve the gravest commercial failures (e.g. Railtrack and Northern Rock) and control of interest rates has been abnegated. Budget deficits serve the purposes of investment and do not operate to manage aggregate demand. The taxation system is not employed to eradicate inequalities in income. In a climate of economic globalisation, EU-isation and rapid technological change, 'New Labour's partnership with business is critical to national prosperity' (Blair, 1998, p. 8).

Yet New Labour does not completely repudiate traditional social democratic political economy. Economic stability accompanies a fundamental commitment to secure full employment which is in turn coupled to a vision of an 'active welfare state' (Giddens, 1998). New Labour's system of tax credits serve to incentivise paid employment and operate in tandem to its New Deals which render benefits contingent upon obligations to accept reasonable job offers or undertake voluntary work or training. However, it does not follow that New Labour's ambition to tackle poverty is timid or that the social security and tax systems serve no purpose beyond facilitating (re-) entry into the labour market. Ambitious targets have been set to halve child poverty by 2010–11 and eliminate it by 2020. It has established minimum income guarantees for pensioners and has pledged to restore the earnings link for the state pension abolished in 1981 by 2012.

New Labour presents itself as the guardian of the NHS's founding principles, asserting that 'Healthcare is too precious to be left to chance, too central to life chances to be left to your wealth' (Labour Party, 2005, p. 57) while also recognising 'the impact that poverty, poor housing, unemployment and a polluted environment have on health' (Labour Party, 1997, p. 21). Yet while New Labour conceives of 'the NHS as a public service working co-operatively for patients, not a commercial business driven by competition' (Labour Party, 1997, p. 21), its institutional reforms – particularly the creation of

NHS Foundation Trusts and the pragmatic use of private sector providers – have undermined the principle of universalism which social democrats have traditionally prized. In education, the creation of specialist schools and (city) academies has also eroded universalism. The latter require private sector sponsors and are indicative of New Labour's view that education must enhance the nation's economic performance. Yet New Labour also views education as a vital motor of social mobility and equality of opportunity and has sought broader access to higher education, aspiring to 50 per cent of young people attending university by 2010.

New Labour's approach to law and order is complex. Determined not to appear 'soft' on crime, it has heightened emphasis on individual responsibility for criminality and sought to respond to the public's perceived desire for punitive criminal justice. Yet, New Labour lays considerable stress upon the social environment, particularly unemployment and poverty, in generating criminality and is addressing these through initiatives such as the New Deal for Communities. Moreover, New Labour maintains a characteristically social democratic faith in the potential for rehabilitation, extending programmes to prevent re-offending, particularly among young offenders and drug addicts.

Policy outcomes

As should be evident from the above, New Labour's Third Way contains much which is recognisably social democratic. Its rapprochement with the market, its focus upon plurality in service delivery and its heightened individualism nevertheless represent a clear revision of that ideological tradition.

Such shifts neutralised the attacks of a dogmatically neoliberal Conservative Party and its press supporters and allowed Labour to present itself as pitched on the centre ground of British politics. They also disarticulated the party from its past experiences of office, particularly under Wilson and Callaghan, when socialist rhetoric went largely unrealised. But these digressions from social democratic tradition were not merely matters of electoral calculus. They also marked a belief on New Labour's part that the changes wrought by neoliberalism over the last three decades could not be easily unpicked. For New Labour social democratic change was possible in this new environment, but required these adjustments as its precondition.

Accordingly, gauging New Labour's ideological character also requires consideration of the outcomes of the policies which it has implemented in this environment. Whereas the policy programme of the Blair governments has been studied in detail elsewhere (Driver and Martell, 2006; Shaw, 2007) and in other chapters of this volume, we will focus our attention here on three key areas as markers of New Labour's ideological character.

Public spending

For New Labour the primacy of the economy has been the precondition for both social justice and electoral success. During its first term (1997–2001), the party followed the restrictive spending plans of the outgoing Conservative government, and buoyed by healthy growth rates and falling unemployment managed to significantly reduce the national debt. Thereafter, the chancellor continued to insist on low inflation and sound public finances while his golden rule was largely maintained. In the context of an open and de-regulated economy and with the highly influential City of London an internationally exposed financial centre, New Labour sought to create a favourable environment for business. This saw, for example, cuts in corporation tax (33p to 30p), small business tax (23p to 19p) and capital gains tax for long-term business assets (40p to 10p) (see Brown, 2006).

Such prudence is evidence enough for some of the neoliberal character of New Labour. However, its approach was more nuanced and social democratic in practice than many critics allow. Rather, the party regarded the economy as the precondition for achieving greater social justice through public investment. Increases in public spending during their first term were modest, not significantly higher than those under the Major governments, and targeted towards key areas earmarked for social investment (e.g. health and education) (*OECD Economic Outlook No. 81* (OECD, 2007a)). In 2001, however, by which time the economy was on a stable footing and New Labour had established its reputation for fiscal prudence it could substantially increase spending. Public spending overall increased in real terms by an average of 4.8 per cent per year between 2001 and 2005, health spending grew by 8.2 per cent per year and education spending by 5.4 per cent (HM Treasury, 2007) with the aim that this additional investment would promote equality of opportunity and equalise life chances.

The Labour market, social security and poverty reduction

As noted above, New Labour has sought, in line with traditional social democratic aspirations, to secure full employment and reduce poverty. Viewing citizens as holding both rights *and* responsibilities, it decried both welfare dependency and unbridled individualism (Blair, 1995). For New Labour social inclusion demanded equality of opportunity and decent living standards, but it also sought 'to transform the safety net of entitlements into a springboard for personal responsibility' (Blair and Schröder, 1999, p. 173) by re-ordering the benefits system around employment ('welfare to work').

The creation of a minimum wage, which has gradually increased from 46.2 per cent to 52.3 per cent of average earnings (Low Pay Commission, 2007, p. 148), and a system of tax credits (including Child and Working Tax Credits) have sought to remove the poverty trap by offering a minimum guaranteed 'take-home pay' for those willing to accept low-paid work (Labour Party, 2001, pp. 26–7). In addition, New Labour has targeted initiatives on key groups of the unemployed. For example, its Sure Start programme and enhanced childcare provision have been directed to mothers returning to work.

But not only has New Labour permitted the value of benefits to decline relative to average earnings (Department for Work and Pensions, 2006a), it has also introduced stiffer requirements to actively seek and accept work. Indeed, since the Third Way holds that any job is better than none (Blair and Schröder, 1999, p. 174), the Labour government has been an active proponent of labour market flexibility.

The third element of welfare-to-work has been training and guidance for the unemployed through the 'New Deal'. This is a traditional social democratic demand-side programme, investing in skills and training, initially funded by a £5 billion 'windfall tax' on recently privatised utilities. Although there is evidence that the New Deal's success rate was diminishing in Labour's third term (House of Commons Committee of Public Accounts, 2008) New Labour's overall success in reducing unemployment is undeniable. New Labour's impact in respect of wealth and poverty is somewhat more complex. Overall, the distribution of wealth in the UK has remained much the same. The Gini coefficient in 2005–6 stood at 0.35, slightly higher than the 0.33 New Labour inherited in 1996–7 (Brewer et al., 2008, p. 2) and the least wealthy half of the population has continued to share just 7 per cent of marketable wealth (Self and Zealey, 2007).

Yet New Labour has stemmed the dramatic rise in income inequality that occurred under the Conservatives. Without New Labour's progressive and redistributive tax and benefit reforms the Gini coefficient would have risen considerably higher (Brewer et al., 2007). Moreover, such measures have proven significant in addressing poverty. The overall percentages of households in relative poverty (incomes below 60 per cent of the median) dropped from 25 to 22 per cent from 1997–8 through 2005–6 (after housing costs). Relative poverty among pensioners dropped dramatically (from 29 to 17 per cent), and although its aim of halving child poverty by 2010 is unlikely to be met, the 34 per cent of children living in households with incomes below 60 per cent of the median in 1997–8 had fallen to 30 per cent in 2005–6 (Department for Work and Pensions, 2007).

Public services – health, education and criminal justice

We saw above that government expenditure has risen during a decade of New Labour government, particularly in respect of health and education. Much of the new investment dealt with perceived under-staffing. Tens of thousands of new doctors, nurses and teachers were thus recruited through the provision of 'better pay and conditions' (Blair, 2002, p. 26). In return public sector workers would often have to commit to more flexible working hours and assessment of the effectiveness of their work. A second principle of public sector reform was 'national standards' (Blair, 2002, p. 17). Increased resources were accompanied by performance targets assessing the success of investment, for example, in reducing hospital waiting lists, increasing pass rates for exams and reducing school class sizes.

In respect of the NHS these increased resources, greater than any committed in the last three decades, delivered reduced waiting lists, extra staff and improvements in the population's overall standard of health. Furthermore, as signalled in the 1998 Acheson report, New Labour also sought to address traditional social democratic concerns regarding health inequalities. While inequalities in mortality rates from heart disease, strokes and cancer subsequently narrowed, inequalities in infant mortality and life expectancy at birth have nevertheless grown (Department of Health, 2007, pp. 198–9).

Increased resources for education saw general improvements in achievement, falling class sizes and additional teachers. Grammar schools persist however and despite the abolition of the Assisted Places Scheme, the percentage of pupils educated in independent schools actually rose marginally from 6.74 per cent in 1997 to 7.07 per cent a decade later (Department for Children, Schools and Families, 2007). New Labour's recognition that social background generates educational inequalities nevertheless triggered a plethora of initiatives including the Sure Start programme, Excellence in Cities and Educational Maintenance Allowances, and there is evidence of slow progress in a social democratic direction. For example, the proportion of state school entrants into higher education increased from 84 per cent in 1998–9 to 87 per cent in 2005–6, the proportion from lower social classes rose from 25 to 29 per cent and the proportion from low participation neighbourhoods increased from 11 to 13 per cent.

Quantitative support for public services has been accompanied by qualitative change in the delivery of those services (Shaw, 2007). Believing that 'where private-sector providers can support public endeavour, we should use them' (Labour Party, 2001, p. 17), the private sector has become increasingly involved in providing public services through Public-Private partnerships and in particular in financing capital-intensive programmes through PFI. Indeed, New Labour's refurbishment and construction programmes for schools and hospitals have heavily relied on PFI, despite questions regarding its long-term financial logic (House of Commons Committee of Public Accounts, 2007). Yet elsewhere private sector involvement has faltered. Educational Action Zones were abandoned after failing to attract significant private sector investment and involvement while academies have grown slowly, educating less than 1 per cent of pupils by 2007.

New Labour's criminal justice policies have had similarly complex outcomes. The prison population in England and Wales increased from 60,130 in May 1997 to 81,106 a decade later, despite the government signalling its preference for non-custodial community sentences to the courts. Yet New Labour has nevertheless exhibited a characteristically social democratic focus upon rehabilitation of offenders through enhanced in-prison education and drug treatment and monitoring orders, for example. Such efforts have had some success. Between 1997 and 2004, proven re-offending fell by 6.9 per cent, although the majority (55.5 per cent) of offenders had still been re-convicted within two years (Cunliffe and Shepherd, 2007).

New Labour in a European context

Placing New Labour in a European context is particularly revealing. Despite Tony Blair's fondness for associating with those on the political right (for example, George Bush in the US, José María Aznar in Spain and Silvio Berlusconi in Italy), New Labour also encouraged its sister social democratic parties to embrace the Third Way, not least through a sequence of 'Progressive Governance' summits and collaboration engineered by Tony Blair's most trusted adviser, Peter Mandelson. Such efforts were frequently met with rejection in Europe. But Labour's electoral success and that of the UK economy began to make its policies more attractive, particularly for centre-left parties, facing not only the external challenges encountered by New Labour but also relatively high levels of public spending, public debt and unemployment. Between 1997 and 2004, public spending as a proportion of GDP was on average 25 per cent higher in France and 12 per cent higher in Germany than in the UK, while public debt was 46 per cent higher in France and 33 per cent higher in Germany over the same period (*OECD Economic Outlook No. 81* (OECD, 2007)). Therefore European social democrats have frequently implemented programmes resembling the British Third Way in government, even though their unique institutional constraints and national social-economic starting points often place them on different trajectories (Paterson and Sloam, 2006). What has been evident, however, is that in implementing *modern* agendas, they have generally encountered much higher political costs than New Labour, as Jospin in France (2002), Schröder in Germany (2005) and Prodi in Italy (2008) discovered.

We will take the German Social Democratic Party (SPD) and the French Socialist Party (PS) as our two comparators. The former has been in power since 1998 and the latter between 1997 and 2002. Gerhard Schröder, the former SPD Chancellor (1998–2005), was initially a key figure in the international Third Way network that began to meet from 1999 and the Blair-Schröder paper (1999) was published at a time when Schröder's 'Neue Mitte' was in the ascendancy in the SPD (Hombach, 2000). The Blair-Schröder paper, while fairly uncontroversial in the Labour Party, precipitated a summer of internal turmoil in the SPD (Sloam, 2004). SPD politicians balked at the constraints placed on social policy by the argument that public spending as a proportion of national income could not increase, as well as the business-oriented commitment to labour market flexibility. At this time, the *Neue Mitte* agenda was defeated in the SPD – institutional constraints prevented the imposition of a new approach – and it appeared that the party would take a different policy path to British Labour. Yet the *Neue Mitte's* defeat only proved to be a hiatus, as many of the ideas initially put forward in 1999 were implemented as part of the SPD-led government's 'Agenda

2010' reform programme from 2003 to 2005. Agenda 2010 represented a serious effort to rein in public finances (e.g. freezing pension rates) and introduce welfare-to-work employment policies (i.e. the so-called 'Hartz reforms') (see Streeck and Trampusch, 2005). In the face of the resource crunch in German public finances and the (perceived) constraints of economic globalisation (Watson and Hay, 2003), Schröder warned that Germany (and his own party) must 'modernise or die' (Schröder, 2003).

The political costs of these reforms were nevertheless very high for the SPD. The introduction of penalties for those not accepting jobs, through the Hartz reforms, was largely responsible for the haemorrhaging of support among the party's traditional constituency. It also indirectly assisted the emergence of a new (hostile) electoral coalition on the hard left of the spectrum (the Left Party). In 2005, the party was, thus, keen to reassure its supporters that it would 'preserve the welfare state' (whose 'main role remains that of social levelling') (SPD, 2005, p. 9). However, despite the political costs, the SPD programme demonstrated clear convergence with Labour's Third Way (Paterson and Sloam, 2006) – from the commitment to place 'equality of opportunity' at the heart of its 'Politics of the Centre' (SPD, 2002, p. 10), to support for an 'active state ... that helps people to lead an independent life' (SPD, 2005, p. 9), to the central argument that 'economic prosperity and social justice are not contradictions' (SPD, 2005, p. 8). Though, as junior partner in the current (Christian Democrat-Social Democrat) 'Grand Coalition', it has been nervous about advertising its policies as *revisionist* (given its new rival on the left), the adoption of Third Way-type policy platform was largely confirmed in the SPD's new Basic Programme (SPD, 2007).

The French Socialist Party has a (deserved) reputation as a more left-wing party. The PS-led government under Lionel Jospin (1997–2002), though implementing some more leftist policies (e.g. the '35-hour-week') nevertheless also sought to cap public spending and deregulate some areas of the labour market and the economy. In fact, Jospin's formulation of '*réalisme de gauche*' (leftist realism) (Clift, 2001) indicated that the party was at least trying (despite its socialist rhetoric) to adapt to the realities of the modern world. Jospin's 2002 presidential manifesto sought to balance an emphasis on 'inequalities in income' with 'equality of opportunity': ending poverty with special regard to housing while promoting social investment through (particularly) education (Jospin, 2002, pp. 3, 15–7, 25). Tellingly, the PS-led government managed to increase social investment through a 'leftist savings policy' (Merkel, 2000) that channelled more resources to social democratic priority areas without adding to overall levels of public spending. Therefore, the PS in government also converged towards a Third Way-type approach – even if it maintained a more 'dirigiste' (statist) belief in the role of the state. In other ways, the *Parti Socialiste* continued to proclaim a more traditional social democratic outlook – for instance, viewing the benefits system only in terms of citizens' rights and the state's responsibilities. The general approach was characterised by Jospin's dictum 'Yes to the market economy, no to the market society' (PS, 1999). This agenda was not, however, sustainable outside government given the 'federating tendencies' (Knapp and Wright, 2001) of the PS (with factions rallied around potential presidential candidates), the extreme competition on the left of the political spectrum (increasing the demand for socialist rhetoric) and the nature of France's two-round electoral system (increasing the need to appeal to core voters before the first round of voting). Thus, Jospin suffered a humiliating defeat in the first round of the 2002 French presidential elections for promoting a programme regarded as too centrist. Conversely, Ségolène Royal in her bid for the 2007 presidency found that her overall popularity sank when she was forced to unite the party's diverse factions around a more traditional leftist programme (Royal, 2007).

In the context of larger, more regulated welfare states, the SPD and PS in government have introduced liberal economic reforms without the Labour Party's capacity to increase overall public spending. European integration has also been significant – the completion of the Single Market and the stability-based ethos of the European Central Bank have further constrained government policy. The impact of globalisation is less tangible, but the (perceived) threat of tax competition and outsourcing has also affected the social democratic mindset. New Labour has been able to pursue a more recognisably social democratic strategy of increased public spending, allowing Blair to boast that 'Britain is the only European country where public spending as a proportion of national income in education and health will rise this year and next' (Blair, 2002, p. 16). However, as he also recognised, such increases only served to narrow the gap with average European levels of funding. These social democratic parties – moving along different trajectories – have thus converged towards similar political-economic-social models. Though this might at first seem counter-intuitive – for tactical reasons, Labour has *spun* its policies to the right while the SPD and PS have *spun* to the left – the real story has been the development of a new social democratic consensus in Europe. The major problem for the SPD and the PS has been the political cost of new programmes. Agenda 2010 resulted in the emergence of a new electoral threat on the left in Germany, while Jospin's denial that his programme was 'socialist' contributed to the electoral disaster of PS in 2002. Labour, in contrast, has proved more effective in packaging its new policy programme into a politically acceptable formula.

Conclusion

The analysis offered here is far from comprehensive and readers will have the opportunity to consider our arguments in the light of the more detailed studies of particular policy areas in the chapters that follow. However, we argue that despite its limitations our study sustains three broad conclusions.

Firstly, we have shown that New Labour represents a coherent project, both strategically and in terms of policy. Under Tony Blair's leadership the party undeniably retreated from key elements of the party's historic ideological prospectus. However, as we have shown, social democracy has wide ideological perimeters and it does not follow that the shift from Old to New Labour has taken it beyond these boundaries. New Labour's accommodation to the market represents its greatest departure from social democratic tradition. But as we have argued, the primacy of a prudently managed market economy has been, for New Labour, the precondition for realising its broader and more characteristically social democratic programme. In the altered context of the 2008 financial crisis, the Labour Government under Gordon Brown was quite prepared to opt for large-scale intervention and regulation of the markets when it was deemed prudent for the economy.

Secondly, on the basis of its achievements in office, we conclude that New Labour also emerges with some social democratic credit. It is certainly far from the most radical social democratic government. As the 2004 Higher Education Act, the 2004 Warwick Agreement and compensation for the abolition of the 10p tax rate in 2008[1] have shown, it has also needed parliamentary and trade union pressure to settle upon a progressive path. Yet we must recognise the context in which New Labour has governed. Internationally it has operated in an environment of increasingly open and de-regulated markets which many had regarded as foreclosing any possibility of social democratic advance. Domestically it inherited a polity in which the writ of neoliberalism had run further and longer than virtually anywhere else in the world. From such a perspective New Labour's achievements seem slightly more significant and its disappointments more intelligible.

Finally, if these conclusions appear discomforting and counter-intuitive it is because they run counter to the presentational strategies of both New Labour and its sister European social democratic parties. New Labour has found it most politically useful to downplay its social democratic credentials in favour of presenting itself as a moderate centrist party. This has invited and heightened a contrast with apparently more radical social democratic parties elsewhere in Europe. But as we have shown in the German and French cases, behind such appearances lies compelling evidence of social democratic convergence. Indeed, should the concern about the insecurities and risks of financial globalization triggered by the 2008 financial crisis persist, we may witness a further convergence of policy rhetoric and party programmes.

Note

1. Backbenchers won concessions on enhanced bursaries for students from low-income families during the passage of the Higher Education Act 2004 which introduced 'top-up' fees for university students. The Warwick agreement was a deal brokered under trade union pressure covering enhanced fairness at work, pensions and the public services.

Part II   Policy

7
Blair and the NHS: Resistible Force Meets Moveable Object?

Calum Paton

Introduction and perspective

The record of New Labour under Tony Blair's premiership from 1997 to 2007 can be viewed from the vantage point of what happens under his successor, Gordon Brown. Was there a 'Blairism' which applied to health policy and the NHS, keeping in mind Ted Marmor's wise aphorism that it is better to consider 'politics in health' rather than the 'politics of health' – given that the politics affecting health policy is unlikely to be unique to health. This is true even though politics and health policy are 'mutually embedded' (Moran, 1999), whereby developments in one sphere affect the other.

Was the Blair era (whether or not one can pin down a 'Blairism') distinct; and, if so, have its characteristics laid down a precedent for the future (that is, has Brown continued the Blairite direction of travel?). Or was it an aberration, at least in health policy and as regards the steering of the NHS, based on the breathless 'initiative-itis' which stemmed from the 'sofa government' of the era (Butler, 2005) and from the dominance of political advisers-cum-aspiring ministers who dominated policy (Benn, 2003) and moreover represented a 'neo-liberal cuckoo' in the Labour nest?

The New Labour legacy to the NHS is best described not as a continuation of the Conservatives 'new public management' (NPM), but the creation of 'the new public administration'. While some of the classic tenets of NPM are aspirationally present in some of New Labour's policy statements, (both 'business-like techniques' and the use of the market), the policy culture under Blair was too chaotic and 'post modern' to be characterised as NPM.

New Labour arrived at the Department of Health in 1997 and pledged to 'abolish the internal market' (long since reversed – an example of the confusion and circularity pointed to by the Better Government Initiative which reviewed executive policy and implementation as well as by academic studies (Paton, 2006.)) New Labour had an ambivalent attitude, however, to the 'new public management' in a number of ways. They continued the 'managerialist' institutions which they inherited from the Conservatives, such as

Table 7.1   Key New Labour health policies

POLICY INITIATIVES/'REFORM'	AIM/ORGANISATION IMPLICATION
The NHS: Modern and Dependable (1997)	Builds on institutions such as the purchaser/provider split created at end of Conservative tenure, but rejects market culture in favour of collaboration.
Department of Health (2000)	Sets targets to accompany increased investment.
Shifting the Balance of Power (2001)	Devolution (of responsibility, not power) to local commissioners (Primary Care Trusts – PCTs); removal of regional tier.
Implementing the NHS Plan: Next Steps for Investment, Next Steps for Reform (2002) *Commissioning a Patient-Led NHS* (2005)	The beginning of the 'neo-liberal turn' in health policy – the 'New Market'. Reverses *Shifting the Balance of Power* by merging PCTs and restoring regions in all but name.
Our Health, Our Care, Our Say (2006)	Shifting to Primary and Community Services (reaction to hospital deficits).
Health Reforms in England (July 2006)	New 'overall framework' for reforms creating a 'new market'.
The Future Regulation of Health and Adult Social Care in England (November 2006 and October 2007)	Attempt (partial) to provide a regulatory framework for the 'new market'.
Darzi Review of English NHS 2007–8	Essentially a planning approach, led by the Department of Health via the Strategic Health Authorities (regions in all but name), to reconfiguring hospital, primary care and community services.

the 'purchaser/provider split' and even extended the 'total purchasing pilot' projects of the mid-1990s into Primary Care Groups (later Trusts.) Yet they supplanted the last surviving pretensions of the 'new public management' towards diminished political interference and devolution of responsibility to and down the management chain. By 2000 the 'central admin' culture (and it was 'admin', for ministers such as Alan Milburn were administering initiatives geared to different targets 'commanded and controlled' down different central 'silos' of the Department of Health and Treasury) was more compelling than ever in the 1990s.

And the apotheosis of central command came with the merging of the jobs of the permanent secretary to the Department of Health with that of the chief executive of the NHS, when Nigel Crisp was appointed in October

2000 – removing the last vestiges at central level of Sir Roy Griffiths' 'new public management' reforms set out in 1983 (DHSS, 1983).

Instead of the Weberian tramlines of traditional 'public administration', we have had directives, targets and 'standards' which are both centrally set and almost (were it not for New Labour's earnestness in believing its own rhetoric) whimsically changing. This is not just a rhetorical point: changing targets – and, for example, separate and often inconsistent targets for purchasers/commissioners of care, on the one hand, and providers such as hospitals, on the other hand – have specifically affected both behaviour and outcomes in local health economies across England (much of this, although not all, is an English analysis.)

Further exploration of the points raised in the paragraphs above occurs in Paton (2008). It remains to be seen whether the renewed aspiration of a 'marketised' NHS, prefigured in Department of Health, (2002) but only implemented from 2007 onwards, will change the trajectory of growing command and control from 1948 to the present day (see Table 7.1 for a summary of the major NHS reforms under Blair).

New Labour and the NHS

So what was the essence of the New Labour NHS? We should distinguish different levels of policy: political economy, the policymaking (and implementation) process, the nature of public management and the means – the structures and incentives – used for steering the NHS.

Political economy

At this highest level, the New Labour project has essentially consisted in making Labour policy compatible with capitalist globalisation as opposed to national social democracy, recognising the passing of the Keynesian national welfare state and the move to what Bob Jessop called the Schumpeterian workfare state (Jessop, 2002.) Tony Blair's Labour party career began during the heyday of the Bennite left in the Labour party, and his abiding obsession was to 'modernise' the party until it represented the (arguably right-of-centre) political mainstream in Britain (or was it England?). He was at one with Gordon Brown, his colleague, rival and successor, on this, although Blair's relative lack of Labour party baggage and later ideological predilection towards many of the tenets of neoliberalism made this a voyage of choice for Blair rather than (perhaps) a voyage of necessity for Brown.

For the NHS, this meant ensuring that it retained a political constituency among the contented majority (Galbraith, 1992), who expected high levels of service in other walks of life and would not forever accept Fordist rather than Rolls Royce, or at least BMW, healthcare. The mission of the NHS moreover (although this point was probably subconscious for most New Labour ministers) had to include investment in those cadres of the workforce who were most central to the country's economic success. If they, or their employers, went private, it would not free up public funds for the rest – that is, the poorer – so much as reduce the tax base for the NHS altogether, as those paying privately in time came to embrace the politics of the tax-revolt.

Therefore – if the NHS were to retain its mission for the poor or what the European Union might call the 'social model' stressing solidarity if not equity and equality – the pressure on the public purse to fulfil a tripartite mission for the NHS (social model, economic investment and keeping the affluent happy) would be great. Hence came the NHS Plan (DoH, 2000), calling for more money and also greater efficiency ('investment plus reform').

It is not tax-funded healthcare which is the problem; it is tax-funded healthcare in a political economy where there is significant inequality and where there is a 'right-of-centre' voting majority concerned more with lower taxes than with social investment. This is in essence the 'dilemma' remarked upon by Tony Blair seven years ago in the Foreword to the NHS Plan (DoH, 2000.) The challenge for the NHS in such a setting is to combine quality and efficiency to such an extent that the better off are prepared to pay publicly for the NHS for all, with some redistribution to the worse off as part of the deal, and still get as much for themselves as they would if insuring themselves alone in private markets.

Therefore, the question is not, 'is the NHS more efficient than alternatives?'; the question is, 'is the NHS so significantly more efficient than alternatives that it can do this?' The Labour government has rightly perceived the challenge (investment and reform must be linked); the problem in England is that the reform process has been confused and expensive (Paton, 2006.)

From 2002 onwards, there was an increasing split between the Blair and Brown camps, with the latter content to rely on public targets and performance management, but the former increasingly attracted both to neoliberal ideas and to neoclassical economic doctrine (Le Grand, 2007) leading to a stress on market structures and incentives. This was uber-Blairism, if you will – the Third Way (a middle way between markets and statist social democracy) being superseded by a 'fourth way', or rather the earlier second way of market reform to state institutions.

The policy process

In terms of New Labour's approach (deliberate and otherwise) to health policymaking for England (the rest of the UK is a different story (Greer, 2004)), I have argued that the metaphor of the 'garbage can' is useful, albeit incorporated into a 'macro 'framework which renders it compatible with the longer-term trends to be explained (Paton, 2006): that is, how can we combine the short-termist focus of the garbage can with the longer-term evolution of the shape of policy as influenced by external factors such as political economy.

The garbage can theory (Cohen et al., 1972) of the policy process has been effectively illustrated by Kingdon (1984), who distinguishes the three 'streams' of politics, policies and problems. In my own words: when a decision making or policy-influencing opportunity arises (when a policy window opens), solutions are peddled by the 'usual suspects' and ideologists with a tailor-made solution or answer, often offered before the problem or question has been 'rationally' analysed. How politics, problems and solutions come together at such opportunities is neither (necessarily) rational nor linear (in the sense of analysing solutions as responses to problems, with 'politics' a mediating factor at most). Instead, politics and rationality are distinct arenas.

The New Labour health policy era from 1997 to 2007 seems to exemplify a hyperactive approach to policymaking, with 'policy windows' of opportunity created frequently by a government concerned with short-termist 'rebuttal' as well as, or instead of, longer-term strategy. For example, the abolition of NHS health authorities and regional offices in England in 2001–2 seems to have been motivated less by a grand plan than by a desire to 'get in first' when the government got wind of the Conservatives oppositions' to health authorities, in order to make a symbolic anti-bureaucracy announcement to similar effect. As a result, New Labour imposed on itself arguably the most dysfunctional reorganisation in the history of the NHS which was (partially) reversed three years later, again in a short-termist manner which created new problems (Paton, 2007).

Additionally, New Labour – perhaps reflecting a secular trend – has seen policy as a centralist exercise despite periodic homilies about 'listening', 'public participation' and the like. Talking of the Miliband brothers whom he liked at a personal level (advisers to Blair and Brown respectively before they became ministers), as typical of the 'world of the Prime Minister's advisers, Tony Benn (2003) recorded, '… they see policy as something they work out, push through the policy forums, push through the Conference and then, having had an election victory, they push it through the Cabinet and the Commons. There's no real participatory element in it' (p. 643).

New Labour's centralist solipsism has arguably been responsible for its genuine mystification when things go wrong of which many people outside their rarified 'consultations' were aware. An example is the deficit crisis of 2005–7 (Paton, 2007; Select Committee on Health of the House of Commons, 2006), when the health secretary seemed not to see coming what parts of the NHS were keen to tell her but often were excluded from the orthodox channels of consultation – to use a US term, the 'kiss up, kick down' hierarchies – where bad news was not welcome until too late. Even the titles of institutions and initiatives reflect this self-congratulatory (and incidentally un-British, schmaltzy) tone – such as 'WORLD-CLASS COMMISSIONING' (2007). If it's really world class, do we need to say so? It smacks of desperation as well as bad taste.

Politicised management

The real story of the NHS from 1948 to the present day is not one of central control from 1948 to 1990, then Tory internal market from 1991 to 1997, then increasing sharply, right through the Tory 1990s and even more so under New Labour (Paton, 2006). This makes the 'third way' of 1997–9 a minor rhetorical distraction covering a period of stasis or drift in the NHS, rather than a distinct approach. The high noon of Alan Milburn's centralism (1999–2002, when he thought or pretended that he was beginning to devolve) was, on my reading, the apotheosis of Thatcherite centralism as described by Simon Jenkins (1995). And Brown, Son of Thatcher (Jenkins, 2006), is likely to go further.

The New Labour approach, especially from 2002 on, was to preach (and seemingly believe in) what was called 'devolution' (actually de-concentration, not even decentralisation) – for example, the cumbersomely named and disastrously devised Shifting the Balance of Power (to the 'frontline', of course) (DoH, 2001). Yet the reality was to abolish, or fail to restore, the regional institutions which could effectively steer and/or plan health services. Thus only the centre was left as the means to direct and clear up messes.

The key achievements of the NHS under New Labour have been occasioned by an amalgam of traditional public administration and the 'new public administration' (not the new public management) which emphasises central targets (Barber, 2007), changing central initiatives and clinical strategies (note the Department of Health's clinical Tsars, making the approach pre-Leninist rather than Stalinist) which are personally led by agents of the central state. The appointment of Lord (Ara) Darzi – as undersecretary of State for Health (2007) but more significantly as 'modernizer' of NHS provision in, first, London and then the rest of England entrenches a 'centralist' trend on a larger scale, as well as (potentially) driving a coach and horses through the 'health reform programme' characterised by choice, payment by results and arms length regulation (Harper, 2006).

Despite New Labour's policy mantras of 'what counts is what works', and 'joined-up government', New Labour's major structural and institutional initiatives on the NHS (for the present use of the terms 'structural' and 'institutional', see Tuohy, 1999) have been largely evidence-free and occasioned by the 'politics of the garbage can' rather than by a 'rational' approach to using means (eg 'joined-up government') to achieve clear ends. Practice-Based Commissioning, the latest 'fad' towards the end of the Blair tenure, embraced by former Health Secretary Patricia Hewitt in 2006–7, is a good example of an answer without a question – a solution without the problem being clearly defined. This insecure faddishness bedevilled Labour in opposition, from the time of Blair's accession to the leadership of the party in 1994 to the present day. In the language of football, Labour needed to play its own game rather than worry about the opposition – especially during their landslide majority from 1997 to 2005.

New Labour policymakers have almost subconsciously assumed that the NHS should mirror in its organisational forms what they assume the 'post-modern organisation' to look like. But this is a psychological rather than logical approach: to play its role in a post-Fordist political economy, the NHS arguably has to be neo-Fordist (Paton, 2006).

Conflicting policy regimes

What were the 'policy regimes' which New Labour adopted one after the other? Labour had inherited the structure of the previous Conservative government's internal market and never removed it. In essence this was the 'purchaser/provider split' between what were now to be called commissioners of health care and the agencies (such as hospitals) which actually provided it.

To this, New Labour added three distinct policy 'regimes', not all of which were new but which were emphasised at different times between 1997 and 2007. It added exhortations to collaborate (at first, via the NHS 'third way') from 1997–9; then central control, the heyday of which was from 1999 to 2002 (although de facto central control continued to 2006 and arguably to this day); and – trailed in 2002, yet only really implemented in 2006/7 – the 'new market' of patient choice buttressed allegedly by a new system of reimbursing healthcare providers. (In this chronology we are lacking the 2001–2 initiatives to 'devolution' prior to the implementation of the 'new market', but this was, on my argument, a chimera.)

Taken together, these stages have been presented by the ideologists and advisers of the Blair regime as a 'cunning plan' to move through central standards, to 'pull up the NHS by the scruff of its neck', towards the relaxation of central control and reliance on consumerism and the new market to ensure standards (and financial control.)

The 'garbage can' approach to interpreting New Labour's first ten years (Paton, 2006) however depicts each of these policy regimes as short-termist in origin and deriving most of its justification ex post. Moreover, and crucially, the four regimes – old and new markets, local collaboration and central command and/or control – have co-existed, to an extent that causes confusion – certainly in implementation of policy and arguably in policy itself.

The alleged hierarchy (that-never-had-been) of the 'first way' was at least in line with traditional public administration. The central control-by-targets which New Labour instigated in 1999–2000 – as the 'collaborative' third way failed, bluntly, to make much difference (especially to waiting-times) – was more like a version of the Sun King's 'l'etat – c'et moi', with the health secretary of the time seemingly saying to a bewildered and battered community of clinicians and managers, 'l'NHS – c'est moi'! We might call this the

New (Labour) Public Administration, rather than either traditional public administration (misleadingly classified as hierarchy by the New Labour spinmeisters) or the new public management. Furthermore the struggle between Blair's premiership and then chancellor Gordon Brown's treasury piled up complex and contradicting 'performance management regimes' for the NHS in England (based on the treasury's public service agreements, and more detailed performance assessment frameworks, on the one hand, and the prime minister's policy fads, on the other hand).

New Labour: Same old Tories?

There is a myth which has gradually gained the status of orthodoxy, concerning the health service reform which started with the Conservative NHS reforms (trailed in the White Paper, *Working for Patients*, in February 1989; enacted into legislation in the NHS and Community Care Act of 1990 and officially introduced on 1 April 1991) and which – eventually – continued in more virulent form under New Labour, trailed in 2002 by the deceptively brief and informal Department of Health Paper, *Implementing the NHS PLAN: Next Steps for Investment, Next Steps for Reform* (DoH, 2002).

That myth, comprising interrelated and unproven assumptions, is that the NHS was failing, that reform was driven by a desire for greater patient involvement, that this in turn necessitated market-like reforms to challenge 'provider capture' and that (in the Labour version) hospitals were the epicentre of elitist interests which were best challenged by emphasising primary care as the 'answer'.

In fact the Tory 'market reforms' born between 1988 and 1991 were occasioned by two influences. Firstly, there had been, from 1984 onwards in England, a technical debate about the best means by which health authorities (which in those days both planned services and provided them) could be reimbursed for patients who flowed across administrative boundaries. This created the option – one among many – of 'cross-charging', which created the technical prototype for the more ideologically rooted 'internal market'.

Secondly, the American adviser Alain Enthoven (1985) straddled the technical and ideological camps and was responsible for introducing the idea into mainstream politics – although this was only the immediate cause. The underlying cause was central government's ideological search for market reforms in the public sector. Even so, it was initially the fledgling Social Democratic Party, via former health minister David Owen, which took up Enthoven's idea in early 1985: only four years later did the Conservative Government, led by Mrs Thatcher, adopt the idea.

Almost two decades later, the Blair government's 'new market' reforms were no more born of a 'bottom up consumerism' than the Thatcher government's had been. Similar to the attack on the Thatcher regime by the medical Royal Colleges, there was widespread professional dissatisfaction with the scattergun approach to health reform under Blair – high on announcement, low on coherence motivated by a mistrust of public sector professionals (Blair, 1999c).

To the extent there was ideology, it was centrally imposed. The practical expression of this (neo-liberal) ideology – in terms of individualism and consumerism applied to public services – was not forced on Blair by public pressure, although the public rightly expected more of the NHS as citizens and as users than their grandparents in 1948. Instead, it was his way of proactively seeking to 'dish the Tories'.

The empirical record

The 'bottom line' of the story of Blair's ten years is: much new money, partial achievement and limited cost-effectiveness (Wanless, 2007). The Right uses this generalisation to suggest that 'state medicine' is intrinsically flawed (they mean the NHS itself, although think tanks such as the neoliberal Reform seek to have their cake and eat it here; sometimes talking of replacing the NHS with 'social insurance' and sometimes talking of improving it). But the real lesson is less ideological, or rather friendlier to the Left: more could have been done with the money if it had been spent on services rather than permanent 'redisorganization' inspired by New Labour's increasingly neoliberal leanings. NHS policy, in clinical terms, has suffered from irritable bowel syndrome.

Inputs and outputs

Let us consider what the achievements were, for there were real achievements; what the main quantitative qualifications are and what underpinned these.

Between 1997/8 and 2007/8, NHS annual expenditure rose from c. £30 billion to c. £90 billion, at 'current prices'; at constant prices, the rise was to c. £55billion, and when taking additional account of 'NHS inflation' above the level of economy-wide inflation, the rise was to less than £45 billion (Wanless, 2007). In real terms, therefore, the budget nearly doubled over the ten years, but NHS inflation accounted for at least two-fifths of this. As well as the costs of drugs and supplies, pay inflation – especially occasioned by new clinical contracts and the Agenda for Change workforce pay reform – was an important component.

But we must also add in: high costs of capital occasioned by widespread use of the Private Finance Initiative (set to 'kick in' more significantly over the coming 30 years); 'pump priming' of new private sector providers at higher-than-tariff initial reimbursement, for guaranteed volumes of work which was not always forthcoming, and – significantly – large non-recurring and recurring 'administrative costs' born in continual reorganisation (Paton, 2006).

By the end of 2006, as reported in the British Medical Journal of 25 November, the then health secretary Patricia Hewitt claimed that the NHS was employing far more hospital doctors than it should be. Quite apart from the fact that the figures were a direct response to the targets of the NHS Plan and later pre-election targets in 2005, there was policy confusion here. International evidence, including from Kaiser Permanent in California (British Medical Journal, 2002), suggests that reducing lengths of stay significantly but also safely in health care systems, and thereby saving resources, depends on significant investment in senior doctors so that patients can be 'managed' more 'proactively.' The NHS still lacks this, and ministers are confused, facing both ways on the issue in response to short-term pressures.

In terms of 'outputs' – the services delivered – there has been much commentary since 2004 to the effect that productivity has not been what it should be, and even that it has declined by some measures. The picture is more complex. Firstly, the unit of measurement – the finished consultant episode – only tells part of the story. Secondly, quality needs to be taken into account, but this is difficult. Thirdly, an equivocal record on 'numbers of electives treated' (targets met in a majority of cases, but average waiting-times falling less significantly) has been counterbalanced by the high 'productivity' of the hospital system in treating emergencies, which have increased significantly. Overall, the reduction of long waits (with England doing better than Scotland and Wales, but having to spend to do so) has been a success for the 'central target regime' rather than for the more recent 'new market', whose consequences have yet to be determined.

Concerning 'outcomes', cancer mortality rates have fallen but only at similar rates to other 'advanced' countries, with countries like the US, Germany and (especially) France remaining ahead by similar proportions as before up to 2004. The picture may have improved since then. A similar story may apply for other conditions which the government targeted, such as coronary heart disease and stroke. Concerning the wider social, environmental and personal health determinants, 'public health targets' have been set both on behaviour (such as smoking cessation and teenage pregnancy) and on health consequences (such as inequalities, as measured by low birth weights and variations between social classes). Wanless (2007) reports that, in the language of Wanless (2002), public engagement falls somewhere between the scenarios of 'solid progress' and 'slow uptake' – perhaps we can call this a C+!

Overall Labour has achieved some significant successes for the NHS, but less than that might have been achieved with greater consistency of purpose and confidence in a social democratic strategy rather than an obsession with 'dishing the Tories'. Thus New Labour's wider political strategy – seen to be deficient by 2008 – affected its detailed NHS record, which might be summed up as 'part success, part failure', giving grist to the mill of anti-NHS commentators.

How distinctive have Blair's New Labour been?

To be fair, health policy and the NHS always provided a less likely location for the apotheosis of New Labour as a distinctive creed or practice. For as Blair rightly said (Department of Health, 2000), 'the NHS was the greatest act of modernization ever undertaken by a Labour government'. The challenge of 'modernizing' the NHS has not lain in a 'third way', fourth way or whatever; it is more prosaic than that. But as Toynbee and Walker (2005) have pointed out, New Labour has undersold its progressive achievements – and, I would argue in the case of the NHS, diminished these – by apologising for the public sector rather than bolstering it.

Despite having been in opposition for 18 years, Labour's health policy on assuming office in 1997 was sparse. Essentially, it was tactical, consisting in 'we are not the Conservatives; we will save the NHS' (for consumption by the audiences of the clinical professions and the general public) and 'we will recognise our inheritance and avoid debilitating reform' (for an audience of NHS managers, especially those high-flying Chief Executives whom New Labour admired but who had tied their colours to the mast of Tory reform.)

Labour pledged to abolish the 'internal market' introduced in 1991 and 'reintegrate the NHS without reorganisation'. This was either contradictory or platitudinous: if there was a rampant internal market, abolishing it would require structural reorganisation; and if the internal market had already withered on the vine by 1997, then the policy was an inert one (a sheep in wolf's clothing), perhaps an acceptance of the 'forces of conservatism' which PM Tony Blair would excoriate in his party conference speech two and a half years later in October 1999.

To understand why health policy was not characterised by a distinctive, cohesive approach under New Labour, we have to remember the origins of the 'third way'. The overt part of the ideology of New Labour was derivative in two senses. Firstly, it was not based on values per se but derived from the dictates of political strategy. Secondly, this strategy was derived from the Clinton campaigns in the US. The Blair 'project' sought to 'triangulate' between two polar opposites – defining itself by what it was not. Clinton had rejected not only Republicanism but also 'traditional tax-and-spend Democratic policy'. The Blair project rejected not only (Thatcherite) Conservatism (at least on paper) but also the social democracy of what the Blairites were the first to call Old Labour.

Anything that was to the left of New Labour or based on the institutional interests of the Labour coalition was conveniently called Old. It was a short step in the world of spin, therefore, to adopt the word 'modernisation' as New Labour's mantra. But, just as Herbert Morrison (a post-war cabinet minister and grandfather to the spinmeister of New Labour's Peter Mandelson) had defined socialism as 'what Labour governments do', 'modernisation' could now be described as everything New Labour governments do – and everything that they disapproved was 'old' (whether Old Labour or – to try to keep the party faithful onside – the Old Tories.)

But modernisation also had a harder edge – it was not just the pragmatism, or opportunism, of Morrison in a modern setting. 'Modernisation' was part of the (initially) more covert part of New Labour ideology: it was at root a term alluding to political economy – in particular, the need for New

Labour policy to conform to the dictates and constraints of capitalist globalisation. Thus the 'forces of conservatism' included not only 'conservative' social groups such as fox-hunters (and, more importantly, wider rural interests and ways-of-life) but also (of course) the trade unions (Labour's paymasters, past and future, once Blair's rattling of the box in the citadels of capitalism came to grief) and – even more significantly – all those who believed in, or were based in, national economic and welfare institutions which were in tension with the international market of global capitalism.

Meanwhile, in 1997 and for the next ten years, Labour talked of 'old values in a new setting', but this was just rhetoric geared to the party faithful. When elected as party leader in 1994, Blair had still used the word socialism, but inserting a hyphen, that is, 'social-ism', as in his address in 1994 at the launch of the report of the Commission for Social Justice, chaired by Sir Gordon Borrie, previous chair of the Monopolies and Mergers Commission fame, at the invitation of Blair's predecessor John Smith.

At a postmodern stroke of a pen, he had reduced the 'hard' ideology of Labour to a woolly belief in the 'social'. Who could differ, apart from the Aunt Sally version of Margaret Thatcher, quoted out of context by her enemies, as believing that there is 'no such thing as society'?

Later, social democracy too fell by the wayside, to be replaced by the 'triangulated' concept of the Third Way. It was this concept which was initially applied to health policy – mechanistically and again derivatively, as a political strategy rather than a policy development. (This belief in 'politics as policy', with implementation looking after itself, to boot, would come back to haunt Blair and New Labour, in general and especially the NHS). Later on, New Labour was characterised by breathless and persistent 'modernisation' and legislative and administrative hyperactivism.

The 'third way' may indeed be a fig leaf for neoliberalism. Twentieth-century Marxism explained 'social investment' by the state as a means of saving capitalism from its own short-termism. Seen in those terms the 'third way' is just the longer-term logic of the capitalist state. We can note with amusement what Fidel Castro had to say when asked what he thought of Blair: 'I read Anthony Giddens' book, which contains the theory of the so-called "Third Way". There's nothing of a third way in it – it's the way taken by every turncoat in this world' (Castro and Ramonet, 2007, p. 500).

Has New Labour influenced the future of health policy?

New Labour has been responsible for co-opting Conservative policy in favour of both the NHS model and its own (Labour) levels of expenditure. This is quite an achievement, which mirrors in reverse New Labour's initial acceptance of Conservative levels of public expenditure in 1997–9. It remains to be seen whether the Conservatives will maintain this consensus, if and when they have been in power for a few years.

To emphasise this, the Conservatives have dropped their 2005 proposal for a 'patient passport', in effect a subsidy for private health care. This differed from the Labour government's use of private providers. Whereas the government policy uses the private sector in the context of NHS financing and NHS 'rules of access', the dropped Conservative policy would have allowed individuals to 'go private' through personal purchase, perhaps 'queue jumping' and perhaps topping up their 'state voucher' with additional private money.

Conclusion

New Labour has set the terms of debate on expenditure on the NHS, which has constrained the Conservatives to promise at least to match, and possibly exceed, its spending plans. This is a major success, and the mirror image of its own constraints in sticking to the outgoing Conservative government's fiscal plans in 1997.

It is in the policy through which this expenditure has been mobilised that various own goals – born of policy overload, with incompatible policies being adopted and overlaid on each other – have been scored. And the use of policy as 'Prime Ministerial and Ministerial announcement' – for example, in the recent 'anti-hospital', pro-primary care policy of Our Health, Our Care, Our say (DoH 2006) – often sets the management of the NHS upon 'must do' tasks which are at odds with local needs (e.g. contracting hospitals without adequate extra-hospital care). 'Post-modern shopping' for policy often leads to adopting overseas 'good practice' (such as the approach of Kaiser Permanente in the US as an alleged example of integrated care) at the level of rhetoric and 'local experiment' in environments which are hostile (the rest of English policy is disintegrating, not integrating, local health economies, as an overt part of 'marketising' the NHS) or in ways which are not true to the originating model. Kaiser's success, such as it is, is based upon employing many more senior doctors per weighted capita than in the UK, to achieve more active patient management and shorter lengths of stay. English policy however has recently been based on an assumption that there has been over-investment in doctors (from a much lower start-point, and of course as a result of an earlier phase of New Labour policymaking).

Some of the long-term (political) challenges for the NHS have been well understood by New Labour. But the devil has been in their policy detail. And Tony Blair's *imprimatur* is on the style of making and implementing (or failing to implement) policy between 1997 and 2007. Centralist policy changes have been the order of the day, and New Labour's deliberate political amnesia has condemned it both to repeat mistakes of earlier eras and to accumulate incompatible rafts of policy.

8
Reformulating Social Policy: The Minimum Wage, the New Deal, and the Working Families Tax Credit

Jerold Waltman

Few areas of public life were touched more profoundly or more directly by the Blair governments than the welfare state. Indeed, in a sense, re-engineering the welfare state was the very essence of New Labour. For in that domain its emphasis on going back to the party's basic ideals but finding new policies to bring them into fruition was on full display.

By the time Tony Blair left office, the Beveridge-inspired welfare state had been significantly reshaped. In place of a regime founded on social insurance and public assistance, there was one emphasizing work and responsibility. It was uncertain, though, whether either the policies that have been put in place or the political bases supporting them would endure. In the first part of this chapter, I will lay out the policy and political inheritance that greeted the first Blair government when it took office in 1997. I will then turn to a brief portrayal of the ideas that informed New Labour's approach to the welfare state. Following that, I will survey three central components of the new strategy—the New Deals, the refundable tax credits, and the minimum wage—including an analysis of their impact and, finally, speculate on what their futures might be.

The policy inheritance

Although the welfare state can be traced to the initiatives of the last Liberal government before the First World War, the modern welfare state was the product of the famous *Beveridge Report* (1942) and the 1945–51 Labour government. Beveridge pointed to eight primary causes of need: unemployment, disability, loss of livelihood by someone not employed, retirement, marriage needs of women, funeral expenses, childhood, and physical disease or incapacity. To address these conditions, he proposed a large social insurance program filled in around the edges with public assistance. When Labour left office in 1951, virtually the entire system he proposed was in place. The essential prop for the system, full or near-full employment, was to be maintained through careful manipulation of Keynesian style aggregate demand management.

While parliament was enacting the Beveridge program, a tract was published that would do much to shape the subsequent ideology of the welfare state. The sociologist Thomas H. Marshall (1950) argued that "rights" had gone through a three-stage evolution. Basic civil liberties had been won first and then political rights were added. The mid-twentieth-century's contribution would be the right to receive state benefits. The implications of accepting Marshall's position are enormous. First, it put the receipt of payments from the public purse on a par with freedom of speech and voting. Second, it demolished the distinction between social insurance and public assistance. Third, it detached the obligation to work from the receipt of benefits. While it is uncertain that Marshall himself accepted the last of these (Powell, 2002), his disciples certainly did. By the late 1960s, Beveridge's policies and Marshall's ideas had become a quasi-religious orthodoxy among the Labour Party's intelligentsia.

However, by the 1970s the postwar welfare state was experiencing serious problems, at least four of which were critical. The first element was financial; no matter whether measured in absolute or percentage terms, its costs were steadily growing. Part of this growth in expenditure was attributable to simple demographic factors, the lengthening life span, and the growth in one-parent households, for example. Another part came from the natural tendency of programs to grow, as bureaucrats and politicians make incremental adjustments. But another part was that the number of people claiming benefits climbed. The stigma attached to public assistance melted away in much of the population, abetted to a degree, no doubt, by the spread of Marshall-type ideas among much of the populace.

Second, there was increasing evidence that people who stayed on benefits for sustained periods of time developed a "dependency culture." What was atypical before became normal for many people (Lindbeck, 1997). Thus, drawing benefits rather than working became merely expected behavior.

Third, there was the persistence of poverty despite substantial public expenditures. And, to many, the most telling datum about those in poverty is that they did not work. Stephen Nickell (2003), for example, showed that among those who were workless, poverty stood at 64 percent, compared to 29 percent where one family member worked just part-time, and a miniscule four percent when all adults in a household worked full-time.

Finally, there was rising public resentment about some facets of the welfare state. While the public remained basically committed to helping the less fortunate, ordinary people could see around them (and could read sensational stories in the press about) people living on public assistance and making no visible effort to find and keep work.

The Conservatives tapped into such feelings as part of their successful election campaigns of 1979, 1983, 1987, and 1992. In office, they pursued a relentless attack on the welfare state. The stated goals were to get people off benefits and into work, achieving at once the creation of a pool of low-wage workers that would make British industry more competitive, a cut in expenditures, and more upright lives among the previously workless. Specifically, obtaining and staying on benefits was made more difficult and the few props against very low wages, such as the Wages Councils, were abolished. In order to cut expenditures further, the Thatcher and Major governments put more emphasis on means-tested benefits. Consequently, between 1980–1 and 1996–7 means-tested benefits went from 15 to 25 percent of the social security budget (Adler, 2004, p. 91). Ironically, though, because of the high unemployment of the period, the total amount of expenditures on welfare state programs overall hardly budged.

New Labour thinking on the welfare state

Anthony Giddens spoke of creating a *positive welfare* society. What Beveridge had sought to guard against were the misfortunes of life, offering public policies to soften life's negatives. Giddens (1998, p. 117) argued that

> Welfare is not in essence an economic concept, but a psychic one, concerning as it does well-being. Economic benefits and advantages are therefore virtually never enough on their own to create it. Not only is welfare generated by many contexts and influences other than the welfare state, but welfare institutions must be concerned with fostering psychological as well as economic benefits. Quite mundane examples can be given: counseling, for example, might sometimes be more helpful than direct economic support.

Giddens was therefore severing the connection between welfare policies and the provision of cash benefits. Although he spoke of how public assistance might foster dependency, he did not really address the obligation to work.

Tony Blair and Gordon Brown made this connection, however. In their first pronouncement on welfare policy, the 1998 Green Paper *New Ambitions for Our Country: A New Contract for Welfare*, the two leaders' message was clear, "The Government's aim is to rebuild the welfare state around work" (Department of Social Security, 1998, p. 23).

As for Blair himself, clear indications of his thinking on welfare state reform can be gleaned from his Beveridge lecture of 1999, given at Toynbee Hall (where both Beveridge and Clement Attlee had worked). "We believe," he said, "that the role of the welfare state is to help people help themselves, to give people the means to be independent. We are creating an active welfare state focused on giving people the opportunities they need to support themselves, principally through work" (*The Times*, 18 March 1999). At the same time, he made clear that he recognized that merely getting people into work was not enough; work must carry adequate pay. By doing both of these, he argued that the welfare state could be rescued from the dead hand of the left that merely wanted to continue and expand the Beveridgite policies and protected from a right that had no sense of social justice. It was the only way, he felt, to make the welfare state popular again.

Blair was certainly right that the benefit system had lost favor among the public. Those who believed that "if welfare benefits weren't so generous, people would learn to stand on their own two feet" rose from 33 percent in 1987 to 42 percent in 2003, mirroring a climb from 67 percent to 78 percent over the same period for those who thought that "many people falsely claim benefits" (Taylor-Gooby, 2005, p. 15). Support for the welfare state had even fallen among those who identified with the Labour Party. Among them, for instance, endorsement of spending "more money on welfare benefits even if this means higher taxes" went from 73 percent in 1987 to 50 percent in 2002. Additionally, 65 percent of the general public agreed in 2002 that most of the unemployed could get a job "around here" if they wanted one, whereas only 40 percent had thought so in 1987 (Sefton, 2004, p. 4 and pp. 15–6).

Policy

Translating a preference for work over state benefits into policy resulted in three important initiatives: the New Deals, a series of earnings-related tax credits, and a minimum wage. The New Deals were designed to urge the unemployed into work and prepare them for better-paid positions. The tax credits were a public subsidy to the employee to make work more economically attractive, while the minimum wage sought to create a floor under wages throughout the economy.

The New Deals were in many respects simply a more humane version of what the Tories had been pushing for during their tenure. But the tone and the purposes were rather different. Nonetheless, they incurred the wrath of much of the traditional left within the Labour Party. The tax credits were more politically acceptable to both the party regulars and the Conservatives. The minimum wage was long opposed by most unions (Bowlby, 1957), since they feared it would undermine collective bargaining, but they had now come out in favor of the measure. It still, though, encountered ferocious opposition from business interests, a key group New Labour was trying to mollify. The whole policy matrix was therefore fraught with political difficulties.

The new deals

Payments to the unemployed, called Job Seekers Allowance (JSA) since the mid-1970s, had long been a staple of the British welfare state. Indeed, it was in many ways the most basic of the benefit programs, inasmuch as the fathers of the postwar welfare state had worried endlessly about a repeat of the massive unemployment of the 1920s and 1930s. However, few of them had envisaged a time when people would stay on unemployment benefit if work were available. By the 1960s, though, the Marshall-inspired idea of entitlement had undermined, at least for many, the idea of obtaining work if at all possible. There were indeed some weak work requirements in the law, but they were hardly ever enforced. As a result, a certain number of people simply stayed on Job Seekers Allowance virtually indefinitely.

New Labour's approach was to get people into jobs, but to do so with a more positive, and hopefully more effective, blueprint. The scheme was designed to guide people into work gradually and to support them as they made the transition from benefit recipient to self-sufficient employee. The centerpiece was the New Deal for Young People (NDYP), applying to 18–24 year olds. Established in 1998, it is compulsory for all those in this age bracket receiving Job Seekers Allowance.

With NDYP, a clearly defined three-step process is in place with rigid timetables. The first is a six-month period called "open" unemployment, in which the person receiving JSA is free to search (or not search) for a job on his or her own. At the end of six months, the person enters the Gateway phase of the program. The recipient is assigned a counselor, whose task it is to help the person obtain any needed basic skills (such as punctuality, how to compose a CV, and so forth) and engage in a serious job search. The recipient must meet with the counselor bi-weekly and report all actions taken to secure a job. During this period the JSA benefit continues, although it can be terminated if the person fails to co-operate with the counselor. Gateway is limited to four months. The third stage is called Options. Here there are four choices, and depending on the choice the time period can be between six and twelve months. The first is a subsidized job, in which public funds are given to an employer to hire and train the recipient. The second is a specific job-related education or training program. This can last up to twelve months, and the JSA continues. The third is a job, usually secured by the counselor, in the voluntary sector. The fourth is the so-called Environmental Task Force, which is essentially a government job. Although the government initially mandated that one could only exit the Gateway phase through a regular job, it later changed the guidelines and allowed people to select an Option during Gateway. To underscore the government's commitment to the program, the employment offices were combined with the offices paying benefits into a Jobcentre Plus network.

In addition to the NDYP, a number of other New Deals were rolled out, the most important of which was for the long-term unemployed over 24. Launched in 1998 as well, it was reformed in 2001, and now bears the title New Deal 25 Plus. The basics of the program are very similar to those of the NDYP, except that the open period of unemployment can be stretched to 18 months. New Deals are also in place for lone parents, disabled people, those who are over 50, and partners. However, none of these is compulsory, although there is strong encouragement for lone parents to participate. In addition, a program enacted in February 2008 called Pathways to Work applies to those receiving incapacity benefit.

Evaluating the success of the New Deals is, of course, tricky. The government, naturally, claims enormous success. Celebrating the program's tenth anniversary, the government crowed: "The New Deals have been the most successful innovation in the history of the UK labour market. In the last decade, the New Deals have helped more than 1.85 million people into work. Overall, employment is at record levels and the total number of people on key out-of-work benefits has fallen by a million since 1997" (Department for Work and Pensions (DWP), 2008b, p. 5).

It is true that the employment rate has risen, and the rise has been spread over the country. It is true, in addition, that the number of people on all the major benefit programs has fallen. More analytically, the two most sophisticated studies of the NDYP (Blundell, et al., 2004 and De Giorgi, 2005) concluded that the programs had increased the employment rate among the target group by six to seven percent. Another study (Coleman, Wapshott, and Carpenter, 2004) sought to find out what happened to those leaving NDYP and ND 25 Plus. They found that 46 percent of the youths and 41 percent of the older people left to start or return to a job not found through the New Deal. Another nine percent of the younger people and 19 percent of those over 24 moved onto another benefit program, while six percent and three percent respectively took up education or training unrelated to the New Deal program. On a discouraging note, though, the overall employment rate among the least skilled has actually fallen (Brewer, 2007, p. 14).

More evidence that the New Deals were now facing the daunting task of moving the hard to employ into stable jobs surfaced in early 2008. Forty percent of those leaving JSA, it was found, make another claim within six months, and 20 percent do so within 13 weeks (House of Commons Public Accounts Committee, 2008b, p. 7).

Tax credits

Getting people into employment and keeping them there is only half the task, though, if a welfare state is to meet its minimal goals of providing a way out of poverty and lessening inequality. The jobs must provide enough income to allow people to become self-sufficient. The first measure for meeting that objective was a tax credit geared to earned income.

This policy was borrowed from the US, where the Earned Income Tax Credit (EITC) has existed since 1975. The basic idea is that if you work but your earnings fall below certain income thresholds then you receive a refundable credit (that is, a check from government if the credit exceeds the tax liability). The proposal thus strikes a political chord with both the right and the left. For the right, it stresses work and avoids the bureaucracy associated with income support programs. For the left, it offers an attractive way to add to the cash income of those at the bottom of the income scale without the stigma of periodic visits to the benefits office. A Treasury report of 1998 noted, "that the US EITC had much to recommend it. Although the differences between the UK and US tax and benefit systems need to be recognized, there is no overriding reason why the UK should not have a tax credit payable through the pay packet to families in work" (HM Treasury, 1998, p. 22).

Accordingly, the old Family Credit (FC) was replaced by the Working Families Tax Credit (WFTC) in 1999, with the administration moving from the social security office to the tax collecting agency. To qualify, a family had to have one adult working 16 hours a week and have dependent children. The credit was withdrawn at a rate of 55 percent (of net income) up to a certain threshold, at which it phased out entirely. (That is, for each pound earned, the benefit was reduced by 55 pence up to the threshold.) The generosity of the credit and the more lax eligibility requirements (such as the earnings disregard) made it much more expensive to the public purse than the previous policy.

The major drawback of the WFTC was that it ignored those on low incomes who had no children. Therefore, in 2002, the government proposed adopting a new system, a combination of a Child Tax Credit (CTC) and a Working Tax Credit (WTC) (HM Treasury, 2002), a plan that was put in place in 2003.

Calculating the amount of WTC a recipient is entitled to starts with the "basic element," £1800 in 2008–9. (All subsequent figures are also for 2008–9.) Then, various other "elements" are added in for couples, lone parents, disabilities, working 30 hours per week or more, returning to work after 50, and child care. For CTC, there is a "family element," of £545, with other elements added in for additional children and disabled children. Moreover, the two credits can be combined.

For those claiming either WTC only or both WTC and CTC, there is a first income threshold of £6240. For those claiming CTC only, the first threshold is £15,575. Below these numbers, that is, no withdrawals occur. Above those thresholds a withdrawal rate of 39 percent (raised from the 37 percent in place between 2003 and 2008) kicks in; however, the 39 percent is now calculated on gross income (which can make the marginal tax rate on additional earnings approach 70 percent when National Insurance Contributions and income tax are figured in). For both groups, the second threshold is £50,000, at which point the withdrawal rate becomes 6.67 percent.

As even this truncated survey shows, no matter how simple the policy appears in principle, in practice the design and operation of the system is enormously complex, and it cannot be made simple. The various components are inherently complex, and this says nothing about how people's changes in circumstances are to be reported and checked. Furthermore, the program is quite prone to fraud, as some people claim more children than they have or contend they earned a little self-employment income.

The raw numbers of people drawing one of the two credits or both is substantial, around 5.9 million families (HM Revenue and Customs (HMRC), 2007, p. 5). In the bottom income quintile of households, 37 percent are affected, and even in the second and third quintiles, 36 and 33 percent respectively receive the payments (House of Commons, 2008c). This number falls to 26 percent in quintile four and only four percent in quintile five. Nearly half the total payments though, 48 percent, go to those in the bottom quintile. Still, there are people who are eligible and do not participate. Revenue and Customs puts the official number of those eligible for CTC at 21 percent and those eligible for WTC at 44 percent (HMRC, 2006, p. 7). Nonetheless, together the tax credits cost the treasury £24.2 billion annually.

In 2008, the Commons Public Accounts Committee reported that six billion pounds had gone out in overpayments in the first three years of the program (House of Commons, Public Accounts Committee, 2008a). Part of that was attributable to a huge computer foul up early in the program and Revenue and Customs' inexperience in administering such a program. Still, despite an increase in staff connected with the program from 7300 to 10,120 and an increase in administrative costs from £406 million to £587 million, one billion pounds a year was still being sent to unworthy claimants.

The minimum wage

British minimum wage policy began in 1909, with the adoption of the Trade Boards Act 1909 (Morris, 1986). Separate boards were created for four industries and empowered to set minimum rates of pay. A slow expansion of the system occurred through the years, with the bodies being renamed Wages Councils in 1945 (Bayliss, 1962). Conservative animosity to this breach of market fundamentalism, however, led to their being wound up in 1993.

The Labour Party, bowing to the wishes of the major unions, had given up support for a national minimum wage in the 1930s. As noted above, Beveridge did not believe low pay to be a major cause of poverty in the 1940s, and hence ignored it in his report.

Leaders of the public sector unions began a campaign in the 1980s to resurrect the idea, and the 1987 Labour manifesto included the proposal (Waltman, 2008, chapter 3). John Smith endorsed the idea while he was leader, and Tony Blair concurred. Thus, the 1997 manifesto made a minimum wage one of its key provisions. In 1998, parliament adopted the National Minimum Wage (NMW) statute, which went into effect in 1999.

The Act establishes a 12 member Low Pay Commission (LPC), all of whom are appointed by the government. Each spring the government hands the Commission a charge. The Commissioners then take submissions from all concerned and gather data from various sources. After deliberating, they make recommendations both for the rates and for any policy changes they deem warranted. The government must respond to the report publicly and provide a rationale for accepting or not accepting the recommendations.

Structurally, at the outset there were two distinct rates, the adult rate, applying to those over 21, and a development rate, applying to 18–21 year olds and adults who were new hires. Later, the development rate was made applicable to youths only (it was seldom used for adults anyway) and a new band was instituted for 16–17 year olds.

While the government has continued to emphasize how important the NMW is to New Labour's vision, it has in fact been quite cautious in terms of policy development. For example, it has been keenly sensitive to business interests when making appointments to the LPC. Furthermore, despite union pleas to set a target of half male median wages, the government has steadfastly refused to establish any guideposts at all, much less provide for any kind of automatic uprating. In addition, in spite of continual suggestions from the LPC to make the adult rate reach 21 year olds, such a move has been vetoed each time. A group of ministers, led by Gordon Brown, has successfully argued that the party must be careful not to offend its business allies.

Each rise in the minimum wage has affected about 1.3–1.5 million workers, around five percent of the workforce. Importantly, the households containing these workers, contrary to what many critics say, are strongly skewed toward the lower reaches of the income ladder. The lowest two deciles contain 45 percent of all minimum wage workers with another 15 percent falling into the next decile (Bryan and Taylor, 2004). There is a pronounced gender gap among minimum wage workers, with two-thirds being women. In fact, 47 percent of all minimum wage workers are the spouse of a head of household while 33 percent are themselves head of a household.

The minimum wage has had none of the calamitous effects opponents predicted when the measure was being debated. There have been no negative employment effects (Metcalf, 2007); no traceable inflationary effects have been unearthed (Wadsworth, 2007); and the health of businesses, even those in the low-wage sectors, is as robust as ever (Draca, Machin, and Van Reenen, 2005).

Poverty and inequality

Taken together, have these new policies had a significant effect on poverty and inequality?[1] The answers are uncertain and mixed.

Relative poverty, defined as 60 percent or more below median income, has declined since 1997. Measured after housing costs are deducted, the number of people in poverty fell from 25.3 percent to 20.5 percent in 2005 (Brewer, 2007, p.18). However, there has recently been a slight upturn in these numbers, to 21.6 percent. When it comes to inequality, there have been relatively greater gains by the less well off. However, this has had only a miniscule effect on overall income inequality. Moreover, wealth inequality has continued to grow apace (Dorling, et al., 2007).

However, two additional questions must be faced. First, what would have happened in the absence of Labour's policies? Concerning poverty, had the income growth patterns of the eighties and nineties continued, a likely possibility without a Labour government, there would have been even more people in poverty today. Regarding inequality, the Institute for Fiscal Studies (Brewer, et al., 2007, p. 22) concluded that had the previous policies been in place, rather than the slight increase from 0.333 to 0.347 the Gini coefficient exhibited, it would have soared to 0.378. Thus, outside factors, such as globalization, seem to be playing a significant role in the growth of poverty and inequality; consequently, governments, at least with the policy tools now at their disposal, can only mitigate, not abolish, them.

The second is more psychological. The Tory message from 1979 to 1997 was one of a thinly veiled hostility to the less well off. While many of New Labour's actual policies have been similar to those of the Conservatives, the approach has been markedly different. It is not "Get a job and go away," but a genuine attempt to make people more productive members of society. There has been talk of inclusion, and the New Deals do take a humane approach to helping people obtain and keep a job. Furthermore, the tax cred-its and the minimum wage make an attempt, perhaps a cumbersome and by some measures an inadequate attempt, but nonetheless an attempt, to make the job pay an adequate income. Thus, comments like that of a barmaid in Swansea regarding the minimum wage may be the most telling of all, "you can hold your head up high and say that you are earning £5 an hour" (*The Observer*, 20 November, 2005). New Labour may have forced many people off the public assistance rolls and into jobs, often, to be sure, dull and dead end jobs, and it may not have reduced poverty as much as it wished to nor made much of a dent in inequality, but if it has made people feel more like citizens of a democratic polity, that surely counts for a great deal.

A lasting impact?

It is doubtful that a Brown government will retreat on either the New Deals or the tax credits. From the beginning, Brown was even more adamant than Blair about emphasizing work. He told an interviewer for the US Public Broadcasting System in 2001, for example, "in every civilized society that works, rights and responsibilities must go together. If you're getting help to find a job, you've got a duty to look for a job. These are rights that come with responsibilities and not without responsibilities" (Public Broadcasting System, 2001). Thus, if anything, he is likely to strengthen the New Deals, perhaps by making the one for lone parents compulsory. During his time at the Treasury, he was one of the key backers of the tax credits; hence, unless they become administratively completely unmanageable, he would not likely throw out his baby.

In contrast, his stance on the minimum wage has been much softer. His was the most strident voice in cabinet for keeping the initial rate low in 1999, and he continued to counsel caution. He was adamantly opposed to lowering the age for the adult rate to 20, and he argued strenuously on several occasions that raising the youth rate by too much would contribute to unemployment.[2] Furthermore, as chancellor he cultivated the support of business, and being reticent on the minimum wage was one way to build and maintain these bridges.

The other question for the future is what the Conservatives might do when they return to office. For starters, there is no evidence that any of these policies, except possibly the minimum wage (Waltman, 2008, pp. 206–9), has become sacrosanct, politically untouchable by a parliamentary majority.

The real question, then, is: What is the ethos of the Conservatives regarding the welfare state likely to be when they again assume power? Perhaps the period out of office will have spurred a process of rethinking similar to that that led to New Labour. Perhaps New Labour will have shifted the ideological ground as much as Thatcherism did, and a "New Tory" orientation will emerge which will accept the goals of welfare policy enunciated by New Labour while only tweaking the methods.

There is some evidence that a partial rethinking has been going on inside the party, but it is only partial. For example, a perusal of the two major documents produced by the party's Social Justice Policy Group, *Breakdown Britain* (2006) and *Breakthrough Britain* (2007) provide some interesting clues, especially inasmuch as the latter contains 190 specific policy recommendations.

One thing that is immediately evident is that the rancor of the Thatcher years is largely gone. In tone at least, the documents evidence a sincere concern for poverty and sympathy for those mired in it. Moreover, they address areas that are much in need of discussion, such as addiction, family breakup, and the need for early intervention. However, when it comes to how the Tories would actually deal with poverty, a good bit of the old baggage slips in.

The group declares that New Labour's "aspirational targets are well intentioned but flawed" (Vol. 2, p. 4). New Deal incentives to work are inadequate, they claim, and the follow-through to make sure people stay in jobs is weak. Their solution is twofold: to force more participants into work sooner and to turn to the private sector to operate much of the program. Thus, one might expect that a Tory government would overhaul the New Deal program, making its work requirements more draconian and move much of the administration to business and the voluntary sector. As for the tax and benefit system, it is to be a key tool to get people out of poverty, but one of its central goals, so it is said, must be to create financial incentives to keep families intact.

Even though the Conservatives vociferously opposed the minimum wage when it was under consideration, they have dropped their pledge to repeal it. David Cameron told *The Observer* in 2005 that he thought, "the minimum wage was a success, yes. It turned out much better than many people expected." However, that is not an endorsement, and *Breakthrough Britain* underscores that: it is mentioned nowhere. Hence, it is likely that a future Conservative government would let the minimum wage atrophy, by stacking the LPC with those opposing a minimum wage, crafting charges that would stress the costs to the economy, and simply not implementing any changes it deemed objectionable.

The following paragraph capsules *Breakthrough Britain*'s section on welfare and dependency as well as any:

> Work is the primary route out of poverty. There will be no end to poverty in the UK without a jobs revolution. Our aim must be that every working-age household capable of earning a decent living must be both able and obliged to do so. Government policy must, therefore, focus on getting those who are unemployed and long-term economically inactive people, into employment.
>
> (Vol. 2, p. 20)

In sum, if this is an accurate guide, a workfare state is in store under future Tory rule, but one without much if any attention to low wages.

Conclusion

New Labour began its reign by retooling the welfare state. Jettisoning the unthinking support of public benefits, its policy planners placed a renewed emphasis on work and responsibility. Its three-pronged policy was designed to get people into work and have work supported by, on the one hand, a remolded tax and benefit system that would make work more financially rewarding than benefits and on the other by a general wage floor.

Politically, this left the Conservatives temporarily becalmed. However, it antagonized much of Labour's traditional "heartland." Thus, it was more controversial within the party than without. In time, though, most Labour elites came round. Meanwhile, the Tories attacked the implementation and the details of the New Deals and the tax and benefit system, not its objectives. Labour's leaders responded with ever more emphasis on work and responsibility in order to defang the opposition. For example, the 2006 Green Paper *A New Deal for Welfare: Empowering People to Work* (DWP, 2006b) reiterated the desirability of work, and in early 2008 the Department for Work and Pensions announced a new initiative to partner with business to offer more subsidized jobs for the hard to employ (DWP, 2008c).

Blair's three governments thus have indeed remade the welfare state. Nonetheless, its New Deals and tax and benefit systems are quite vulnerable to any change in government, as dramatic modifications to the programs could be easily adopted. As for the minimum wage, by not putting it on some type of automatic pilot through indexing or some similar mechanism, it can be eviscerated by a future government.

New Labour's policies are therefore on two tracks. It is hard to see how a reversion to the old benefit system would come about while the party remains in power. Gordon Brown and his major allies are firmly committed to the work-first approach, even if there is sniping about the edges on the minimum wage. A small coterie of MPs and supporters on the left are still dissent, certainly, from making work a central component of social policy, but they are a distinct minority. At the same time, New Labour's ideas have not established a new orthodoxy that crosses party lines. Tory support for an emphasis on work easily derives from their standard approach, and there is no evidence that they have embraced either the more humane aspects of the New Deals or an injection of government into the labor market via the minimum wage.

Thus, while Britain's welfare state has been largely refashioned, unless and until New Labour's underlying philosophy creates a new consensus in the wider polity, the reforms remain important but tenuous.

Notes

1. Of course, many other policies affect poverty, such as pensions.
2. In fairness, the youth unemployment rate was slightly higher than the adult rate throughout the time he made this argument.

9

New Labour and the British Model of Capitalism

Terrence Casey and Alistair Q. Howard

Britain's economy was clearly transformed during the Thatcher-Major years, but what difference did a decade of New Labour make? Building on the comparative capitalism literature, this chapter offers an empirical index to compare British capitalism to other advanced economies, and to track changes over time. We show that Britain remains a liberal economy, although somewhat less so than in 1997. We offer a narrative of key changes during the Blair years, focusing on role of the state, the organization of labor, and the regulation of business. The most notable changes were substantially increased government spending (mainly on social welfare) and greater business regulation. Turning to outcomes, we argue that the Blair government's macroeconomic record was solid, transforming Britain from a laggard to a leading European economy. The chief blemishes were continued high inequality and an inability to alter the underlying productive capacity of the economy. Finally, we argue that New Labour's attempt to reconcile globalization with social democracy has created a hybrid form of capitalism best described as an "Anglo-Social" model.

Mapping British capitalism

The comparative capitalism literature offers useful organizing concepts and ideal types to systematize national variations in political economy (see Jackson and Deeg, 2006, for an excellent review). The literature is premised on the idea that economic activity is embedded in institutional configurations providing economic strengths and weaknesses. Understanding institutional variation—mapping the "varieties of capitalism"—is central to explaining comparative performance. Beyond this, disputes arise regarding the key distinguishing traits, appropriate levels of analysis, optimal methodology, classification schemes, and the number and types of capitalism. The most widely used framework is Hall and Soskice's (2001) dichotomy of liberal market and coordinated market economies. Schmidt (2002) distinguishes between market capitalism, managed capitalism, and state capitalism, the latter encompassing

Asian economies and France. Amable (2003) gives Asia its own category and subdivides Europe into Scandinavian, continental, and Mediterranean economies. Others go so far as to treat each economy as *sui generis* (Perraton and Clift, 2004).

Most noteworthy for our purposes is the "consensus across the literature ... on the character and membership of the liberal economies" (Jackson and Deeg, 2006, p. 32). Liberal economies are characterized by "small states" that eschew market regulation and pursue low taxation and modest welfare spending. Rejecting corporatist coordination or industrial policies, the liberal state strives to be a neutral arbiter, promoting open, competitive markets. On the business side, inter-firm relations are distant, contractual, and competitive. Coordination between firms is discouraged and even criminalized through antitrust laws. Financial systems are dominated by equity capital, leading to a short-term profit orientation, a focus on price competition, and arguably also radical innovations to reap first-mover advantages. Labor relations are decentralized, individualistic, and adversarial, with weak trade unions; labor-management relations are a private matter. In sum, the liberal economies are market driven, rather than state led or formally coordinated with social partners. Economies fitting this characterization include Australia, Canada, Ireland, New Zealand, the United States, and, of course, Great Britain.

After 10 years of New Labour is this still an accurate characterization of British capitalism? The existing literature has difficulty dealing with such questions, as the placement of countries in particular categories is largely subjective and based on broad historical patterns (Amable being the notable exception). A more objective framework is needed. Casey's (2009) "comparative capitalisms index" is based on the three key domains most commonly examined in the literature: the organization of labor (including labor markets, labor-management relations, and skills), the organization of capital (including financial systems, corporate governance, and inter-firm relations), and the role of the state (in terms of government spending, market regulation, and welfare policies). Data on various indicators in each of these domains were gathered for the Organization for Economic Cooperation and Development (OECD) countries, then normalized and combined to create a single index score from 0–10 for each country (see Casey, 2009, Table 1 for a full list of variables and sources). The index was scaled so that more coordinated economies received higher scores and more liberal economies lower scores.

Table 9.1 shows results for the Blair years, noting the change over time in the right column. Britain is clearly on the liberal end of the scale, ranked only slightly higher than the US. Yet by 2007 the UK index score showed it as somewhat *less* liberal, a result mainly of increased economic regulation and government spending. Blair's critics (for example, Hay, 1999) accuse New Labour of being neo-Thatcherites. The evidence produced here suggests this is only partially correct. To get a better understanding we need to look more closely at the changes during the Blair years.

Table 9.1 Comparative capitalism index scores, 1997–2006

	1997	2006	Change
Finland	7.09	6.78	−0.31
Belgium	7.09	7.02	−0.07
Norway	6.95	6.43	−0.52
Austria	6.93	6.93	−0.01
Sweden	6.75	6.82	0.07
Portugal	6.73	6.56	−0.17
Italy	6.65	6.49	−0.16
Denmark	6.60	6.48	−0.12
Germany	6.19	6.40	0.22
Greece	5.97	5.70	−0.27
France	5.86	6.06	0.20
Netherlands	5.75	6.16	0.41
Spain	5.72	5.86	0.15
Iceland	5.59	5.15	−0.44
New Zealand	5.05	4.61	−0.43
Australia	4.84	4.05	−0.80
Korea	4.63	4.49	−0.14
Ireland	4.55	5.08	0.52
Luxembourg	4.04	4.17	0.13
Japan	3.98	4.18	0.20
Switzerland	3.73	4.86	1.12
Canada	2.98	3.52	0.55
United Kingdom	2.66	3.48	0.81
United States	2.15	2.41	0.26
AVERAGE	5.35	5.40	0.05

Note: Index derived from the normalized values of 12 variables related to the state, labor, and business. Scores ranges from 0–10, with higher scores indicating more coordinated economies.
Source: Casey, 2009

British capitalism under New Labour

Tony Blair's approach to economic management entailed a fundamental rejection of the Old Labour methods. "Tax and spend" policies, activist industrial policies, income policies, and intimate connections with the labor unions were swept aside. Conversely, the Blair government accepted most of the Thatcherite political-economic settlement. Privatization was here to stay, and was even expanded through Private Finance Initiatives (PFI) for infrastructure development. Fiscal conservatism and monetary stability were the rule at least in the short term. Ministers argued that prosperity under globalization required open, flexible, and competitive markets (Hay, 2001). But critics are wrong to see New Labour as merely "neoliberalism with a human face" (Callinicos, 2001). To see why, we explore each of the domains used above: the state, labor, and business.

The state

New Labour gained office during an economic upswing and enjoyed ten years of global growth. Still, the new government learned from Labour's historic failures. The "stop-go" cycles of the 1960s and 1970s were politically as well as economically damaging, destroying Labour's economic reputation even as its base endured spending cuts. Blair and Brown therefore wanted to establish economic credibility *before* increasing social spending. Fiscal and monetary policies were aimed at establishing stability and confidence.

The key monetary policy decision was Brown's immediate grant of independence to the Bank of England; politics would not be allowed to spoil the macroeconomic fruit. The Monetary Policy Committee gained interest rate responsibility and an explicit inflation target, entrenching sound money at the heart of policy. In fact, the bank exercised greater monetary restraint than the US Federal Reserve. This was possible in part because, again, Labour benefited from good timing. Thatcherism and the exit from Exchange Rate Mechanism (ERM) had finally crushed price inflation, just as rapid growth in the world's labor force tamed wage expectations. Concurrently there was an international savings glut, reducing interest rates. Thus, despite expansion in the real economy and asset price appreciation, inflation and long-term interest rates remained exceptionally low. Consumer price inflation averaged only 1.6 percent between 1998 and 2007, down from 4 percent between 1989 and 1997 (ONS). Not until April 2007 did the bank miss its 2 percent target, requiring the bank's governor to write an explanatory "open letter" to the chancellor.

Low domestic inflation and market confidence helped sustain Sterling's post-ERM recovery. A strong pound in turn enhanced consumer purchasing power and fueled growth at home. But exporters found it harder to compete on price, and by 2007 Britain had the G7's worst trade deficit. It gained a mere 3.1 percent of global merchandise exports—the same proportion won by Belgium ("Top Exporters"). A growing service sector surplus was not able to compensate for the worsening goods deficit.

Financial flows through the City made the trade deficit tolerable, and Labour did nothing to challenge the significance of the City as a site for investment and source of capital. With its financial services specialization and admired financial regulations, Britain could exploit global liquidity and the search for higher yields (Commons Treasury Committee, 2007, p. 10), leading Europe in hedge fund and private equity activity, for example. This helped produce massive surpluses on the nation's capital accounts.

On the fiscal front, New Labour reversed Old Labour's approach: famine proceeded, rather than followed, feast (Stephens, 2001, p. 193). Before the election Brown committed to Conservative spending limits, insulating Labour against voter and market skepticism alike, and getting the books in order to allow more spending later (as the chancellor put it, "prudence with a purpose"). Two fiscal rules were introduced. The "golden rule" confined government borrowing to investment only over the economic cycle—not consumption. The "sustainable investment rule" would keep public debt below 40 percent of GDP (Lea, 2007, p. 28). Following these rules, it was hoped, would repair Labour's reputation.

Brown stuck to the script in Labour's first term. Spending was exceptionally tight in the first two budgets, dropping from 41.6 percent to 37.5 percent of GDP by 2000. Extra revenue was also raised, including a £5.2 billion windfall tax on privatized utilities and a further £5 billion raised from "raiding" pensions by abolishing dividend tax credits (Smith, 2005a, p. 170). There were also notorious "stealth taxes," mainly the ending of exemptions, such as married couples allowance. But this meant the taps could be opened without frightening the markets prior to the 2001 election. The spending spree has continued since, with much of the extra money going to education and the NHS, especially as Blair committed to bringing overall health care spending up to continental levels. By 2007, UK government spending as a percentage of GDP exceeded that of Germany.

The fiscal situation deteriorated during the second term, with revenues falling short of spending. The IMF reports net government debt in 2006 as 38.4 percent of GDP, up from 32.5 percent in 2002, while gross debt was 43 percent of GDP in 2006, up from 37.6 percent in 2002. This apparent violation of Brown's own prudential rules was rationalized by "adjusting" the terms of the business cycle, meeting the letter if not the spirit of the "golden rule" (Lea, 2007, pp. 29–30). But whether appropriate or not, Chancellor Brown thus limited the options of Prime Minister Brown.

Labor

The government wanted to preserve labor market flexibility, while improving protection for bottom-tier workers and addressing market (and government) failures on training and social exclusion. There were several headline regulatory initiatives, and active labor market policy was enhanced to increase employment. But most significantly, nothing was done to restore unions to their pre-Thatcher status and membership continued to decline.

The major new regulations were a national minimum wage, the (European) Social Chapter, an EU directive limiting work weeks to 48 hours, and an EU measure on employee information and consultation. The left welcomed the minimum wage, although it was set initially at the cautious rate of £3.60. By 2008 this had risen beyond inflation to £5.73—worrying to CBI members and economists alike. Still, employment losses were not great. It is evidence of New Labour's timidity that the other significant new regulations came from Europe, and were, moreover, weakly interpreted. Ending the Tories' opt-out of the Social Chapter was of chiefly symbolic importance. It did, however, result in new sex discrimination rules, parental leave, and some benefits for part-timers. The Working Time directive was actually forced on Britain by the courts, and anyway included an opt-out permitting longer hours. Finally, the worker consultation directive was introduced grad-ually beginning in 2005, with wide managerial scope for interpretation. The Tories joined CBI opposition to these and other regulations, but they could hardly deny their minimal impact. More troubling was the "red tape" involved in compliance—a topic discussed below.

Active labor market policy was more important under New Labour. Moving people from welfare to work was not just about reducing the num-ber on the dole; it was their means of achieving social justice (Coates, 2005, p. 61). The flagship was the New Deal, a scheme aimed primarily at youth, but also helping the handicapped, single mothers, older long-term unem-ployed people, and even unemployed musicians. Participants are offered employment counseling, job training, continuing education, even subsi-dized employment, with reduced benefits for those refusing. The govern-ment claims 2.9 million individuals have started New Deal programs (National Audit Office, 2007, p. 20), but these programs are criticized for being costly and creating few new net jobs (Riley and Young, 2001).[1] More recent efforts included reducing incapacity benefit take-up, which was 2.6 million by 2005 (OECD, 2005). Overall, funding for active labor market poli-cies is not historically high, and remains well below the high-end European spenders. Yet employment rates increased substantially during the Blair decade, outstripping the average for the previous decade by 2.3 percent (ONS, 2008, Fig 4.1).

Employment policy also focused on "human capital" formation—basic education, vocational training, and lifelong learning—to promote both social integration and competitiveness (HM Treasury, 2004). Britain suffers from an "hour glass" distribution of skills: lots of university graduates and early school leavers, but too few with intermediate and vocational skills. The OECD cites this to explain "the comparatively low proportion of UK firms engaged in suc-cessful innovation" (OECD, 2005, p. 9). To correct this, the government plowed money into basic education, nearly doubling spending (in cash terms) over ten years. As a percentage of GDP, education spending rose from 4.9 per-cent during 1990–7 to 5.5 percent in 2006/7 (ONS 2008, Fig 3.20).

There is some evidence of success. According to the OECD, by 2004 the average adult has completed 12.6 years of formal education, up from 9.09 in 1995. The Program for International Student Assessment (PISA) ranked the UK 5th among OECD countries on reading and 9th in science in 2003 (PISA, 2007). There has also been progress on training. The number of National or Scottish Vocational Qualifications awarded has increased dramatically between 1997 and 2006, particularly at the middle and higher end (Levels 4 and 5, equivalent to first and higher degrees, increased 158 percent) (ONS, 2008, Fig 3.16).

The labor market flexibility imperative precluded any return to the unions' previously privileged position in policymaking. In principle the new approach was pluralist—unions would be consulted like any other interest group. In practice, they remained weak, given long-term economic changes and the legacy of Conservative legislation. New Labour did nothing to alter this, and union discontent rose through the second term. Before the 2005 election unhappy union leaders extracted from the party the "Warwick Agreement" to do better on a list of regulatory enhancements (Hall, 2004). These included extending statutory leave and ensuring striking workers would not be quickly fired. Such initiatives were phased in slowly and with wide managerial discretion. Yet overall, labor relations remained good, with the average number of days lost to strikes annually well below preceding decades.

Business

Blair and Brown wholeheartedly embraced the virtues of efficiency and globalization, promoting "light-touch regulation" and encouraging investment (Owen, 2001, p. 209). Both were seen as necessary for prosperity as well as economic fairness. Endogenous growth theory lay behind this approach (Dolowitz, 2004): an activist state would correct market failures but with very few exceptions (such as energy policy); the state would follow rather than lead markets. Regulation and industrial policy promoted competition. Government spending was allocated by market means and with private cooperation where possible. Underperforming firms would not be saved by the government, despite plant closures and redundancies (e.g. Rover, Corus). The key distinction, then, is the relationship between policy and markets. For New Labour, policy was seen as market-led but actively pro-market; for Thatcherite neoliberalism, active policy was seen as inevitably anti-market.

One priority was increasing low rates of investment, blamed for Britain's longstanding productivity gap. Given the correlation between investment and business cycles, Brown believed macroeconomic stability would help (HM Treasury, 2001, pp. 25–6). Unfortunately, the aggregate investment record is mixed. Gross domestic expenditure on R&D, for example, was actually slightly lower in 2007 than when Labour took office and much lower than competitor economies (Maher and Wise, 2005, p. 12). On the other hand, the majority of UK R&D investment is in the promising high technology sector. Foreign direct investment was also healthy across the period, bringing both higher productivity (compared to home-owned operations) and positive spillover effects (Pain, 2001).

An additional problem for investment is transport infrastructure, an area where policy failure creates significant private costs, estimated by the British Chambers of Commerce (BCC) at £17 billion annually (BCC, 2007). The government's 2006 Eddington Transport Study, for example, found that reducing business road travel times by just 5 percent would produce annually £2.5 billion in savings (0.2 percent of GDP) (HM Treasury, 2006).

Business people stress two additional impediments to investment: taxes and regulation. Both tax levels and filing costs are unpopular. The tax code is complex and has doubled in length to 10,000 pages under Brown's chancellorship.[2] But tax levels are low by international standards and have not increased dramatically (OECD Tax Database, various tables). For most of the Blair years the combined corporate tax rate was 30 percent; down 3 percent since 1997 and lower than that in the US (39 percent), Germany, and France, but higher than Sweden's 28 percent (the UK dropped its rate to 28 percent in April 2008). Although taxes on company dividends are higher in Britain than in the US, they remain well below most in Europe. Payroll taxes are also comparatively low (12.8 percent compared to 13.85 percent in the US), although they have increased since 1996. Smaller enterprises are taxed at 19 percent, the same as the US rate. Finally, the top marginal rate of income tax is the same as in the US (40 percent; although the UK rate applies to a lower multiple of average earnings) and much lower than in Continental Europe. Still, the Confederation of British Industry argues that the net tax position of business had deteriorated ("Help or Hindrance?", 2005). And as other countries have cut their corporate tax rates—the average was 27.1 percent in 2006—Britain's 28 percent top rate no longer gives the economy much advantage (Lea, 2007, p. 23).

Regulation or "red tape" draws still louder criticism, especially from small and medium enterprises. The BCC estimates costs at £10.4 billion annually, with as much as £65.99 billion in new regulatory costs since 1998 (BCC, 2008). Cited as especially costly are the Data Protection Act (1988), the Flexible Working Regulations (2002), the Working Time Regulations (1999), the Vehicle Excise Duty (Reduced Pollution) Regulations (2000), the Control of Asbestos at Work Regulations (2002), the Disability Discrimination Regulations (2001), and the Employment Act (2002). Similarly, 82 percent of the members surveyed by the Institute of Directors cited employment regulation as their biggest burden ("Help or Hindrance?" 2005), and Labour's implementation of European Union mandates is particularly resented.

It is helpful to distinguish "policy costs" from "compliance costs" of regulation. The former include profits forgone when some activity is proscribed, while the latter are expenses arising from demonstrating compliance, such as tax preparation fees. The Blair government actively sought to reduce policy costs by insulating regulators from political influence and by implementing European Union regulations with great deference to business rather than unions or consumer advocates.

Compliance costs are a more legitimate concern. A 2002 OECD report found that, although "entrepreneurs generally face a better business environment in the UK than in most other OECD countries," red tape costs were a real burden (OECD, 2002, p. 6). This was true especially for smaller enterprises, where economies of scale increase compliance costs. Part of it also stems from poor regulatory design, a function of New Labour's well-deserved reputation for "control freakery" and reflexive rule making. Additionally, technological advances mean companies keep more operational data—and this data is more easily requested by government. For New Labour transparency is essential to both efficient markets and regulatory accountability. Extensive reporting—paper work—is the result.

The government agreed that compliance costs were too high and implemented a comprehensive regulatory reform program (OECD, 2003). Initiatives included the 1997 Better Regulation Task Force (now Commission), the 2004 Hampton Review, and the 2007 Davidson Review of EU legislation. Trade and Industry was even re-branded as the Department for Business, Enterprise and Regulatory Reform. In important areas the record is positive. Financial services regulation is widely admired, particularly in contrast with the US regime. Britain is, for example, an exceptionally good place to raise money. The Milken Institute's Capital Access index ranked Britain above all countries except the Hong Kong SAR (with the US in 11th place) (Milken Institute, 2006).

Yet broader comparative evidence suggests a real, if not extraordinary, regulatory burden. The World Bank's "Doing Business" index ranked Britain 6th for overall business regulation in 2007, with lower rankings for taxation (12th), employment regulation (17th), and licensing (46th). Complaints about regulatory costs are probably exaggerated, with the exception of restrictive planning rules that limit business expansion (Crafts, 2007). But neither profits nor business creation has suffered. Corporate profitability in 2006 stood at 15.1 percent—higher than at any period since 1989 (ONS 2007). The net rate of return to non-financial companies accelerated throughout the 2000s, with the 1997–2006 average standing at 13.58 percent (excluding oil companies) as opposed to 11.42 percent between 1987 and 1996. Finally, company creation, including the small business and self-employment sector, remains healthy.

Economic performance under New Labour

Given this policy record, how well has Britain performed? Chancellor Brown's 2004 budget statement claimed the longest period of sustained growth since the Industrial Revolution. Hyperbole aside, the economy performed extremely well over the decade. On most major macroeconomic indicators, the UK outperformed her major competitors (other than the US) (see Table 9.2). Growth and employment were above average; inflation and unemployment below. Even per capita GDP ($37,328 at purchasing power parity [PPP]) now rested comfortably above France ($33, 077), Germany ($33,022), and Italy ($32,319). Low inflation meant real incomes grew—after tax take home pay increased on average 3 percent between 1997 and 2002 (Bank of England, 2007, Table 4.A). This is higher than the 2.7 percent average for the previous 20 years, although there was a worrying slowdown after 2002 to a mere 1 percent on average (Brittan, 2008). Still, in comparative terms—international and historic—the economy did very well.

Table 9.2   Comparative economic performance, 1997–2007

	United Kingdom	Eurozone	G-7	United States
Income and Inflation				
Growth (Average Annual Change, 1997–07)	2.87%	2.25%	2.25%	3.04%
GDP per capita at PPP (2007)	$37,328	$34,282*	$35,931	$44,764
Inflation (Average Annual Change, 1997–07)	1.60%	1.90%	1.80%	2.50%
Employment				
Unemployment (Average, 1997–06)	5.40%	8.86%	7.16%	4.94%
Employment (Employment/ Population, 2006)	72.5	65.7	67.9	72.0
Equality and Poverty Inequality (Gini Coefficient, 2000)	32.56	27.78	31.35	35.67
Poverty Rate** (2000)	11.40%	9.70%	12.00%	17.10%
Productivity				
Labor Productivity (Average Annual Change, 1997–07)	1.82%	0.83%	1.25%	1.87%
Productivity (Real GDP per Person Employed, 2007)	$74,129	$71,965*	$75,695	$92,978
Relative to US (US = 100)	79.7	77.4	81.4	100.00
Productivity (Real GDP per Hour Worked, 2007)	$46.13	$44.12*	$46.24	$52.80
Relative to US (US = 100)	87.4	83.6	87.6	100

*Figure excludes Luxembourg, which is an extreme outlier on these measures.
**Below 50 percent of median income.
Source: IMF, OECD, GGDC Database

There are two dull spots in this otherwise bright picture—inequality and productivity. In contrast to the Thatcher years, Labour presided over a general improvement in incomes, and a flattening of income distribution. During the first term, incomes rose most for people in the two upper income quintiles, while more recently the poorest did better than those at the top. Yet both wealth and income inequality are still high. Measured by the GINI index, inequality rose during the first term before falling somewhat in the second and third. The Institute for Fiscal Studies (IFS) reports that, as Blair left office, inequality was "effectively unchanged and at historically high levels" (IFS, 2007). But the important political fact is that Labour's redistributive policies prevented even worse inequality emerging for demographic and structural reasons. This involved rising means-tested benefits and tax credits in the second and third terms (IFS, 2007, p. 22).

Poverty also fell during the decade. In 1997 approximately 19 percent of the total in Britain lived at below 60 percent of the median income, including 27 percent of children and 25 percent of pensioners. The comparable figures for 2005/6 were 18 percent, 22 percent, and 21 percent (ONS, 2008, Figures 5.18 and 5.19). Relative poverty, measured this way, fell for eight consecutive years beginning in the mid-1990s. Beginning in 2004–5, however, income growth slowed dramatically and this resulted in the first increase in the number of poor since 1997—by about 600,000 people. Moreover, childhood and pensioner poverty rose in 2006–7 (DWP 2008a). These figures suggest Labour will not meet its long-term poverty reduction targets, and show how difficult eliminating downward mobility is.

Redistribution, moreover, was a secondary consideration to getting people into work, growing the economy, and, most of all, increasing productivity. These were the ultimate means of achieving social cohesion (Stephens, 2001, p. 185). Labour's economic grand strategy entailed: (1) stabilizing the macroeconomy; (2) promoting capital formation (human and physical) to enhance productivity and increase the growth rate; and (3) use the increased tax revenue from a growing economy to expand social welfare spending. Increased productivity was thus New Labour's Holy Grail (Coates, 2005, p. 102). Unfortunately, the record is mixed. Productivity growth kept pace with America's and stayed well ahead of the eurozone (see Table 9.2). But in absolute terms Britain started well behind. Figures 9.1 and 9.2 show the trends in GDP per person employed and GDP per hour worked. The Blair years saw a narrowing, but not a closing, of the gap with the continental economies.[3] The absolute difference with the US remains substantial and most of the narrowing occurred during the Major years. Since then the economy was running to stand still.

America's rapid productivity growth is driven by the widespread application of information and communication technology (ICT). Continental European economies have both lower ICT investment and have been slower to implement process and organization changes to fully realize the benefits of ICT investment (Atkinson, 2007, p. 6). British business is investing in ICT—at rates very close to those in the US—but has been unable to maximize its productive potential. In the US much of this came from the retail sector, especially the expansion of 'big box' operations, such as Wal-Mart (Gordon, 2004, p. 9). As noted above, planning restrictions on out-of-town retail development in the UK hinders productivity in that sector, dragging down national productivity (Crafts, 2007, p. 286). Beyond retail, one ONS study showed that US firms in the UK gain more productivity from computer investments, suggesting that what matters is how ICT is used rather than the amount invested (Clayton, 2005).

The EU's Innovation Scoreboard ranks the UK as 11th out of 25 EU states on innovation in 2005 (EU Innovation Scoreboard, 2006). It criticized Britain for the lack of business-financed university research and its ability to translate knowledge generation into products and services. An Economic and Social Research Council report (ESRC) (2004) report pointed the finger in many

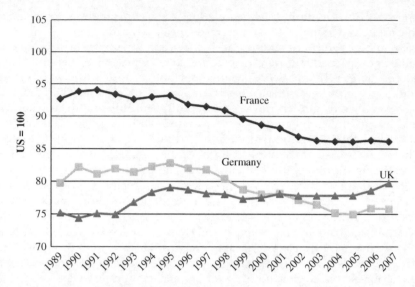

Figure 9.1   GDP per person employed
Source: GGDC Total Economy Database, January 2008.

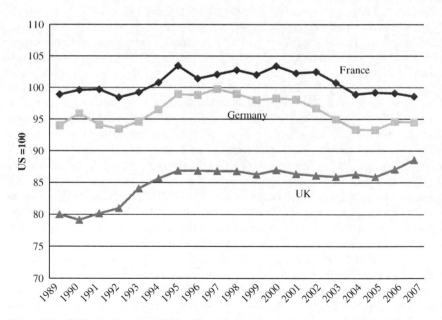

Figure 9.2   GDP per hour worked
Source: GGDC Total Economy Database, January 2008.

directions: low capital intensity, not enough R&D, short-termism discouraging investment, poorly trained managers and workers, higher barriers to entry and exit in some sectors (such as retail), and low productivity in the public sector (Economic and Social Research Council, 2004). The latter may be especially significant given Labour's vast increase in public spending, adding one million people to the public payroll (Lea, 2007, p. 3; Crafts, 2007, p. 286). The picture is not entirely gloomy; Britain is generally doing better than many of its EU counterparts, keeping pace with the US while others fall behind. Moreover, Britain's productivity gap derives from deep-seated economic and social factors that many governments have been unable to tackle; similar problems would have been noted in 1997 or 1987. Viewed positively, the government's policies worked, particularly by improving human capital, but this may take a generation to fully bear fruit. A less generous view suggests that Blair was bequeathed a strong economy that he did little to improve (Smith, 2005a, p. 183). Time will be the ultimate arbiter of this debate, but the Blair government demonstrably failed to meet its own objective of increasing the productivity of the British economy in the near term.

British capitalism into the 21st century

So what are the broad contours of British capitalism into the early 21st century? Blair's political economy was, it turns out, distinct from both Thatcherism and Old Labour. New Labour accepted the economic and moral virtues of market allocation. It encouraged competitiveness for an open, global economy. Yet it also extended the state's regulatory reach—ostensibly to correct market failures rather than steer markets per se. Instead of interventionist industrial policies, government would offer businesses and workers the tools to compete. At the same time Labour renewed the political and fiscal commitment to the welfare state. Especially after 2001, the government increased efforts to ameliorate inequalities associated with growth (Riddell, 2006, p. 87). Yet in contrast to Old Labour, Blair's governments did not try to redistribute wealth that had yet to accumulate.

A combination of somewhat increased business regulations and vastly increased government spending meant that the UK economy was less of an ideal-typical liberal market economy at the end of Blair's tenure. At the same time the emphasis on the primacy of markets, a rejection of formalized bargaining between the social partners, and the belief in an enabling (not interventionist) state precluded mimicking continental or Asian models. Britain is becoming (or returning to) more of a social welfare state, nudging closer to the models found in the Antipodes and Ireland than the US.

How to describe the new pattern? Nick Pearce, the Blairite former director of the Institute for Public Policy Research, has suggested the label "Anglo-Social." "This emergent new 'Anglo-Social' model secures high employment in flexible labor markets, with open and competitive product and service markets, and mixes these US-style features with strong public services funded through general taxation and a Scandinavian-style active welfare state" (Pearce, 2005). The Anglo-Social model very successfully captures the aspirations which lay behind New Labour's political economy (Hopkin and Wincott, 2006, p. 63). It does have its limitations, of course. The Anglo-Social model describes the New Britain that New Labour was aiming to create, but never quite managed to produce. The UK has not matched the productivity of the American economy or, even after a deluge of spending, the quality of Scandinavian public services (or, for that matter, its universalism). This moniker represents the hopes as much as the reality of the Blair years.

Ultimately, as prime minister, the legacy is Tony Blair's. But given his unprecedented control over domestic and economic policy, the economy post-1997 was truly Gordon Brown's (Coates, 2005, pp. 56–7). Those waiting for some great transformation with Brown in Number 10 will wait in vain. Nor will an alteration in government likely matter, as a new consensus seems to have developed in terms of the appropriate balance between state and market. David Cameron's Tories might tinker at the edges, but, barring some cataclysmic economic events, this Anglo-Social model will be with us for some time.

How well will this model work over the long-term? There is reason for optimism. Britain's economy has adapted well to globalization. But the Anglo-Social model is something of a delicate balance. The liberalization begun in the 1980s has effectively been taken as far as is politically feasible. Alternately, the re-expansion of the state pursued by Blair has now bumped up against fiscal limits. The economy is essentially prosperous, although as in the US, Britain's housing and asset price bubble burst in 2007–8. More importantly, the underlying structural performance, in terms of innovation and productivity, appears to have plateaued. Perhaps patience is warranted, but the question—really a political question—is what happens if this transformation does not occur? The basic equation for the Anglo-Social model is for free markets to produce enough growth so as to provide ample revenue for an enlarged welfare state. Can that equation hold over the long term if fundamental structural improvements do not materialize? If not, what then? If the balance between market and state is to be reconsidered, in which direction should it be recast? This is the fundamental challenge for the Anglo-Social model, and it may be a challenge that Gordon Brown—or David Cameron—faces all too soon.

Postscript

In October 2008, as this book went to press, the world financial system skirted total collapse, with credit markets frozen, bank capital evaporating, and share prices plummeting. Prime Minister Brown responded by partially nationalizing the country's largest banks and guaranteeing deposits, moves supported by the Conservative opposition. (His decisive action earned him a reprieve from his flagging poll numbers.) Popular condemnations of the irresponsibility of financial institutions revived calls for new regulation. Some, most prominently columnist Will Hutton, even went so far as to suggest that this marks the end of neoliberalism. Either way, after decades on the offensive, British free market forces were beating a hasty retreat.

It is too early to measure the depth and breadth of the recession that will follow this crisis. Nevertheless, what do these events tell us about the future direction of British capitalism? The UK is particularly susceptible to a meltdown of this kind. With an economy heavily dependent on financial services, the tumultuous restructuring of that sector will have a greater impact on the economy. Second, consumption is closely correlated with housing wealth, so falling house prices cut more sharply into real GDP. The poor state of public finances, moreover, leaves little leeway for fiscal stimulus without substantial debt increase. While the debt to GDP ratio is lower in the UK than the rest of the G7, massive borrowing by Western economies may induce a global rise in interest rates.

This crisis raises two fundamental questions for Anglo-Social capitalism. This model is premised on long-term growth sufficient to support a generous welfare state. Is this a temporary downturn driven by problems arising in the US housing market, or an indication that the growth under Blair was founded on unsustainable debt-based consumption? Second, after years on the sidelines, is the state returning as an active economic player? In the crisis atmosphere of October 2008, the Brown Government took an unprecedented role in restarting financial markets. New financial regulation, especially of hedge funds and other obscure financial instruments, is highly likely. But what sorts of regulations will be imposed? Will these be aimed more at increasing transparency or limiting risk? Similarly, how 'temporary' is the direct stake that government has taken in the banks, and will political pressures push them to intervene in the day-to-day management of financial institutions? The answers to these questions will determine the future contours of British capitalism, which for now remain opaque. We must await events for clarity.

Notes

1. The New Deal for Young People had 1,175,000 participants from 1998–07, but only placed 732,000 in jobs at a cost of £2620 per job (National Audit Office, 2007, p. 7).
2. Martin Winter of Taylor Wessing, quoted in *The Times*, "What lawyers really want now", 26 June 2007, p. 3.
3. Although labor market distortions keep less productive workers out of the workforce in these economies, boosting net productivity (Crafts, 2007, p. 283).

10
Judicial Reform and Human Rights

Mark Bevir and Richard Maiman

Immediately following the 1997 election, the New Labour government began to pursue a series of radical constitutional reforms with the intention of making British political institutions more effective and more accountable. As a result of these reforms, the judiciary has witnessed more change in the last ten years than in the entire past century. The Human Rights Act (1998) dramatically extended the practice of judicial review. The Constitutional Reform Act (2005) overhauled the Lord Chancellor's office and the process of judicial appointments while also setting the scene for the creation of a Supreme Court.

In this chapter, we review the changing status of human rights and the judiciary within the UK. We begin with an account of the places ascribed to them within the constitutional theory of A. V. Dicey and the looser concept of a Westminster model of government. We then look briefly at challenges to Dicey and the Westminster model prior to the 1997 general election. The bulk of the chapter then considers the formal changes introduced by New Labour and the practical debates and issues that have followed on from these changes.

The judiciary before New Labour

Dicey and the Westminster model

Relatively few general accounts of the British constitutional and political system were published before the middle of the nineteenth century. When they came, they rushed in. The year of 1867 alone saw the appearance of William Hearn's *Government of England*, Alpheus Todd's *Parliamentary Government in England*, and Walter Bagehot's *English Constitution*. Erskine May's *Constitutional History of England* had appeared a few years earlier in 1861. During the next two decades, several other classic studies were published, including Edward Freeman's *The Growth of the English Constitution* (1872), Sir William Anson's *The Law and Custom of the Constitution* (1886), and, most importantly for us, A. V. Dicey's *Introduction to the Study of the Law of the Constitution* (1885).[1] These classic works were characteristically written against the background of Whig historiography, and they entrenched the broad outlines of what became the Westminster model.

The main source of concern with the constitution was, of course, the debates around the Reform Act of 1867. During the nineteenth century, from early fears of Jacobinism to the late rise of socialism and the New Unionism, the British state constantly faced the threat and reality of popular protests demanding an extension of political and social rights. These protests were met by a series of Reform Acts, such as that of 1867, which extended the franchise to an ever-larger proportion of adult males. Yet, the Reform Acts, because they extended the franchise, exasperated a widespread anxiety about the entry of the lower classes into government. Even radical liberals were affected by this anxiety, with, for example, J. S. Mill advocating a system of plural voting as a means to preserve the competence of the electorate (Mill, 1963–91). One component of the anxiety was the idea that the extension of the franchise would disrupt social stability and constitutional principles.

Dicey tried to alleviate fears over the spread of democracy by appealing to a constitution within which popular participation was restrained by parliamentary sovereignty, the rule of law, and informal constitutional conventions. In doing so, he provided the classic account of the place of the judiciary within what was to become the Westminster model.

Dicey begins his analysis of the British legal system by looking at parliament. He writes, "The sovereignty of Parliament is (from a legal point of view) the dominant characteristic of our political institutions" (1902, p. 34). Parliamentary sovereignty means that parliament (composed of the King, the House of Lords, and the House of Commons) can make or unmake any law it chooses and no other person or institution can overrule its laws.[2] Parliament is the only body with the authority to make laws. Hence parliamentary sovereignty implies the subordination of the judiciary. The judiciary cannot challenge an Act of Parliament.

The attempt to subordinate the judiciary might appear to fail in light of the common law. The common law appears to allow judges to make laws by establishing precedents that are then binding upon their successors. Dicey argues, however, that the practice of the common law does not really contradict the supremacy of parliament since "judicial legislation is ... subordinate legislation" to Acts of Parliament (p. 58). Crucially, for Dicey, there is nothing in the constitution akin to the judicial review provided by the Supreme Court in the US. To the contrary, parliament ultimately has supreme authority in every jurisdiction, including the rights of the individual.

At this point parliamentary sovereignty begins to resemble just that kind of despotism which so enraged many eighteenth and nineteenth century radicals. Parliament appears to be a leviathan against which individuals have no appeal and from which they can expect no redress. Dicey argues, however, that two limitations circumscribe the actions of even the most despotic ruler. First, no prudent monarch or government would knowingly pursue a morally repugnant law that may incite the people to revolt. Secondly, even tyrants who may possess the power to make unilateral decisions are unlikely to take certain actions given the cultural context in which they govern.

If parliamentary sovereignty appears as a counter to popular participation, the rule of law is, for Dicey, something of a counter to parliamentary despotism. The rule of law describes the relationship of the government to the courts. Dicey identifies it, rather narrowly, with known rules, equality, and respect for precedent. For a start, Dicey argues that government operates in accord with known rules rather than arbitrary caprice or even discretion. Dicey also argues that Britain, unlike its counterparts, has long boasted a notion of equality before the law, according to which all individuals are treated similarly regardless of class or rank. Finally, Dicey associates the rule of law with the way in which the principles that protect individual liberties have become entrenched over time through the decisions of judges. In his view, although some other states rely on enumerated powers and formalized rights, Britain's use of precedent is in fact a more effective way of ensuring individual liberties.

It is difficult to see how Dicey's account of the rule of law can be reconciled with his principle of parliamentary sovereignty. To mention just one issue: if parliament is bound to follow known rules rather than make and unmake laws on a whim, how can it be free to do as it pleases? Dicey himself argued that far being in conflict, the two ideas actually reinforced one another: "The sovereignty of Parliament ... favours the supremacy of the law, whilst the predominance of rigid legality throughout our institutions evokes the exercise, and thus increases the authority, of Parliamentary sovereignty" (p. 402). Yet his argument here is vague, controversial, and arguably implausible. To say that parliamentary sovereignty favors the supremacy of the law is not to say it favors a rule of law based on formal equality and respect for precedent. Likewise, it is far from clear why parliament requires a strong legal system rather than, say, a strong executive branch of government.

The final section of *Introduction to the Study of the Law of the Constitution* is in part an attempt to explain how the rule of law can operate alongside parliamentary sovereignty. Dicey's explanation consists of an appeal to the importance of constitutional conventions. He argues that the legal system consists not only of the procedural enforcement of rules and precedents but also of the informal "customs, practices, maxims, or precepts which are not enforced or recognised by the Courts, [and which] make up a body not of laws, but of constitutional or political ethics" (p. 413). The unwritten constitution of Britain is one in which these conventions and implicit rules are vital to the operation of democracy. Indeed, Dicey elevates the customs and conventions into a "constitutional morality" to which he then appeals to limit the powers of a popularly elected parliament (p. 424). A sovereign parliament that adheres to these constitutional precepts will not oppose the supremacy of law and so the individual liberties secured by precedent.

Dicey's constitutional views proved extremely influential among both academics and political actors. Even if Bagehot loomed as large over the imagination of political scientists interested in government, Dicey clearly defined the agenda for legal scholars and others interested in the constitution and the judiciary.[3] Indeed, for most of the twentieth century the dominant image of the British political system was of a Westminster model defined in terms of parliamentary sovereignty. Within the Westminster model, the courts are expected merely to interpret acts of parliament to the best of their abilities. Judges are meant to rule in accord with the intention of the legislature: their decisions are meant to reflect how a given act was designed to function. Judges are not meant to challenge, let alone overturn, legislation as they can in, for example, the US. Indeed, by combining parliamentary sovereignty with a concept of the rule of law that was based on precedent, Dicey's followers implied that a judge should never actually challenge an existing law, regardless of whether that law arose from a legislative act or from the past decision of a judge. Any attempt by the courts to reexamine the content of law appeared to be an abuse of power.[4]

A new governance?

New theories and worlds of governance had done much to undermine the Westminster model before the election of New Labour in 1997. New theories of governance drew attention to the ways in which the law plays a more extensive role than that suggested by Dicey and the Westminster model. Gaps in Dicey and the Westminster model became visible in the 1930s as modernist social scientists began to pay more attention to behavioral topics such as policy networks and political parties. It is surely no accident that the most famous early twentieth century critic of Dicey, Sir Ivor Jennings (1936, 1939), was one of the social scientists writing between the wars who focused on the actual behavior of political actors (individuals and institutions) rather than their formal constitutional roles. He was almost a precursor of contemporary scholars of public administration and governance who evoke a core executive and policy network in ways that challenge the Westminster model.

Various new theories suggested that the courts always had played an active role in British politics. While early twentieth century constitutional lawyers focused on topics inherited from Dicey, paying little attention to administrative law, social scientists began to pay more and more attention to public administration and the policy process. Once legal scholars too began to take note of the administrative state, Diceyan opposition to a distinct administrative law seemed implausible, as did the idea that the judiciary remained above politics.[5] Among the roles that the judiciary has long played in British politics are, first, judicial review based on case law, and, second, administrative regulation by ombudsmen, tribunals, and inquiries.

In so far as Dicey inspired constitutional lawyers to pay attention to administrative law, they concentrated on the case law of judicial review by the courts. As we saw, Dicey's attempt to reconcile parliamentary sovereignty with the rule of law was unconvincing. The courts use case law as the basis for a type of judicial review, and judges review government actions against procedural values such as proportionality and reasonableness. Lord Reid, as a member of the judicial committee of the House of Lords, played a notable role in the development of just such judicial review after the Second World War. More recently, in 1993, when the Home Office proceeded with a deportation despite having assured the court that it would not do so, the courts even decided that ministers could be in contempt of court.[6]

The influence of Dicey meant that constitutional lawyers were slow to recognize the extent to which law intervened in politics, not only by judicial review but also by ombudsmen, tribunals, and inquiries.[7] It is true that some of the tribunals and inquiries that judges lead are fairly uncontentious investigations into national disasters such as that into the collapse of crowd barriers at Hillsborough football stadium. Even these inquiries can have direct policy and legal implications, however, such as the requirement that certain stadiums be seating only. What is more, judges also head tribunals and lead investigations that concern the actions of government ministers, parliamentarians, civil servants, and street-level bureaucrats. Macmillan initiated such an inquiry into the Profumo affair. In the Thatcher years, Lord Justice Scarman examined the causes of race riots in Brixton, London.

New worlds of governance have given the law a more extensive role than it had previously. New policies, such as contracting-out, and new institutions, such as the EU, extended the role of law in political decision making. The neoliberal reforms of the public sector often transformed administrative relations into legal ones.[8] For example, contracting-out replaced the hierarchic relationships of a bureaucracy with a contractual one between purchaser and provider. The rise of such legal relations meant that the courts had to play a greater role in defining where formal powers and liabilities lay in a range of public services.

A far more dramatic impact came about as a result of Britain joining the European Union.[9] Legal appeals then could be made to two European bodies. These are the European Court of Justice (ECJ) in Luxembourg, which is the judicial branch of EU government, and the European Court of Human Rights in Strasbourg, which upholds the European Convention on Human Rights (ECHR), an instrument of the Council of Europe. When Britain entered the EU in 1973, parliament accepted EU law into the British constitution. In principle parliament was (and, as we shall see, by and large, still is) free to vote not only to leave the EU but also to reject any part of EU law, although equally, of course, other members of the EU would probably see any attempt by Britain to reject significant EU laws as a breach of its treaty obligations. Still, over time EU law has come in practice to act as something akin to a higher law for Britain. The most dramatic moment in the assertion of the supremacy of EU law came with the *Factortame* cases of 1990 and especially 1991. The *Factortame* decision arose out of a dispute about fishing rights. The Merchant Shipping Act of 1988 effectively barred foreign companies from fishing in British waters in a way that seemed contrary to EU law. When a Spanish company, *Factortame,* appealed, the British courts deferred the issue to the ECJ while saying that they could not strike down an Act of Parliament. The ECJ declared that the House of Lords did have the authority to overturn parliamentary legislation so as to uphold EU law. In 1991, the British courts decided the case by declaring that when domestic and EU law appeared to conflict, the courts should assume that parliament intended to give precedence to EU law.[10] Hence the courts have come to adjudicate differences between national and supranational legislation.

New Labour's reforms

The genesis of the Human Rights Act 1998 occurred some three decades earlier with the publication of Anthony (now Lord) Lester's 1969 Fabian pamphlet, *Democracy and Individual Rights,* calling for legislation to codify individual rights in the UK. A number of prominent political and legal figures subsequently took up the cause, most notably Lord Justice Scarman in his 1974 Hamlyn Lectures (Searman, 1974). By the 1980s, supporters of a written bill of rights were generally agreed that their goal could best be achieved through incorporation of the ECHR into domestic law, perhaps to be followed by the development of a set of "home-grown" statutory rights. A number of private members' incorporation bills were debated in parliament in the 1970s and 1980s, though without the backing of either the Labour or the Conservative Party. The Tories objected to ECHR incorporation largely on the ground that as a European charter subject to continental jurisprudence it posed a threat to Britain's national sovereignty; Labour's opposition was based on concerns that incorporation would dangerously expand the authority of British judges. The prevailing Labour view of the judiciary, reflected most prominently in the writings of John Griffith (1979, 1997), was that it was an unrepresentative and reactionary elite that had and would continue to use its power to thwart progressive legislation.

Labour's position on incorporation shifted under the leadership of John Smith. Turning the traditional argument on its head, Smith claimed that ECHR incorporation, by shifting authority for determining the content of fundamental rights to parliament, would actually *check* the power that judges exercised through the common law. When he became party leader

Tony Blair embraced Smith's commitment to incorporation, though Blair's support was less than that of a committed civil libertarian than of an ardent modernizer. Blair viewed the more efficient delivery of rights as one of a number of constitutional reforms that would make Britain a more up-to-date democracy. This connection between human rights and modernization was explicit in a speech Blair delivered in 1997 to the Council of Europe:

> The new Labour Government is committed to a major decentralization and devolution of power across the United Kingdom, as well as to a Freedom of Information Act. I believe that by bringing decision-making closer to the people, we will be better able to protect their fundamental rights and freedoms. Remote, centralized Governments, cut off from their citizens, are much more likely to infringe those rights than local administrations responsive to people's needs (Blair, 1997b).

The Human Rights Act

In the fall of 1997, as the new government was completing the drafting of the human rights bill promised in its election manifesto, considerable internal debate was still taking place about how to reconcile the entrenchment of Convention rights with the principle of parliamentary sovereignty. Despite the considerable erosion of Dicey's Westminster model over the previous decades, the principle of parliamentary sovereignty still loomed large for a Labour Party eager to exercise its hard-won power without undue judicial interference. Finally it was decided that the Human Rights Act would first oblige judges to interpret legislation in accordance with Convention rights "so far as it is possible to do so" (Section 3); if that proved impossible, judges would be authorized to issue "declarations of incompatibility" with the convention, but not actually to strike down the law as in American-style judicial review (Section 4). What happened next—whether and how to remedy the point of incompatibility—was left to the discretion of the parliament and the executive. In the words of one of the bill's chief proponents, the then Lord Chancellor Derry Irvine (2003, p. 114), the model "retains Parliament's *legal* right to enact legislation which is incompatible with the Convention. But it dramatically reduces its *political* capacity to do so." Thus Irvine, whether deliberately or not, echoed Dicey's notion of a "constitutional or political ethics" that would effectively limit the power of parliament in ways that the law itself cannot.

This version of "soft entrenchment" proved sufficiently reassuring to Labour skeptics to secure the legislation's passage, but its inherent tensions remained unresolved. As the Blair decade progressed, the relationship between the judiciary and the government became increasingly strained as the Human Rights Act was invoked in legal proceedings challenging parliamentary and executive actions. By the time Blair left office, the courts had issued 17 declarations of incompatibility. In 11 of these instances the government had already accepted the declaration and amended the point of incompatibility; in the remaining six cases the government had appealed the decision or was still considering remedial legislation. The most dramatic example of a declaration case was the Law Lords' ruling in 2004 that a section of the anti-terror law permitting indefinite detention of foreign nationals who could not be deported to their own countries, was incompatible with European Convention Articles 5 and 14.[11] Another notable declaration came in a 2002 judgment of the House of Lords that the statute authorizing the home secretary to determine the mandatory minimum sentence to be served by a life sentence prisoner was incompatible with Article 6 of the Convention.[12]

The Constitutional Reform Act

The Human Rights Act might have seemed no more than a reluctant response to international pressure for adherence to the ECHR. Yet, New Labour continued to attempt to reform the judiciary's lack of formal, independent, and transparent procedures. Finally, after years of opposition from the House of Lords, the government passed its Constitutional Reform Act (CRA) in 2005. The Act introduced dramatic changes to the office of the Lord Chancellor and the judicial appointment process, and it even proposed the creation of a Supreme Court. Once again, the government justified the reforms in large part by appealing to effectiveness and to trust. The reforms, especially those to the office of the Lord Chancellor, were intended to make the operations of the judiciary both more efficient and more transparent.

The Lord Chancellor

No proposed feature of the Act met anywhere near as much resistance as the elimination of the office of the Lord Chancellor. Ultimately the government kept the office while radically limiting its powers. Historically, the Lord Chancellor has served as an important inter-branch actor with responsibility for coordinating the judiciary's actions with the government's agenda. The Lord Chancellor has had a wide variety of duties as both speaker of the House of Lords and head of the judiciary. The CRA separates these two roles, giving the duties of the latter to a Lord Chief Justice. The government argued that one person could not adequately serve the interests of both the judiciary and the government especially after the HRA increased the independence of the courts. They also suggested that making the head of the judiciary more independent would address concerns about centralization and a lack of transparency. Hence the new Lord Chief Justice has become the central figure in upholding the autonomy and independence of the judiciary.

The Lord Chief Justice is now responsible for reporting before parliament to discuss issues of great importance to the judiciary. It is also the authority of the Lord Chief Justice to give "designated directions" over the procedural operations of the judicial system. Additionally, in what may seem like a trivial point of semantics, the CRA attaches an addendum for numerous alterations to previous Acts that refer to the Lord Chancellor as a parliamentary equivalent to the speaker of the House of Commons. It replaces such references with "Speaker of the House of Lords." Yet other facets of the Lord Chancellor's historic duties, like control over judicial appointments, are now shared between the Lord Chancellor and the Lord Chief Justice through procedural consultation. Finally, in addition to inheriting powers, the Lord Chief Justice has been imbued with new rulemaking powers meant to address British needs in an age of judicial autonomy from parliament. The reduced role of the Lord Chancellor further reinforces the clearer separation of powers among the branches of government.

Judicial Appointments

In addition to circumscribing the Lord Chancellor's statutory powers, the CRA has also transformed the method of judicial appointments. Although the Queen was nominally in charge of appointments, in practice the Lord Chancellor determined them by advising the monarchy. Here too the Lord Chancellor has lost ground—this time to a new Judicial Appointments Commission. The process has become more formal and independent. The Judicial Appointments Commission screens potential candidates on the basis of merit. (In an attempt to increase accountability and representation, the Commission will include legal scholars, judges, and laymen alike.) The role of the Lord Chancellor is largely restricted to rejecting nominees deemed unfit. The CRA has also modified the process for disciplining judicial actors. The power to remove and suspend jurists is now shared between the Lord Chancellor and the Lord Chief Justice.

A Supreme Court?

The CRA hints at an even more formal separation of powers in its proposal for a Supreme Court. Historically the highest court in Britain has been composed of the Law Lords, all of whom are also, by virtue of being Law Lords, members of the House of Lords. The proposed Supreme Court will consist of 12 senior judges who will be selected through consultation between the Lord Chancellor and the Judicial Appointments and only then recommended to the Queen by the prime minister. This same appointment process will apply to the president and deputy president of the proposed Supreme Court. Once in office, Supreme Court judges will serve for the duration of their lives unless they are removed through a bicameral decision. The president of the Supreme Court will decide all other operating principles and rules within the court after consulting with the Lord Chancellor. The Lord Chancellor will have little direct impact upon the cases heard or the procedures adopted by the Supreme Court. Indeed, his role appears to be limited to securing proper accommodation for the court (Part 3, Section 50) and administering its costs (Part 3, Section 53). The jurisdiction of the Supreme Court will cover the responsibilities presently held by the Law Lords together with matters arising from the new forms of judicial review and others arising from devolution—the latter of which are currently covered by the Judicial Committee of the Privy Council.

Human rights and judicial authority after Blair

The judicial reforms introduced during the Blair governments have provided the British judiciary with unprecedented structural independence and functional authority. These changes reflected and reinforced patterns of expanded judicial authority that had already been underway for decades. But whereas the earlier evolutionary developments had attracted relatively little attention outside of the legal community, Blair's highly publicized reforms touched off vigorous debate among government officials, judges, lawyers, journalists, and academics about the judiciary's appropriate role in Britain's democratic system.

On its most prosaic level, this discussion was simply about whether judges had used their powers under the HRA "correctly." A series of controversial rulings (not always directly involving the Act) prompted a succession of home secretaries, and the prime minister himself, to complain that judges sometimes went too far in substituting their views for those of elected politicians, and had failed to achieve a proper balance between the rights of individuals and those of the public. The right-wing tabloids noisily agreed that that judges had forgotten their proper place in the constitutional order.[13] In 2006 Blair ordered the Department of Constitutional Affairs and the Home Office to review the Human Rights Act to determine whether the statute might have to be revised to ensure that its application by the courts did not interfere with appropriate treatment of terror suspects. Although the government ultimately rejected the draconian option of repealing the HRA, it did not rule out amendments to the law that would put judges on notice that "public safety comes first." However, the prime minister took the view that the HRA, as written, *already* permitted such an approach, and no such amendments had been tabled by the time Blair left office.

Breaking with a tradition of reticence about discussing their rulings in public, senior judges stoutly defended themselves and each other against government criticisms. Two successive Lord Chief Justices, Lord Woolf and Lord Phillips, argued in a number of speeches and press interviews that, contrary to the government's claims, judges were doing nothing more than the Human Rights Act required of them. While judicial authority undoubtedly had increased under the Human Rights Act, it was parliament and not the judiciary that had made that policy choice.[14]

There was a more scholarly dimension to this debate that transcended, and indeed preceded, the Human Rights Act itself. For some time legal commentators had argued about whether judges were already empowered (or required) under the constitution to challenge parliamentary sovereignty through judicial review. A leading proponent of the affirmative view, Sir John Laws, based his case on the principle that "[t]he constitution, not the Parliament, is ... sovereign." Embedded in Britain's constitution are "the imperative of democracy itself and those other rights ... which cannot be denied save by a plea of guilty to totalitarianism" (1995, p. 92). According to Laws (and quite contrary to Dicey), judges must be prepared to use the power of judicial review to protect the fundamental rights of citizens against legislative encroachment, even to the extent of denying the validity of parliamentary actions that violate such rights. Reacting strongly to such expansionist views, Griffith—joined now by a new generation of judicial restraintists—warned of the dangers to democratic values in the further growth of judicial authority.[15]

This debate—both scholarly and otherwise—about the scope of judicial authority will no doubt grow in intensity over the next few years because of its close connections to a piece of unfinished business left over from the Blair reforms. Back in 1997, Labour had proposed to follow its ECHR incorporation bill with further legislation that would supplement the convention with a bill of codified rights. However, once the HRA was adopted, the government dropped the bill of rights issue and never addressed it again. To the surprise of most observers, it was resuscitated by Gordon Brown shortly after he succeeded Blair as prime minister. As chancellor, Brown's capacious domestic policy brief did not include constitutional matters, and for a decade he managed to avoid public involvement with most of the government's constitutional policies, with the exception of his strong support for Scottish devolution. In one of the first policy initiatives of the Brown government, a green paper prepared by Justice Secretary and Lord Chancellor Jack Straw (2007), included a commitment to developing a "Bill of Rights and Duties" for submission to parliament.

This proposal, unlike some other parts of Brown's program of "constitutional renewal," is intended to unfold "over an extended period of time." Thus it is not yet known what the government means by its proposed statutory "duties"; if and how such duties would be related to the codified rights; and whether they would be merely hortatory or legally enforceable. The green paper makes it clear that the legislation will be limited to civil and political rights because to include social and economic rights would "involve a significant shift from Parliament to the judiciary in making decisions about public spending and, at least implicitly, levels of taxation" (p. 61). This invocation of the traditional Labour bugaboos of an emasculated parliament and an unfettered judiciary carries faint echoes of Blair's battles with the judiciary. But since the document makes no other mention of judges, it leaves unanswered crucial questions about the role they might be expected to play in the interpretation and enforcement of these newly codified rights, and what limits, if any, would be placed on their powers. Whether the Brown government maintains its commitment to the bill of rights or not, and regardless of Labour's electoral fortunes, the issue will probably remain alive because the other two major parties also are on record as favoring adoption of codifying a bill of rights of some sort. The Liberal Democrats have long supported a written constitution including a bill of rights. David Cameron has said that a Conservative government would adopt a statutory bill of rights after first repealing the Human Rights Act. It is difficult to imagine that any of these plans will go forward without reigniting the now familiar clashes over judges and democratic values. But based on nearly a century's worth of experience, it seems equally certain that the inexorable march toward greater judicial authority will continue apace.

Nevertheless, it will be some time, if ever, before judges in the UK exercise the kind of power they do in, say, the US. Even without such authority, however, in recent years British judges arguably have been at least as effective as their US counterparts in upholding challenges to executive authority based on human rights claims. In the post-9/11 period the US Supreme Court has decided several cases about the president's constitutional authority to conduct the so-called "war on terror."[16] Although the Court has rejected the government's sweeping claims that detained foreign nationals may be denied access to federal court review and that the president can unilaterally establish military commissions to conduct trials for war crimes, its rulings have had little practical effect because subsequent legislation by Congress has essentially codified the president's positions. In the UK, by contrast, the ruling by the House of Lords that the government could not detain foreign national indefinitely resulted in the prisoners' immediate release (though they continued to be monitored electronically). Similarly, the Law Lords' emphatic statement that evidence based on torture could not be used in court was accepted by the government without protest.[17] This evidence, though hardly definitive, suggests that the absence in Britain of constitutionally codified rights and judicial authority to overturn legislation has not produced any less protection of human rights than has the presence in the US of a bill of rights, separation of powers, and judicial review.

Cases cited

R v. Secretary of State for Transport, ex p. Factortame Ltd (No. 2) [1991] 1 AC 603.
M v. Home Office [1993] 3 All ER 537 (HL).
R (On the Application of Anderson) v. Secretary of State for the Home Department [2002] UKHL 46.
A (FC) and others (FC) v. Secretary of State for the Home Department [2004] UKHL 56.
A (FC) and Others (FC) v. Secretary of State for the Home Office [2005] UKHL 71.
Rasul v. Bush 542 U.S. 466 (2004).
Hamdi v. Rumsfeld 542 U.S. 507 (2004).
Hamdan v. Rumsfeld 548 U.S. 557 (2006).

Notes

1. General studies of nineteenth century political thought include Collini, Winch, and Burrow (1983) and Francis and Morrow (1994).
2. Dicey here followed Sir William Blackstone, an earlier conservative Whig.
3. Bagehot (1963) did not discuss either parliamentary sovereignty or the rule of law, and he showed no interest in the constitutional role of courts and judges.
4. Compare Davis (1961, p. 202).
5. See, for example, Harden and Lewis (1986).
6. *M v. Home Office* [1993] 3 All ER 537 (HL).
7. A fine exception is Harlow and Rawlings (1997).
8. Compare Vincent-Jones (1994).
9. Among the extensive literature on the impact of the EU, see Nicol (2001) and, for a comparative perspective, Slaughter, Sweet, and Weiler (2000).
10. *R v. Secretary of State for Transport, ex p. Factortame Ltd (No. 2)* [1991] 1 AC 603.
11. *A (FC) and others (FC) v. Secretary of State for the Home Department* [2004] UKHL 56.
12. *R (On the Application of Anderson) v. Secretary of State for the Home Department* [2002] UKHL 46.
13. For detailed analysis of these controversies, see the House of Lords Select Committee on the Constitution (2007, pp. 18–20; 46–7).
14. See, for example, Travis (2005).
15. See, for example, Griffith (2000), Gearty (2006), and Bellamy (2007).
16. The cases are *Rasul v. Bush* 542 U.S. 466 (2004), *Hamdi v. Rumsfeld* 542 U.S. 507 (2004), and *Hamdan v.Rumsfeld* 548 U.S. 557 (2006).
17. *A (FC) and Others (FC) v. Secretary of State for the Home Office* [2005] UKHL 71.

Part III Governance

11
Tony Blair as Prime Minister

Mark Bennister

Making sense of Tony Blair as prime minister is a tricky task. Political commentator Peter Riddell warned of the danger of making the leap from describing a particularly strong or assertive prime minister to concluding that the office itself had changed permanently. Equally he warned against the opposing view that a change of prime minister will return a style of governing back to an ideal of collective collegial rule (Seldon, 2001, p. 21). Each prime minister brings his or her own style to the position, and institutional change is inevitable. But how much institutional change or stretch is attributable to the individual incumbent and how much of this outlives the tenure of office? And does the Blair premiership fit into trends in prime ministerial leadership evident elsewhere?

Peter Hennessy, the doyen of British prime ministerial study, commented that 'Tony Blair's style of government has been so full of paradox and controversy that it has fostered a cottage industry of commentators spread between my trade, the top slice of political journalism and the interviews and memoirs of those who have departed his cabinet room' (Hennessy, 2005, p. 6). Some downplay the level of personalisation, preferring to stress the rise of interdependency under Blair in the core executive, describing the 'court politics of the Blair fiefdom' (Fawcett and Rhodes, 2007); others such as Michael Foley have drawn presidential parallels (2000). The purpose of this chapter is to find a way through this avalanche of commentary on the Blair premiership and arrive at an understanding of Blair's legacy as prime minister.

Blended or interactionist approaches are key to finding a framework that marries the institutional and personal aspects of prime ministerial leadership. Drawing on the work of Kevin Theakston, personal skill is viewed within the context of institutional resources and the leadership environment within which Blair operated. As such 'though structural, institutional and contextual factors are important, individual prime ministers' personalities, political skills and leadership styles are key and relevant variables' (Theakston, 2002, p. 283). Assessing personality alone is inadequate, while the prime minister is more than an institutionally determined actor. The skill in context approach, developed at first in relation to US presidents, asserts that 'the individual prime minister has to be understood in his or her institutional setting and political and economic context' (Theakston 2002, p. 286; Hargrove and Owens, 2002). Theakston argues that prime minister-ships and the achievements of successive British prime ministers can only be understood by analysing the circumstances in which the individual advanced to the leadership, the strategical and tactical aims of the prime minister in office, the political skills and style of the prime minister and the operating environment faced by the leader.

Contrasting epithets have been used to characterise Tony Blair as prime minister: from tales of the 'command' premiership of 'President' Blair to narratives of an unfulfilled, frustrated prime minister (Riddell, 2006; Stephens, 2004). These, however apt, may only capture a moment or phase of his tenure. It is better to assess Tony Blair as prime minister in a more sys-tematic and measured way. Borrowing from classical literature on political leadership: a predominant prime minister needs to marry the institutional and personal capacity at his disposal. Tony Blair stretched and manipulated the institutional capacity and personalised his leadership to create an autonomous premiership; aspects of his style of leadership will undoubtedly endure as will many of the institutional reforms. However, he remained a constrained prime minister boxed in domestically by his chancellor and frustrated by a system slow to respond to his prompting. When his per-sonal appeal was high he was empowered as an autonomous leader, but – post-Iraq – it waned and he became weak as authority seeped away and constraints reemerged.

The Blair premiership was based on creating a strong centre from where, surrounded by a loyal coterie of advisers (termed the 'denocracy' by Anthony Seldon), he could attempt to influence and direct the machinery of government. Informality and circumscription characterised the style of government, one which eschewed any collegial emphasis in favour of bilat-eral relationships. As such, Blair, rather than the formal cabinet system, was the hub through which all matters passed, but always with Gordon Brown as the obstacle. Policy units and a highly centralised media operation set the agenda from the core of the core executive, in an attempt to impose prime ministerial will and break down the inherited departmentalism. Although his leadership was highly personalised, many of the characteristics of the Blair premiership are evident in other countries, in particular the increase in structural capacity around the leader.

Asquith famously remarked that the office of prime minister is what the holder chooses and is able to make of it, but Blair was both enabled and con-strained by the position. He was at his peak when he could blend his 'stretched' institutional resources with his personal capacity, but these are contingent and moveable rather than fixed points. This chapter will analyse the two strands of Blair's predominant prime ministerial leadership: the institutional and the personal, drawing attention to the application of political skill within the operating context. Such an analysis of Blair's political 'skill in context' demonstrates how he personalised the premiership and built his political capital on a combination of increased institutional capacity and personal autonomy. Yet the British Prime Minister's ability to 'make the weather' is always contingent on a range of factors.

'I make no apology for a strong centre'

Andrew Turnbull, one of four cabinet secretaries who served under Blair, suggested the prime minister could have posed two questions on his arrival in office in 1997. Is this all I have to lead the fifth largest economy in the world, 60 million people, a public sector of 5 million and a civil service of 500,000? And even if the centre can cope with day to day operations, does it have the capability to develop strategy and to lead a reform programme for the public services? (Turnbull, 2007).

The institutional resources at Blair's disposal were small, but this was no surprise. The blueprint for the strong centre was set out by Peter Mandelson and Roger Liddle (1996). They called for a formalised strengthening of the centre of government giving greater personal support to the prime minister and the means for greater strategic government action. Downing Street is physically constrained and its bureaucratic structure had been neglected by John Major. It remains smaller than most comparable world leader's offices, in terms of both staff and structure. Mandelson and Liddle recommended beefing up the political unit and extending into the Cabinet Office to make it 'more akin to a Department of Prime Minister and Cabinet, charged with actively carrying forward cross departmental policies' (1996, p. 242). By 2003 Blair had assembled 27 special advisers (out of the 81 who worked across all central government departments) in the Prime Minister's Office, which by 2004 contained 190 staff in total (compared to 130 under Major) (Heffernan and Webb, 2005; Burch and Holliday 2004, p. 12). Yet by the end of the Blair premiership Michael Barber, Head of the Delivery Unit was still lamenting the continued lack of capacity at the centre of government (Barber, 2007).

In the intervening years Blair established a new style of premiership. In evidence to the Liaison Committee of the House of Commons in July 2002, he was unapologetic about increasing the capacity at the centre.

> I am not disputing the fact that we have strengthened the centre considerably; but I say that is the right thing to do; it is necessary if we want to deliver the public service reform that is essential for us and given the totally changed foreign policy and security situation.

Blair transferred his team in opposition into government creating key advisory positions for Alistair Campbell (Chief Press Secretary), Jonathan Powell

(Chief of Staff), Sally Morgan (Political Secretary), Anji Hunter (Special Assistant) and David Milliband (Head of Policy) (Kavanagh and Seldon, 2000). Powell and Campbell had their central positions further enhanced when given power to direct civil servants. Blair then created strong advisory positions in foreign affairs, strategic planning and delivery, responsible directly to himself. British prime ministers have always had trusted individuals and small groups of confidants. Margaret Thatcher had Bernard Ingham and, before her, Harold Wilson had Joe Haines as forerunners of the Campbell style of media management. However Blair's relationship with his advisers was more visible and more central to his style of governing. The appointments reflected not the structural nature of the positions that had been created, but more the individuals that held them. The impact of these individuals depended on their closeness to the prime minister at any given time. Similar trends of advisory support have been identified in other comparable countries. In Germany the chancellor's office has developed from a rudimentary support unit into a formidable centre for executive power with sufficient manpower to screen and coordinate government policy (Poguntke, 2005, p. 70). Similarly in Australia 'support for the prime minister has expanded considerably since the 1970s', and in Canada staff in the Prime Minister's Office and Privy Council Office increased and 'remained strong even when line departments were cut back in the 1990s' (Tiernan, 2007, p. 8; Bakvis and Wolinetz, 2005, p. 208). The capacity for the prime minister to coordinate and direct from the centre has increased considerably across countries and this trend is not confined to majoritarian systems (Poguntke and Webb, 2005, p. 340).

The institutionalisation of this type of policy advice can be seen in the establishment of small policy units close to the prime minister. Blair's policy advice units were fluid, often disjointed and fragmented. The series of machinery of government changes made to the centre resulting in a 'department of prime minister in all but name' have been well documented (Burch and Holliday, 2004; Hennessy, 2000; Kavanagh and Seldon, 2000). By his third term, the centre looked a little more coherent with a single strategy unit providing longer-term policy advice to augment the policy directorate in Downing Street, but Fawcett and Rhodes concluded that the centre was yet to mature after ten years of 'permanent revolution' (2007, p. 103). By 2007, units and advisers still straddled the Cabinet Office and the Prime Minister's Office, but the arrangements had become more embedded and policy advice more institutionalised without the creation of a formal prime ministerial department.

Cabinet government? 'I shudder to think'

Blair sought to reengineer the capacity around the prime minister by increasing the number and authority of those who served him directly. The growth in such capacity came, in the eyes of many commentators, at the expense of cabinet collectivity. The weaknesses of cabinet meetings are well established: too little time, too much information, too many busy people (Kavanagh and Seldon, 2000, p. 321). Measured by frequency of meetings and papers received, the cabinet as a set of arrangements has steadily declined over time (Weller, 2003). Former cabinet secretary Lord Butler described Blair's approach to cabinet as reverting to the 18th century, when advisers would group around the monarch. It is perhaps more modelled on Thatcher, who took an unapologetically strong approach to managing her cabinet business. She entered office promising not to waste time on internal arguments, and making it plain that she did not want cabinet by committee but government by herself in concert with selected ministers, brought together semi-informally (Young, 1989). Formal cabinet meetings under Blair in the first two terms tended to be short and informal meetings to discuss the business of the day, involving round the table stocktake reports which lasted no more than 40 minutes.

Many traditionalists have bemoaned this demise of collective engagement around the cabinet table, but as Jean Blondel has pointed out the notion of cabinet government can be over idealised: 'If the principles of cabinet government were applied to the letter, the system would not merely be grossly inefficient, but truly not viable' (quoted in Andeweg, 1997, p. 64). Under Blair, and certainly up to 2003, it had essentially been a political tool to avoid conflict and ensure stability and cohesion within a single party setting.

Jack Straw, when home secretary, insisted early in the Blair years: 'Cabinet still has an important role, but fewer decisions are informally endorsed there.' He made the connection between a Callaghan government which needed to be more collegial because of the context of Labour Party divisions and a stable Blair one that did not need such collegiality (Hennessy, 2000, p. 522). The implication was that a greater reliance on consensual decision making would be a sign of weakness. Although it may be that, as with Callaghan, the precariousness of the political context necessitated using the cabinet structures to generate unity (Blick and Jones, 2007). Blair, ignoring the context, was dismissive of any overly procedural approach to governing:

> But you know, the old days of Labour governments where, I think the meetings occasionally went on for two days and you had a show of hands at the end of it. Well I mean I shudder to think what would happen if we were running it like that.
>
> (Blair in Hennessy, 2000, p. 520)

The demise of formal decision making in cabinet is supported by the figures, pointing to a steady decline in formal cabinet activity. During the late 1940s cabinet met for an average of 87 times a year with 340 papers being formally circulated, in the 1970s it met 60 times a year with 140 papers and by the

1990s no more than 40 times a year with only 20 papers. This downward trend continued under Blair with most of the formal business being moved to cabinet committees and ad hoc groups under the prime minister's chairmanship (Turnbull, 2007; Heffernan 2003, p. 359). Such a shift away from traditional collegial decision making is not unique to Britain. Donald Savoie famously described the Canadian cabinet as little more than a 'rolling focus group for the prime minister' and even in Australia cabinet became more of an advisory committee under John Howard, with new institutionalised units involved in the decision-making process (Savoie in Bakvis and Wolinetz, 2005; and Bennister 2007).

'Between 1997 and 2005 it is impossible to cite a meaningful collective decision that has been taken by the full cabinet by a truly collegial means. The exception may be the fully supported decision in 2003 to embrace the London Olympic bid (Heffernan, 2006b, p. 35).' The early predominance of Blair over cabinet was demonstrated in a well recounted incident from June 1997. Blair had to leave the cabinet room towards the end of discussions on whether to proceed with the Millennium Dome project, inherited from the previous Conservative government and supported keenly by Blair and Mandelson. There was considerable opposition from around the cabinet table to the project, but after a long and vigorous debate on the merits of the project, even in his absence Blair's wishes prevailed and the project went ahead (Campbell, 2007, p. 212; Rawnsley, 2001, p. 56).

Cabinet was not the political centre under Blair, but sometimes meetings went through painful manoeuvres to present cabinet as a collective decision making body. In May 2002 cabinet ministers were presented with 1982 pages of the economic assessment on whether the five tests for Britain joining the euro had been met. Despite Blair's keenness to present a 'yes, but not yet' Brown had already interpreted the assessment as a clear 'no'. The involvement of the whole cabinet was a presentational issue to bind the cautious together with the euro enthusiasts and make it look like a collective decision (Seldon, 2007, p. 212). Avoiding internal cabinet fallout and the power struggles that dogged John Major's government had always been a priority, yet this served to stifle and homogenise collegiality in the largely subservient cabinet of the first two terms. Outside formal cabinet meetings Blair presided over an extensive committee structure which he dipped in and out of, chairing up to 14 of them himself. Cabinet committees were popular with ministers who battled to join them as 'a passport to involvement' (Dunleavy, 2003, p. 344).

Cabinet as defined narrowly as the weekly meeting of ministers can be both a source of strength and weakness for a prime minister. If debate, discussion and decision-making are absent, political battles will necessarily be played out in other forums and the propensity for disputes to spill out into the public arena is enhanced. As authority and control ebbed away post-Iraq, opposition within (and without) the cabinet was evident. Former senior cabinet ministers (such as Charles Clarke and David Blunkett) were happy to describe cabinet internal differences in print. Others began to jockey for position in advance of the Brown premiership.

'Informality and circumscription'

The formal structures of the cabinet system may have diminished, but where then did Blair gain his institutional predominance from? In one sense by ignoring collective cabinet structures, he avoided the constraint of bureaucratic process. He wanted delivery and results with as little institutional impediment as possible. It took a while for the civil service to take this on board and craft a flexible centre around the prime minister that reflected this desire.

Those close to Blair deny that his approach was any less collegial than previous prime ministers. They emphasise the amount of work that went on outside full cabinet meetings, particularly later in the Blair premiership and the need to respond swiftly to a fast moving global agenda. Senior civil servants may have bemoaned the lack of formality and structure, but Blair's advisers painted a picture of irritation with process. Results and delivery were what mattered, particularly in the second and third term. If these were achieved in an ad hoc fashion pulling on board different individuals at different times, then so be it. Interdependency and network governance lay at the heart of the Blair style.

But Blair was not an equal in these dependency relationships; he was always the predominant player. Blair's preferred method of engaging with colleagues was via bilateral interaction. He expected to hear of any minister's concerns personally and well before any formal meeting. The bilateral relationship between Blair and Brown set the style, tone and agenda for government and was reflected in the emergence of 'policy fiefdoms'. Hennessy (2005, p. 10) assigned schools, health, crime, transport, Northern Ireland, foreign and defence and intelligence and security to Blair and pensions, child and youth policy, welfare to work, enterprise, science and technology, structural change and regional development to Brown. The personal relationship between the two had a constant impact; those close to them commented: 'the business of government was smooth when they are getting on and bumpy to the point of paralysis when they are not. The main responsibility of other ministers is to navigate between the two centres of power' (Edwards, 2004, p. 274). Outside the relationship with his chancellor, Blair cultivated his own way of operating as prime minister. Lord Butler most famously commented on the Blair style in the 2004 review of intelligence on weapons of mass destruction:

> We are concerned that the informality and circumscribed character of the government's procedures which we saw in the context of policymaking

towards Iraq risks reducing the scope for informed collective political judgement.

(Butler, 2004, p. 160)

This 'informal and circumscribed' style ebbed and flowed over the ten years of Blair's premiership. Blair was not interested in structures or 'governing by committee' (Rawnsley, 2001, p. 53). He preferred to buck convention and work informally conducting bilateral meetings with cabinet ministers, or in small informal groups. Civil servants were often not present at these meetings which tended therefore not to be minuted. Latterly bilateral stocktakes with specific departments became important in keeping on top of the agenda, but these were prime ministerial committees and not cabinet committees. The informality was derided as 'sofa government'. Blair's aspiration was that relationships with cabinet colleagues would be managed through individual meetings in Number 10 Downing Street to ensure that the 'writ of the prime minister ran through government' (Hennessy, 2000, p. 525).

Cabinet government as a system of relationships between key actors was clearly in evidence under Blair. Those close to the prime minister saw a form of cabinet government being enacted to varying degrees under Blair. Yet former cabinet ministers, such as Mo Mowlem and Clare Short, were particularly scathing about the lack of discussion in meetings; 'no real collective responsibility, no collective, just diktats' (Short in Heffernan, 2006b, p. 17). Advisers were indeed prickly about suggestions that cabinet meetings did not discuss matters. The response was often to highlight occasions when cabinet received full briefings on matters (such as the decision on the euro). This tended more to emphasise the times when major decisions had not been through full cabinet meetings (decision on having an EU constitution referendum) and times when full cabinet sentiment was disregarded (decision to proceed with the building of the Millennium Dome).

The fact that cabinet meetings did not function as a decision making body or even as a forum for robust discussion under Blair was no accident. Cabinet ministers, at least in the first term, were happy to acquiesce to the Blair-Brown agenda – the tone was set early by the decision to make the Bank of England independent without any cabinet consultation. Also Alistair Campbell attended cabinet meetings (the first time such an official had attended) 'acting as a restraint on debate and a deterrent against leaks' (Rawnsley, 2001, p. 53).

Leadership style

Blair played to his strengths like no other previous incumbent. He was a gifted communicator, telegenic, populist in his rhetoric and skilled at demonstrating empathy at key moments (Theakston, 2007, p. 232). But

Blair never got to grips with the hiring and firing of ministerial colleagues and wider issues relating to his powers of patronage (the relationship between party donors – who had been so courted early on – and peerage appointments came back to haunt him). The power of Brown to set the tone for all ministerial appointments to be considered as either Brownite or Blairite demonstrates the level of duopoly in the relationship. Blair may have had the formal power to appoint, but he had a strong political constraint in the shape of his powerful chancellor. Blair was a poor personnel manger – a fact readily accepted by his advisers who commented that 'he hated sacking people' and that 'his boldness in his advisory appointments was not matched in his cabinet appointments'. His reshuffles over the years proved less than successful (the worst example being the June 2003 reshuffle that abolished the post of Lord Chancellor and gave birth to the Department for Constitutional Affairs), as he tried to instigate machinery of government changes at the same time as balancing personnel matters. Blair was not helped by the loss of key confidants from his cabinet (Mandelson twice, Blunkett twice, Byers and Milburn). Meanwhile older stagers John Prescott and Margaret Beckett were the only survivors, alongside Brown, from Blair's first cabinet, still in his last. Blair was always more comfortable working with his advisers than his cabinet colleagues.

An essential part of establishing Blair as the autonomous embodiment of the government came with the creation of a powerful media operation centred on Number 10. Such a resource is only available to the prime minister. As Heffernan (2006a, p. 590) notes, 'government-centric political communications help strengthen the prime minister's institutional prerogatives by setting the government's agenda and so further circumvent the very real collegial constraints of parliamentary government'. The media was used in a coordinated fashion to trail policy, 'interpret' speeches and announcements, and as an informal conduit.

For Hennessy (2000, p. 483) and others (Riddell, 2000) the intersection between media management and Whitehall came with the publication of the new *Ministerial Code of Conduct* in 1997. For many traditionalists, like Peter Riddell, this represented 'the biggest centralisation of power seen in Whitehall in peacetime' (Hennessy, 2000, p. 484). Arguably, however, it was merely the transference of the strict command and control system of media management that had been conceived and put into practice in opposition by New Labour. Structural changes were swiftly implemented, with the creation of the Strategic Communications Unit (SCU) in Downing Street, accountable to the prime minister through Campbell, as chief press secretary. The SCU replicated the Millbank system of strong central coordination and key headline messages that the New Labour elite had been familiar with in opposition (Kavanagh and Seldon, 2000, p. 255). The focus on media relations translated into a big rise in the number of staff employed in the Press Office and SCU (Hennessy, 2000, p. 485). The operations were designed to be highly efficient in both reactive and proactive relations with the media, being able to respond and set the agenda from the centre. Although the obsession with 'spin' may have lessened over time and post-Hutton, media management stretched the institutional mechanisms to the extent that communication strategy became an embedded function of the Blair government. Blair by comparison with his predecessors was the most media-conscious of all British prime ministers.

While the development of a strong public profile for prime ministers was not new, Blair took image projection to a new level. Foley (2000, p. 205) describes this propulsion of leaders into the public arena and away from government as 'spatial leadership' and asserts that the possession of a public identity is a political resource in its own right. The greater the public identity, the more powerful the political resource. The contemporary context is well described by Heffernan (2006a, p. 582), 'An interest in political celebrity, backed by an ever more prevalent interest in process journalism, magnifies the modern prime minister, placing him or her centre stage in key political processes'. Central to Blair's style was this autonomous connection with the electorate beyond the office of prime minister. Blair sought to represent the collective will on the basis of a certain kind of individualisation and intimacy (Finlayson, 2002). McAllister (2007) points to the substantial evidence supporting the view that leaders are increasingly visible to the mass public during elections and research has shown a consistent trend towards more candidate than party mentions in news stories across a range of countries. Such personalisation driven through the mass media is reflected in the leadership styles of Blair's early contemporaries, Clinton, Berlusconi and Schroeder.

Blair as prime minister appeared less rooted in idealism and dogma than any of his predecessors. He was a more postmodern, pragmatic and rhetorical prime minister. Blair has been described as both everything and nothing. Robert Skidelsky likened him to Keynes' description of Lloyd George as '... rooted in nothing; he is void and without content; he is an instrument and a player at the same time' (Seldon and Kavanagh, 2005, p. 439). Often regarded as a chameleon politician, much of the New Labour project rested on Blair's broad personal appeal and importantly his lack of Labour Party baggage. From the start Blair had an autonomous relationship with his party, for Tony King he was 'the perfect leader for the Labour Party in the 1990s. ... He was young. He was classless. He was squeaky clean. He had no ties to the trade union movement. He carried virtually no ideological baggage' (quoted in Theakston, 2002, p. 307). Blair, as he said himself, chose the Labour Party rather than being born into it. The way Blair emerged as leader is instructive. He, together with Brown, had been planning their reform of the party for some time; he displayed a level of opportunism, and he quickly reached out beyond the constituency that elected him to establish his credentials.

Biographical study of Blair is rich and historical journalists have shown a certain fascination with his leadership. Blair had a legal background, as a barrister, but his education at a fee-paying Edinburgh school and Oxford represents a traditional (though not necessarily Labour) route to the top. Attention is often drawn to the moral and religious conviction that underpinned Blair's life: 'he conceptualises the world as a struggle between good and evil in which his particular vocation is to advance the former' (Seldon, 2005, p. 700). It came to the fore most notably in his second term of office, one dominated by foreign policy issues. Seldon (2007) suggests that this conviction led to a greater decisiveness on the international stage than domestically, reflecting Elgie's (1995, p. 9) theorised view of political leaders who 'steer a course towards 'high' politics (defence, foreign policy, constitutional reform) and away from 'low' politics (domestic affairs).

Blair though has been most often characterised as the 'barrister-actor'. His legal training and, albeit limited, acting career (as a student), combined to make him a powerful persuader and an impressive public speaker. Presentation and single-minded belief have been hallmarks of his public persona (though leadership for Blair was about demonstrating strength of resolve and character). Displays of humility were rare, since for Blair a demonstration of weakness was a sign of poor leadership. His acceptance of Ken Livingstone back into the Labour Party for the 2004 London Mayoral election was more pragmatic than real humility. Also his apology for faulty intelligence on Iraq was left ambiguous and in 2003 he echoed Margaret Thatcher in announcing to Labour Party Conference that he had 'no reverse gear'.

Skill in context

Circumstance and events combined to propel Blair to the top position, and 'such circumstances can have a crucial effect on [a leader's] political standing, their political objectives and their scope in office' (Theakston, 2002, p. 314). His personal character traits were clearly reflected in the style of governing: the legal approach, the moral strand, the rhetorical oratory and the informality ('call me Tony'). As a performer he excelled, but he did benefit from the context of big Labour majorities and a weak Conservative opposition. Hargrove and Owens point out that while context may be important, political skill needs to be able to successfully exploit a favourable context to make a leader effective. Indeed context may even be shaped in part by political skill (2002, p. 205).

Blair was more than a rhetorical construct; he attempted to redefine the office of the prime minister, increasing the government's central capacity and establishing an informal network of dependency around his persona and authority. Yet, he was a poor personnel manager and uninterested in administrative detail. His political skill related more to the imposition of his force of personality than the more traditional values of political management. He may have set the bar high for emotional leadership leaving a powerful personal imprint, but his institutional impact is less coherent.

The prevailing view of the core executive in Westminster systems emphasises interdependent networks at the core of the executive. Such analysis sees leaders not as unfettered, but constrained by new informal mechanisms and accountable in a system of governance, whereby power is relational and diffused (Smith, 2003). Indeed in a 'hollowed out state' prime ministers may have less power as decision making is located elsewhere. Blair was often portrayed as frustrated by his inability to progress the New Labour agenda domestically, while he could assert his will in foreign affairs. However constrained he may have been domestically, his autonomous actions in foreign affairs (and on Iraq in particular) eroded both his public standing and support within the Labour Party.

We have seen a growing trend towards greater centralisation of institutional power resources around the leader across countries, often with differing political systems. Poguntke and Webb's consideration of 'structural presidentialisation' in 13 different countries found that 'in almost every case, leaders' power resources and autonomy within national political executives have increased and/or were already at a high level' (2005, p. 340). They make two compelling arguments for this trend: the internationalisation of political decision making and the growth and complexity of the state. This has not just been driven by institutional imperatives, but by the force of personalised politics and strong agency factors too. The Blair premiership fits into such cross-nation comparisons well and leaves Britain as one of the more executive dominant and personalised regimes (Bennister, 2008).

Strong contemporary leaders are not dictators and neither are they modern day revolutionaries, they must work within the existing structural constraints. Interaction with colleagues, followers and the public are key to gaining authority and trust. But dominant prime ministers, like Blair, can stretch and shape the institutional capacity at their disposal. Techniques of leadership are now well established and essential for modern successful election campaigns and media strategies which aim to maximise the benefits of incumbency.

Personal and institutional political capital, painstakingly acquired over time, can however quickly disappear. Blair stretched the capacity of the prime minister's office further than any other previous incumbent and created a premiership based on his individual charisma and personalised appeal (in common with Margaret Thatcher, he did not talk about what 'we' the party might do but about what 'I' Tony Blair would do (Finlayson, 2002)). But his autonomy bred a sense of dislocation. Greater institutional constraints enveloped the prime minister in his third term. Some core elements of the command and control nature of the premiership were questioned.

'A perceived mismatch between rhetoric and substance in policy achievement, and divisions over Iraq produced a haemorrhaging of trust' (Theakston, 2007, p. 232). Communications strategy, particularly the corrosive impact of 'spin' in the Campbell era, came under scrutiny, while prime ministerial patronage and party funding also cast a shadow over Blair's last months as prime minister. Blair's successor, as a consequence, inherited greater levels of scrutiny and constraints over powers of patronage in particular, accompanied by calls for a return to greater cabinet collegiality.

In British politics a prime minister's power is crucially contingent on tolerance by the party, as Bob MacKenzie famously pointed out. Parties will tend to be tolerant as long as the leader appears an electoral asset; a view backed up by Robin Cook in his prediction in 2002: 'The danger for Tony [Blair] is that the sole reason he has retained the affection and support of the party is because he has delivered phenomenal popularity for the party. The risk is that if he ever loses that popularity, there will be no other reason left for the party to give him their support' (Cook, 2004, p. 79).

Blair chose not to put this to test with either his party or the electorate, reasoning that three election wins were enough. The operating environment had shifted over ten years, his personal standing had slumped, the opposition had regrouped and the economic context was beginning to alter. His ability to 'make the political weather' had run out. In retrospect it was not such a bad time to leave the premiership.

12
The Role of Parliament under Blair

Mark Stuart

'In every generation, the British parliament seems to be dying.' So spoke Hugh Berrington, the doyen of British political science at a rare gathering of parliamentary scholars held in the British Academy in the summer of 2007 (Berrington, 2007). For decades now, academics, political commentators and even parliamentarians themselves have routinely bemoaned the decline of parliament, yearning for a fictitious 'golden age' when men of independent means held the executive to account (Hollis, 1949; Hill and Whichelow, 1964). Near the end of the Blair decade, the populist Power Commission claimed that 'the executive in Britain is now more powerful in relation to Parliament than it has been probably since the time of Walpole' (Power Inquiry, 2006, p. 128). And yet, even if one accepts that the Blair government set about modernising parliament with the intention of reducing its power relative to the executive, the eventual outcome of the Blair decade was rather different from the picture painted by most contemporary observers: parliament became a shade more responsive to an increasingly media-orientated world; a more rebellious House of Commons emerged, alongside a more assertive House of Lords; the Commons became slightly more representative of the population as a whole, especially of women; with parliamentarians now better resourced than ever before, reflecting their growing focus on constituency work.

Modernisation

New Labour's 1997 manifesto claimed that the House of Commons was 'in need of modernisation' (Labour Party, 1997, p. 33). A cross-party committee of the Commons, the Select Committee on the Modernisation of the Commons, was established in June 1997 to consider how its practices and procedures should be modernised.

However, parliamentary reformers immediately smelt a rat: unlike normal select committees, the new chair of the Modernisation Committee would be a member of the Cabinet – the Leader of the House of Commons. Doubts were strengthened by the fact that the first two incumbents of the post – Ann Taylor (1997–8) and Margaret Beckett (1998–2001) – took an executive view of parliament: that parties which enjoyed a majority in the House of Commons were entitled to get their business through as efficiently and smoothly as possible. Beckett, in particular, became locked in a battle with the Liaison Committee, consisting of all 33 chairmen of Commons committees, over the role of select committees. In 2000, she blocked the more radical ideas set out in the Liaison Committee's report, *Shifting the Balance* (Liaison Committee, 1999–2000, HC 300), which proposed allowing membership of select committees to be determined by senior backbenchers rather than by the party whips.

Critics argued that the net effect of the modernisation reforms in Blair's first term was to make it easier for the government to get its legislative programme through, rather than enhancing scrutiny. They had a point. The most important reform was to introduce automatic timetabling for every bill, curtailing backbench power to scrutinise legislation. The existing system was being abused, particularly by a renegade band of Conservative backbenchers, led by Eric Forth, who tried to keep the government up late at night, calling Commons divisions on the most trivial matters (Cowley, 2002). Late night divisions on non-legislative matters were also deferred to later in the week. Members only had to turn up to sign a ballot paper on a Wednesday afternoon – in what became known as a 'mass vote-in'. Initial resistance to the introduction of deferred divisions and the automatic programming of government bills petered out, and both reforms were subsequently made permanent.

But the key criticism of New Labour's approach to modernisation in Blair's first administration was an apparent lack of an overall clear vision. The outcome was a hotchpotch of reforms.

The most positive reform in terms of scrutiny, however, was the creation in 1999 of Westminster Hall, a parallel debating chamber, semi-circular in shape, based on the model of the Australian legislature and intended to deal with non-legislative business. MPs sat in a horseshoe arrangement, intended to encourage constructive, rather than confrontational debate. Although there were no formal votes, backbenchers were able to grill junior ministers for an extended period, particularly on matters that closely affected their constituencies.

The pace of modernisation quickened markedly in Blair's second administration (2001–5), with the prime minister submitting himself to more scrutiny than any previous incumbent. Twice a year, Blair was quizzed alone for two-and-a-half hours in front of the Liaison Committee. It was felt that this format would facilitate more in-depth cross-examination of the prime minister than the superficial exchanges at Prime Minister's Questions (Liaison Committee, 2001–2, HC 984, p. 6), which Blair had unilaterally cut from two sessions per week to one at the beginning of his premiership.

The Liaison Committee format suited the charismatic prime minister: he regularly worsted his senior parliamentary colleagues, who would ask too many disparate questions, instead of concentrating their fire on a limited number of topics. Nevertheless, such sessions enhanced scrutiny because they allowed for sustained questioning on a range of topical questions. These appearances seem set to become a permanent feature of Commons scrutiny, Gordon Brown having signalled his willingness to carry on with this welcome innovation.

Yet the positive impact of the Liaison Committee reforms was largely eclipsed by another Blairite innovation: the monthly Downing Street press conference, providing more fuel to those who argued that parliament was increasingly being bypassed. Ministerial statements, it was pointed out, were being routinely trailed in advance in the media; parliamentarians became increasingly irritated that they had not been told first. Towards the end of her term of office, Betty Boothroyd, speaker of the House of Commons from 1992 to 2000, even wrote to Margaret Beckett, the Leader of the House to make it clear that when the government announced changes of policy, ministers should first provide the House of Commons with the details.

But what media commentators and traditionalists failed to see was that parliament had, over the previous few decades, slipped down the pecking order of importance in the view of ministers and civil servants. Power had ebbed away through devolution and successive European treaties. Quite understandably, ministers became more interested in media management, and parliament had failed to catch up. A great deal of the thinking behind the reforms of the second Blair term were therefore about making parliament more responsive to enable it to cope with a more media-focused world.

Robin Cook, Leader of the House from 2001 to 2003, understood the importance of bringing parliamentary procedures and practices into the twenty-first century. In 2001, Cook's Memorandum (Cook, 2001–02) set out its reformist stall, introducing new ways of making the Commons more responsive to press and public alike. Radical changes were made to the parliamentary timetable, including an earlier start to Prime Minister's Questions (at noon on a Wednesday, instead of 3 p.m.) in order to generate better press coverage. Cook wanted parliamentary time to be used more efficiently, by making greater use of mornings, instead of late evenings, and through the introduction of time-limited speeches in the main chamber. Cook's reform proposals also made ministerial question time more topical by reducing the shorter notice period for oral questions from ten days to three.

Other parts of Cook's reform package met stiff resistance from the Government Whips' Office, especially when it came to attempting to remove their power over appointments to select committees. Unofficial government whipping ensured that these proposals were defeated, but many other parts of Cook's reform package survived. In particular, better funding for select committees, including extra remuneration for select committee chairs (usually an additional £12,500 per annum) helped to make backbench careers an attractive alternative to entering government.

And at long last, some of Cook's proposals addressed the need to modernise the scrutiny of legislation: more bills were to be published in draft form, allowing for earlier and more routine pre-legislative scrutiny (Smookler, 2006); and the sessional cut-off was relaxed, allowing bills to carry over from one session to another, designed to stop the legislative log-jam that routinely occurs at the end of each parliamentary session. In practice, however, only a couple of bills per session were carried over, and the traditional legislative 'ping-pong' between both houses of parliament at the end of every session continued unabated (Whitaker, 2006).

Not all of Cook's reforms survived, particularly in relation to changes to parliamentary hours, and more broadly, to the annual parliamentary timetable. A pilot scheme had allowed for earlier starts from Tuesdays to Thursdays – at 11.30 a.m. instead of 2 p.m. – but many backbenchers quickly objected to the idea of early Tuesday starts, because of the late finish on Mondays (10 p.m.). In 2005, MPs voted narrowly to return to the old hours of business on a Tuesday, that is 2.30 p.m. to 10 p.m. The idea of early September sittings also failed to take root, and by 2006, an attempt to revive the practice was decisively rejected.

But overall, despite these minor reversals, the Cook reforms constituted the most significant phase of modernisation in the Blair period. It was a pity then, that Cook's immediate successor as Leader of the House, John Reid, who was only in post for a few short months, and Peter Hain, took little interest in furthering that reform process.

It wasn't until Jack Straw's period as Leader of the House that the modernisation process regained some momentum. Straw correctly identified one of the key weaknesses in the Commons' scrutiny of legislation, namely the role of standing committees, that part of the legislative process between the principle of a bill on Second Reading and its consideration on the Floor of the House. Most MPs who serve on these so-called standing committees (which are not permanent, as their name might suggest) did so because they were selected by the whips. Debates were notoriously partisan, and levels of scrutiny poor. Straw's reforms not only involved a change of name (from 'standing committee' to the more sensible 'public bill' committee), but also permitted the committees to receive oral and written evidence.

It's probably too early to assess how well some of these reforms have worked in practice. The success of Jack Straw's changes to standing committees, for instance, will depend on the willingness of future governments to cede genuine powers to backbenchers. More broadly, the changes represented part of a discernible shift away from a chamber-based legislature to a more European, committee-based legislature (Norton, 2005, p. 123–5).

Overall, the reforms have been a mixed bag: after a slow start in which the needs of the executive seemed to have taken precedence over enhancing Commons scrutiny, the Cook and Straw reforms at least attempted to 're-balance' (a favourite phrase of the Blair decade) matters in the opposite direction.

A more assertive House of Lords

If modernisation of the House of Commons produced an incoherent mosaic of unrelated reforms, then the government's management of modernisation of the House of Lords was positively cack-handed.

It all began smoothly enough, as the first Blair government enacted what it termed Stage One of Lords reform, removing hereditary peers from membership of the upper chamber. Some 655 hereditary peers departed, leaving only 92, leading to a much smaller second chamber now dominated by life peers. At the beginning of the second Blair term, the groundwork was then laid for delivering Stage Two – a partly elected chamber. A Royal Commission, chaired by Lord Wakeham (Royal Commission on Reform of the House of Lords, 2000, Cm. 4534) had failed to agree on the precise proportion of directly elected peers, so Lord Irvine of Lairg, the lord chancellor, produced a Government White Paper that would have allowed only 20 per cent of peers to be elected. (HM Government, 2001, Cm. 5291). This reform package was effectively mauled apart by angry Labour backbenchers (Cowley and Stuart, 2003). Robin Cook, the Leader of the House, set about trying to find what he termed the 'centre of gravity' among Labour MPs, which seemed to coalesce around a 60 per cent elected upper chamber.

In a major U-turn, the government announced the establishment of a 24-member joint committee, drawn equally from both houses of parliament which drew up a range of options for Lords reform. The committee recommended a series of seven votes in both houses on composition, ranging from a fully appointed chamber to a fully elected chamber. However, the process ended in high farce in February 2003 when the Lords voted decisively 3-1 in favour of a fully appointed chamber (and against all other options), but MPs rejected every option on the table. Despite a majority of MPs favouring an elected chamber, they failed to co-ordinate their preferences into one of the options on offer (McLean, Spirling and Russell, 2003).

Tony Blair's reputation as someone with scant regard for the wishes of the House of Commons was cemented. A week before the votes on Lords composition, he came out in favour of a fully appointed second chamber. In the run-up to the votes, which were technically free, Labour whips privately urged MPs to 'support Tony'. Although Blair's preferred option also fell by the wayside, such unofficial whipping probably made the difference between the success and failure of the 80 per cent option (Cowley and Stuart, 2005, p. 36).

It would be another four years before the Blair government's other reform-minded Leader of the House, Jack Straw, returned to the thorny question of composition. In 2007, the government published yet another White Paper, advocating a second chamber with half of its membership elected and half appointed (HM Government, 2007b, Cm. 7027). In March 2007, the House of Commons voted decisively in favour of a fully elected upper chamber, but the Brown government moved cautiously: a White Paper on Lords reform was delayed until the summer of 2008.

While the government's handling of the debate over Lords composition was at times calamitous, observers of the half-reformed House of Lords began to notice a much higher degree of assertiveness among peers. In particular, Meg Russell, a former adviser to Robin Cook, based at the Constitution Unit at University College London, uncovered a wealth of evidence to back her claims of greater assertiveness among peers (Russell and Sciara, 2006). The abolition of hereditary peers in 1999 removed a large number of Conservative 'backwoodsmen', such that the Conservatives fell from being the largest group in the Lords to the third largest. More significantly, instead of being a Conservative-dominated chamber, post-1999 the Lords became 'hung' in its composition – a no-overall-control chamber: crossbenchers and the Liberal Democrats held the balance of power. With the change in composition came a change in peers' attitudes. In the past, peers had been willing to back down when facing a stand-off with the Commons, abiding by the 'Salisbury Convention'; now they insisted in having their say most of the time. As a result, they inflicted over 400 defeats on the government between 1999 and 2007. For their part, the government began to realise that it had to negotiate with peers, routinely giving way on key aspects of government legislation (Russell and Sciara, 2007).

A more assertive House of Commons

By almost any measure, the Blair decade turned out to be an extremely rebellious one in terms of Labour backbench dissent. From May 1997 until June 2007, when the prime minister finally left office, there had been no fewer than 6520 dissenting votes cast against the Labour whip. That compares with 4259 rebellious votes during the eleven-and-a-half years of Margaret Thatcher's premiership (which ran from May 1979 until November 1990). In percentage terms, whereas Mrs Thatcher's three administrations had witnessed backbench dissent in 14 per cent of divisions, Blair's three administrations saw a rebellion rate of 16 per cent. Labour MPs rebelled over issues ranging from immigration and asylum to welfare reform to defence and foreign policy.

And yet, in May 1997, the hope among the New Labour leadership was that their MPs would exercise a new self-discipline: new because during past spells in government, Labour MPs had been very rebellious indeed (Norton, 1975; Norton, 1980), and also new because John Major's second administration had seen historically high levels of backbench dissent, especially over the issue of Europe (Baker, Gamble and Ludlam, 1994).

Just six days after he became prime minister, Tony Blair urged his troops not to repeat the mistakes, both of Labour's past and the Conservative government that had come just before (Blair, 1997a). Initially, Labour MPs heeded their leader's advice: even highly rebellious left-wingers held back from opposing the legislation giving the Bank of England operational independence over the setting of interest rates.

However, the mood in the Parliamentary Labour Party changed in December 1997 when 47 Labour MPs voted against a cut in lone-parent benefit, with at least 20 MPs abstaining. Although the rebellion was not especially large by historic standards, and failed by a wide margin (the Conservatives supported the government in the division lobbies), it had huge significance for the rest of the Blair decade in power. For their part, the government realised that coercion alone could not deliver iron discipline among its MPs. As a result, government ministers began to display a marked willingness to grant concessions to disgruntled MPs. So, although in 1999 proposed reforms of incapacity benefit caused the biggest rebellion of Blair's first parliament – involving some 67 Labour MPs – Alistair Darling, the social security secretary responsible for the legislation showed a greater tendency to negotiate and engage than his predecessor, Harriet Harman had done.

By the second Blair term in 2001, Labour backbenchers had become increasingly emboldened. They felt, often mistakenly, that they had retained their constituencies as a result of their own efforts, rather than coming in on Tony Blair's coattails. They were joined by a new intake of MPs – smaller than 1997, but generally more politically experienced. By now, the ranks of disgruntled ex-ministers had swelled, along with the ranks of those overlooked for ministerial office. Add in a group of around 30 perennial dissenters, ideologically hostile to the government, and these disparate groups had the capacity to cause the government a real headache (Benedetto and Hix, 2007).

The mood in the Parliamentary Labour Party (PLP) was about to get nasty. The government whips assumed that their huge overall majority (down from 179 in 1997 to 167, but still very large indeed) would cushion them from any potential revolts. Surely, they would be able to govern with relative ease?

The whips were sadly mistaken. The 2001 parliament saw Labour MPs vote against their whips on 259 separate occasions, more than in any other post-war parliament save that between October 1974 and 1979. A total of 218 Labour MPs voted against their whip at least once from 2001 to 2005, and 21 per cent of divisions witnessed Labour dissent, a higher rate of rebellion than in any other parliament since 1945.

The largest rebellion occurred in March 2003, when 139 Labour MPs supported an amendment urging the government not to go to war in Iraq, the largest rebellion by MPs of any governing party – Labour, Conservative or Liberal – on any type of policy for over 150 years. The subsequent government motion – formally approving of military action – saw 84 Labour MPs defy the whip. Parliamentary historians had to search as far back as 1846, to the time of Sir Robert Peel, and the Tory split over the repeal of the Corn Laws to find a bigger rebellion.

Very large Labour rebellions were also witnessed over key aspects of government legislation. The rebellions in 2003 over the introduction of foundation hospitals broke the record for the largest health policy rebellion ever by Labour MPs against their own government. In 2004, the 72 Labour votes against the Second Reading of the Higher Education Bill, the bill that introduced top-up fees, was precisely double of what had until 2001 been the largest education rebellion ever by Labour MPs.

Yet despite these huge rebellions, the government survived the 2001 parliament undefeated, if only just.[1] In the run-up to important votes on Iraq, foundation hospitals and education reforms, the whips played on backbenchers' fears of the consequences of defeat, threatening its rebellious backbenchers with victory, predicting dire consequences, including prime ministerial resignations, votes of confidence and a general election, should the government be defeated.

In May 2005, when Labour's majority was dramatically cut from 167 to just 66, the line from the Government Whips' Office was that the smaller majority would 'concentrate the minds' of Labour whips. Self-discipline, they believed would re-assert itself. But despite significant number of Labour rebels losing their seats and retiring at the 2005 general election, Philip Cowley observed in November 2005 that there were still 60 Labour MPs who had survived the 2005 election who had rebelled on 10 or more occasions between 2001 and 2005, enough to defeat the government should they mishandle legislation, particularly on anti-terrorism legislation (Cowley, 2005, p. 246).

As Cowley predicted, the government went down to two defeats during the Report Stage of the Terrorism Bill in November 2005. The government had proposed extending the maximum length of time for which a terrorist suspect could be held without charge from 14 days to 90 days; in two separate votes, Labour MPs limited the extension to 28 days. These were the government's first defeats in the Commons on whipped votes since Labour came to power in 1997; and, with the government losing by 31 and 33 votes, the largest substantive Commons defeat since 1978.

In January 2006, the government was again twice defeated, during the Lords Amendment Stage of the Racial and Religious Hatred Bill. The whips had miscalculated, allowing too many Labour MPs to be absent from the vote. The government was doubly embarrassed: the prime minister was present for the first vote but did not vote in the second – which was lost by a majority of just one.

The defeats were a wake-up call to the government; they no longer enjoyed the cushion of landslide majorities. Even greater efforts were made to prevent further defeats, with the government further compromising over a number of bills, particularly concerning a Government Green Paper over Welfare Reform (HM Government, 2006, Cm. 6730) where ministers abandoned plans to extend means testing for the long-term sick.

Sometimes, the concessions were still not enough. This was most obvious with the Government's Education White Paper (HM Government, 2005, Cm. 6677), and the subsequent Education and Inspections Bill in the 2005–6 session. Several leading government backbenchers produced what they termed an 'Alternative White Paper' (AWP), demanding changes to the policy. The government met many (although not all) of the rebels' demands, and the Education and Inspections Bill that followed was significantly changed from the White Paper. Despite further considerable movement from the government prior to Second Reading, the bill saw several large backbench revolts (the largest comprising 69 Labour MPs), and the bill only passed at both Second and Third Reading thanks to Conservative support.

Other issues, however, made compromise difficult, most notably the government's decision to proceed with the renewal of Trident – which produced the largest revolt of Blair's truncated third term, with 95 Labour MPs defying their whips on one vote. It meant that three key policy decisions taken during Tony Blair's Premiership – encompassing foreign policy (Iraq), defence (Trident) and domestic policy (schools reform) – were only passed thanks to Opposition votes.

Throughout the Blair decade, Labour backbenchers also flexed their muscles on unwhipped votes, over Lords reform in the first parliament, and then hunting with dogs.[2] But the most dramatic demonstration of growing Labour backbench power occurred in February 2006 when the government allowed its MPs a free vote on the introduction of a total ban on smoking in public places, despite a manifesto commitment to introduce a partial ban. A remarkable 91 per cent of Labour MPs – including the prime minister – voted in favour of a total ban – against the position on which they had fought the election under a year before. The second vote, introducing a total ban on smoking in private clubs, saw 84 per cent of Labour MPs vote against the Labour manifesto, which had promised an exemption.

Throughout the Blair decade then, ordinary Labour backbenchers wielded real and measurable influence over a whole range of government policy. Much of this influence was exerted behind-the-scenes, without formal rebellions in the Commons. As such, the larger rebellions represented a failure of the usual channels of communication between the government and its backbenchers.

Composition and constituency role

One of the most dramatic changes in the composition of the House of Commons at the beginning of the Blair parliament was the increase in the number of women MPs, which reached 120 in 1997, or 18 per cent of the Commons, double the percentage achieved at the previous election. All except 19 of these women sat on the Labour benches. In 1993, Labour had adopted All-Women Shortlists (AWS) for parliamentary constituencies, whereby a proportion of local parties were required to shortlist only women candidates for selection. The process was applied in half of all Labour's 'winnable' seats in 1993–6. The process ran into difficulties in 1995 when an industrial tribunal declared AWS in breach of the Sex Discrimination Act 1975 (Lovenduski, 1997). Nevertheless, the percentage number of women in the House of Commons was maintained at 18 per cent in 2001, and rose slightly to one fifth in 2005, as all three main parties were able to increase their representation of women (House of Commons Information Office, 2006).

In Blair's second term, the Sex Discrimination (Election Candidates) Act 2002 amended the Sex Discrimination Act 1975 to enable political parties to take positive action to reduce inequality in the numbers of men and women, although it does not compel parties to do this. Such methods of positive action to redress inequalities are now in use in many European Union countries, although the issue has not yet been tested in the European courts.

Following New Labour's landslide victory in 1997, 101 'Blair's Babes' were famously photographed with Tony Blair in 1997. Expectations of what women could achieve were extremely – perhaps too – high. The sense of disappointment came swiftly. After the marked failure of Labour women MPs to rebel in the lone-parent division in December 1997 (a cause that many critics argued should have incensed and galvanised women), 'Blair's Babes' were derided and dismissed collectively as an 'uncritical mass': clones who did whatever the leadership told them to do (Perkins, 1999). Hard evidence showed that the 1997 Labour women were half as likely to rebel against the government as the same cohort of Labour men.[3] However, that did not reveal the whole story: according to Joni Lovenduski, women MPs did politics differently from men, arguing behind-the-scenes for policy changes, rather than engaging in public rebellions (Lovenduski, 2005). The problem with such theories was the absence of any reliable means of measuring such gender differences (Cowley and Childs, 2003). Nevertheless, research appeared to show that women MPs performed an agenda-setting role, pushing certain issues up the political agenda, such as childcare and equal pay that would not otherwise have been tackled (Childs, Lovenduski and Campbell, 2005).

Whatever their supposed failings, there is no denying the assault that Labour women more generally have made on the ranks of government since 1997. A decade ago, women ministers occupied just 18 jobs in government from a talent pool of 418 Labour MPs; at the time of writing they occupy

31 jobs from a total of 352 Labour MPs. That represents a doubling of female ministerial representation. Nearly every department of state has now seen a minister from the 1997 intake. And with Gordon Brown's new government, one of their number – Jacqui Smith – has become the first ever female home secretary.

If the story of female representation was one of significant progress during the Blair decade, then the story of the under-representation of ethnic minorities remained one of 'could do better'. In 1997, the number of ethnic minority MPs stood at nine, up from four at the 1987 election a decade before. By 2001, that number had crept up to only 12, and by 2005, the rate had not accelerated, as the figure staggered to 15. Too many ethnic minority candidates suffered from 'ghettoisation' – being placed in largely unwinnable seats, destined never to enter the House of Commons. In contrast to positive discrimination for women, no such institutional arrangements exist for ethnic minorities, and so the progress on this front is likely to be painstakingly slow.

One final change marked out the Blair decade, but once again it was one that the media painted in negative terms. Labour MPs elected from 1997 onwards spent far more time in their constituencies than had occurred in previous parliaments, a trend mirrored by newly elected Conservatives, such that one study of the 2005 Tory intake found that almost half of their available time was spent on constituency work (Rosenblatt, 2006, pp. 31–2).

New Labour's hierarchy went as far as to actively encourage this through the introduction of 'constituency weeks', and by allowing their MPs time off to campaign in key marginal seats (Johnston, Cowley, Pattie and Stuart, 2002). At times, the Labour Whips' Office was left regretting the increasing focus on constituency work to the point where they began to fear that it might distract Labour backbenchers from their responsibilities at Westminster.

In tandem with the greater constituency role came greater funding for MPs. The Blair decade saw a sizeable increase in the allowances paid to members. Unfortunately, just as these allowances were beginning to take effect, the government, forced by its own Freedom of Information Act (which came into force in 2005), started to publish the details of the expenditure claims made by each MP.[4] The bare statistics for 2003–4 revealed that the 659 members of the House of Commons claimed an average of £118,000 in allowances and expenses on top of the standard backbench salary of £57,000. The bulk of MPs' expenses were not really 'expenses' at all, but went primarily on staff costs (around £72,000), on allowances for second homes if they live outside London (up to £20,000), office space (again, about £20,000), plus stationery and travel expenses. The media headlines were predictable: Members were widely were seen as lining their pockets with taxpayers' money; and each year the newspapers printed the names of 'Britain's most expensive MPs'. But while the media's focus was almost entirely negative, the more positive development was that MPs were now properly resourced, and that this growth in resources reflected the increasing constituency focus of MPs.

Conclusion

The idea of parliament in decline is one of the most resilient themes in British political science. As has been demonstrated, Blair's decade in power was to prove no different. Criticisms abounded of an overweening executive that had variously introduced permanent guillotines, which was not properly held to account by MPs who now enjoyed shorter hours and had asked for yet more money to do less work.

Under Tony Blair, the executive had undoubtedly strengthened its role in relation to the legislature in terms of controlling the timetabling of government legislation, but as has been shown, MPs were not nearly as supine under Blair as the media supposed, but were instead rebelling in record numbers. Meanwhile in the House of Lords, the government's reforms, though ill-thought through, had the unintended effect of producing a more legitimate chamber, and one more willing to inflict defeats upon the government than in the past.

On balance, parliament's dominance at the centre of public life probably diminished slightly under Tony Blair. But that trend would have occurred without Blair. Arguably, it took a media-savvy prime minister, ably assisted by the reform-minded Robin Cook, to force both chambers to adapt to a world where the media was no longer automatically interested in what parliament said and did. Had the format of Prime Minister's Questions not been changed, had the introduction of Liaison Committee scrutiny of the prime minister not been made and had MPs not accepted major reforms to their hours of business, then it is arguable that parliament could have continued to slip even further in importance. The Blair decade ended with parliamentarians better resourced than ever before, and if not wholly representative of the wider public, then a great deal more so than they had been previously. The biggest failure, however, lay in the paucity of initiatives to enhance the scrutiny of government legislation at the expense of reforms which tended to make the executive's job easier at the expense of parliament.

Notes

1. In November 2003, the government scraped home by 17 votes on the closest foundation hospitals vote, and by an even narrower margin of just five on the Second Reading of the Higher Education Bill (introducing top-up fees) in January 2004.
2. Labour backbenchers consistently refused to allow their government to wriggle out of a total ban on hunting with dogs. After a seven-year battle, and despite Tony Blair's stated preference for licensed hunting, foxhunting was banned.
3. By 2001, 17 per cent of the 1997 New Labour women had rebelled against the government as against 34 per cent of the Labour men from the same cohort. By 2007, however, the gap had narrowed considerably, 46 per cent of Labour women having rebelled, as against 58 per cent of Labour men.
4. From January 2005, all public employees had to submit their expense accounts to public disclosure.

13
The Blair Government, Devolution and Regionalism in the United Kingdom

Jonathan Bradbury

One of the principal reforms introduced by the Blair governments was the devolution of power from Westminster to elected institutions representing the UK's territorial nations and regions: a Parliament for Scotland (1999), an assembly for Wales (1999) and an assembly for Northern Ireland (1998). At the same time in England, the Blair governments established regional development agencies in all nine regions (1999). In London this was accompanied by an elected Greater London Authority (2000), although elsewhere a purely administrative regionalism developed. The chapter seeks to review the significance of this major series of innovations to the Blair legacy. Section one provides a historical context to reform. Section two considers the approaches adopted in introducing devolution and regional reform over the period 1997–2007. Section three then considers the implications of devolution and regional reform for UK territorial politics, judged from competing theoretical perspectives.

Historical contexts and the Blair agenda

Originally, the UK came together on the basis of territorial unions between England with Wales, (1536), Scotland (1707) and Ireland (1800), revised to Northern Ireland (1921). Constitutionally, the UK governmental system rested on the sovereignty of the UK parliament, and British-wide parties became central to the development of a largely unitary political system. Even so, relations between Westminster and the nations and provinces always embraced territorial differentiation. In Scotland this was reflected in the conditions of the Act of Union, and from the late 19th century in the Scottish Office as a territorial office of central government. The idea of the territorial office of state was replicated in Wales in 1964. The politics of Northern Ireland were most distinctive of all, resting on a division between unionism and nationalism and closely related in turn to the schism between Protestant and Catholic religion. In England, by far the most populous nation in the UK, national identity became melded with that of Britain as a whole. English regionalism did develop, but primarily on a functional basis, resulting in a disparate swathe of regional field offices and agencies.

The politics of territorial identity always posed at the very least a latent threat to the stability of the UK state. Nationalists promoted the reunification of Northern Ireland with the rest of Ireland, and independence for Scotland and Wales. In response, the UK centre sought to block nationalist separatism and ideally sought the maintenance of the constitutional tradition based on parliamentary sovereignty rather than any embrace of territorial federalism. The granting of more political rights associated with national identities focused narrowly on the policy option of devolution. This is an explicitly constitutional and legislative act which involves 'the transfer to a subordinate elected body, on a geographical basis, of functions at present exercised by ministers and Parliament' (Bogdanor, 1999, p. 2), but crucially without theoretically compromising the legal sovereignty of parliament. Devolution was seen in the 19th century as a means of accommodating what the former Liberal prime minister, William Gladstone, famously characterised as 'local patriotism'. Nevertheless, despite its consideration for Scotland and Wales in the early 20th centuries, and again in the 1970s, devolution was formerly employed only in Northern Ireland between 1921 and 1972.

In reflecting on the reform options for England, the term 'devolution' should only be properly used with reference to establishing an English parliament. This has had few supporters. Instead, analysts have primarily observed debates about regionalism at the sub-English level. Regionalism is a governmental process involving the 'formulation of public policy for, and the administration of policy in, large geographical units consisting usually of a number of neighbouring counties defined by geographical, sociological, administrative and political criteria' (Smith, 1964, p. 2). This may involve an elected tier of government but not necessarily so; even if it does, it will focus on executive capacity and not compromise the legislative powers of central government. In practice the development of a coherent English regionalism during the 20th century was frustrated by the interests both of central and local government. Only between the mid 1960s and 1979 when regional planning councils were created was consolidation of regional governance seriously on the agenda, but after 1979 Mrs Thatcher's first government soon put a stop to that.

Such was the backdrop to the modern era of UK territorial politics. By the mid-1990s, however, arguments for devolution and regional reform were much more forcefully put (Keating, 1998). First, devolution was argued for on identity grounds: as a response to the UK's relative decline and to recognise the rights of stateless nations. For separatist nationalists devolution was a stepping stone to independence; for reformist unionists it was a means to gain autonomy within a reconstructed state. Second, devolution was argued for on democratic grounds: that the experience of the Thatcher and Major governments (1979–97) revealed the extent to which interests could be over-ridden by a central UK government essentially elected on English votes and pursuing an unpopular form of neoliberal state reform. Third, there was an instrumental case: that devolution would create strategic institutions that could promote territorial interests in a single European market, create more co-ordinated regional development policies and represent more diverse interests in a multilayered order of governance in the European Union.

These arguments for reform were compounded by resentments at Mrs Thatcher's staunch unionism and opposition to devolution except in the special case of Northern Ireland. The Major government did seek to show more respect for Scottish and Welsh identity. Equally, they made more effort to achieve devolution in Northern Ireland. John Major was a co-signatory of the Downing Street Declaration in 1994, which renounced both British and Irish claims on Northern Ireland and helped to create the conditions for the peace process later in 1994. Even in England, again in 1994, the Major government introduced the Government Offices for the Regions (GORs) as a means of integrating the field operations of central departments. Yet, the Major strategy still appeared too little, too late to diminish support for devolution in Scotland and Wales; in Northern Ireland the Major government's perceived closeness to Unionism led to Nationalist/Republican frustration and the end of the IRA ceasefire; and in the English regions the GORs were seen as instruments of central control. Overall, the legacy bestowed to the Blair government was one of inflamed territorial politics in each part of the UK (see Bradbury and Mawson, 1997).

When Tony Blair became leader in 1994, the Labour Party under his pro-devolution predecessor, John Smith, had already developed commitments on devolution. Out of power since 1979, and with party strongholds in both Scotland and Wales, a majority in the Labour Party in each territory moved towards principled support for devolution. Participation in the Scottish Constitutional Convention after 1989 led to agreement on a final report in 1995. In Wales, Ron Davies as shadow secretary of state organised debates purely within the Labour Party that also resulted in proposals by 1995. On Northern Ireland, Blair inherited a policy sympathetic with Republican arguments for gradual UK disengagement. Only on England was policy still relatively lacking in commitment and form.

It remains unclear whether Tony Blair himself was a principled advocate of devolution. Accounts of court life appear to indicate that he was not proactive on the matter and consequently devolution should not generally be seen as an integral part of the New Labour project as Blair himself defined it. Rather it should be seen as a policy pushed into the Blair programme by a variety of pressures. James Naughtie's *The Rivals* (2001) reveals the extent to which the Blair premiership incorporated significant power for the chancellor, Gordon Brown, and that for him Scottish devolution was non-negotiable. Blair had a more instinctive support for devolution in

Northern Ireland, but he was profoundly uncomfortable with the party's apparent sympathies with republicanism. He wanted to move the party to a more even-handed honest broker role. John Prescott, the author of the early 1980s alternative regional strategy, and now deputy leader was also in a position to press the case for regional reform in England.

On this basis it is probably more accurate to suggest that except in the special case of Northern Ireland, Blair was of a piece with former Labour leaders like Neil Kinnock in not being a natural supporter of devolution. Rather, the Blair leadership was penetrated by powerful representatives of territorial interests, notably Brown and Prescott. That Blair still had to wrestle with the issue before satisfying himself that it was consistent with his broad ambitions for a Labour government is reflected in a note in the dairies of his press officer, Alistair Campbell. After reading a biography of Gladstone by the Liberal Democrat peer, Roy Jenkins, Blair appeared to have finally accepted devolution in terms of the idea that 'power devolved was power retained at Westminster' (Campbell and Stott, 2007, p. 105). Whatever aspirations there were for devolution out in the country, for Tony Blair it was ultimately intended to conform to assumptions of state stability and the sustained authority of the centre.

Consequently, between 1994 and 1997 Blair confirmed his party's support for devolution proposals prepared in the Scottish and Welsh parties, and allowed regional reform proposals for England to be prepared by Jack Straw, then the shadow home secretary. At the same time Blair was influenced by caution; he insisted that devolution proposals should be enacted only after gaining a mandate in separate referendum votes. Blair appointed Mo Mowlam as his Northern Ireland spokesperson, and defined Northern Ireland policy as one that sought to reach consensus. In each case devolution was intended to give expression to identity politics and improve governance, but it was expected that this would also rebind the ties of the UK. Even in Northern Ireland Blair did not expect Irish reunification in his lifetime. It was hoped that devolution would not raise the English question too strongly and that regional reforms would answer any pressures from that direction (Bradbury and Mawson, 1997).

The Blair government's policies on devolution and regional reform

The electoral landslide of 1997 and subsequent election victories in 2001 and 2005 meant that the Blair government was able to see much of their plans to fruition. This programme of reform raised a number of issues relating not only to the devolved institutions themselves, but also to the development of inter-governmental relations, approaches to public policy variation, and debates about the further development of devolution. A number of key components of the Blair government's record can be identified (see Trench, 2007; Bradbury, 2008 for a fuller elaboration of trends in the politics of UK devolution).

First, all three of the devolution settlements were introduced rapidly in the period 1997–9. It is important to note also that devolution was introduced on an asymmetrical basis. Under the 1998 Scotland Act, the Scottish parliament received primary legislative powers in all areas outside of those specifically reserved for the Westminster parliament. This meant the parliament gained the power to amend or overturn existing legislation in a wide range of domestic policy areas as well as legislate on new areas that came up and were outside Westminster's reserved areas. The parliament was reliant on a block grant from Westminster but it did have the power to vary the level of income tax from the UK level by plus or minus three pence in the pound. In contrast the National Assembly for Wales received secondary legislative powers on an itemised basis under specific policy headings. This meant that the assembly had the power to pass statutory instruments and take executive decisions under primary law still made at Westminster. The assembly was also reliant on a block grant from Westminster, but did not have any fiscal powers of its own.

Devolution in Northern Ireland was different again. Under the terms of the 1998 Belfast Agreement (also known as the Good Friday Agreement) the Northern Ireland Assembly received a mix of primary legislative and executive powers and was reliant on a block grant from Westminster. The institutional structure was highly distinctive in including a North-South Ministerial council, bringing together ministers from the Northern Ireland Assembly and their counterparts from the Irish government, as well as a British-Irish council, providing for meetings between representatives of the UK and Irish governments and all of the devolved institutions. The Belfast Agreement also stipulated that all three institutions had to be operational, or they all fell together.

Second, the legal character and institutional mechanisms of the devolved institutions was also developed on a highly varied basis. In Scotland devolution was to the first minister, as the leader of Her Majesty's government in the Scottish parliament. In Wales devolution instead was to the assembly as a corporate body. In both countries, mixed member proportional electoral systems, using simple plurality constituency seats and regional lists, were adopted to make the new institutions more representative and encourage more inter-party co-operation. However, in Scotland the proportion of list seats was 44 per cent, virtually guaranteeing expectations that no party could win a majority in the parliament. Meanwhile in Wales, the proportion of list seats was only 33 per cent, leading to the expectation that the Labour Party, with its long-standing domination of constituency seats, would still win a majority. In both Scotland and Wales arrangements sought to put some flesh on 'new politics'; mainly this focused on encouraging consensual work in committees.

In Northern Ireland, these issues were dealt with again in even more distinctive fashion. All members had to designate themselves as unionist, nationalist or neither. Devolution was made to a diarchy of first minister and deputy first minister, comprising the nominees of the unionist and nationalist blocs, and the executive was then composed on a proportional power-sharing basis of representatives from the different parties. Voting in the assembly was also defined according to rules that required unionist and nationalist consent. Such arrangements suggested that devolution was expected to operate a consociational form of democracy as opposed to the majoritarian form in Scotland and Wales. With the added North-South and East-West institutions, this was characterised as consociationalism plus. Northern Ireland was also distinctive for adopting the single transferable vote (STV) electoral system, as well as institutional features to further embed power sharing.

Third, the Blair governments put considerable political resources into successfully introducing the new devolved institutions. In the case of Scotland and Wales this was relatively straightforward. Following successful referenda in 1997 the first elections were held in 1999 and each four years thereafter. In contrast, in Northern Ireland, despite a 'yes' vote in the referendum in 1998, the implementation of the Belfast Agreement was beset by difficulties arising from tensions between unionist and nationalist parties. These arose from differences in interpreting their obligations, and unionist demands that the paramilitary republican organisation, the IRA, decommission its weapons and support law and order. The assembly went through a period of halting existence until its most lengthy suspension between 2002 and 2006. The Blair government, in concert with the Irish government and the Northern Ireland parties, nevertheless, secured a breakthrough with the St Andrew Agreement in late 2006. IRA decommissioning was acknowledged; Sinn Fein declared its support for the police and the Democratic Unionist Party agreed to go into power-sharing government. In May 2007, a DUP-Sinn Fein led executive finally took office to re-establish devolution, at least for the foreseeable future.

Fourth, the Blair governments operated a machinery of inter-governmental relations that in most important respects endured until 2007, but in fact contained relatively little change from past practice. There were formal innovations. At the political level, territorial secretaries of state were retained to manage relations between central government and the devolved institutions. From 2003 these positions in Scotland and Wales were henceforth to be done on a part-time basis by cabinet ministers holding other briefs as well. A new feature was the Joint Ministerial Council (JMC) which was established as a basis for ministerial-level discussions between central and devolved ministers. The judicial committee of the Privy Council was given the role of arbitrator of any disputes that occurred. At the bureaucratic level memorandums of understanding (MOU) and concordats were introduced as a basis for working relations between civil servants. The Northern Ireland civil service had long been separate, although senior officials continued to observe developments in the British civil service very closely.

In practice a new formal machinery of intergovernmental relations (IGR) did not emerge. The JMC was barely used and there were no notable disputes before 2007. Instead, a culture of informal relations developed, no doubt helped by Labour ministers being in office at both the UK and Scottish/Welsh levels up to 2007. Equally, the unity of the British civil service was retained. Early initiatives in central government to set up staff units with an explicit remit on devolution were relatively quickly downgraded. MOU and concordats tended not to be consulted formally, but instead were incorporated into the common sense rules of dealings between civil servants across the UK. On the key issue of territorial finance, continuity was also a predominant theme. Despite some requests for a needs-based approach, the system of allocating territorial finance on a block grant basis according to the population and expenditure-based Barnett formula that had pertained with the Scottish, Welsh and Northern Ireland Offices was continued. In the circumstances of reasonably buoyant public finances, favourable comprehensive spending reviews and a new round of EU regional funding, public finance allocations to the devolved institutions were in practice very favourable during the Blair years (Trench, 2004).

Fifth, the Blair governments' approach to the new devolved executives, despite having preferences, was largely characterised by an acceptance of the need to work with whoever was elected. In Northern Ireland, the Blair premiership sought to build up the moderate unionist and nationalist parties, the Ulster Unionist Party (UUP) and the Social Democratic and Labour Party (SDLP), but it was always aware that because of its links with the IRA, the support of Sinn Fein had to be courted. In practice, in both the 2003 and 2007 assembly elections not only Sinn Fein, but also the more hard line Democratic Unionist Party (DUP), emerged as the leading parties in the nationalist and unionist blocs respectively. These parties' more extreme positions made gaining a compromise appear more difficult. Nevertheless, the Blair strategy ultimately was agnostic on which parties were being dealt with as long as they could be trusted to lead their communities in stabilising power-sharing government.

In contrast in Scotland and Wales, the Blair premiership was naturally keen to see Labour in power. The approach to the first elections in 1999 was to have extensive British party leadership involvement. This covered an actual or perceived strong role in leadership and candidate selection, manifesto development, electoral strategy and campaigning. However, after 1999 this close interest subsided. Labour was the largest party in both the Scottish Parliament and the Welsh Assembly, forming a coalition with the Liberal Democrats in Scotland that would last in renewed forms until 2007 and in Wales governing first as a minority administration and then in coalition with the Liberal Democrats from 2000 until 2003. But Labour's position was not as strong as had been hoped for in either country in 1999, and the intervention of the British leadership was seen as a problem. In Wales the retreat of the central party was strongly associated with particular Welsh party resentments at having Alun Michael 'imposed' as their leader and the subsequent poor result in the 1999 Assembly election.

After 1999 the Scottish and Welsh Labour parties gained much greater autonomy over party organisation, policy and electoral strategy. The party in Wales arguably made more use of this autonomy to assert a more avowedly socialist politics than that of Blair's modernising New Labour. In neither of the 2003 elections was the hand of the Blair leadership present; following which Labour retained power in a coalition administration in Scotland and were able to form a majority administration in Wales. Only in the Scottish parliament election in 2007 did the Blair leadership intervene in devolved Labour politics again. Faced with polling evidence that suggested the Scottish National Party (SNP) could become the largest party, both Blair and Gordon Brown took a high profile role in supporting the Scottish Labour campaign. This was judged in Labour circles to be helpful, but it still failed to stop the SNP emerging as the largest party and going on to form a minority administration. In Wales, the Labour Party experienced an even worse result in 2007 than in 1999, eventually going into coalition with Plaid Cymru. Despite the 2007 intervention in Scotland, the Blair government by 2007 had still generally moved away from seeking to exert direct control over the Scottish and Welsh Labour parties.

Sixth, the Blair governments developed an approach to devolved public policy that was largely permissive. There were some notable points of friction. For example, the Scottish parliament's decisions to adopt different policies on student funding in higher education and care for the elderly very clearly cut across UK Labour government policies. In each case, the Treasury declared that there would be no additional funding to pay for these decisions. Equally, the divergence in approaches to the National Health Service in Scotland and Wales caused Labour MPs considerable anxiety in the run up to the 2005 UK general election. In the main, however, the Blair government was not perceived to interfere in the policies pursued by the Labour and coalition administrations in Edinburgh and Cardiff, a fact evidenced by the general lack of controversy regarding the role of the UK government.

Seventh, while pressures for change varied, the Blair government's approach to the development of devolution was generally characterised by flexibility and a desire to reach accommodation. In Scotland, debates emerged primarily about fiscal powers but they did not develop into a concerted campaign. At the time that Blair left office the SNP's call for a referendum on independence met united opposition. In Northern Ireland, the DUP and Sinn Fein argued about the validity of the Belfast Agreement as a basis for returning to devolution. Ultimately the Blair government helped to find a compromise in the St Andrews Agreement, which reassured unionists on such matters as the controls to be placed on ministerial behaviour. Nevertheless, these were seen as minor amendments to the Belfast Agreement, which was still seen as the bedrock of devolution.

The biggest pressures for concerted change came in Wales. In response to the 2004 Richard Report, which pressed for a change in the Assembly's legal status, more powers and a move to an STV electoral system, the Blair governments passed the Government of Wales Act 2006. This abandoned the concept of the assembly as a corporate body for a clearer devolution of power directly to ministers. It asserted that the powers of the assembly were still to be developed gradually, but adding new procedures for using orders in council at Westminster to give the assembly powers in additional areas. A new referendum was required to grant primary legislative powers, which even then could only be held if there was a 2/3 majority in the assembly and if Westminster agreed. Labour rejected the proposal for an STV electoral system; instead the 2006 Act retained the existing electoral system, with the revision of allowing only single candidacy for constituency or list seats but not both. Following the 2007 assembly elections the Labour-Plaid Cymru administration set up a convention to review support for the move to primary legislative powers, with the intention of holding a referendum before 2011.

Finally, the Blair governments' plans for regional reform in England were implemented, generally with the minimum of fuss. These included the creation of regional development agencies, regional chambers and in London a new greater London authority with an elected mayor. Referenda for elected regional government were promised in the North-East, North-West and Yorkshire and Humberside, but they were abandoned in the latter two because opinion polls showed low support. In the North-East the referendum was held in November 2004 but resulted in a devastating 78 per cent 'no' vote.

A more concerted campaign for a different deal for England was promoted by the Conservative Party, which saw English regional institutions as an expensive distraction. Instead, they raised the West Lothian Question, first raised by Tam Dalyell, MP for West Lothian, in November 1977, which asked how could it be right after devolution that Westminster MPs from Scottish constituencies could vote in the House of Commons on matters relating only to England which in Scotland were devolved matters and could not be influenced by English votes. The Conservatives sought to develop some way of allowing only English MPs to vote for laws only affecting England in the House of Commons. Latterly, public opinion polls and UK press coverage have raised the spectre of English resentments at the different deal for university students in Scotland. In response to these pressures, the Blair government remained fairly resolute. They refused to give any oxygen to a political debate about reform of voting rights at Westminster or indeed an

English parliament, stating that giving succour to English nationalism was the clearest way to destabilising the Union (Hazell, 2006; Falconer, 2006).

Taking all of these issues together, the approach of the Blair governments appears to have been characterised by a general determination to combine robust support for devolution and regional reform with flexibility in how it should be applied in each part of the UK, and a desire to leave the devolved institutions to do largely as they wished. There was no attempt to centrally impose a uniform prescription for devolution; and in developing devolution thereafter, this approach of following local origination was maintained. Equally, in developing a system of inter-governmental relations, the Blair governments leant heavily on approaches of the pre-devolution era, notably civil service approaches to the former territorial departments, and the financial rules of the Barnett formula. They were revised for a new era rather than reconsidered as part of a programmatic engagement with discussing first principles and devising new systems.

The Blair government embarked on central intervention only selectively, primarily in the start-up phase of devolution in Scotland and Wales and in moments of possible territorial crisis such as in Scotland in 2007. Otherwise, substantial latitude was given to Scottish and Welsh party organisations and devolved executives to follow their own wishes. In this light, such interventions as did occur appeared more like occasional gunboat diplomacy than evidence of a systematic intent to meddle in devolved affairs. Finally, English regional reform obviously did constitute a desire to respond to an English case for better governance and public policy, and to dissipate any resentment about devolution elsewhere in the UK. But the Blair governments did not impose regionalism further than was given consent by public demand, and they eschewed any debate about an English parliament.

Overall, throughout Tony Blair's term of office all of these implicit priorities appeared to have been sustained. It put the flesh on the bones of the idea of 'power devolved was power retained', and suggests that the Blair government hoped that by taking a benign and non-programmatic approach to devolution it would be relatively smoothly adapted to the gradualist contours of the British political tradition.

Blair's legacy for UK territorial politics

Devolution was a controversial innovation, fiercely opposed by the Conservative party in 1997–8, and hotly contested between reformist unionists and separatist nationalists as to its future implications. In practice it led to many changes in UK politics, the significance of which is open to dispute. A transformative perspective suggests that the 'suspended revolution' in UK territorial politics, a term coined originally by Jim Bulpitt (1983), is being relatively quickly overturned (Nairn, 2000; Rawlings, 2003; Keating, 2005). Devolution and regional reform have facilitated variations in party systems, voting behaviour and/or public policy across the UK, creating dynamics of divergence across a wide range of political variables. Events in 2007 added considerably to perceptions of the possibility that the UK might actually break asunder. The 2007 elections resulted in a sea change in devolved politics as the SNP, Plaid Cymru and Sinn Fein entered government. One could plausibly argue that at the very time that he was just about to leave office Blair's hopes that devolution represented an approach by which the state could be reformed to conserve were unravelling. Nationalism appeared to be on the march, with potentially transformative implications for the UK as centrifugal pressures overcame centripetal ones.

This perspective has fuelled a critique of the Blair government that the approach to devolution devoted too few resources to managing and controlling the new UK state. Jeffery (Jeffery and Wincott, 2006; Jeffery, 2007) suggests that the initial apparent success in bedding down devolution and regionalism largely was the result of good fortune. During the Blair era Labour was consistently in power at the UK and Scottish/Welsh levels, the economy was relatively strong and public spending allocations to the devolved institutions were generous. However, the situation by 2007 was entirely predictable and the key legacy of the Blair approach was to leave the UK system of government ill prepared to manage the dynamics released by devolution. He focused on two major problems.

First, Labour's lack of engagement with fundamental principles by which the new intergovernmental system should operate or set legitimate boundaries for the development of devolution reflected a fundamental lack of strategic thinking and a preference for piecemeal development. Jeffery suggested that the lack of an integrated approach to charting what devolution implied for the future of the UK meant that it left a great deal of uncertainty, which could be exploited in a period of economic downturn, and when different parties were in office at the UK and devolved levels. 'Piecemeal answers to specific empirical questions do not appear ... to provide the basis for an enduring devolution settlement' (Jeffery, 2007, p. 95). Second, the needs of England and the relationship of England to the rest of the UK after devolution had been largely unaddressed, leaving the UK as a lopsided state in which only the territorial periphery had received political devolution. He warned that England is 'not just an elephant compared to the much smaller occupants of the UK boat, but also an inadequately tethered and potentially wilful version of that beast' (Jeffery, 2007, p. 96), whose reactions to devolution elsewhere in the UK were unpredictable, further potentially undermining the stability of future territorial politics.

Overall, Jeffery argued that the ad hoc and uncoordinated nature of the Blair government's reforms meant that the rules of the new territorial system were ill-defined and that at some point a more formal approach would be required. The Blair government had, in other words, failed to grasp that it was becoming like many other states that had federalised or regionalised, and needed to embrace the practices of federal or quasi-federal systems such as Canada, Belgium and Spain. Without such a change, devolution threatened to make the UK one of the established democracies in which the strengthening of regional politics presented fundamental challenges of fragmentation and potential state break up rather than simply greater state complexity.

Alternatively, a sceptical perspective emphasises the fact that post-devolution territorial politics during the Blair era was instead mainly characterised by stability relative to the pre-1997 period. Bradbury (2006) suggests that the dynamism of devolution co-existed with considerable continuity in the underlying themes of UK territorial politics, and that the assertiveness of the periphery can be exaggerated. Even the significance of the rise of the nationalist parties in 2007 should be questioned. Over the 1997–2007 period public opinion in Scotland, Wales and Northern Ireland showed little decisive move to separatist identity formation or support for independence. Indeed, the SNP and Plaid Cymru's assent into government may be better seen primarily in terms of swing of the pendulum politics against Labour, the relative weakness of the Conservatives and the necessity of semi-proportional electoral systems requiring coalition politics. In Northern Ireland, Sinn Fein's position was heavily constrained by the opposing pressures of the DUP. Blair would not have wished to leave the SNP, Plaid Cymru and Sinn Fein (rather than the SDLP) in prime positions to mobilise political support for their political causes. Nevertheless, it is reasonable to argue that analysis of the Blair legacy should still primarily stress continuity and relative stability in state territorial politics, albeit with a raised eyebrow to the implications of 2007.

This perspective underpins a more sympathetic appraisal of the Blair government's approach to the introduction and early management of devolution; that it was in fact more subtle in being informed by the peculiarities of UK politics that make it different from other states than Jeffery and other critics have acknowledged. Bulpitt (1983) suggested that the English/British centre was a reluctant imperialist and that historically not only has peripheral assertion been weaker than its promoters would often hope for, but that the centre, in having highly unusual preoccupations for an offshore island state of a major global role, had limited resources for dealing with any peripheral assertion that did exist. This means that UK governments have sought satisficing rather than ideal approaches to territorial management in order to retain a relative autonomy from peripheral concerns and to have the freedom to pursue high politics aim of a global role, whether it is that of a worldwide empire or a role as a post-imperial junior partner to the US.

From this perspective, devolution was not at all desirable because of the threats it posed to the territorial stability of the UK and the requirements it potentially raised for engaging in close territorial management. But there is nothing new in the Blair government seeking to create a stable duality even after devolution; between the politics of the centre and the ambitions of the New Labour project and a modernised Britain on the one hand, and the territorial periphery and its political preoccupations on the other. While there were problems, primarily in making the historic achievement of power-sharing devolution in Northern Ireland, the Blair governments in the early years of devolution at least successfully stuck to the employment of 'traditional' centre autonomy methods to attempt to manage the potentially deeply disruptive influence of devolution on UK territorial politics in such a way as to allow the UK centre to get on with its main preoccupations. Arguably, it did this with reasonable success (Bradbury, 2006).

At the same time this perspective may highlight the dangers of the UK following international leads in how to manage intergovernmental relations. Given the nature of territorial challenges in the UK, recipes for the long-term central imposition of prescriptions for the rules of governance in each territory are fraught with danger. It is possible that the Blair government's approach produced a relative tranquillity in territorial politics precisely because of its respect for local authorship of developments in devolution in each territory. Equally, in the face of concerns about territorial threats to the UK, it is logical that central policy might continue to seek to allow local unionist answers to these challenges, and that compromises between centripetal and centrifugal pressures within the UK are worked out not between centre and periphery but between actors within the periphery. In dealing with the lopsided state and the English question it is questionable whether the Blair governments could have done other than they did, without being perceived to impose further unpopular policies on England. The Blair government's management of UK devolution may look very messy from an international perspective but it is symptomatic of the particularities of a geographically small offshore island seeking to continue to punch above its weight internationally, while not being held down by the increasing saliency of its complex internal identity politics.

Conclusion

Devolution and regional reform were among the most significant constitutional reforms passed by the Blair government. They made the territorial dimension of the state, always an integrally important aspect of the peculiar make-up of the UK, politically explicit for the first time. They also represented a fair reflection of what Labour planned to do while in opposition before 1997. The reforms were marked by flexibility in how they were applied in each part of the UK, and a desire to leave the devolved institutions to do largely as they wished. The implications of the reforms are, nevertheless, contested. This is not surprising as devolution represented such a potential disjuncture in the politics of Scotland, Wales and Northern Ireland and their relationship with the UK. As Tony Blair left office, intriguingly the apparent smoothness with which devolution had been achieved, topped by the extraordinary achievement of power-sharing devolution in Northern Ireland, were cast in a potentially fresh light by the success of the nationalist parties in the 2007 devolved elections. But mainly the legacy of devolution was successful seen in Tony Blair's terms. Devolution was granted, but the stability of the state for the time being, at least, was achieved; 'power devolved was power retained'.

Instead, what comes of the dynamics of devolution will be more closely associated with Tony Blair's successors, perhaps fittingly so in the case of Gordon Brown, for it was his very support for devolution to Scotland that made devolution all round a part of the New Labour project, and thus a key part of the Blair legacy. The question is whether the Blair approach will provide lessons or problems for centre objectives in the future. Certainly in the short term, Brown's premiership appeared to embrace only a cautious upgrading of the Blair approach to territorial politics; focusing mainly on rhetorical and symbolic attempts to build up a culture of unionism, through such devices as the promotion of British values and flying the union flag on public buildings (Ministry of Justice, 2007). Largely, the onus was left on reformist unionists in the territorial periphery to embed devolution more strongly in a reformed UK rather than in a trajectory towards national separation. Even so, Brown showed considerable consternation at the high-risk strategy of the Scottish Labour leader, Wendy Alexander, who announced in May 2008 her view that a referendum on Scottish independence should be held soon to meet this challenge head on and defeat it. A major overhaul of central policy and a fundamental constitutional debate may be the ultimate result of such renewed territorial troubles. On balance, though, it may be worth continuing with strategies of benign neglect even, or perhaps particularly, if territorial challenges become ever stronger. For UK central government, if it cannot retain an integrated state, would probably rather have an amicable divorce and territorial stability on a transformed state basis than unending conflict and heavier internal territorial management responsibilities that undermine the UK government's capacity to act on a global scale.

14
Mayors, Monitors and Measurers: Blair's Legacy to Local Democracy

Chris Game

The past is a foreign country

The observation originated in the opening lines of L.P. Hartley's best-known novel, *The Go-Between*, but for academic local government expert Tony Travers it summed up the Blair administration's record of dashed hopes, missed opportunities, and almost unremitting central control:

> It is hard to believe just how optimistic people were during New Labour's early days ... The end of capping was in sight; compulsory competitive tendering would be abolished; it was possible business rates might be returned to local government ... new ministers spoke encouragingly about the need to strengthen and enhance local government – a new Enlightenment perhaps? ... The past is indeed a foreign country.
>
> (Travers, 2007, p. 20)

In fact, as Blair left office, ministers were still capping the budgets and council taxes of individual local authorities and still setting business rates (property taxes). Indeed, all the most democratically detrimental essentials of the local finance system remained untouched. Compulsory competitive tendering (CCT) had disappeared, but been replaced by immensely expensive regimes of performance measurement and external monitoring. As this chapter will contend, local government had certainly been changed, possibly modernised, but hardly strengthened and enhanced, because, like authoritarian parents, ministers simply could not bring themselves to trust their dependents and let go.

The irony is that this governmental authoritarianism is precisely the accusation that, in opposition, Labour levelled at their Conservative predecessors – as in a book seen in 1996/97 as almost a blueprint for a New Labour Government, *The Blair Revolution: Can New Labour Deliver?*:

> [T]he Tories came to power on a firm pledge of freeing local government from constraints. [They] promised: 'We will sweep away tiresome and

excessive control over local government. Local councils are directly elected. They do not need the fussy supervision of detail that now exists.' However, far from rolling back the central state, over 150 acts of parliament since 1979 have reduced local government powers ... The Thatcher government took away Londoners' rights to elect a voice for their city, abolished metropolitan authorities, and introduced rate capping ... The Major government took powers to limit every local council budget.

(Mandelson and Liddle, 1996, p. 196)

The book's authors were Peter Mandelson, a future cabinet minister and a co-founder, with Blair and Brown, of New Labour, and Roger Liddle, a Blair advisor. Both happened also – unlike, Blair, Brown and most of the party's parliamentary leaders – to have been Labour councillors. So when, under the heading 'Reviving local government' (p. 197), they stressed New Labour's firm localist commitment to reverse the Conservatives' record and bring about a fundamental cultural change in central-local government relations, it was taken as more than mere rhetoric:

Labour must act to reinvigorate local government ... The closer politics – and power – is to people, the more chance there is of interaction between them ... Bringing such closeness about has to be a top priority of a government that genuinely believes in a bottom-up, not top-down, approach ... that celebrates diversity and local initiative and believes that uniform solutions won't work.

The party's manifesto for the 1997 general election, *New Labour – Because Britain Deserves Better*, was presumed to share this localist commitment, and to be the main instrument for its realisation. If some of its detailed 'Good local government' pledges did come with a measure of 'wriggle room', this was, after all, a manifesto, and in the event relatively little was needed. As shown in Table 14.1, only one pledge was completely abandoned – as demonstrably impracticable. All the others – most at least mentioned in this chapter – could be ticked off, by the end of the government's first term in 2001, as being already or *en route* to being achieved.

In the 2001 general election Labour's 1997 vote fell by over 20 per cent, to the lowest total won by any elected government since the 1920s. Under a more proportional electoral system the party, instead of having a 165 Commons majority, would have been out of government. As a snapshot summary at that time of the Blair legacy, Table 14.1 would record that most pledges in a substantial reform programme had been progressed at least as far as legislation, and the local government world shaken up to probably positive effect. The likely overall verdict would have been favourable.

This goes to show not the worthlessness of legacy evaluation by manifesto, but definitely its limitations. For a start, a more careful reading confirms

Table 14.1   Labour's 1997 manifesto pledges concerning 'Good Local Government'

	Achieved (✓) or not (x)
1. New duty for councils 'to promote the economic, social and environmental well-being of their area' ['well-being power'].	✓
2. Councils 'should work in partnership with local people, local business and local voluntary organizations'.	✓
3. 'To ensure accountability, a proportion of councilors in each locality will be elected annually.'	x
4. [a] We will encourage democratic innovations, [b] 'including pilots of the idea of elected mayors with executive powers in cities'.	✓x
5. [a] 'Although crude and universal council tax capping should go, [b] we will retain reserve powers to control excessive tax rises.'	✓✓
6. 'We will make no change to the present [national] system for determining the business rate without full consultation with business.'	✓
7. [a] 'Councils should not be forced to put their services out to tender, [b] but will be required to obtain best value.'	✓✓
8. 'Every council will be required to publish a local performance plan with targets for service improvement, and be expected to achieve them.'	✓
9. [a] Additional powers for the Audit Commission 'to monitor performance and promote efficiency. [b]On its advice, government will where necessary send in a management team with full powers to remedy failure.'	✓✓
10. All local authorities encouraged 'to adopt [Local Agenda 21 – sustainability] plans to protect and enhance their local environment.'	✓
11. A joint attack by central and local government 'against the multiple causes of social and economic decline – unemployment, bad housing, crime, poor health, and a degraded environment' [Neighbourhood Renewal].	✓
12. Following a confirmatory referendum, 'there will be a new deal for London, with a strategic authority and a mayor, both directly elected'.	✓

Source: Labour Party (1997), p. 34.

that this manifesto never was the kind of local revivalist tract required to further Mandelson and Liddle's localist ideals. Few pledges (maybe 1, 4, and 12) involved a real furtherance of local democracy. More were framed in the 'top-down' language they denounced: councils 'should', 'will be required' or 'expected to' do the government's bidding. Two (5 and 6) seemed almost designed to provide ministers, if challenged by their own dissatisfied supporters, with a useful record of what was *not* promised. Then there is the fact that judgement of the whole three-parliament New Labour local government story is necessarily heavily influenced by key chapters that were still undrafted even in 2001, let alone 1997; also by those that have remained unwritten. The outcome is a verdict that, for most, is likely to be considerably less charitable than it might have been at the end of that first term of office: that the gap between promise and practice has been at least as great as that of which Mandelson and Liddle found the Conservatives guilty.

The local government modernisation agenda (LGMA)

Sticks and carrots

If Tony Blair's reborn New Labour Party, entering office in May 1997, had summarised its mission in a single-word slogan, that word would surely have been 'modernisation'. New Labour would modernise all outdated institutions and practices, and high on both lists was local government. Immediately, however, there was a problem. Following years of Conservative government unpopularity and the collapse of the party's local election support, most of the nation's principal local authorities were either controlled or dominated by Labour councillors. Having fought in the metaphorical front line against the depredations wrought by the Thatcher/Major administrations, these Labour activists certainly wanted reform. 'Older' Labour members even hoped for a reversal of some of the Conservative policies that their party's shadow ministers had once opposed so vehemently. They could hardly be expected to welcome, therefore, ministerial pronouncements that they and their councils were as much part of the problem as part of the solution.

From the outset, New Labour made it clear that the traditional ways of 'doing' local government had to change – and according to the detailed prescriptions to be set out in the government's 'modernisation agenda' with its attendant 'sticks and carrots' incentives (Wilson and Game, 2006, pp. 174–8). Councils embracing the government's remedies would be rewarded with the carrots of additional 'freedoms and flexibilities'. Resisters, though, would be sharply reminded that, in the UK's unitary governmental system, the national government had both the superior mandate and the ultimate power. Ministers could and would intervene, and, in the last resort, wield the big stick and handover the management of the recalcitrant local authority to another agency.

Just as the LGMA initialism gained currency only during the government's second term of office (2001–5), so the agenda itself took time to acquire its eventual full-grown form. The 23 projects and initiatives listed on the relevant web page of the Department for Communities and Local Government (DCLG) – the subjects of the government's comprehensive programme of evaluation studies – were developed and launched over several years. Neither the incremental nature nor the full scope of the LGMA, though, will overly concern us here, for this chapter's purpose is not detailed history, but an overview of the indisputably major elements of the LGMA from the vantage point of 2007/08.

Of the several ways of thematically grouping LGMA initiatives, the chapter adopts the simplest division possible, reflecting local government's two basic functions: its service function and its political function. Most of the policies that demand consideration in the Blair legacy were aimed at *service improvement* – a prioritisation directly carried over from the Conservative government. Considerably fewer – and this in itself is a feature of the legacy – were directed towards *democratic renewal* and councils' role as institutions of local self-government, as well as organisers of services.

LGMA policies aimed at service improvement

While many LGMA initiatives have aimed at directly or indirectly improving service performance, their means have varied. Some have sought changes *within* the local authority – more effective performance management and measurement systems, better strategic planning, more efficient procurement, and more user involvement. Others have specifically advocated partnership working *across* agencies, between local authorities and the private, voluntary, and community sectors. Yet others emphasise organisational learning and 'technology transfer', or the notion of 'stretch targets' and performance-linked rewards (Martin and Bovaird, 2005, pp. 24–5).

The Best Value regime

Best Value (BV) was New Labour's replacement for the Conservative governments' transformative policies of Compulsory Competitive Tendering (CCT) – that required local authorities to compare in-house provision costs of specified (mainly technical 'blue collar') services with those of interested private contractors, and to award the service contract to the most competitive – that is, the lowest – bidder. While only some 40 per cent of contracts (and 25 per cent of overall contract value) actually went to private bidders, CCT was totemically unpopular within the Labour movement, and its abolition became a political imperative. This presented a dilemma for Tony Blair's ideologically more centrist New Labour Party, and Best Value was devised as an overt compromise: abolishing the Compulsory part of CCT, but retaining the Competitive part (see Table 14.1, item 7 above).

Best Value involved councils making arrangements – in the form of regular service-specific and cross-cutting reviews and an annual BV Performance Plan (see Table 14.1, item 8) – to secure *continuous* improvement in the way they undertook *all* their service responsibilities. The italics highlight the key distinctions between CCT and BV, which made the latter, at least initially, more acceptable to the government's own supporters. They soon realised, however, that the BV regime was just as centrally prescriptive as CCT had been, and potentially even more interventionist. It applied, moreover, to every single council service.

Introduced in New Labour's first major Local Government Act (1999), the BV regime required all 409 principal local authorities in England and

Wales – Scottish local government being by now a responsibility of the devolved Scottish Parliament – to review all their functions over a five-year period, applying in each instance the 4Cs:

- **Challenging** why, how, and by whom a service was being provided and showing that alternative delivery approaches had been considered;
- **Comparing** its performance with that of similar authorities across a range of BV performance indicators;
- **Consulting** local stakeholders in setting new and demanding performance targets and an action plan to deliver continuous improvements;
- **Competing**, wherever practicable, to secure efficient and effective services.

BV Performance Plans are subject to external audit, and all council functions to regular inspection by either the independent Audit Commission or another specialist inspectorate. Where inspectors identify persistent failures to comply with the regulations or to secure improvement, they can refer services, and ultimately whole authorities, to the minister, who has powers to intervene directly (see Table 14.1, item 9) (Wilson and Game, 2006, pp. 361–7).

Implementation of BV presented a major challenge for most authorities, and particularly smaller councils with fewer corporate staff. On the 4Cs, most councils unsurprisingly proved better at consulting and comparing than at challenging and competing, and few appeared to have examined rigorously the underlying need for a service, as opposed to thinking up ways of improving it. There was also concern about the net value, if any, added by the policy and particularly by its resource-intensive inspection regime – concerns that would be massively heightened in respect of BV's post-2002 successor programme: Comprehensive Performance Assessment.

Comprehensive Performance Assessment (CPA)

CPA has been termed 'BV Mark II', which is partly accurate, partly not. CPA did not replace BV so much as incorporate it. Most obviously incorporated was the dual scoring system used by all BV service inspections, with four-point scales for 'quality of service' and 'prospects for improvement'. CPA, which developed entirely during Labour's second term of office, applied a BV-type regime to the performance of the whole local authority, rather than to individual services. Using similar four-point scoring scales determined by external inspectors, every English local authority – the Assembly for Wales having opted for a separate Wales Programme for Improvement (WPI) – would be assigned to one of just five performance categories: initially labelled Excellent, Good, Fair, Weak and Poor.

Following the 'sticks and carrots' approach noted above, councils judged Excellent and Good were 'rewarded' with such 'freedoms and flexibilities' as lighter-touch inspection regimes, exclusion from budget- and council tax-capping, less ring-fencing of government grants, and extended trading and charging powers: 'privileges' that in other European countries would mostly already be theirs by constitutional right. Councils deemed Poor or Weak received not exactly punishment, but intensified scrutiny and external 'engagement' – a kind of corrective therapy programme provided by ministerially appointed officials who oversee and assist the authority in implementing a recovery plan.

CPA assesses and scores three main spheres of a council's activities: its core service performance in six key service areas, its use of resources, and its ability to improve. Not surprisingly, attempting officially to characterise large multi-functional, multi-service organisations by one-word adjectival descriptions was, even in Britain's highly centralist political culture, controversial. The most excellent organisations have their shortcomings and underperformers their oases of good practice. CPA requires, however, not just a centralist culture and a central government that feels it necessary, desirable and appropriate to monitor and measure – as the chapter title puts it – in this detailed way the activities of democratically elected local authorities. It requires too a scale of local government organisation to make the exercise feasible. As shown in Table 14.2, the UK, uniquely in Western Europe, fulfils that precondition as well, with a scale of sub-central government that most other countries would have difficulty recognising as 'local', even without the most recent tranche of mergers that will increase that scale still further.

Table 14.2   Measures of local government scale and fiscal centralisation

	Pop. (mill.)	Number of lower tier (most local) principal councils	Av. pop. per council	State/local taxes as % of:	
				total local income, 2005	total taxation, 2005
France	63	36,780 Communes	1,720	45	11.5
Spain	44	8,111 Municipios	5,400	50	30.2
Germany	82	12,312 Gemeinden	6,600	41	29.2
Italy	58	8,101 Comuni	7,300	44	16.6
Belgium	10	589 Communes/ Gemeenten	17,800	n/a	29.0
Sweden	9	290 Kommuner	31,400	53	32.2
Netherlands	16	443 Gemeenten	37,000	13	3.9
UK (2008)	61	468 All councils	130,000	15	4.8
UK (2009)	61	433 All councils	140,000		

Source: Wilson and Game, 2006, p. 263; Bauer and Rudorf, 2006, Table 7; OECD, 2007b, p. 28.

The most obvious way, of course, to convince local government sceptics that CPA was not only an important stimulus to continuous service improvement but actually in their own interests would be to ensure that assessments would start off generally favourable and become annually more so – thereby proving officially that local government performance was much better than its critics alleged. Interestingly, this is precisely what happened – with the result that, within four years, despite a recalibration of the scoring system to make CPA literally 'a harder test', 79 per cent of authorities had reached the top two categories, with none at all left in the lowest (Wilson and Game, 2006, pp. 166–7; Audit Commission, 2007). English local government was apparently approaching the enviable state where the government's own statistics showed there was little room for further improvement. The unanswered questions were: at what costs, and had the public even noticed?

Local Public Service Agreements (LPSAs)

CPA was, within local government, probably the most divisive LGMA initiative. An informal *Local Government Chronicle* survey of mainly local government officers, for example, ranked it as both the government's fourth most positive achievement and its fourth biggest mistake (Game, 2007, p. 8). Another incentive-based initiative, but one whose limited number of negotiated targets and cash rewards for success made it considerably more appealing than CPA, has been the Local Public Service Agreement. LPSAs are a form of partnership between government departments and individual local authorities, based on matching commitments.

The authority agrees to deliver in a specified time period about a dozen measurable service improvements, *beyond* any targets in its BV Performance plan. The relevant government departments agree, first, to provide 'pump-priming' grants to help the authority achieve these agreed improvements, and then to pay performance reward grants if/when the improvements are verifiably attained. First piloted in 2000, LPSAs were quickly taken up by almost all major councils and subsequently formed part of the model for the flagship public service project of Labour's third term, Local Area Agreements.

Local Area Agreements (LAAs)

LAAs are LPSAs writ large. They are LPSA-type central-local service delivery agreements, but negotiated not between individual government departments and single local authorities, but between altogether more complex partners. Representing the local area are Local Strategic Partnerships (LSPs) – the non-statutory, council-led bodies that have become the principal vehicles through which public, private and voluntary sector representatives endeavour to work together, preparing Community Strategies and addressing the multi-faceted problems facing their area: industrial decline, unemployment, poverty, crime, failing public services and family breakdown (see Table 14.1, items 1 and 2). Across the negotiating table are the Government Offices for the Regions (GORs) – the regional 'outposts' of the major domestic central government departments.

LAAs themselves are three-year agreements of up to 35 detailed improvement targets in policy areas such as Children and Young People, Healthier Communities and Older People, Economic Development and the Environment – the targets being drawn from a national set of performance indicators that was reduced in 2007 from an almost incredible 1200 to 200. This relative streamlining, set alongside the government's other LAA commitments, can be read as a belated attempt to reduce some of the excessive central direction and national target-setting that characterised its first two administrations. LAA targets would be more locally determined, multiple funding streams into an area would be channelled into a 'single pot' and the ring-fencing of grants greatly reduced, and council-based CPA performance inspections would be replaced by lighter-touch area assessments of the overall quality of public services experienced by local citizens.

It sounds like something approaching the 'fundamental cultural change in central-local government relations' called for by Mandelson and Liddle nearly ten years earlier, but even – or especially – after such a time lapse, there must be doubts about its realisability. The greater likelihood is that many LAAs will prove a further demonstration of the deep-rooted differences of perspective – localities looking for enhanced means and resources with which to tackle intractable long-term problems, and the centre seeking contractual delivery of short-term efficiency gains.

LGMA policies aimed at democratic renewal

Increasingly during the Blair administration, its Modernisation Agenda came to be dominated by the kinds of measures outlined above – including other initiatives squeezed out of this summary: beacon councils, the procurement agenda, e-government, and the Innovation Forum. All were initiated by central government – in precisely the top-down, diversity-suppressing manner execrated by Mandelson and Liddle – and all aimed at increasing the quality or efficiency of local services. Which is why 'service improvement' led these central sections of the chapter, and why, if accorded proportionate space, it would unbalance the whole in the same way as it unbalances the Blair legacy.

Back in 1997, though, that was not what was generally expected. New Labour's modernisation programme seemed then more about what the very first of its local government consultation papers termed 'Democratic Renewal': attacking the 'culture of apathy' pervading local democracy, increasing the public's awareness of and engagement with their councils, raising local electoral turnout, and boosting councillors' community leadership role (DETR, 1998a).

Democratic Renewal thus took pride of place in that earliest version of the LGMA, and, as with service improvement, New Labour was confident it had the remedy. Councils' political structures and processes – particularly British local government's distinctive and longstanding committee system – must be replaced by something maybe less inclusive, but capable of capturing the public imagination and providing visionary community leadership. What was needed were strong, directly elected executive mayors:

> Such a mayor would be a highly visible figure. He or she would have been elected by the people, rather than the council or party, and would therefore focus attention outwards in the direction of the people, rather than inwards towards fellow councillors. The mayor would be a strong political and community leader with whom the electorate could identify.
>
> (DETR, 1998a, paras 5.13–5.14)

The Greater London Authority and the London mayor

In fact, the UK's first directly elected executive mayor proved to be about the most highly visible figure imaginable. He was elected, moreover, not just by 'the people' but as an Independent, standing against all other parties, including the one of which he himself had been a lifelong member, but whose leaders – Blair and Brown in particular – had rejected him as its mayoral candidate. The figure was, of course, Ken Livingstone, Labour leader of the Greater London Council (GLC) when the Thatcher government abolished it in 1986, detested *provocateur* of Blair and New Labour, who in 2000 returned triumphantly to a new City Hall as the capital's first elected mayor.

As already noted, Labour in opposition had pledged to recreate an elected city-wide London authority (see Table 14.1, item 12), but ministers were determined it would not be a GLC Mark II, with the power and tax base to challenge seriously the policies of their own national government. The Greater London Authority (GLA) is therefore a strategic body – regional as much as local government. The 32 London Borough Councils continue to run most day-to-day local government services, while the GLA's chief responsibilities are public transport, policing, fire and emergency planning, employment, and economic development and regeneration.

The GLA comprises two distinct parts. The mayor – since 2008 the Conservative, Boris Johnson – sets an overall vision for London and develops various policy strategies: for example, on spatial and economic development, culture and tourism, transport, and waste. The 25-member assembly acts principally as scrutineer of the mayor's budget and policies. It amounts to a unique organisation and one that, on structural grounds alone, could not serve as a model for mayoral government elsewhere in the country, which required altogether different legislation.

Councils' political management arrangements and elected mayors

The government's position on this more general legislation split into what it insisted should happen and what it merely wanted to happen. The imperative was that at least all major councils in England and Wales should abandon their traditional committee systems – in which no individual elected member, not even the council leader and committee chairs, had delegated decision-making powers – and adopt executive-based systems in which, for the first time, councillors would be *either* executive *or* non-executive members. Within that imperative, councils would have some choice regarding the actual executive model.

But despite the manifesto reference to councils piloting mayoral and possibly other executive arrangements (see Table 14.1, item 4), the Local Government Act 2000 proved narrowly prescriptive, presenting authorities – in another example of ministers' instinctive authoritarianism and predilection for local uniformity – with a choice of just three executive models:

- directly elected mayor *plus* personally appointed cabinet of between two and nine councillors;
- directly elected mayor *plus* council-appointed council manager;
- indirectly- or council-elected leader *plus* appointed cabinet.

All councils, whichever model they adopted, were to establish a structure of 'overview and scrutiny' committees or panels of non-executive members to hold the executive to account. Ideally, this overview and scrutiny function would complement and have parity of esteem with the executive, both having vital roles to play in any optimally functioning executive system. Unsurprisingly, it didn't and still doesn't, which helps to account for both the strong councillor opposition to elected mayors and the lingering antipathy of many non-executive members towards the executive reforms in general.

Directly elected mayors may have appealed to ministers and been interesting in principle to many voters. But within local government, councillors of all parties were critical and concerned: critical of the 'dangerous' introduction into British local government of concentrated power in the hands of a single individual, and concerned that, if they were not among the small minority of executive councillors, they could find themselves largely excluded from the policymaking process. The mayor/council manager model suffered the additional handicap of being based partly on another alien institutional novelty, the council manager – an unelected official.

Following the 2000 Act, all authorities had to consult their electorates and select one of the three executive models. If they did opt for a mayoral model, they would have to get the referendum approval of their voters, five per cent of whom could also trigger a referendum by signing a petition.

The outcome of these not always entirely balanced consultations was that the overwhelming majority of councils opted for the leader/cabinet model, and just 11, following endorsing referendums, chose directly elected mayors: ten mayor/cabinets and one mayor/council manager. The government's palpable disappointment was compounded by the fact that, while the mayoral authorities (12 as of 2008) are all sizeable towns and boroughs, they include no really large city – such as Birmingham, Manchester, Leeds, or Liverpool – that might serve as a national role model.

Of all the LGMA initiatives, elected mayors was the one with which Tony Blair associated himself most personally, and he must share therefore its relative failure. Local government has not been transformed or reinvigorated by the installation of mayors across urban England, while the one mayor he went to extreme lengths to thwart, Ken Livingstone, had, during his two terms of office, the strongest personal mandate of any politician in the country. But if the initiative generally failed, the mayors themselves have mostly been fairly successful and have undoubtedly achieved a far higher local political profile than they would have done as 'merely' council leaders. Significantly, and surprisingly in Britain's party-dominated political culture, half the mayors elected in 2002 were Independents of various kinds who defeated candidates from all the major parties. Most have been re-elected with comfortable majorities, and in some cases their own supporters have won council seats on their metaphorical coattails. Most too have made a local policy impact, launching personal service initiatives in relation to economic development and regeneration, environmental improvement, crime, and anti-social behaviour.

Increasing electoral turnout

A key claim advanced by ministers for executive-based local government, particularly if headed by elected mayors, was that it would increase public interest in local government and thereby raise the worryingly low (30–40 per cent) turnout levels in local elections. There is little evidence of any of this having happened. No mayoral contests, either referendums or the subsequent elections, have attracted higher turnouts than might have been expected in ordinary local elections, and most have been slightly lower. Average turnout in the first 30, mainly postal, referendums was 28.7 per cent (Game, 2003, p. 22). The average for all mayoral elections except those coinciding with the 2005 general election is 28.6 per cent, which shows consistency but is hardly an endorsement of a supposedly more engaging model of local democracy. If local turnouts have increased at all recently, the explanation almost certainly lies in changes in the conduct not of council government but of elections: in particular the introduction in 2000 of postal voting 'on demand' – an immensely controversial measure and no part whatever of the LGMA (see Wilson and Game, 2006, p. 227).

Local finance – sins of omission

In the *Local Government Chronicle* survey cited earlier in relation to CPA, the government's biggest mistake, according to one in every four respondents, was its failure to reform the Council Tax. With another sizeable group nominating tax-capping, about a third of all respondents saw local finance as the area of Labour's greatest culpability or missed opportunity (Game, 2007). The latter description is probably the more correct, for these issues involve more than broken manifesto pledges. In fact, as Table 14.1 shows, there was no mention in Labour's 1997 manifesto of reforming or restructuring Council Tax, any more than there was a commitment absolutely to abolish capping. What the Blair government is accused of here, then, are not so much broken promises as sins of omission.

The UK 'system' of local finance that New Labour inherited is as exceptional in its centralisation as is the population size of its local authorities. Indeed, the two characteristics are closely linked. Just as CPA could only be attempted in a country with the UK's centralist culture and its scale of local government, so too could 'capping', requiring as it does the detailed concern of ministers and their civil servants with the budget-setting of every individual local authority. The degree of the system's centralisation can be summarised in its defining features:

- **Less than five per cent of the tax paid by UK taxpayers goes to local government** – roughly a quarter of the Western Europe average (see Table 14.2).
- **UK local authorities have access to just one local tax** – since 1992 a domestic property tax known as the Council Tax – instead of the range of taxes with differing tax bases (income, profits, goods and services) available to local governments in most developed countries.
- **Council Tax funds under one-sixth of local authorities' total spending** – roughly a third of the Western Europe average (see Table 14.2) – and under a quarter of current/revenue spending. The remainder comes from central government in the form of general and specific grants and the Uniform Business Rate, a commercial and industrial property tax set since 1990 by central government at a standard national rate.
- **The central/local funding balance for current spending has a gearing effect**, so that, for every additional one per cent of spending, a local authority must raise its Council Tax by almost four per cent, there being no other short-term source of additional income.
- **Ministers may 'cap' the proposed budget – and thereby the council tax – of any principal local authority in England and Wales,** meaning that the budget parameters of every authority are effectively determined by central government.

The local accountability in this regime is clearly minimal. Local voters see no direct relationship between any changes in their Council Tax and the services provided by their councils, and many sense that the really meaningful budget decisions are made by ministers in London rather than by their own councillors. If an authority is permitted to raise its Council Tax by more than the inflation rate, then householders on fixed incomes, such as pensioners, are hit particularly hard, prompting almost annual protests and demonstrations.

Reformers had – indeed, still have – various demands, depending on their interests. Those concerned with the health of local democracy and the constitutional relationship between central and local government want the immediate abolition of capping and a major redress of what they see as the damaging central-local imbalance of funding, possibly through returning the setting of business rates to local government. Others focus more on Council Tax and its increasing 'unfairness', as the 1991 property valuations on which it is based become ever further out of line with current house prices.

Capping simply had to go – at least in the 'crude and universal' form deployed by the Major government (see Table 14.1, item 5). For constitutionalists, it had been one of the most outrageous Thatcherite inventions, involving ministers overruling the budgetary decisions of elected councillors and substituting *their* judgements of how much individual councils should be spending and their local voters paying in tax. Introduced in 1984, it was initially used as a selective post-budget device, to force (mainly Labour) councils planning to spend what ministers considered to be 'excessively' to think again. By the 1990s, however, it had become 'universal': capping criteria and ceilings were announced for all councils at the start of their budget-making process, with the inevitable outcome that most simply adopted the government's figures as their own.

The abolition of this 'crude and universal' capping was included in the same 1999 Act that introduced Best Value, but in its place, just as pledged in the manifesto, there would be a return to 1980s-style selective capping of any councils budgeting for 'unacceptable' tax increases – a commitment acted upon in 2004 and subsequent years. In the 1998 White Paper preceding the Act (DETR, 1998b) the government also announced two other policies that would remain in place throughout the Blair premiership, and, more remarkably, would survive intact through the three-year inquiry into the central-local balance of funding that culminated in the 2007 Lyons Report. First, there would be no significant changes in the Council Tax system – not even the addition of new property value bands, as proposed by Lyons – for ministers pronounced it to be operating satisfactorily enough. Secondly, and even more significantly, business rates would not be re-localised, notwithstanding the manifesto's acknowledgement of the 'sound democratic reasons' for doing so (Labour Party, 1997, p. 34) or the fact that it could on its own have redressed the funding imbalance to approximately 50:50.

The fact that all the big financial reforms – abolition of capping, Council Tax, business rate re-localisation, additional local taxes, revaluation – were either ruled out or indefinitely postponed does not mean there were no noteworthy changes at all. There were, some of which were undoubtedly to local authorities' benefit – greater stability of grant distribution and a series of favourable grant settlements, self-financed borrowing for capital invest-ment – but they pale into relative insignificance when compared to what might have been.

The Blair legacy and the Granita inheritance

This chapter has sought to suggest that there are two components of the Blair local government legacy – neither very creditable – that outweigh all others. Both were prominent features of the Thatcher/Major governments' dealings with local government that were persistently attacked by Labour in opposition, but that in most essential respects have been continued. The first has been New Labour's seemingly incurable addiction to central direction, micro-management, target-setting, and ceaseless measuring and monitoring; or, put another way, its reluctance to trust local government with any degree of unsupervised responsibility. The second is the most centralised local finance system in Western Europe, left essentially unreformed after three terms of office. Between them, these two features produce a striking irony.

It is widely accepted in British politics that, following Labour leader John Smith's death in 1994, the two leading rivals to succeed him, Tony Blair and Gordon Brown, met in an Islington restaurant and came to an understand-ing subsequently known as the Granita Pact. Brown would not contest the leadership, while Blair agreed to stand down after a certain period of time and would also allow Brown, as Chancellor of the Exchequer, almost unfet-tered domestic policy powers in a future Labour government. Now consider the legacy. Brown is the micro-manager supreme, a self-confessed 'details man', while Blair, with his reputation for 'sofa government', is instinctively almost the opposite. As for finance, simply nothing of any consequence happened without Brown's say-so. The conclusion has to be that, in this case, Blair's legacy to Brown was substantially of Brown's own making.

15
The Constitutional Revolution of Tony Blair*

James E. Alt

Never one to exaggerate, Tony Blair promised the Labour Party Conference (4 October 1994) that New Labour's proposed Constitutional Reform would be "[t]he biggest programme of change to democracy ever proposed." It was at least a big program, and much of it—though by no means all of it—actually happened; indeed some other changes also took place that were not even contemplated in the plans. How important was it? Some believe the Blair-years changes were part of a "radical discontinuity" as a result of which the "traditional British Constitution ... no longer exists" (King 2007, pp. 2–3). In that discontinuity Britain's membership in the European Union was the source of many sweeping changes, some of which were themselves the foundation of many of Blair's changes.[1] But not everything came from Europe, and other sources, some unplanned, contributed to the degree of change. There can be no doubt that the program as a whole has made a significant difference to how Britain is and will be governed. Whether it has made nearly as much difference to the essential nature of the British constitution is harder to say. Partly that depends on what one believes was previously essential, and opinions differ, as we shall see. However, at this level, there is also a great deal (perhaps a surprising amount) of continuity. Is the essence of the British constitution still that the executive power respects only those rights built up through a process of convention and case law? Largely, the answer is yes.

We begin with a close look at Labour's promised program in 1997. We consider which among the promises they did and did not carry out, thinking always about three possible motives for action or inaction: principles, practical politics, and obligation (as in, the EU made them do it). We also glance at the future under Gordon Brown, and ask especially what the on-hold-but-by-no-means-gone-forever EU constitution might portend for the British constitution. Having described what has happened, we then ask what parts of received constitutional theory are still valid. Is Britain's constitution still unwritten? Is it representative and responsible (Birch, 1964)? Has devolution made Britain federal? Foreshadowing the direction our analysis will take, the

25-word executive summary might be that the more you believe the part of Dicey (1915) that said the essence was the "rule of law" rather than simply "parliamentary sovereignty," the less you need rethink.

Promises, promises

Labour's 1997 general election manifesto proposed a dozen changes of substance, which are listed below.[2] The same list, with some additions noted below in *italics*, appeared in a Labour/Liberal Democrat Joint Consultative Committee document that same March. The list included:

- Scottish Parliament *with legislative and tax-varying powers*
- National Assembly for Wales
- Support for the peace process and devolution in Northern Ireland
- More accountable and democratic local government
- Strategic authority for London
- Regional chambers leading to directly elected regional assemblies in England *if supported by regional referendum*
- Reform of the House of Lords
- Modernization of the House of Commons
- Controls on party funding
- Referendum on a *proportional* voting system for House of Commons
- Freedom of Information Act
- Incorporation of the European Convention on Human Rights into UK law *(this was put first in the joint list)*
- *Independent National Statistical Service*
- *A Civil Service Act*

Some of the electoral and administrative reforms did not happen. One other that did happen, unpromised and unplanned in the list but by no means unimportant, is the creation of a Supreme Court. However, the dominant foci of intended actions include government beyond the center (devolution, regions), parliament and elections, and rights and freedoms.

In many cases Labour did not face a dilemma between its broader ideological commitments and its constitution promises. For example, in many respects devolution and local democracy offer a good fit with the community part of a stake-holding theme, while Lords reform had long been a part of Labour's traditional support of a classless society. However, it is also easy enough to see why this was good electoral politics in 1997. Labour (and the LibDems) faced a Conservative government that was out of touch: for example, new interest groups were replacing parties as foci of political activity. The emphasis on sleaze in the campaign made the promise of a Freedom of Information Act competitively valuable in the short term. The emphasis on devolution can be seen the same way, given the accumulation of

Conservative-sponsored centralization in administration. Civil Service Protection was similar, though it turned out to be largely the opposite of what Labour wanted to do *ex post*. On the other hand, in retrospect (perhaps even in prospect) the promise of proportional representation feels totally tactical: a good method for pulling votes back from the LibDems in a moment when Labour could not yet be confident of the coming landslide.

In any event, after the election they got a lot done, and quickly. Within a year the overarching strategy of constitutional reform, devolution, the European Convention on Human Rights, Freedom of Information, London governance, and Lords Reform respectively were managed by half a dozen new Cabinet committees (comprising a fifth of the total). A significant amount of constitutional legislation passed, almost all in Labour's first term.[3] Devolution was carried into force by several separate Acts, including the Referendums (Scotland and Wales) Act 1997, Government of Wales Act 1998, Scotland Act 1998, Northern Ireland (Elections) Act 1998, Northern Ireland Act 1998, and Regional Development Agencies Act 1998. The Human Rights Act 1998 incorporated the European Convention on Human Rights into UK law. Electoral reforms included the Registration of Political Parties Act 1998 and the European Parliamentary Elections Act 1999 while the Greater London Authority Referendum Act 1998 and Greater London Authority Act 1999 brought in elected mayors and an assembly. There was a House of Lords Act 1999 and a Local Government Act 2000, a Freedom of Information Act 2000 and a Data Protection Act 1998, and controls on party funding: implemented by the Political Parties, Elections and Referendums Act 2000. By any standards it remains a significant, even remarkable legislative achievement.

Government beyond the center

Many of the biggest changes in governance relate to devolved powers for Scotland, Wales, and even Northern Ireland. Scotland now has a parliament, elected by an additional member system, with law-making powers including defined and limited financial powers to vary revenue. This new arrangement extends democratic control over responsibilities exercised administratively by the Scottish Office. The "reserved" responsibilities of the UK parliament in London remain unchanged over UK policy, for example economic, defense, and foreign policy. The National Assembly for Wales now similarly provides some democratic control over existing Welsh Office and other administrative functions, with secondary legislative powers. In Northern Ireland, the Good Friday Agreement smothered the province in government, with power sharing, two axes of consultation within the UK and also Ireland, and complex super-majoritarian requirements for Northern Ireland Assembly actions reducing the probability of sweeping unilateral policies. There have been assembly elections and, very recently, some progress toward ongoing regional government.[4]

However, as far as regional government in England in concerned, the story is quite different. The Regional Development Agencies Act 1998 created eight new RDAs by April 1999, all to be appointed by ministers, and not accountable to "Regional Chambers," voluntary, non-statutory bodies, which if so "designated" by the Secretary of State must be consulted by the RDA in formulating a regional plan. In the summer of 1999 eight Regional Chambers were so designated, one for each RDA. However, this was not intended as, nor has it become, a first stage toward elected regional government. In November 2002 the government introduced the Regional Assemblies (Preparations) Bill. It did not define the powers or functions of regional assemblies but instead enabled regional referendums to be held on whether assemblies were desired. One such referendum was held, in the North-East in 2004, and was a disaster for those hoping to see elected regional governments empowered.[5] Possibly many of those voting judged the regional schemes in place to be expensive and of little practical value, and did not believe that further development would improve them. The issue appears dead for now.

For London, it is quite a different matter. There is now a strategic Greater London Authority with a Mayor of London and an assembly, both directly elected, and staff which has had significant planning (though by no means exclusive or even major revenue-raising) responsibility for London-wide issues since November 1999. As a consequence, some distinctive policies, like the congestion charge for motor vehicles, have come about, and the third elections for London Mayor were held in May 2008.[6] Though empowered to do so, only a dozen other large towns chose to have elected mayors (Norton 2007).

In that sense the overall picture is mixed: the flagship developments are the Scottish Parliament[7] and the Greater London Authority, with the Welsh Assembly less significant, but at the level of local or regional government in England, nothing at all has happened to alter a half-century-long drift toward greater centralization. Despite initial promises, local authority reform has been mostly focused on performance evaluation, but improved performance has not been matched by greater responsibility for implementing local preferences or indeed for locally raising the revenues to implement those preferences. "Community" was a major theme in New Labour politics early on, so this lack of development of local initiative, capacity, and responsibility is all the more remarkable.

Parliamentary reform

The reform of the House of Lords opened to banner headlines and world-wide interest with the House of Lords Act in 1999. Under the Act most of the rights of hereditary peers to sit in the Lords disappeared: 92 remained (selected by vote of the rest) in a transitional second chamber of 700 peers.

The "second stage" of permanent reform was referred to the Wakeham Commission, which reported in January 2000: it recommended a part-elected, mostly appointed House of Lords, with elected members to represent nations and regions and appointed members (including party nominees) to be selected by an independent Appointments Commission. The government created a non-statutory Appointments Commission, but only to select cross-benchers, some 12 appointments a year. A subsequent White Paper, *Completing the Reform*, appeared in November 2001 but was strongly criticized by the Public Administration Committee of the House of Commons three months later.

As a consequence the government announced that the next stage of Lords reform would be considered by a joint parliamentary committee; in December 2002 the joint committee presented a report giving seven options for different mixes of elected and appointed Lords. Both Houses voted on these options in early 2003, but the combination of varying preferences and no mechanism forcing a final choice saw all seven voted down. After the Lords elected a speaker in summer 2006 to resolve another constitutional dilemma (below), in spring 2007 another vote was held. On this occasion the Commons voted for an elected Lords, while the Lords continued (more strongly than before) to vote for an appointed Lords. A minimal consensus is emerging on some points: the need for a statutory appointments commission and 15-year terms are examples. Nevertheless, the reform is far from complete, and appears to be on hold again.

What has signally not emerged is any consensus on what one wants a second chamber for. This is not a surprise, since thinking about bicameralism (like federalism) has only occasionally had a role in British constitutional analysis. Some seek a Lords to add a dimension of expertise, perhaps to strengthen legislative examination, amendment, and scrutiny (that argues for appointments) while others want elected representation, though there is no evident agreement on exactly how the basis of this representation should differ from that of the Commons, though a second chamber that duplicates the first is not of evident value (Tsebelis and Money 1997).

There were also supposed to be some significant empowering reforms to procedures in the Commons, but less came of this. Both the Norton Report and Ann Taylor's Modernisation Committee largely stalled. Robin Cook was defeated over plans to move nominations to Select Committees away from the Whips. Select Committees did receive some wider freedoms and resources, along with the ability to take evidence. Developments of some significance intended to strengthen the legislature included the introduction of two-year planning for the legislative program. Details, some still up in the air, involved changes to sitting hours (morning sittings) and timetabling for bills.

These efforts to provide more pre-legislative scrutiny have to be set against a bigger change, the new procedure allowing the carryover of bills from one session to the next, which, in fact, relatively though minimally empowers the government by eliminating any possibility of backbenchers' using delaying tactics to frustrate legislation. While it is a little too early to say if there will be a significant increase in delegated legislation as well, a similarly government-empowering consequence might attach to the Legislative and Regulatory Reform Act 2006, which expands the role of Ministers' Orders (more or less comparable to the growing use of Executive Orders in the US). Overall, however, none of this has made much difference to the position of the government in parliament: there is certainly no real sign of any drift away from executive dominance.

Freedom of information and human rights

Following passage of the Data Protection Act in 1998, a Freedom of Information Bill was introduced in December 1999 and passed the next year. By international standards it was a somewhat restrictive measure, having a big gray area over what Americans would call the "national security exemption": ministers retain the ability to declare some information out of bounds.[8] The Act came into full force in 2004 and ever since there have been arguments over exemptions (for instance, for parliament, which failed), arguments over the cost to fulfill requests, and arguments over fees. Nevertheless, the Act seems to be working. Whether because of this Act or because the Act itself is just part of its time, the preference given to broad confidentiality in state affairs has declined somewhat over the last 20 years.

The Human Rights Act 1998, implemented by 2000, embodied or incorporated the European Convention on Human Rights (ECHR) into UK law. This had some smaller and larger consequences. For one thing, less was heard about the need for a separate, written British Bill of Rights. For another, 9/11 happened and the (December 2001) Anti-Terrorism Act provided for indefinite detention without trial (subsequently narrowed in some highly acrimonious debates and votes), secrecy, limited rights of appeal and access to lawyers, and a burden of proof placed on the defendant. In sum, what was seen to be a state of emergency justified early withdrawal from Article 5 of the ECHR, and for a time the British constitutional tradition of empowered government appears to have prevailed over any conception of inalienable rights. The controversy re-emerged after the Law Lords found that parts of the 2001 Act contravened the Human Rights Act, and ultimately that Act (and ECHR rights) prevailed over some of the most extreme anti-terrorism measures (Norton 2007, pp. 117–18).

However, it would be somewhat misleading to conclude therefore that Human Rights Act would have only a marginal effect. The HRA creates a *potentially* huge change in the constitutional role of courts, even if so far it is not immediately observable in actuality. The Act imposes on British public authorities the duty to promote policies and practices consistent with EU law. As a constitutional principle, that was older than the Act, having arrived with Britain's membership in the European Union. The HRA establishes that British courts can declare the noncompliance of British with EU law, unless parliament has explicitly derogated from EU law. This implements the classic *Factortame* decision that said, colloquially, "if Parliament had wanted to overturn the 1972 treaty, all they had to do was say so; since they didn't, they didn't mean to." While (still colloquially) the law already is that the European Court of Justice should deal with nations, in fact the European Court of Human Rights will deal with individuals who claim to be deprived of Euro-rights by their nation and not redressed in national courts.[9] In general, things should still be dealt with at lowest level consistent with EU law (that is the principle of subsidiarity) and it is always much better if the legislature fixes the problem, according to Section 3 of the HRA. Without attracting much attention, this protection has led to declarations of noncompliance sustained after court appeals perhaps three or four times per year since its inception, and the needed results have always been implemented by the government.

But, speculatively, this could grow in the future. The ECHR lists a large number of rights. Certainly in the US we are used to asking, what if rights are in conflict? Suppose that there is a conflict between two listed rights and parliament legislates that the British way to fix it is as follows: Would a court (or the European Court of Human Rights on appeal) intervene to impose a European order of precedence among rights? Possibly. Could this create a crisis? It might. It feels like an expansion of court power. But even more, Section 6 of the HRA creates a significant broadening of standing by giving *an individual* remedies against any public authority that had a choice and impaired the individual's Euro-rights. The possibility of appeal to the European Court is always there, if case is alleged to be based on an "erroneous" decision of highest national court. So while the forecast that Britain will become as litigious a society as the US is probably exaggerated, it is not too hard to see that down the road a variety of cause groups could come to use this channel to lobby for political change, and that would certainly be a big change in political life if not necessarily in constitutional theory.

One that didn't really happen: Electoral reform

We saw above that Lords reform was left hanging by uncertainty over what purpose the second chamber should serve. Another early, possibly tactical, commitment was to extend the use of proportional representation from local, regional, and Euro-elections to parliamentary contests, at least to some degree. The government-created Jenkins Commission recommended a system dubbed "AV-plus": the Alternative Vote for single member constituencies, plus a relatively small number of top-up seats to provide a further element of proportionality. Once safe with a large majority, the Blair government dropped the issue, which has been dead for a while. It will be interesting to see if it makes a comeback in Labour's reduced electoral circumstances.

There were also meant to be controls on party funding, at least to the extent of obliging political parties to reveal the source of all donations above a minimum figure. The Nolan Committee on Standards in Public Life, subsequently chaired by Lord Neill, recommended an Electoral Commission as the main watchdog and enforcement body to ensure spending limits are observed in elections and referendums. Nevertheless, curbs on funding led directly to the design of an end-run by replacing donations with loans (on which there was no limit) and not having the loans repaid (who would know about that?). This led not to better practice but instead to a long-running scandal and a lot of embarrassment for the Blair government, and may well have contributed to increasing opposition (especially in the Commons) to various degrees of appointed Lords.

A constitutional affair: The Supreme Court

As King (2007, Chapter 6) elegantly recounts, the road to court reform and the creation of a Supreme Court was not part of the 1990s constitutional rethinking at all. It did, however, follow a period in which (after they were allowed to appear more broadly in the media) judges became more prominent in political debates, and in which judges and elected politicians had frequently been on opposite sides of arguments involving sentencing and other issues of criminal justice. Whatever the precise origins, following the 2001 election, in a reorganization of the central administration, the Home Office lost all constitutional functions to the Lord Chancellor's Department, which in turn took over responsibility for human rights, freedom of information and data protection, the monarchy, church and state, and relations with the Channel Islands and the Isle of Man. In May 2002, the Lord Chancellor's Department was given responsibility for electoral matters: in effect it became the Department of Justice and Constitutional Affairs. December 2002 saw the creation of a new post: Director of Constitutional Affairs. Consolidating control, four other Cabinet Committees on constitutional reform were all chaired by the Lord Chancellor Lord Irvine, who among cabinet ministers probably had the greatest interest in constitutional reform (Norton 2007).

However, in June 2003 Lord Irvine was sacked as Lord Chancellor, following a row over the progress of reforms. The subsequent cabinet reshuffle abolished the Office of Lord Chancellor. Responsibility for constitutional questions was transferred to a new Department of Constitutional Affairs, under a Secretary of State, Lord Falconer. The Department of Constitutional Affairs was to handle civil law reform, the court system including criminal courts, and legal aid, but not criminal law (a Home Office function, though sometimes in conflict with domestic policies like race relations). Amid the confusion it became clear that until the necessary legislation had been passed Lord Falconer would have to retain the title of Lord Chancellor and continue to act as speaker of the House of Lords until one could be elected, in 2006. He thus remained head of the judiciary, sat in parliament as a Law Lord, and remained a senior member of the cabinet until the Department of Constitutional Affairs was absorbed back into Ministry of Justice in May 2007.

This shambles of a process should not mask a significant reform of the court system, one that includes separation of the political and judicial functions of the Lord Chancellor, the creation of important diversity goals for judges accompanied by the recommended appointment of judges by an independent commission (which has been the practice since about 2006), plus, finally, the creation of a separate Supreme Court. What is this Supreme Court? Essentially, it is a unified court of final appeal for the UK. It absorbs the Appellate Committee of the House of Lords (familiarly known as the "Law Lords"), but it also has the devolution functions of the Judicial Committee of the Privy Council. Nevertheless, probably altering the appointments power and the incorporation of diversity goals will be more important down the road than the fact that the court for most purposes just moves across the road to a new building. It could also turn out to be in conflict with future Lords reform, since an elected Lords holds no promise of including enough qualified individuals to fill a Supreme Court, though this, if it comes about, will probably just lead to further appointments reform.

Portents for the future

A review of constitutional change would be incomplete without considering briefly what the future might hold: first, whether the change of prime minister from Tony Blair to Gordon Brown alters the situation significantly and second, what a future European constitution portends (were the Treaty of Lisbon to be adopted and, perhaps, become one). Some thought Brown might do more, citing his "history of interest" in reform and a written constitution; early on he gave a speech indicating his intentions. He promised to upgrade the Ministerial Code and give up some prime ministerial prerogative powers, especially those relating to war and appointing bishops. Parliament itself was promised a role in treaties, the oversight of intelligence and appointments, and recall on demand, while the Attorney General was to be removed from prosecution decisions and the public got the right to demonstrate at Westminster. What Brown did not mention was a constitutional convention (some had hoped to see one write a formal document), a further Bill of Rights in the near future, speedy Lords reform, or the long-promised Civil Service Act.[10] On the last point, it is worth recalling that Brown as chancellor greatly expanded the number and role of (political) special advisors in the Treasury. In any case, the omissions are bigger than the inclusions, suggesting that not too much departure from the recent past should be expected.

The future of a European constitution, embodied in the currently contested Lisbon Treaty, encapsulates the past process of adjustment between Britain and European law. The Treaty would bring big changes in the harmonization of criminal law, and immigration laws and policies, but little in the way of uniform policies for taxation, foreign policy, and defense. Voting weights for countries change, but not the principle of qualified majority voting. The Charter of Fundamental Rights becomes legally binding in principle if not in all details, though the protocol negotiated by the Blair government says the charter cannot be used by a court to declare a provision of British law noncompliant. This desire to state explicitly what you believe you are signing onto is a healthy sign, in contrast to the debates over European membership in the early 1970s which never mentioned the significance of European law for Britain (Nicol 2001). It reflects the legal presumption discussed above, that the government will be assumed to have agreed to something unless it explicitly says it has not. But will this work? Practically, of course, the question is to what extent the charter will add rights to those already respected under (sometimes recent) British law. "Free job placement" might be one. One can imagine the future patchwork of legal challenges that continue the situation of parliamentary adjustment for cases of noncompliance with the ECHR that make it through the legal system. Constitutionally, of course, the executive power still respects only those rights built up through a process of convention and case law. But the sources of that case law and convention have changed.

The nature of the constitution: A new order?

Returning to the quotation opening the chapter, Blair was certainly right to point out the magnitude of the changes proposed. But did it actually create a new order? Devolution, the emphasis on rights, the prominence of the courts, and diminished secrecy feel close to it even if reform of the Lords, the Civil Service, and the electoral system are on the back burner. The distance already traveled is by past British standards remarkable. Breach with past precedent has gradually assumed major proportions, even if no single document or event proclaims the birth of a new constitutional order. It seems fair to say that there is a new context within which British politics is conducted. Pressure for further major changes will likely build in the years ahead, over freedom of information (administrative issues and the privileges of ministers), the voting system for Westminster, the composition and purpose of the second chamber, the powers of the devolved administrations and their relationship with the center, and perhaps more of the prerogative powers wielded by the prime minister.

But how much has actually changed, at a deeper, constitutional level? Flinders (2006) calls it "half-hearted," while Norton (2007) stresses "falling short," "lacking in coherence," and "unintended consequences." Indeed, some of it is incomplete. Indeed, some of its most important features, like incipient federalism and developed bicameralism, lurk in dark corners of British constitutional scholarship. As King (2007) points out, perhaps partly because of the discontinuous, gradual, and often unintended nature of the changes, no one has risen to the challenge of writing the equivalent of the *Federalist Papers* to provide uniformity and coherence, though some, like Hazell (1999) made a serious effort to elevate the debate about rights, at least. But to call the situation unstable because so much remains to be worked out is somehow to miss the point of the first decades after the ratification of the American constitution: even though it was more uniformly authored and adopted (more) all at once, years of decentralized political entrepreneurship revealed what it actually meant. It will be no different in Britain, where gradualism and adaptation have always been seen as important aspects of constitutional evolution.

But again, how big is the discontinuity? Suppose you read a book on the British constitution in the past, what would be the key features of British government that it identifies? First, surely, would be that the constitution was "unwritten." This is still "true," in the sense that there is no single constitutional document with that name, and what is written is now in even more places than before. Probably a higher proportion than before is written somewhere, as reliance on unwritten convention or norms, for example those governing questions of procedure for ministers, has declined. You might well also have found that Britain had no Bill of Rights: it doesn't call it that, but the 1998 Human Rights Act surely codified one, although it did not privilege it in any way.

Had the core principle of parliamentary sovereignty disappeared, as Powell (1991) incautiously claimed? Constraints are indeed imposed by the need to respect other authorities: for example, the EU has qualified majority voting and determines where unanimity offers member states a veto. But this is not new: any pretense to unconstrained national discretion as part of parliamentary sovereignty had been gone for a long time, whether one uses exchange rates or nuclear policy or even just membership in NATO as examples. Parliamentary sovereignty more pertinently meant that no parliament could bind its successor, nor "protect its statutes from repeal," as Hart (1961) put it.

Now, some point to referendums as a "significant feature of the constitutional landscape" (Norton 2007, p. 114), and they have indeed—despite some notable failures—become customary for institutional changes below the national level like devolution and local elections. As part of national politics they still seem heavily tactical, like the original one on the EU itself in 1975. Most that were recently discussed or promised—on the electoral system, joining the euro, plus the controversy over the draft EU constitution—never happened. Would the successive general elections, insisted on by monarchs before assisting Lords reform a century ago, today be replaced by insistence on a prior referendum? Quite possibly, though, as then it might depend on political preferences over what appeared to be the likely outcome.

McLean and McMillan (2007) document the rise of "entrenched" statutes, those which set the rules for recognizing valid statutes or involve treaty or referendum-based commitments. Theirs is a very good way to see how much and how little has changed: each twentieth-century step in the reduction of power of the Lords followed the procedures set out in the previous step (though it took some extraordinary threats to take the first step in 1911). In much the same way, nothing short of derogating from the European Union Treaty can allow the British government to escape from the duty to fix non-compliant statutes, but withdrawal does not require extraordinary steps, and in fact the draft European constitution created a procedure for doing so. Of course withdrawal, like violating a treaty or reneging on a referendum-based commitment, is very costly, which consequentially makes it less likely to happen. However, there is an essential continuity here: parliamentary sovereignty, whatever it was, was always limited in this way.

The way it was limited emphasizes the continuing significance of "the other side of Dicey": his emphasis on the rule of law interpenetrating parliamentary sovereignty as a principle. Paraphrasing him for brevity, all government actions must be authorized by law, no one can be lawfully interfered with by the authorities except for breaches of law, but no one is above the law and everyone is subject to the ordinary laws of the land. There is no need for a bill of rights; government decisions are made according to written law and rules and sanctions cannot be *ex post facto*; and rules are applied as much as possible consistently to all. Courts provide a consistent process and provide reasons based upon the law for their decisions. To whatever degree this actually held then or holds now, the principle in Britain was that for the rule of law to be supreme, parliament must legislate or would have already done so. Any lack of clarity or inconsistency means either that implicitly parliament has consented or that there is a need for parliamentary action. This is not a consequence of European law or recent reform.

Moreover, British government is also still parliamentary, that is, it has no separate executive. The center still has strong party government but parties were hardly legally recognized until very recently. It is still "representative": there have been some big changes in mechanisms, like different electoral systems below the national level. However, the central assumption of *ex post* accountability still holds, and the exact form of the electoral system was never a point of constitutional law. It is also still "responsible": individually there is less force to resign than before, and the collective practice is also shifting, as witness cabinet working in committees, agreements to differ, deferrals to referenda, and the constant battle between news sourcing and leaks. What feels like a bigger source of change is the drift away from secrecy toward revelation. The Official Secrets Act set the tone for politics in the 1980s, and while it is still there, the tone today is set by the Freedom of Information Act.

Indeed, you would have read also that parliament was "bicameral with a dominant House" and this will almost certainly remain true, while we wait and see what direction the far-from-complete reform of the House of Lords takes. Less clear (and probably less stable) is the future of the "unitary" nature of the constitution. This is weakening, but the UK is not nearly federal yet in spite of some devolution. Ten per cent of the population lives in regions that have some special powers, not altogether unlike Catalonia in Spain. But devolution plus diminished roles for the Secretaries of State for Scotland and Wales has been accompanied by the disastrous failure of regional assemblies and the complete absence of any sign that local authorities might gain the power to finance some degree of desired and/or desirable diversity. This leaves dangling that part of the stake-holding program that swapped obligations to contribute for opportunities to participate meaningfully, and leaves Britain one of the most centralized countries of its size.

Summing up, if the rule of law was the essence of the constitution a century ago, it still is, even if the source of some of the law has changed. If it constrained what a parliament could validly do then, it does so now. One big change is that the rule of law now encompasses a set of explicitly listed rights. Others include the extent of devolved powers and the death (more or less) of the hereditary principle in the Lords. Both of those remind us that sweeping changes in governance accompany more partial and uneven constitutional changes, and indeed that the process of change is ongoing.

Notes

* Thanks to Iain McLean for helpful comments and suggestions.

1. For a detailed review of constitution evolution over the last century, see Bogdanor (2003).
2. Norton (2007) gives an excellent review of the importance of the organization Charter '88 in expending support for constitutional reform and its appeal to Labour leader John Smith and others (probably more than to Tony Blair himself) as sources of these reforms. See also Blackburn and Plant (1997).
3. One can refer to a variety of publications of the Constitution Unit and Norton, 2007 for more comprehensive treatments and chronologies of these events.
4. The assembly created by the Northern Ireland Act 1998 began work in December 1999, but was suspended briefly the next year and again from October 2002 to May 2007. Under the Act various measures must have "cross-community support," which can be required for any measure by petition of 30 members.
5. On the question of whether there should be an elected assembly for the North East region, nearly 78 per cent of those voting voted no, on a healthy turnout of 47 per cent.

6. In the 2008 mayoral election, the Conservative candidate, Boris Johnson, defeated the two-term Labour incumbent Ken Livingstone.

7. In creating a Scottish parliament, Labour opened the door to future constitutional tinkering, as Scottish Labour leader Wendy Alexander conceded after losing seats in the May 2008 election. To reduce the number and power of Scottish MPs at Westminster, some English Conservatives now argue outright for Scottish independence. While independence enjoys only minority support in Scotland, Labour has joined the other non-nationalist parties in creating a new Constitutional Commission to advocate more powers for the Scottish parliament. Electoral politics aside, the process has initiated a whole range of constitutional questions unlikely to subside.

8. The weaker bill reflected the preferences of the minister bringing it about, Lord Irvine: Norton (2007) explains how this came about.

9. Because the EU as a whole has not joined the Convention on Human Rights, EU institutions technically are not yet bound by it. If the Treaty of Lisbon is ratified, the EU is expected to sign the convention. Then the Court of Justice will be bound by the Court of Human Rights and subject to its human rights law, ending a gray area around possibly inconsistent case law between the two courts.

10. Most of the list Brown mentioned eventually appeared in the March 2008 White Paper on "The Governance of Britain – Constitutional Renewal" (Ministry of Justice, 2008, Cm. 7342). Though less ambitious than the 2007 Green Paper (Ministry of Justice, 2007, Cm. 7170) it followed, the White Paper did promise to put the civil service on a statutory basis, enshrining the principle of merit hiring.

Part IV   Foreign Affairs

16
What Difference Did He Make? Tony Blair and British Foreign Policy from 1997–2007

Stephen Benedict Dyson

Several years after the Iraq intervention, the *Guardian* columnist Peter Preston conjured from his imagination a hypothetical world where Tony Blair had not joined George Bush:

> It is March 2003 and the US has 100,000-plus crack troops poised in the zone. Australians, Poles and numerous small fry are there or thereabouts. But France and Russia and—now—Britain are staying out. The weapons inspectors need more time, they say. Resolution 1441 doesn't sanction invasion. (Lord Goldsmith is quite clear on that.) So what happens next? What was always going to happen. The Americans, too committed to permit delay, blast in anyway. Saddam folds. That toppling statue stars on TV screens around the world. "Mission accomplished!" cries George Bush. Freedom lives! And, at a subsequent press conference, he voices his sorrow over "what must be the end of our special relationship. Since Winston Churchill, Great Britain has been our staunchest friend. We gave it our bomb, our help in the Falklands. We came to its rescue in 1944. But now, in our own war after 9/11, that friend has turned its back. All Americans will be specially saddened and shocked."

There follows an unfortunate tale of cancelled trade and Iraq reconstruction contracts, a decline in the numbers of US tourists visiting the UK, and the ending of the visa waiver program. Nicholas Sarkozy, the new French president, is able to flamboyantly proclaim "Moi! Je suis le special relation maintenant." In this hypothetical world, Blair is hounded from office a broken figure, harangued for having failed to give the US the wise counsel it required at its time of greatest need, with every insurgent attack on US troops in Iraq evidence of the folly of leaving the US alone to manage the postwar (Preston, 2007).

It is a fascinating speculation, and raises the perennial issue of how precisely individual choice shapes world historical events. I argue that Blair was in fact never likely to keep Britain out of Iraq, because his personality and

235

worldview—vividly demonstrated in the pre-Iraq wars he fought—disposed him to become involved.[1] Others who could have occupied the post of prime minister, however, might well have made a different choice. Indeed, the argument of this chapter is that Blair has a distinctive worldview and leadership style, and that this shaped British foreign policy from 1997–2007, in particular in the three crises of Kosovo, 9/11, and Iraq. It follows, then, that the major foreign policy issues of that decade would have been dealt with differently had another person been prime minister.

As with Preston's scenario above, we cannot know for sure how history would have turned out if someone else had been in office and had faced those foreign policy challenges, but we can speculate in a more or less disciplined fashion by asking the counterfactual question: what would another prime minister, faced with these decisions, have chosen to do? There are two ways to ensure this is done in a reasonable fashion: to compare the choices made by different individuals faced with similar situations, and to consider the policies advocated by other individuals who could plausibly have been prime minister in Blair's place as the key March 2003 decisions were made. Employing the first strategy, I compare John Major's Balkan strategy with that of Blair in Kosovo, and Harold Wilson's Vietnam choice with Blair's Iraq decisions. Both Major in the Balkans and Wilson in Vietnam faced similar situations to those that confronted Blair in Kosovo and Iraq but made very different choices, and this provides some evidence for the influence of Blair as an individual.

Employing the second strategy, I consider the views of prominent individuals from Blair's cabinet who could plausibly have been prime minister in his place as the choices on Iraq were made, in particular the views of Foreign Secretary Jack Straw and Chancellor (now prime minister) Gordon Brown. I suggest it is unlikely that either individual, had they been prime minister, would have made the same decisions as Blair, although we cannot, of course, know for certain. The overall goal is to isolate those decisions made by Blair that were shaped by his distinctive individual characteristics in order to consider "what difference he made". I conclude that the difference was rather large in Kosovo and Iraq, while after 9/11 Blair's worldview shaped the detail, but probably not the broad outline, of the British response. The first step is to isolate the Blair worldview and approach to international politics.

The "Blair style"[2]

Many explanations of international affairs assume away the individual idiosyncrasies of the political leader. The situations they face, it is often argued, compel policy choices based upon *raison d'etat* that any rational person in the job of leader would make. Know the power of the state relative to others, the threats it faces, and the alliances it has made, and one can know the policy of the state regardless of the name of its leader (Waltz, 1979). Others—and here I tip my hand as to the perspective adopted in this chapter—argue that individual personality, experiences, and beliefs can often exercise a decisive influence on the direction of a state's foreign policy. Overall goals, and the means employed to achieve them, are not deducible from objective circumstances but are subjectively constructed by the key individuals making state policy. Therefore, political leaders are not interchangeable.

If, as I contend, individuals matter in world politics, it is a worthwhile investment of our energies to develop some metrics by which to understand them. The subfield of political psychology has as one of its primary aims the application of insights concerning human cognition and personality to the special case of political leaders. This, of course, presents some challenges, but nonetheless substantial progress has been made in understanding the way in which the worldview and leadership style of political leaders impact upon their choices (Schafer, 2000).

Previous research on Blair's personality, conducted by systematic content analysis of his House of Commons performances for patterns of speech associated with specific beliefs and personality traits, has found that he is distinctive in several major ways, two of which bear directly on his foreign policy choices. Firstly, he has a very high belief in his ability to control events, a perception of personal and national efficacy that has been linked to the pursuit of proactive and ambitious international policies. Secondly, he has a low conceptual complexity, an element of cognitive style linked to strongly held schema that are essentially dichotomous and unequivocal, and that has been observed in those with Manichean and absolutist foreign policy worldviews (Dyson, 2006).

Indeed, Blair has been judged by almost all who have worked with and studied him to be an unusually proactive prime minister, the author of a highly interventionist foreign policy doctrine, and a leader much more comfortable leaning forward into rather than reacting to events. Sir Jeremy Greenstock, the former UK ambassador to the United Nations, felt he had a "sense of mission in his underlying psychology" (Author Interview), while Chris Smith, a cabinet colleague who supported Blair's earlier interventions but broke with him over Iraq, says that the prime minister's approach could be "characterized as a duty to intervene, even when the direct interests of the UK are not being threatened" (Author Interview). John Kampfner (2003, p. 385), a chronicler of Blair's deeds, argues that he "acquired a passion for military intervention without precedent in modern British political history and without parallel internationally."

Blair's sense of mission, colleagues and observers judge, was compounded by a highly personalistic style, in which Blair regarded the prospects for progress on an issue as a function of his personal involvement in it. "Tony is the great persuader," a close aide comments. "He thinks he can convert people even when it might seem as if he doesn't have a cat in hell's chance of succeeding. Call him naïve, call it what you will, but he never gives up. He would say things like 'I can get Jacques (Chirac) to do this' or 'leave Putin to me'". Another observer suggests that "there is not a single problem that Blair thinks he cannot solve with his own personal engagement—it could be Russia, it could be Africa." A subjective belief that one is uncommonly effective is not, however, necessarily the same as the objective reality: "the trouble is, the world is a little more complicated than that" (Kampfner, 2003, p. 127–8). Blair has, his biographer Anthony Seldon (2005, p. 698–9) judges, an "almost limitless belief in his ability to persuade," but these are powers he has tended to "exaggerate greatly." This was true of Blair throughout his time in office: in his final year in power, faced with the Lebanon–Hezbollah war, and one might think chastened by Iraq, his instincts were again toward personal involvement: "Every time he was in the car between meetings," an aide recalled, "it was Lebanon, Lebanon, Lebanon. He wanted to talk to this person, talk to that person. 'Get me Merkel, I'll phone Bush, get me Chirac'" (Seldon, 2007, p. 475).

The second key element of the Blair style, buttressing and shaping his interventionism, is the certainty of his judgments and the explicit and overt moralism he brought to his policy choices and justifications. A Downing Street insider says the key to Blair's worldview is "that the PM is a conviction politician" rather than a pragmatist. Seldon (2005, p. 599) agrees: "his very certainty often militated against him seeing other truths and perspectives." Seldon continues: "He conceptualizes the world as a struggle between good and evil in which his particular vocation is to advance the former" (Seldon, 2005, p. 700). Lord Guthrie, who served as something of a military mentor to the inexperienced prime minister during his early years in office, says that Blair "believed in making the world a better place. He thinks if good men do nothing, bad men prevail. He is driven by that" (Author Interview).

Blair therefore exhibits a comfort with clear-cut division of the world into unambiguous categories, and this was perhaps important in his relationship with the similarly uncomplicated American president. "No European leader of his generation," Alex Danchev notes, "speaks so unblushingly of good and evil" (Danchev, 2007a, p. 48). David Blunkett, a prominent Blair ally for much of the era in question, judges that the prime minister was concerned above all "doing the right thing and doing good, and not tolerating evil" (Author Interview). The former Labour Home Secretary Roy Jenkins gave one of the more definitive assessments of Blair's tendencies toward clear-cut judgments: "My view is that the prime minister, far from lacking conviction, has almost too much, particularly when dealing with the world beyond Britain. He is a little too Manichean for my perhaps now jaded taste, seeing matters in stark terms of good and evil, black and white" (Naughtie, 2004, p. 135).

These key aspects of Blair's worldview are, I suggest, central to his foreign policy choices. Individuals less sure of their command over events, and with a more nuanced cognitive style, would not have made the same choices had they been prime minister. Can we provide some evidence to this effect? Lacking a TARDIS (the fictional time machine from *Dr. Who*) with which to rerun history with someone else in charge, we find ourselves here drawn toward the realm of counterfactual thought experiments.

What difference did Blair make?
Counterfactuals and comparisons

Analyses that focus upon the influence of a single individual upon macro-level events inevitably implicate a series of logical and methodological questions. Can individual choices, even in principle, shape major historical events? Did the specific circumstances of the time permit individual latitude in response? Would other individuals who could plausibly have been in a position to make the decisions have acted in the same way?

Such considerations are inevitably counterfactual: as noted above we cannot rerun the events of 1997–2007 with a different prime minister in post and see what changes, and so must engage in a thought experiment. Strenuous efforts should be made to minimize the fantastical nature of these experiments—thought experiments of the "if Napoleon had a stealth bomber" type involve such a series of implausible leaps as to render the analysis silly. To be useful, the thought experiment must be logically possible, and involve a minimal rewrite of actual history (see Tetlock and Belkin, 1996, p. 1–38). The broader, macro-level environment should not be changed, so a counterfactual along the lines of "would Britain have invaded Iraq if it, and not the US, was the superpower?" is also none too useful. The essence of the individual-level counterfactual is expressed in Fred Greenstein's question: Would a different individual, faced with the same circumstances, have acted differently? (Greenstein, 1998) If, after careful consideration, we cannot make a reasonable case to that effect, then we have to conclude that circumstances, and not individuals, were the drivers of policy. If circumstances drive policy, then giving attention to issues of individual personality and style is more of an interesting parlor game than serious social science—we would be better served by adopting the structural realist viewpoint that individual leaders are essentially interchangeable. On the other hand, major foreign policy events such as crises and war, with their chaotic, non-routine, and highly contingent nature, often do seem to turn on a few key decisions made by prominent individuals.

Considering, then, three of the major foreign policy events during Blair's tenure—Kosovo, the response to 9/11, and the choice in Iraq—what would have been different had another individual, with a different style and worldview, been in power?

One way to make counterfactuals as reasonable as possible is to consider an issue with a policy history, where other individuals made decisions about essentially similar actors and under comparable circumstances. The example par excellence of this is the Cold War, wherein eight US presidents elaborated a strategy for dealing with an ideologically hostile Soviet Union in a bipolar international system. Given the similarity in circumstances, differences in that strategy are then plausible candidates, at least in part, for individual-level explanation (Gaddis, 2005).

Turning to the Blair decade, this is a line of reasoning at least partly possible in the case of Kosovo. The Kosovo conflict was one of a sequence of clashes between the constituent entities of the former Yugoslavia, and several of these clashes took place on the watch of Blair's predecessor John Major. There is agreement that the advent of the Blair premiership brought about a profound British strategy change in the Balkans. Moreover, this change in policy was in a direction consistent with Blair's style: proactive and moralistic. Lord Guthrie, who served as the senior UK military officer under both Major and Blair and so is uniquely qualified to speak to this comparison, suggests that Blair took a "much more forward leaning role" than his predecessor, and was, even prior to the Kosovo conflagration, "prepared and anxious that we should send our special forces out and capture war criminals who were actually being a malign influence on society." Blair, Guthrie confirms, was "prepared to go in unilaterally," and was frustrated both by the caution of the Americans and the torturous processes inherent in NATO decision making. He took bold decisions, and took them quickly, and so "as far as I'm concerned, he was certainly a much easier prime minister to work for than his predecessor John Major" (Author Interview).

This change was also noticed by the Americans. "The British no longer had to be dragged along to confront the Serbs" once Blair was in charge, said a senior State Department official. "We saw a completely different attitude." Indeed, a close advisor to Blair confirms that the new prime minister wanted to follow a very different strategy than his predecessor. "Frankly, we were appalled at the cowardice of the Tories" (Seldon, 2005, p. 393). This advisor also locates the source of the different policies followed by the new Labour government in Blair as an individual: "It was a moral thing with Tony. He believed very strongly that Britain should be a force for good in the world" (Coughlin, 2006, p. 76).

In the Kosovo case, counterfactual speculation can be disciplined by a systematic comparison of Blair's choices in relation to those of his predecessor who, while not facing exactly the same circumstances, did make policy choices on precursor conflicts involving many of the same actors. There is agreement that not only did Blair follow a very different strategy than John Major, but also that the difference was in the direction we would expect given Blair's worldview and leadership style: more proactive and interventionist, and leavened with a strong dose of moralism.

What about 9/11? Would another prime minister have acted differently in the aftermath of the attacks on the US? The unprecedented nature of the attacks makes it particularly difficult to find appropriate historical parallels with which to discipline a counterfactual. Within the US the comparison is often made to Pearl Harbor, but here the circumstances of the British, hanging on grimly for national survival against Hitler's Germany, were very different, somewhat spoiling the comparison.

Perhaps, however, we do not need a close historical referent. An oft-quoted aphorism of individual-level analysis is that "if the room is on fire, everyone will make for the exit." This is to say that on many occasions circumstances will be so overwhelming as to preclude individual variation in response. On September 11th, civilian citizens of the hegemonic power in the international system were killed en masse by a terrorist group with a transnational capacity and agenda, and an identifiable "home base" of operations in Afghanistan. The policy response of the US, in invading Afghanistan and removing the Taliban, was easily deducible from the circumstances. Indeed, the widespread sympathy and support for the US in the aftermath of the attacks is testimony to the clarity of imperatives inherent in the circumstances. This is to say that it is possible to explain Blair's solidarity with the US and his pledge of support without reference to his political psychology—any mainstream individual in the post of British prime minister would almost certainly have responded in basically this way.

However, once we move beyond the broad outline of policy and look at the detail, individual-level influences become more apparent. Blair's response to 9/11 did not stop with the expression of solidarity, but encompassed an incredibly ambitious agenda to eradicate the causes of terrorism—poverty, oppression, and squalor—worldwide. This was seen among colleagues as Blair promising to single-handedly "solve all of the world's problems," an impression enhanced when he launched himself on a diplomatic whirlwind tour in order to rally support for the US. Moreover, Blair accepted the Bush administration's framing of the situation as a "war on terror" to be fought primarily through military means and on a global scale. Not everyone in the UK government felt the same way. Clare Short noted that "all of us were horrified by the events of September 11 but most decent people are very worried by the bellicose statements from Bush and fearful of the US lashing out and killing lots of innocent Afghans and making things worse" (Short, 2004, p. 109). While the broad structure of Blair's response seems to be a "room on fire" instance of situation overwhelming individual, the detail of Blair's response, in terms of its ambition and the acceptance of the Bush administration's stark framing of events, does seem more individually determined.

It is, however, in Iraq that we find the most interesting fodder for a counterfactual. Was Iraq a "room on fire" case? Certainly, aspects of the circumstances surrounding the conflict would have pushed any British prime minister in a westward-leaning direction. The determination of the Bush administration to go to war did force a difficult choice upon the UK leadership—with little chance of persuading the Americans not to attack, the choice was to go along or risk the alliance—a dilemma that drives Preston's counterfactual at the beginning of this essay. Staying out would have been far from the cost-free paradise critics of the decision often seem to have in mind. However, the aspects of the environment pushing the UK toward war were balanced by the restraints on commitment—the hostile domestic political environment and the absence of international support. Other European states with security relationships with the US, most prominently France and Germany, took note of these difficulties and refused to become involved. There does seem to have been some latitude for a different response to that chosen by Blair. Would others have chosen a different course, allowing us to attribute Britain's Iraq choices, at least in part, to the style and worldview of the prime minister? We have a number of ways to discipline such an analysis.

Firstly, we have available the example of a different individual faced with a comparable situation, yet making a very different choice. Blair's Iraq decisions, and the increasingly eerie parallels between that conflict and Vietnam, have revived interest in Harold Wilson's relationship with Lyndon Johnson. LBJ applied much more direct pressure upon Wilson for a UK troop contribution than Bush's quite gentle advances toward Blair, and yet Wilson stood firm in refusing. Wilson's stance cannot necessarily be attributed to prescience concerning the wisdom of the war and had rather a lot to do with his unwillingness to take domestic political risks, given the war's unpopularity, but nonetheless the two situations were broadly comparable and the choice made by the prime ministers was very different (Dyson, 2007). Why, when faced with a senior ally requesting a force contribution for an unpopular war, did Wilson refuse and Blair enthusiastically agree? It seems reasonable to suggest that Blair's proactive foreign policy, sense of personal efficacy, and clear-cut framing of issues are at least part of the explanation. Had the prime ministers been switched around, would Harold Wilson have kept Britain out of Iraq, and Tony Blair gone into Vietnam? It is an interesting premise, and I have argued that the answer may well be 'yes' in both cases.

However, perhaps we are being unnecessarily ambitious in reaching back into history for clues as to how a different prime minister would have dealt with Iraq. There is, after all, substantial evidence that members of Blair's cabinet at the time were uneasy with his policy choices. The distress of Robin Cook and Clare Short has been well documented, and it is safe to assume that neither would have made the choices on Iraq that Blair did. It is also, however, true to say that such an extensive rewriting of history would be necessary to place either figure in the prime minister's chair that the counterfactual is of limited utility.

A more plausible premise, and hence more useful counterfactual, concerns Jack Straw, who as Blair's foreign secretary cannot be considered a marginal figure. Would Straw have made the same decisions had he been left alone to direct Britain's foreign policy? He did remain in post and publicly argue for the policy, so was bound to the decisions of the time, but there is a fair amount of evidence that he harbored, at the very least, some doubt about the wisdom of going to war. The infamous "Downing Street memo" has Straw, in early 2002, as very cautious about the enterprise even in principle. The case against Saddam was "thin." He was "not threatening his neighbors, and his WMD (weapons of mass destruction) capability was less than that of Libya, North Korea or Iran." As 2002 progressed, the foreign secretary made public statements that seemed to be designed to slow down the progress toward war, arguing at the time of Hussein's agreement to readmit UN weapons inspectors, that the chance of conflict had now receded to "60-40 against" (Baldwin and Charter, 2003, p. 14; Rycroft, 2005).

Most interestingly in the present context, Straw outlined a plausible alternative policy for the UK as war rapidly approached in March 2003. Noting that a second UN resolution was now unobtainable and the British public and parliamentary Labour Party were far from persuaded as to the merits of war, Straw wrote a carefully reasoned memo to Blair. Perhaps, the foreign secretary suggested, Britain could continue to offer the US the maximum in terms of diplomatic support, but UK troops should not engage in combat operations, and enter Iraq only as peacekeepers, with a UN mandate, after the conclusion of the fighting (Kampfner, 2004, p. 303).

This is a fascinating point of choice. Straw was effectively recommending to Blair that he follow Harold Wilson's Vietnam strategy. There was no need to break from the Americans in public, but there were options short of fighting alongside them as well. The prime minister, of course, rejected this option as soon as he was presented with it, and called Straw in for a personal conference to stress that he either got on board or left the government. Straw was far from prepared to fall on his sword and had been careful merely to raise, rather than advocate, the "Wilson Option." Straw therefore aped Colin Powell's performance in the US administration and loyally fell into line. It had not, however, gone unnoticed that the foreign secretary, while perfectly loyal in public, had not been an enthusiastic supporter of the Iraq policy, and he was replaced by Margaret Beckett after the 2005 election with the provenance of the decision, so the rumors go, in Washington as much as London. The combination of the Wilson precedent and Straw's contemporary elucidation of it do indicate that other options were available to Blair and, given that the prime minister chose the most clear-cut and proactive of the available options, lend additional support to contentions about the causal importance of Blair's personality to the decisions.

Finally, but perhaps most interestingly as a spur for a counterfactual thought experiment, are the views of Gordon Brown. His is an especially important case as the rewriting of history necessary to make him prime minister is not too severe—he was for several years the senior of the Blair-Brown partnership and assumed to be John Smith's heir apparent. Further, of course, Brown's views are especially relevant given that he has now succeeded Blair. Had Brown been prime minister in early 2003, would the UK have gone to war in Iraq?

Brown played quite a careful game in public over Iraq, avoiding saying anything at all on the matter until the point when Blair, facing an enormously difficult parliamentary vote on the war in mid-March 2003, required of him a commitment to the policy. What of his private views?

Clare Short, who met with Brown in private throughout this period, told me that, perhaps surprisingly, Brown was not preoccupied with the Iraq question, he was instead consumed with an uptick in the constant Blairite–Brownite guerilla warfare:

> [T]here have been different periods in the relationship between Tony and Gordon—and this was a period of estrangement, when Gordon was being pushed away—and, everyone knew I was unhappy because I was also giving occasional interviews to the media, and this was all part of my supposed strategy of holding onto Tony's ankles, which spectacularly didn't work, but that's what I thought I was doing. So Gordon would repeatedly say, we'll have coffee and so on. And he didn't say a lot about Iraq, he was watching closely, was not strongly critical of the policy, but was very agitated about other policies that were coming forward at the time such as top-up fees for students and foundation hospitals. Those were the things he kept mentioning to me. And then he kept saying "I won't accept another job." It was in the press then that they were going to push Gordon out of the treasury and offer him foreign secretary, and he was saying "no, no, no, if that happens, I will go." So, he was very much pushed out, but in all the private meetings I had with him, I was obsessed with Iraq and I was blathering on about it, and he was blathering on about foundation hospitals and top-up fees. And not expressing ... he wasn't saying he was solidly for, he was kind of watching it, and, but not expressing ... and this was in private forum with me, when he was saying things that were sort of indiscreet if you like. He wasn't saying this was completely wrong.

(Author Interview)

David Blunkett, a close Blair ally, agrees that the chancellor was careful on the Iraq issue. "I never heard Gordon resile from the decisions that were being taken ... but it was rather late in the day when he joined in publicly" (Author Interview). It seems that Brown was very cautious, even in private, in expressing either support or opposition to Blair's policy. This was probably a logical strategy—if the Iraq gamble worked, Blair would have been strengthened and Brown could not afford to have opposed him; if it failed, a damaged Blair would eventually make way and Brown would have gained nothing through his disloyalty.

We are forced, then, to speculate about Brown's likely choice had he been prime minister. Brown is at least as much of an Atlanticist as Blair, and perhaps instinctively more cautious of Europe. It is hard to imagine him turning his back on the US and joining Chirac and Schroeder in open opposition to Bush. By the same token, there is little evidence in Brown's worldview and style of either the sense of mission and feeling of control Blair has in regard to international affairs, nor of the black-and-white framing of events to which Blair is drawn. Clare Short suggests this line of analysis is about right: "Gordon would have looked to nuance it more," she judges. "He's much more a details man, he would looked for cleverer ways through. Whether he would've found them is another question. But ... he wouldn't have been as reckless as Blair was" (Author Interview). Chris Smith, another former cabinet minister who worked with both Brown and Blair, says that Brown "probably wouldn't have done it," and that Brown would have fashioned a relationship with the Bush administration that was "cordial, but a little more candid." However, Smith is quick to add, this is "pure speculation" (Author Interview).

Conclusion

What difference did Blair make to British foreign policy from 1997–2007? The question requires us to take full account of those factors of personality and worldview that condition the choices made by political leaders. Blair, with a proactive, self-confident approach to international issues overlaid with a stark, black-and-white cognitive style, fashioned policy responses to the major crises he faced that accorded with his individual characteristics. In Kosovo, 9/11, and Iraq, Blair was consistently in the forward end of the troop, arguing in favor of the more ambitious of the available policy options. His view of these events tended to revolve around a demonized enemy—Milosevic, Al Qaeda, Saddam Hussein—and a virtuous US-UK alliance with pure motives and right on their side.

Certainly in Kosovo and Iraq, the cumulative weight of the counterfactual thought experiments—disciplined by consideration of the choices made by different individuals in similar situations and the expressed attitudes of contemporaneous figures who might instead have been prime minister— point strongly toward a substantial causal relationship between Blair as an individual and British foreign policy. Would John Major have been as aggressive in Kosovo? Would Harold Wilson, or Jack Straw, or Gordon Brown, have followed a similar course to Blair over Iraq? If, as an observer of political affairs, one thinks not, then the case for a political psychology approach to individuals and foreign policy has been made.

The need for caution is also illustrated by the Blair case. We can say the evidence is highly suggestive that much would have been different in Kosovo and Iraq without Blair, but cannot know for sure and so this will not satisfy those who believe individual personality to be either irrelevant or epiphenomenal. Indeed, I have argued that Blair's response to 9/11 was, at least in its broad outlines, situationally determined and that his personality was responsible only for the largely rhetorical (as it turns out) features of a pledge to address the root causes of terrorism and for a lot of talk about good and evil. When making the case for the importance of individuals, one must not get carried away and forget the environmental imperatives that would bear on anyone in a given situation.

Taken as a whole, Blair's choices over his decade in office demonstrate and illuminate the ways in which strong-willed individuals, holding distinctive beliefs concerning international affairs, can shape the direction of events. Britain, it seems fair to conclude, would have been a different actor on the international stage had someone else been prime minister for those ten years.

Author interviews (by telephone)

David Blunkett, MP (1 May 2007)
Sir Jeremy Greenstock (6 June 2007)
Lord (General) Charles Guthrie (20 June 2007)
Clare Short, MP (30 April 2007)
Lord (Chris) Smith (18 June 2007)

Notes

1. As a commentator responded online to Preston's article, the answer to "let's just suppose" Britain had stayed out is "then Blair wouldn't be Blair." http://politics. guardian.co.uk/iraq/comment/0,,2073939,00.html. Accessed 7/19/2007.
2. The portrait of Blair in the next few pages is a much shortened and adapted version of that painted in my book *The Blair Identity: Leadership and Foreign Policy*, forthcoming with Manchester University Press.

17
The Mistake Heard Round the World: Iraq and the Blair Legacy

David Coates and Joel Krieger

It was Enoch Powell who once said that all political careers end in failure. Tony Blair's would certainly appear to have done so. Once hailed as the outstanding Labour leader of his generation, Blair is now widely reviled in the very circles that once treated him as their golden boy; and that change of fortune and standing is normally linked to one thing more than any other— his decision in March 2003 to be George Bush's leading ally in the invasion of Iraq. Both at the time and subsequently, that decision was widely questioned; and because it was, it now needs to be both fully understood and clearly explained.

The decision to join the US in a "pre-emptive" invasion against the regime of Saddam Hussein was certainly questioned at the time, not least because the requirement for a pre-emptive war, an imminent threat, was absent. Behind the scenes in Westminster, cabinet colleagues were uneasy, with many urging caution (Cook, 2004, pp. 285–325). On the floor of the House of Commons, Blair twice faced large-scale rebellions on the issue by backbench Labour MPs. On the streets of London, and in other capital cities around the world, millions protested the folly, even the immorality, of the move on the eve of the invasion itself. In the chancelleries of Europe, powerful voices spoke in favor of delay; and at the UN, the second resolution that Blair sought so diligently as cover for the invasion simply failed to materialize. In the wake of the invasion, the doubts, if anything, intensified. The intelligence on which the war preparations had ostensibly been based turned out to be defective. There were no weapons of mass destruction. The terrorist threat that invasion was supposed to nullify grew stronger by virtue of the invasion itself, and came directly to UK cities in bombings in 2005 and again in 2007. The post-invasion death toll on coalition forces and Iraqi civilians alike turned out to be on a scale that none of the proponents of invasion ever contemplated; and that part of Iraq that UK soldiers "liberated" proved so vulnerable to sectarian fighting and the ruthless imposition of Islamic law that UK troops were eventually discreetly withdrawn by Blair's successor as prime minister (Mahmoud, O'Kane & Black, 2007). By 2007, the

International Crisis Group was reporting that "relentless attacks against British troops had driven them off the streets and into increasingly secluded compounds," leaving the streets of Basra "controlled by militias, seemingly more powerful and unconstrained than before" (Fidler, 2007, p. 9). Eventually, and in the face of overwhelming evidence of this kind, even Tony Blair himself was ultimately obliged to concede to Sir David Frost on Al-Jazeera, reluctantly no doubt, that intervention in Iraq had been "pretty much of a disaster" (Branigan, 2006, p. 7).

So the questions remain—why did he do it, and what consequences follow from the fact that he did?

The rush to war

Why did he do it? At the most obvious level, Tony Blair ordered British troops into Iraq because he made a profound error of judgment. He was "trapped" into war by the intelligence he chose to believe and by the arguments he made on the basis of that intelligence. There was serious error in the evidence used to justify invasion. Of that there can no longer be any serious doubt. Saddam Hussein had no weapons of mass destruction. Nor was he seeking them. He also, of course, had no connection to the events of 9/11: though to his credit, Blair was always clear that Hussein did not. The Bush administration invaded Iraq for a myriad of real and imaginary reasons loosely packaged together as a response to the attack on the World Trade Center and the Pentagon, but the Blair government would not have gone along for the ride had they not been convinced by the claim central to that packaging: namely that Saddam Hussein had and was developing weapons of mass destruction (Coates and Krieger, 2004: 128–9). So the failure to find any such weapons underscores the scale of the error that Blair made. He, like Bush, then subsequently defended his decision to invade by shifting blame: insisting that his decision to invade was based on the best intelligence available at the time. But Blair, unlike Bush, was told ahead of time that the intelligence which drove him to war was highly problematic. Blair chose to ignore that warning. He was even accused of "sexing up" the data by which mobilization for war was justified, and he was certainly warned of the dangers inherent in the rush to war on which the White House was insisting in the early months of 2003. There were also errors of timing and execution as well as of basic strategy: errors about when and how to invade; that were not made in a moment, but errors that were seen coming, warned against and argued about, but made nonetheless.

So why was Tony Blair so resistant to the warnings that the intelligence was problematic and the rush to war too rapid? In the most immediate sense, the answer lies in the public role that he by then had adopted for himself and by which he was then widely recognized on the international stage. Blair took the UK into war because by the time the decision was finalized, he was trapped by the logic of his own earlier positions. He took the UK to war in March 2003 because he had talked himself (and his government colleagues) into a corner from which they could not escape without an intolerable loss of face. Blair *talked* the UK into a premature war with the Iraqi dictatorship, and held to his position because, at the eleventh hour, hubris overtook judgment.

In the immediate run-up to the invasion, the leading UK players—Jack Straw no less than Tony Blair—became victims of their own prior rhetoric. They both signed on to the Bush formulation of the post-9/11 problem— that the world faced a war on terrorism. They both signed on to the "axis of evil" formulation of the world's current dangers. Indeed Blair argued publicly in April 2002 (at George Bush's ranch in Crawford Texas, of all places) that there were certain regimes in the world that were just too dangerous to be left in place, and that it was essential that the international community take action to contain or remove them. By early 2003 Blair then reached the moment that he had spent the bulk of 2002 trying to avoid or postpone. He reached the moment at which the dilemma written into the linkage he established at Crawford could be avoided no longer—the moment, that is, when the condemned regime were still in existence but the multilateral coalition to remove it was not.

How then to jump? Had the status of the regime been changed by the absence of an international will to remove it? No, it had not. Was the regime too dangerous to leave in place? Blair was on record as saying so, and saying so repeatedly. So the case for unilateral action won, as it were, by default. Blair did not want to act without UN backing, but he could not get that backing; and he had argued himself into a corner in which inaction against the regime being criticized was no longer a possibility. Jack Straw saw the danger too, and at the eleventh hour tried to persuade Tony Blair to stop short of full military deployment when invasion was proposed, but UN backing was blocked by the prospect of a French veto (Kampfner, 2003). But Straw too in the end chose to bite the bullet, locked into a military adventure for which he had little appetite by the sheer force of the saber rattling that he and his leader had done so effectively in the months preceding the invasion.

The UK went to war against Iraq alongside the US in 2003 because its prime minister had attempted to recreate the anti-Taliban coalition against a different enemy—Saddam Hussein—and had failed. Tony Blair took the UK to war because by then his public statements had locked him into a confrontation with Iraq from which he could not escape without cost. He could not escape without bolstering the self-confidence of the Iraqi regime that both he and Bush claimed was so dangerous. He could not escape without imperiling the "special relationship" with the US to which, after 9/11, he had given unique priority. In that sense, the UK went to war in a comedy of errors, locked into a sequence of events that its prime minister had worked hard to avoid. Blair ended up where he had no particular wish to be: second-in-command of a ragbag coalition of third-rate nations. Such a view is fully in line with Robin Cook's suggestion, in his diaries, that by the time war became inevitable, Blair was "genuinely puzzled as to how he had got himself into his present dilemma." It was Cook's judgment that Blair "had never expected to find himself ordering British troops into war without UN backing," particularly given that by then—again in Cook's judgment—the prime minister did not believe any longer in the veracity of the claim, made by his own government as late as September 2002, in a much maligned dossier, that Saddam Hussein had weapons of mass destruction that could be deployed within 45 minutes (Cook, 2003, pp. 320, 312). "I am certain," Cook wrote, that "the real reason he went to war was that he found it easier to resist the public opinion of Britain than he did the request of the President of the United States" (Hoge, 2003).

Trapped by his own logic

So why: why was a Labour UK prime minister who was ideologically so different from a Republican president more willing to appease Washington neo-conservatives than to listen to his own backbenchers? Following David Runciman, we can see a space for a *psychological* element in the overall explanation of why Blair went to war; and following Steve Kettell, we can also see a space for a *constitutional* dimension to the explanation. Neither psychological nor institutional explanations suffice, but both contributed critical elements to an explanation that might.

There is room here for some sense of Blair the man (Runciman, 2006, pp. 40–53). By 2003 Blair, the world statesman, clearly expected to play big leadership roles, and actively enjoyed the playing. He had practiced such a role on the world stage at least twice already, in Kosovo and in Afghanistan. He had also practiced it at home endlessly, both before and after 1997, taking and winning one political gamble after another. Iraq was, from this perspective, simply more of the same. Blair imposed himself on the Bush people in 2001 because he wanted a leadership role post 9/11, and though they had initially not known what to do with him, by 2003 the Bush administration had drawn him into their inner circle, using him as their main global commercial traveler. After all, Blair did "sincerity" well—far better than Bush—persuading others with the fluency of his argument because of his capacity, in the moment, to persuade himself. Then, when more traditional Labourites threw up their hands in horror at New Labour's intimacy with so conservative a Republican administration, Blair's own hubris kicked in, reinforcing his commitment to the relationship and the invasion the more that both were challenged. He had shown people before. He would show them again. Leadership was about getting ahead of the curve. Iraq was simply the next curve. A different prime minister, with the same options, would have played it more cautiously, but Blair did not. He became trapped by the logic of what he had already said, all the more trapped because it was a logic of his own *choosing*.

Once trapped in this fashion, Blair then could not be easily blocked in the pursuit of the policy to which that step-lock gave rise. Steve Kettell is entirely correct to argue this: given the patronage and power that modern prime ministers now enjoy, once Blair had set his Iraq policy in train, it was very hard, indeed close to impossible, for anyone to stop him (Kettell, 2006, pp. 178–9). The UK state does have a serious democratic deficit, especially in relation to foreign policy: too few checks and balances, too limited a notion of representation, too great an enthusiasm for strong leadership. Yet too much cannot be made of this in relation to the invasion of Iraq, because in this case at least, parliament did vote. It actually voted twice—26 February and 18 March 2003—and on each occasion Blair's policy decision prevailed. It prevailed because Labour placemen/women in government voted with the Conservatives against the Liberal Democrats and the Labour left. The responsibility for agenda setting may have been Blair's—the product of his own psychology and hubris—but the responsibility for its underwriting by parliament was not solely his. That responsibility he shared with Labour MPs and with cabinet colleagues. Too many Labour members of parliament swallowed their doubts, and no doubt their consciences, to keep their jobs on the eve of invasion and war. Only Robin Cook resigned. Even Clare Short initially did not. The invasion of Iraq tells us therefore about more than Blair the man: or even about Blair the dominant prime minister, though it does tell us much about both. It also tells us about the careerism and mindset of vast sections of an entire parliamentary party, a party still in power as we write. Blair may have gone, but that mindset most definitely has not, which is why, in probing for the long-term consequences on British politics of the invasion of Iraq, there is no escaping an examination of the mindset that made that invasion possible.

Blair's mindset

So what was that mindset, and what role did that play in the taking of this awesome and ultimately flawed decision? There is both an immediate and a deeper answer to questions of that kind.

There is an immediate answer, one focused on the prime minister's attitude to the US. The immediate answer to why Tony Blair went to war alongside George W. Bush is that Blair decided that UK national interests required that he remain standing "shoulder to shoulder" with the US in a context in which the US and UK were already standing "shoulder to shoulder" in the policing of Iraq's no-fly zones. There is a sense in which invading Iraq simply required Tony Blair to go on doing what he had done when Bill Clinton was president, and what an earlier Conservative prime minister had agreed with an earlier President Bush: being America's staunchest ally in dealing with an apparently intractable problem. Blair was simply doing what other UK prime ministers had done before him: not Harold Wilson in relation to Vietnam, but Attlee in relation to Korea and Thatcher and Major in relation to the first Gulf War (Dumbrell, 2006). What Blair added was his own determination to "hug them close" in Peter Riddell's telling term, to get even nearer to the Americans in their moment of geopolitical isolation than he had when the bulk of the international community had stood with America in the immediate aftermath of the attacks on 9/11(Riddell, 2004).

The clearest documentation of this determination to stay so close to the Americans that you couldn't slip a cigarette paper between the two governments appears in Peter Stothard's *30 Days*, where he reports the existence of a list of points on the London-Washington-Baghdad interplay, drawn up in September 2002 by the prime minister, "to which he and his aides would regularly return." The list is worth reproducing in full (Stothard, 2003, p. 87).

- Saddam Hussein's past aggression, present support for terrorism and future ambitions made him a clear threat to his enemies. He was not the only goal, but he was a threat nonetheless.
- The United States and Britain were among his enemies.
- The people of the United States, still angered by the 11 September attacks, still sensing unfinished business from the first Gulf War twelve years before, would support a war on Iraq.
- Gulf War 2 – President George W Bush vs. Saddam Hussein – would happen whatever anyone else said or did.
- The people of Britain, continental Europe and most of the rest of the world would not even begin to support a war unless they had a say through the United Nations.
- It would be more damaging to long-term world peace and security if the Americans alone defeated Saddam Hussein than if they had international support to do so.

The list is a truly remarkable one, and one little commented upon in other analyses of Blair's rush to war. If true, it tells us that even in September 2002 Tony Blair was resigned to the inevitability of war with Iraq. It also demonstrates Blair's determination to stay with the Americans, and to hold them to a multilateral politics in the build up to war. But if that was the Blair intention, it was one that singularly failed; and then the list also indicates the choice that the prime minister had eventually to face. Which point in the list was to be the breaker for Blair: the penultimate one or the final one? Events proved that it was the final one that prevailed. As Martin Kettle put it, the list shows that in the end Britain "went to war to keep on the right side of Washington" (Coates & Krieger, 2004, p. 96).

That Blair was writing lists of this kind, in the midst of a growing international crisis in which he was a major player, tells us something else as well.

It tells us that Blair, like Labour prime ministers before him, found himself comfortable playing this inflated global role, maintaining a world position as close as possible, despite diminished great power status, to that enjoyed by previous prime ministers in the heyday of the UK's imperial past. Blair often described the invasion of Iraq as the new century's first "third way" war; but in truth, for the UK at least, it was not. It was a throwback to an older— actually Old Labour as well as old Conservative—imperial use of UK military power. It was the shadow of imperialism that made it easy for Blair to invade Iraq. Rearranging other people's political furniture is what imperialist powers do best, and what British arms have done many times. Understanding why Blair went into Iraq also involves understanding that New Labour in power had not made a fundamental rupture with ways of thinking that stretch back more than a century. As we said in *Blair's War*, "if the speed and ease with which New Labour went to war in Iraq without a UN mandate makes one thing clear, it is this: that the intellectual furniture of Victorian imperialism still remains a presence in the mindset of the existing leadership of the Labour Party ... a furniture that," in our view, "long ago should have been thrown out and burnt" (Coates and Krieger, 2004, p. 124).

A legacy of empire

So at a deeper level, Blair's decision to invade Iraq, like similar foreign policy decisions made by many of his predecessors, was anchored in the overall worldview that he, like they, brought to the totality of the policy agenda. Blair's role, and that of his ministers, must be grasped as the natural outgrowth of their general understanding of the world they faced around them, a general understanding that gave an underlying unity to the thrust of their entire domestic *and* foreign policy. A full explanation of the rush to war with Iraq is therefore impossible without an analysis of the origin of those more general understandings.

It is our contention that they have to be understood as the outgrowth of legacies left in the mindsets of contemporary Labour leaders by the worldviews prevalent in the minds of previous generations of Labour Party leaders (on this more generally, see Coates 2002); and that in consequence New Labour in 2003 was not as new as it liked to claim. Its general analysis of the world, and of the role of the use of force in advancing UK interests, had new emphases and inflections, but it also carried within it large elements of the imperialist and Atlanticist proclivities left behind by the thinking and practice of Labour leaders in the past. It was this fusion of those new inflections and old legacies that hold the ultimate key to why Blair made Bush's war his war too, despite the large moral and geopolitical divide that separated the two war leaders.

Students of British Labour (ourselves included) have too often in the past separated domestic and foreign policy as objects of analysis. To understand

Blair's move to Basra, we have to bring those separate studies together by developing some general models of Labour politics through which to isolate the manner in which foreign and domestic policy necessarily originate together. In *Blair's War* we developed four such models, organized in a 2 by 2 matrix. To understand how New Labour took the UK to the invasion of Iraq, it is necessary to see how (1) a *Traditional Labour* model was challenged historically by (2) a *Left-Labour* alternative, and how the legacies of that political confrontation left Blair with a new choice: between (3) New Labour's post-1997, pre-9/11 adherence to an expansive view of global interdependence, humanitarian intervention and debt relief (what we call *Offensive Multilateralism*) and (4) a post-9/11 New Labour understanding of the world that generates a foreign policy scarred by residues of imperialism and Atlanticism, and yet still insists on resolute multilateralism, now recast by Blair's new post-9/11 mentality—what we call *Defiant Internationalism*. The four frameworks may be summarized as follows:

Framework #1—British Labourism: Traditional foreign policy

Promote the British state and its national interests, above class and party, by an active defense of imperial and commercial interests, and the effective management of a balance of power in Europe. Enhance Britain's role as an offshore balancer of Europe and as a great power by a dedicated commitment to an Atlantic Alliance and a robust participation in NATO. Britain's international status and security require the commitment to a global military capability and the willingness to use force, backed by the full triad of conventional, tactical nuclear, and strategic nuclear weapons.

Framework #2—British Labourism: The socialist foreign policy critique

Promote the advance of socialism and the advance of the left within the Labour Party by insisting that foreign and domestic policy are integrally and organically connected by a set of core principles: internationalism, international working-class solidarity, anti-capitalism, and anti-militarism. Britain's foreign policy and security interests to be best advanced by the projection abroad of clear ethical principles for the conduct of foreign policy, a commitment to third force neutralism and the building of multilateral institutions, a rejection of nuclear options, and support for unilateral nuclear disarmament.

Framework #3—New Labour I: Offensive multilateralism

Harness the forces of globalization and the practical realities of interdependence to advance internationalism, multilateralism, and cooperation in the economic, environmental, and security dimensions of foreign affairs. When necessary, advance humanitarian policy through resolute military means consonant with the doctrine of international community and advance the strategic goal of enhancing Britain's global power and prestige. Engage the questions of debt reduction and institutional reform that are required to secure the aims of human rights, democratic governance, and security.

Framework #4—New Labour II: Defiant internationalism

Rewrite foreign policy to meet the security threats of the post-9/11 order. The democratic preferences of nation and party—and the commitment to strengthen and reform the United Nations and especially the Security Council—must give way to the "war on terrorism". Whatever differences that may develop between the UK and US (regarding the role of the Security Council, the linkage of the Israeli-Palestine conflict to the War in Iraq, the best mix of instruments to be used in fighting terrorism, the role of the United Nations in post-war peace building, and so on) must all be subordinated to the Anglo-American alliance. War in Iraq is justified by the WMD threats of the Saddam Hussein regime as well as its record of horrific human rights abuses and defiance of the United Nations. British national interests and values are best advanced by its unique partnership with the US.

Pre-9/11 foreign policy thinking within the Labour Party had settled at Framework 3. There seemed to be general recognition in governing circles in Tony Blair's New Labour Party that the great power unilateralism of Framework 1 had to be abandoned, and that the ethical concerns of Framework 2 were now best pursued through multilateral institutions set in a globalized world. New Labour, pre 9/11, was acutely focused on globalization, the thread that pulled together the domestic and international dimensions of its core governing project. Globalization justified (and made necessary) the abandonment of old-style Labourism both domestically and abroad. It forced the shift from Keynesianism to new growth theory and it compelled a distinctive reading of foreign policy imperatives. Interdependence was the order of the day; and Blair was in the forefront of the design of new principles of foreign policy appropriate to it. His much-cited Chicago speech in the midst of the Kosovo crisis is entirely germane here, containing as it did his argument for multilateral interventionism. In Chicago Blair argued that isolationism was no longer an option once financial insecurity in Asia destroyed jobs from Chicago to his own constituency in County Durham, and conflict in the Balkans caused refugees in Germany as well as the US. In Chicago, he extolled the "impulse towards interdependence" and the "new doctrine of international community" which he characterized as "the explicit recognition that today more than ever before, we are mutually dependent, that national interest is to a significant extent governed by international collaboration and that we need a clear and coherent debate as to the direction this doctrine takes us in each field of international endeavour" (Blair, 1999a).

Above all, Blair made very clear in the 1999 Chicago address that New Labour's governing model—as well as its guiding ethical principles—cut both ways, in domestic as well as foreign affairs. "Community" was the normative glue that held together the domestic and foreign policy components of Blair's New Labour project, facilitating a distinctive blend of *individuality* (recast in the international realm as *national interest*), and the *interdependence* that he considered to be the core of socialism. So, in Chicago, Blair insisted:

> We are witnessing the beginnings of a new doctrine of international com-munity ... Just as within domestic politics, the notion of community—the belief that partnership and co-operation are essential to advance self-interest—is coming into its own; so it needs to find its international echo. Global financial markets, the global environment, global security and disarmament issues: none of these can be solved without intense co-operation.
>
> (Blair, 1999a)

In this speech, on the eve of NATO's fiftieth anniversary, Blair noted the "danger of letting wherever CNN roves be the cattle prod to take a global conflict seriously," and argued instead for a sustained effort to advance "the principles of the doctrine of international community and ... the institutions that deliver them." Without specifying the relevant principles in great detail, Blair used the experience underway in Kosovo to lay out five tests against which the international community should use to determine whether or not to intervene in the internal affairs of a sovereign state:

> first, are we sure of our case ... second, have we exhausted all diplomatic options ... third ... are there military operations we can sensibly and pru-dently undertake ... fourth, are we prepared for the long term ... And finally, do we have national interests involved?
>
> (Blair, 1999a)

These were clearly Framework 3 principles. But Blair's hyperactive response to the events of 9/11 changed all that. The attacks on the World Trade Center and the Pentagon, and the loss of lives that ensued, took Blair back to his own version of Framework 1, and so on to Framework 4. Blair responded to the attack on the World Trade Center and the Pentagon by morphing New Labour's offensive multilateralism into what we might call *defiant internationalism*. It was a mindset in which stridency of purpose took precedence over width of support. It was a mindset characterized by a "go for broke" risk-taking strategy to advance British interests and maximize national power, and paradoxically to do so in a world where nation states were seen as having far less power than before. It was a mindset that enabled Tony Blair to enthusiastically join America's unilaterally designed and imple-mented war in Iraq, while simultaneously justifying that war by appeals to the international community, to the demands of interdependence, and to a commitment to multilateral institutions—all of which had been damaged, perhaps irretrievably, by the actions thus justified. In 2003, and at whatever the cost, Blair was content to play Robin to Bush's Batman, fighting masked villains as loyal underling in the dynamic duo: defying the international community, the nation, and the party as he did so. His defiance was the product, we believe, of this fourth mindset.

Will the lessons be learned?

The logic of the argument thus far is that the lesson of the Iraq debacle is this: that New Labour needs to return to its emerging third mindset—the one we term *offensive multilateralism*—and to break decisively with both the *defiant internationalism* of the Blair stance, and with the supine subordination to the dictates of Washington to which it has succumbed. Blair used his last major foreign policy speech as prime minister to advocate a prolonged UK role in both "war fighting and peacekeeping," and to set his face against a retreat into peacekeeping alone (Blair, 2007). Whether that will indeed be the role pursued by Gordon Brown's government or by subsequent Labour or Conservative governments is now the pressing issue of the day.

With the transition from Blair to Brown, the signs of a return to a more principled multilateralism were initially favorable. The appointment of David Miliband as foreign secretary handed the Foreign Office to the party's most powerful young intellectual; and that of Mark Malloch-Brown as minister for Africa, Asia, and the United Nations brought into the center of decision making in London an outspoken critic of the war in Iraq and a UN insider with a robust reform agenda (Brown, M., 2008). On taking office, David Miliband immediately wrote of his desire to make the UK again "a global hub for discussion and decision-making about the great economic, social and political questions we face" (Miliband, 2007); and he spoke openly at the Labour Party conference in 2007 of "moving on" beyond Iraq, promising a second wave of New Labour foreign policy that implicitly conceded flaws in the design and execution of the first wave. Mark Malloch-Brown was at times equally innovative, denying the need for the US and UK to be "joined at the hip," and talking in January 2008 of the likelihood of an inquiry soon into the circumstances that led the UK into war.

But if there has been realignment of this kind, so far it has been marginal and incremental at best. Brown was at pains on his first visit to Camp David as prime minister in July 2007 to reassure his American hosts of the UK's continuing commitment to the alliance between them. The body language may have been less warm, but the message was not. On the contrary, the new prime minister went out of his way to hail and celebrate the relationship with America as the most important bilateral one the UK possessed, and both Mark Malloch-Brown and Douglas Alexander were quickly brought to heel for speeches that implied otherwise. Those who hoped to find a signal that the UK would create a space for disagreement with the US were obliged to take solace in an apparent breach with the US on Security Council reform. In April 2008, a week before Brown's second US visit, the British broke with the Americans, and backed a proposal tabled by Germany for expanded membership (Brown had previously announced support for India's permanent membership on the Security Council while on a visit to India in January, 2008, a position also supported by Cameron). But when the prime minister arrived in Washington, no recalibration in UK-US relations was in evidence. The American president greeted Brown as a "good friend" with whom George W. Bush claimed "a special personal relationship" BBC News (April 2008).

Whether all this means that the invasion of Iraq was not only a mistake, but also a singular one, remains an open question, as it must. Our sense however is that in foreign as in domestic policy, New Labour under new leadership is currently talking a slightly different *language* than that commonplace under Blair, but is not acting or positioning itself very differently from a government in which, after all, most of its key figures were themselves junior members. The inflections have modestly shifted, but the mindset has not. Tony Blair may have gone from the international scene, but in foreign policy as well as in domestic policy, Blairism as a policy stance remains the dominant political orientation.

That said, things are more fluid now in the realm of UK foreign policy than for a decade past. With a new American administration coming into place in January 2009, the pull from Washington may tug London in a direction that will be more compatible with a foreign policy focused on multilateralism, development, and global governance reform initiatives. Moreover, given Brown's travails, it is all the more important to look to the other side of the political aisle, to David Cameron and the Conservatives, to assess the medium and long term legacies of Blair's war in Iraq. Here, as well, to the limited extent that we can usefully describe foreign policy directions for a future Conservative government that may never take office, reappraisal rather than rupture, and a heavy dose of path dependency, seems the order of the day. Cameron, like Brown, projects a deep commitment to the UK's special relationship with Washington. But he also argues explicitly (what Brown and his foreign policy team imply) that the UK must distance itself from the kind of slavish submission to Washington that Blair adopted.

That makes this precisely the time for the UK to consider a genuinely different foreign policy: one grounded in the historic mission of the Labour Party (or of a multilateralist and forward looking Conservative party), mindful of both the strategic and the ethical lessons that can be drawn from the war in Iraq, cognizant of the dangers of unchallenged American power, and willing to reconsider the principles and policies that should orient Britain's global role.

If this process is occurring, as it appears to be, then there is reason for cautious optimism that, in time, Blair's war in Iraq may legitimately be viewed as a mistake, and one not to be repeated. We will know this is the case if and when the UK's traditional imperialist predilections and great power yearnings have been sufficiently downsized and reformed that development goals, climate change, and patient and purposeful diplomacy drive the foreign policy agenda. We will know this is the case if and when UK-US relations remain close but subject to public and private disagreement, when they become no more special than UK-India or UK-EU relations: when, that is, they become simply an important but no longer a unique arena within which the UK can again be a leading force for good in the world.

18

A Just War: Prime Minister Tony Blair and the End of Saddam's Iraq

Ted R. Bromund

Introduction

Serious analysis of prime minister Tony Blair's policy towards the regime of Saddam Hussein must be founded on the fact that, both before and particularly after the terrorist attacks of 11 September 2001, that regime posed a fundamental challenge to the international order established after the end of the Second World War, and revived after the end of the Cold War. Blair recognized this challenge. His response to it was foreshadowed by his leadership in restoring the Labour Party to respectability before 1997, and by his response to other foreign policy crises before 2001. He supported the invasion of Iraq in 2003 because it was based on the liberal international values in which he believed, and which he had twice been elected to pursue. The British disillusionment with the war, which contributed to Blair's resignation in 2007, reflected both the retreat of the left from those values, and Blair's own inability to build a culturally, internationally, and militarily coherent base for his policy.

New Labour abroad before 9/11

Disputes about Britain's armed forces have done as much to keep Labour out of power as they have to endanger it when it was in government. When in 1983, after Britain's victory in the Falklands War, Labour's manifesto committed the party to unilateral nuclear disarmament, the Conservatives, led by Margaret Thatcher, won a 144-seat Commons majority. The lesson Blair took from this defeat was clear: Labour needed to stop opposing sensible and popular Tory policies and stop advancing totemic but wrong-headed and unpopular Labour ones. By 1997, Blair had succeeded in returning to the party the support for liberal internationalism and resistance to dictators that had characterized it in Ernest Bevin's era.

The victory New Labour had in 1997 was not, centrally, a referendum on its proposed foreign policy. But Britain eagerly voted into power a party committed, in the words of its 1997 manifesto, to countering the "proliferation of weapons of mass destruction, ... [and] international terrorism," and to making "the protection and promotion of human rights a central part of our foreign policy" (Labour Party, 1997). On 12 May 1997, incoming Foreign Secretary Robin Cook made the case for foreign policy with "an ethical dimension," arguing that in an interdependent world, it was in Britain's interest to ensure the world lived increasingly by British values. With the Cold War over, Labour would not be seduced by the supposed divide between a foreign policy based on realism and one based on liberal values, and would not be afraid to be "a force for good in the world" (Cook, 12 May 1997).

Cook's speech was, in part, a criticism of John Major's Conservative administration for selling Hawk aircraft to the authoritarian government of Indonesia. It soon became obvious that it would not be easy for Labour to determine how large the ethical dimension of its foreign policy should be. But Labour's contention that the Conservative Party—and the US Republican Party—in the 1990s favored realism as their strategy for pursuing the national interest was fair enough. The democratic world responded haltingly to both the genocide in Rwanda and the rise of the Taliban in Afghanistan, and in the Balkans, it was again too slow to act (Simms, 2001).

The new millennium did not bring a retreat from realism: in 2000, Republican presidential candidate George W. Bush argued that the US should withdraw its forces from the former Yugoslavia ("Europeans say Bush's Pledge to Pull out of Balkans Could Split NATO," *New York Times*, 25 October 2000). Compared with the record Blair had compiled by 2001, Bush's ambitions were distinctly restrained. His claim that US forces should be used to win wars, not to pursue nation building, tried to draw finely the line between interests and values that Cook had dismissed and took little account of what Blair had already achieved abroad. Indeed, Blair's domestic achievements in his first term, given his 177-seat majority, were strikingly modest: his priority was to prove that Labour was a safe pair of fiscal hands, not one that would indulge its old tax and spend instincts.

Blair's advances therefore came in the low-cost realms of Northern Ireland's peace process, Welsh and Scottish devolution, House of Lords reform—and foreign affairs. In September 1999, British forces participated in the Australia-led intervention in East Timor, which stabilized the country and led to its independence from Indonesia in 2002. In May 2000, in Operation Palliser, British forces took control of the Sierra Leone airport to evacuate British citizens trapped by the on-going civil war. The British troops remained to provide support to the internationally recognized government until departing in mid-June.

Neither of these interventions was as risky, or important, as the central role Blair played in bringing the long-running crisis in the Serbian province of Kosovo to an end. After the March 1999 breakdown of the talks at Rambouillet, NATO forces—acting, because of Russian opposition, without authorization from the UN Security Council (UNSC)—began a bombing campaign against Serbia that lasted from 24 March to 11 June. While the US provided most of the aircraft for the campaign, British leadership was crucial to its outcome. When President Bill Clinton was unwilling to commit ground forces, it was Blair, already playing a central role in the air war, who pressured Clinton to reconsider (Seldon, 2005, pp. 392–407). The result was Serbian president Slobodan Milošević's unexpected collapse and a victory—messy, but conclusive—for NATO.

Blair's early successes abroad laid the groundwork, good and bad, for the Iraq War. In the Balkans, he showed he was willing to wage war without UNSC authorization, against the will of great powers such as Russia, in a humanitarian and strategic cause, while taking the lead in the alliance with the US. In all his interventions, the forces employed were limited: quick success was achieved partly because the opposition was weak, partly through bluff, and partly thanks to good luck. Finally, Blair's emphasis throughout was less on post-conflict reconstruction than on defeating the various opposing dictators, rebels, and government-backed militias. In times of crisis, this emphasis was appropriate. But it reflected his argument that the problems the interdependent world faced were caused by failures at the state level, not by deeper social fissures. The challenge the world faced, therefore, was that it needed to find the courage to act, the implication being that action would swiftly eliminate the problem (Bromund, 2008). This optimistic assumption was not to be borne out by the reality of social disintegration and regional opposition in and around Iraq.

Blair, to his credit, acknowledged that not all his wars would be quick. In his most important address on foreign policy, his 24 April 1999 speech on the "Doctrine of the International Community" in Chicago, he cited the need to be "prepared for the long term." As NATO was then only a month into the campaign against Milošević, Blair was less prepared for the long term than he implied. But the address as a whole laid out his belief that "in the end values and interests merge. ... The spread of our values makes us safer," and that, to advance this aim, dictators who were undeniably engaged in widespread violations of human rights, who refused to negotiate seriously, and who posed a threat to other national interests could justifiably be removed by force if that option was prudently available.

Blair's emphasis in this speech was on sustaining US support for operations in Kosovo. But he also drew attention to Saddam Hussein, describing the dictator as a "dangerous and ruthless" man who was personally responsible for the problems Iraq faced. Indeed, Blair's central argument was that the start of the new century was the right time to make a stand against Milošević, so as to deter future dictators, like Hussein, by demonstrating that the democracies would act, and that the post-Cold War era would be defined by resolve, not paralysis. The UN, too, needed to be reshaped, so it would become not a forum for deadlock, but an effective instrument for international co-operation. The alternative, Blair implied, was more Kosovos, more campaigns against dictators undertaken without UNSC authorization (Blair, 24 April 1999a).

For a time, that implication remained unexplored. In May 2001, Blair won a second landslide victory. Though Labour's manifesto referred proudly to the operations in Sierra Leone and Kosovo, it placed more stress on Labour's policy towards the European Union (EU), which it defended, in the traditional style, as the best way to keep Britain relevant in the broader world. The discouraging reality was that Blair had not been able to create a Europe-wide movement inspired by his politics, and that the St. Malo British-French agreement on European defense policy in 1998 had not been matched by European willingness to increase defense spending. Indeed, Labour's manifesto testified to its own first-term spending priorities by conceding that Britain's armed forces had suffered real year-on-year funding decreases for over a decade. In short, Blair's preferences were clear, but, with Europe unresponsive and the newly elected, realist Bush administration emphasizing its suspicion of China, the opportunities for co-operative action appeared to be shrinking.

Blair's victory

The terrorist attacks of September 11, 2001 did not change everything. Rather, for Blair, they vindicated his 1999 analysis and proved that the Clinton and Bush administrations had been too slow to act: the rise of the Taliban in Afghanistan, a state that had dropped out of the modern, interdependent world, was indeed an offense to democratic values and a challenge to the security of that world. So Blair returned to his theme. As he put it in a speech to the Labour Party Conference on October 2, 2001, "interdependence defines the new world we live in." Blair placed himself, publicly and firmly, beside the US, and, in his most portentous metaphor, described the pieces of the post-9/11 world as a kaleidoscope, newly shaken and now in flux, but soon to settle again: before they did, Britain and its allies needed to re-order the world (Blair, 2 October 2001).

The early results of that re-ordering were unexpected. The UN-authorized war in Afghanistan toppled—if it did not quite destroy—the Taliban with shocking rapidity. And, in reaction to 9/11, the Bush administration changed course: having been elected on the assertion that the US needed to avoid using force to build nations, conduct humanitarian interventions, and promote democratic values; it became the apostle of all of these policies. The claim was often made, then and later, that Blair was Bush's "poodle," following in American footsteps to the detriment of British values and interests (Coughlin, 2006, p. 284). In fact, the reverse was true: Blair was in the lead from the beginning, with Bush following tardily behind, brought around not by Blair's arguments but by the persuasive power of events. Blair had been the most consistent and insightful exponent in world politics of the practical and moral dangers posed by dictatorial regimes. The reason why the special relationship was reborn after 9/11 between Bush and Blair was simple: Blair was right, and Bush now knew it.

Bush became, for those who would listen, a forthright proponent, in the Wilsonian tradition, of Blair's doctrine. Bush's clearest exposition came in his June 1, 2002 graduation speech at West Point. His tone—always an issue when American speeches are read in the gentle context of European politics— was more pugnacious, but his vision was Blair's, combining a call for the US to "extend the peace by encouraging free and open societies on every continent" with the warning that, in a more close-knit world increasingly united by common values, the gravest danger to freedom lay at "the perilous crossroads of radicalism and technology" (Bush, 1 June 2002). The price for failing to address this threat, as Blair pointed out, was too high to contemplate. Acting together was preferable to acting alone, but taking action was what mattered. Toppling a brutal dictator, even if the status of his WMD programs was unclear, was good in itself, as well as a contribution to the war on terror. The issue was not simply whether there was a direct link between the dictators and the terrorists; the more important argument was that dictators created terrorism by repressing their own people and then channeling the resulting popular hostility against their neighbors and the international system (Blair, 17 July 2003).

The challenge of Iraq

And that brought Blair, Bush, and the world to the challenge of Iraq. There were both negative and positive reasons to confront Saddam Hussein. The negative one was simple: fear. Hussein's enthusiasm for WMDs was well attested, and he publicly proclaimed his moral and financial support for Palestinian terrorism, which offered no assurances that he rejected terrorism in other contexts. Hussein's attempt to assassinate George H. W. Bush with a car bomb while the former president was visiting Kuwait in 1993 was yet one more piece of evidence to this effect. The positive reasons were more complex: while several dictator states (including Iran and North Korea) were pursuing WMD programs and promoting terrorism, and one autocratic state (Pakistan) that was home to many terrorists had retailed its WMDs around the world, Iraq was the only state of which the UNSC was actively seized. More broadly, while both Blair and Bush made the case against terrorism anywhere in the world, the fact remained that the US had been attacked by terrorists from the Middle East, where—Israel apart—there were no democracies to be found. If the relationship between dictatorial rule and terrorism was to be broken, the Middle East, and Iraq in particular, was the place to start.

But the challenge posed by Saddam Hussein's Iraq went far beyond the question of terrorism, vital though that was after September 11. Nor was it limited to the fact that the Hussein regime was the most relentlessly aggressive and oppressive state in the world, having, since 1979, openly waged war on four of its neighbors (Iran, Saudi Arabia, Kuwait, and Israel), launched campaigns of genocide against the Kurds (during which the regime employed chemical weapons) and the Marsh Arabs, violently suppressed the majority Shiite population, and engaged in a three-decade long pursuit, which included both international purchases and substantial domestic programs, of all manner of WMDs, including nuclear, chemical, and biological weapons.

The central challenge stemmed from the fact that, after the Gulf War— a war unanimously endorsed by the UNSC—the regime had accepted, as a condition of the ceasefire, the obligation to provide, in the words of UNSCR 707 (15 August 1991), a 'full, final, and complete disclosure' of all its WMD programs. The burden was not placed on the UNSC, or the US, to prove that Iraq did have WMDs; the burden was placed on Iraq to prove that it did not have WMDs. This was fair, correct, and inevitable: having launched and lost an unprovoked war that sought to bring to an end the very existence of Kuwait, a member state of the UN, Iraq was presumed to be guilty, and was as such obliged to prove its innocence.

Iraq repeatedly evaded this obligation. Indeed, it demonstrated that the presumption of guilt was justified by conducting a systemic campaign of evasion, concealment, and subterfuge. This campaign extended as far as the murder, on Hussein's orders, of his relative—and overseer of Iraq's WMD programs—Husayn Kamil, along with most of his family. This is not a question of interpretation: it is a matter of well-attested fact. As early as UNSCR 707 (15 August 1991), the UNSC found Iraq in "flagrant violation" of the terms of the ceasefire. The UNSC repeated this finding in UNSCR 1194 (9 September 1998), and again in UNSCR 1205 (5 November 1998). In response to Iraq's obstruction, Britain and the US launched a three-day air campaign, Desert Fox, against Iraqi targets in December 1998. Finally, in UNSCR 1441 (8 November 2002), the UNSC found Iraq to be in "material breach" of its obligations and threatened "serious consequences" if Iraq continued to withhold compliance. In all, Iraq was the subject of 18 UNSC resolutions from the Gulf War to the start of the 2003 campaign.

This was a record of sustained UNSC involvement unparalleled in the history of the UN, an organization founded on the principle of collective security, a principle at the heart of liberal thought—and, in particular, British thought—on international affairs since the late nineteenth century. If the international order established after the Second World War, the order that had fought and won the Gulf War, was to live up to the terms of its Charter, and of its own unanimous resolutions, it had by late 2002 to confront Iraq. If it did not, it would, as Blair had warned in 1999, discredit itself, both as an enforcer of the collective will to be feared by future aggressors and as an arena in which the member states could address their legitimate security concerns. If, with the resolutions the UNSC had compiled on Iraq, and after the shock of 9/11, it did not act, then no one could have any confidence that it would act on any future case. The challenge of Iraq was whether the UNSC would have the courage to live up to the self-imposed responsibilities— including, when necessary, the use of force—of the liberal international order.

To Blair's credit, he refused to evade this responsibility, which weighed particularly heavily on Britain as a permanent member of the UNSC. His 2001 metaphor of the kaleidoscope reflected his recognition that the UNSC, after acting in 1990–1, had fallen into a pattern of piling up resolutions that it did not enforce. 9/11 enhanced the need and created the opportunity to break this destructive cycle by acting against Iraq. Blair was not alone in perceiving the necessity of action, as Democratic senator Hillary Clinton put it on October 10, 2002, "since the [UN] inspectors left ... Hussein has worked to rebuild his chemical and biological weapons stock, his missile delivery capability, and his nuclear program. He has also given aid, comfort, and sanctuary to terrorists ... if left unchecked, Saddam Hussein will continue to increase his capacity to wage biological and chemical warfare, and will keep trying to develop nuclear weapons" (Clinton, 10 October 2002).

Blair, like Senator Clinton, therefore found the status quo unacceptable. Even in 2003, that status quo—a continued UN sanctions regime softened by its Oil for Food Program (OFF)—appeared fragile, both because of Iraq's refusal to comply with the UNSC resolutions and because the sanctions regime itself was under widespread (if misdirected) criticism on humanitarian grounds. In retrospect, OFF was a disaster: Iraq used it to win support in the UNSC by directing oil contracts to French, Russian, and Chinese companies, and by allocating oil to French, Russian, and British politicians, and, most egregiously, to the UN Chief of the OFF (Iraqi Perspective Project, 2006; Duelfer Report, 2004; Independent Inquiry Committee, 2005). The illegal "surcharge" the regime imposed on each barrel of oil sold through OFF contributed to the over $10 billion it earned in illicit revenue between 1990 and 2003 (Duelfer Report, 2004). In short, continued containment of Iraq would have involved a substantial and on-going American and British military commitment and the constant threat of military action. It would also have presumed illogically—and, after 9/11, irresponsibly—that Hussein posed only a conventional military threat. And it would have rested shakily on a sanctions regime that was collapsing because of the eagerness with which three of the five permanent members of the UNSC, and many other UN member states, were subverting it. Given the seriousness with which the UNSC had treated the issue, this was a dereliction of duty without parallel in UN history.

The approach to war

From the first, Blair, as a believer in the UN and the liberal international order, was committed to treating the challenge of Iraq with the seriousness it deserved (Coughlin, 2006, pp. 72–3). The assertion that Blair—an experienced politician and intelligent statesman—was gulled by Bush into war is rooted solely in the visceral contempt that many on the left feel for the American president and, now, for Blair himself. Blair rejected Bush's invitation—offered out of respect for Blair's domestic political difficulties—to drop out of the coalition. He went to war because "it wasn't clear that the whole nature of the way Saddam was dealing with this issue had changed, [so] I was in favour of military action" ("Tony Blair", *Times Online*, 17 November 2007).

The way in which Blair justified this decision to the public continues to be the subject of criticism, some of it fair. In particular, he placed excessive weight on the imminent danger posed by Iraq's possession of WMDs, and used overblown or, retrospectively, inaccurate intelligence to persuade the public of the existence of this danger. Opponents and supporters of the war alike accepted that Iraq had WMDs, as two post-war inquiries have confirmed. Blair did not falsify intelligence, but he did make the most of the unreliable information that was available (Butler, 2004; Hutton Inquiry, 2004). It would have been more accurate, if less gripping, to have emphasized the importance of upholding the UN system of collective security—if necessary, without further UNSC authorization—in the face of Iraq's challenge. But while this error did Blair considerable political damage, and deserves the investigations to which it has been subjected, the fact remains that it was Iraq's duty to prove it did not have WMDs—and that, the UNSC unanimously concluded, it failed to do. There is, in any event, something unreal in the expectation that intelligence agencies will be able to gather full, accurate, and complete intelligence inside a police state, and something dangerous in the belief that, when they are prevented from doing so, that state should be declared innocent and so be allowed to reap the benefits of its repression.

There was also the problem of the UN, where Blair, again for reasons of domestic politics, needed a UNSC resolution explicitly authorizing the use of force. Having persuaded Bush that the potential reward of the resolution was worth the risk of becoming "stuck" in the UN (*Times Online*, 17 November 2007), the US and Britain secured UNSCR 1441, which left the door open for military action without a second resolution. But their efforts to obtain a second, definitive, resolution failed, primarily because of French opposition. As Kosovo had shown, Blair was willing to proceed without the UNSC, but his inability to secure full approval from at least the Western members of the UNSC did him further damage in Britain.

The reasons for the French stance—like the history of the entire post-1991 saga—will not be understood until all the relevant documents, including those from Iraq, are available. But the best explanation revolves around the internal politics of the EU. After German chancellor Gerhard Schröder had a narrow election victory in September 2002 on a platform of opposition to the impending war, France had every reason to continue its historic strategy of aligning with Germany—and against Britain and the US—inside the EU (Coughlin, 2006, pp. 265–6, 268–9). French president Jacques Chirac's explosive response to an Eastern European declaration of solidarity with the US in February 2003—"It is not well brought-up behavior. They missed a good opportunity to keep quiet"—revealed his discomfort that so many European states had not followed the French lead ("Chirac Lashes out at 'New Europe,'" CNN, 18 February 2003).

The fact that, for all their public opposition, neither Germany nor France closed their air space to the US—as both had done in 1986, when the US bombed targets in Libya—implies that both were more concerned with appearing to be anti-war for domestic reasons than in doing anything to impede the ability of the US to wage war. Indeed, they made the war all but inevitable by fracturing the unity of the UN and NATO, which encouraged Hussein not to flee and so eliminated the last plausible peaceful ending to the crisis.

But the French and German opposition does shed comparative light on British politics. The argument that Blair's decisions were shaped by Britain's "imperial legacy," as argued by Coates and Krieger in this volume, has no explanatory power; because this "legacy" can be blamed for anything, it explains nothing. It also ignores the fact that France, the other European power with a legacy of Middle Eastern empire, led the opposition to the war, as well as the fact that Blair was only one of over 30 world leaders—including many in Europe—who supported the war. The problem was that, while many European leaders supported the war, most European publics did not—and those unsupportive publics included the public in Germany, the state that in turn determined France's behavior and so decided the outcome of the struggle in the UN.

The historical legacy that mattered was not the British Empire; it was the Second World War. By winning that war, the US and Britain reasserted their national identities as liberal democracies that had the right to use force to defend their security, to oppose dictators, and to advance their values. As a result, majorities of both their publics supported war in 2003. By losing in 1945, Germany in particular, and much of the rest of Western Europe more broadly, lost confidence in the legitimacy of force as the final appeal for liberal democracies in international relations. As Chirac put it, "War is always an admission of failure. Everything must be done to avoid it" (Coughlin, 2006, p. 269). As France has repeatedly—and unilaterally—used force in West and Central Africa, Chirac's statement did less than full justice to the actual sentiments of French policymakers. But it did complete justice to what, as a Western European politician, he was compelled in public to pretend to believe. Eastern Europe's support for Blair and Bush emphasized the divide; having only recently escaped from Communist rule, the Eastern states had a firmer grasp of the realities of international politics, and the requirements of the liberal international order, than their Western counterparts.

The war and its aftermath

The war itself, and the war after the war, were not primarily Britain's to wage, but Blair made a serious error by failing to press the US to plan more carefully for post-war Iraq (Seldon, 2008, pp. 148–50). The weaknesses of the planning process reflected the Wilsonian bent of both neo-conservatism and Blair's own ideas. By emphasizing Hussein's responsibility for Iraq's shortcomings, both obscured the fact that removing him would reveal as many problems as it remedied. Still, while coalition policy and practice were at fault in many ways, Iraq was inherently a difficult case; better planning would have helped, but the mutual hatred between Sunnis, Shiites, and Kurds; Hussein's cynical Islamicization of Iraq in the 1990s; and the hostility of all the neighboring states to the coalition presence in Iraq meant that the post-war transition could not have been easy (Allawi, 2007).

The widespread hostility the war provoked in the media, and the collapse of the emphasis on defeating terror at its source that prevailed immediately after 9/11, has inhibited analysis of what the war achieved, at a surprisingly limited price. The Falklands War cost Britain over 250 dead, and while that war was productive of many positive results at home and abroad, Iraq has greater inherent significance than the South Atlantic. In Iraq, at the cost of less than 200 casualties, Britain helped uphold the UNSC system of collective security, and so legitimated it as a forum in which to address future crises. The war removed from power a genocidal, WMD-seeking dictator, led Libya to declare and abandon its hitherto unsuspected WMD program, and revealed the endemic corruption of the UN and many of its member states. In Iraq itself, millions of Iraqis participated in free and fair elections, with the result that Iraq is, in 2008, the only Arab country with a legitimate, democratic government. And finally, the result of Al-Qaeda Iraq's intervention after 2003 has been to alienate the Sunnis, and so to cause a collapse of sympathy for Osama bin Laden in the region. Blair intended only some of this, but if he is to take the blame for the war's unexpected negative consequences, he should also be credited with its positive results (Bull, October 2007).

It was the war's aftermath that did Blair the most damage. It slowly eroded his support, and led to his eventual, and long-promised, replacement by Gordon Brown in 2007. The coalition's failure to find the promised Iraqi

WMDs was the most important setback, though the Duelfer Report drew a damning but neglected portrait of Hussein's continued interest in WMDs and other prohibited technologies (Duelfer Report, 2004). The insurgency that began in summer 2003 was the second blow; having called on the public to be "prepared for the long term," Blair found that the British people did not share his desire to stay in the fight, no matter what the consequences of abandoning it might be. And, third, there were the terror attacks in London in July 2005, and the broader evidence of widespread Islamic radicalism in Britain, which critics—ignoring the Muslim-led riots in France in 2005 and evidence of rising radicalism in many other nations around the world—blamed on Britain's participation in the war.

The war had other results, ones that damaged Blair less but will be more important in shaping the future of British politics and foreign policy. In the international realm, the war will be judged by assessing whether it led to the rise of the Shia, backed by a radical Iranian regime with its own nuclear program, across the Middle East. At home, Brown by mid-2008 appeared likely to drag his party down to defeat at the next election. The question for history will be whether Blair's resignation was the end of New Labour as a whole. And, finally, there is the matter of British relations with the US. Here, the inaccurate perception that Blair was Bush's poodle did immense damage to the special relationship, with 36 per cent of Britons surveyed for the *Financial Times* describing the US as the "greatest threat to global security" (Harris Poll, 21 August 2006). This perception poses a central challenge for future British and American leaders.

Blair's contradictory legacy

Blair's downfall was not caused solely by Iraq; no government lasts forever, and by 2007 Blair was the second longest serving prime minister in the twentieth century. While Iraq did much to determine the timing and the manner of Blair's departure, his legacy will not be defined by the war. Rather, it will be shaped by how historians, and the British political system, address the contradictions inherent in his policies.

Blair entered office as a modernizer, intent on reshaping Britain's political institutions and its national identity. There was nothing unusual about this; it has been the declared goal of every prime minister since Harold Macmillan. But Blair, as evidenced by his desire to bring the British public closer to Europe, believed that making Britain more European would make it more willing to support the role he envisioned for it in the world.

Instead, Blair was brought down by the party he had created. For it, being a modern liberal came to mean rejecting the use of force in international affairs; for him, being modern meant standing by this part of the liberal tradition. Deeply moved by his own Christian faith, Blair failed to recognize that the kind of society he sought would distrust both faith and the moral impulses he derived from it (Blair, 1996, Ch. 7). He did not realize that, by encouraging the advance of the European vision, he was in fact undermining his own foreign policy. In this vision, in the international realm, the practical, legal, and moral responsibilities of citizens in democracies center on opposing war—including war in support of the liberal collective security system. Thus, most European states refused to put their forces in harm's way even in the UN-authorized war in Afghanistan. Blair proved himself a better, more courageous liberal than his critics, who refused to address the fundamental dilemma raised by the UNSC's failure to live up to its collective security obligations. Blair's error was to believe that the modern polity he had tried so hard to create was the kind of polity that would support his policies. By 1997, the legacy of the Second World War was still powerful, but it was fading. Under Blair, and in part because of his enthusiasm for modernity, it faded faster.

Blair embarked on the war in the belief that he could win over his opponents both at home and in Europe (Cook, 2003). There was no good reason to think this. Blair was Thatcher's successor; he advanced his policies within the framework she had created. But by 2003, Western Europe had not had a Thatcher, and European voters gave no sign of wanting to emulate the policies of her successor, either at home or abroad. Blair allowed his belief in his own persuasive abilities to override the evidence that Europe was simply not interested in his brand of social democracy and patriotic, liberal internationalism. In 2003, Blair passed the point at which rhetoric could be effective. The problem was that the European vision of domestic policy had a logical counterpart in the realm of international affairs—and this vision was not Blair's. This clash of visions will shape the future of both domestic and foreign policies in the liberal West.

Finally, and most directly, Blair was not willing to pay the financial price to back up his vision. He was committed both to fiscal responsibility and to improving Britain's social services; Britain's armed forces had to make do. By 2007, defense spending as a proportion of Britain's GDP was under 2.5 per cent, its lowest level since the 1930s (Gardiner, 2008). The hollowed-out forces were incapable of meeting the demands Blair placed on them, and sustained damage to their morale, readiness, and operational capacity that will take years to repair. Blair sought to calm domestic opposition to the war by spending as little blood and treasure on it as possible. Except politically, and then only in the shortest of terms, this was a dangerous strategy, as it led the British forces in Iraq to cede control of the city of Basra to Iranian-backed militias. Blair consistently espoused assertive liberal internationalism, but he was unwilling to provide the means to pursue his chosen ends. Sooner or later, his bluff was going to be called.

These contradictions were not unique to Blair's Britain. The left in most advanced democracies is less and less ready to support the use for force. And all democracies cut defense spending after the end of the Cold War. The

272 A Just War

result was that by 2003 most had neither the will nor the means to exercise their right of self-defense, much less to sustain a policy of collective security. Blair offers a particularly pointed illustration of the liberal dilemma, because he remained true to the liberal faith in foreign policy, but not to its political and practical requirements.

But no political program has all the answers. Prime ministers who fail to lead from the front, such as James Callaghan, John Major, or Gordon Brown, do not last long. Parliamentary and popular morale cannot be sustained by a policy of simply getting by. In electing Blair, the British people got what they wanted: a leader with a vision. He will rank as one of the century's dominant, principled prime ministers—not in spite of the war, but because of it, because of his willingness to stand by his convictions. When accused in 2003 of kowtowing to the US, his conclusion was clear: "It's worse than you think. I believe in it." (Coughlin, 2006, p. 284)

19

US-UK Relations: Structure, Agency and the Special Relationship

John Dumbrell

The US-UK Special Relationship embraces formidable accretions of myth, sentiment and emotion. In historical terms, much of the 'specialness' is actually very recent. It was only after meeting Franklin Roosevelt in 1942 that Winston Churchill informed King George VI that 'Britain and America were now married after many months of walking out' (Jenkins, 2002, p. 676). However, the sentimental accretions have developed almost a life of their own. The Special Relationship has its own vocabulary, its own syntactical and attitudinal structure. It ranges from the comic effusions of Stephen Potter's 'hands-across-the-sea-manship' to the view of Churchill (as quoted by Margaret Thatcher) that 'there is nothing more important for the future of the world than the fraternal association of our two peoples in righteous work' (Potter, 1970; Danchev, 2007b, p. 191). There is also a kind of 'hands-across-sea-manship' in reverse: the anti-Americanism of British poodles and spineless prime ministers seeking to please their American masters. It is easy to be cynical about the cultural and sentimental aspects of the Special Relationship, whose story is one of increasing lop-sidedness, with British diplomats seeking to exaggerate and reify the relationship in order to associate Britain with the global superpower. From the US viewpoint, America has 'special relations' with many countries. It is also a simple matter to expose the power relations inherent in the sentimentality. Suez was the most brutal example. On the British side, Special Relations thinking is imbued with the 'Greeks and Romans' mindset whereby London civilises the barbarian intentions emanating from Washington. British leaders have also traditionally been clear that they do expect something more from the relationship than a good feeling about fraternal association. In 1961, Harold Macmillan wrote to Queen Elizabeth II that he had 'always thought about American Presidents that the great thing is to get them to do what we want' (Macmillan, 1972, p. 591).

In international politics, no doubt, interests are all. Yet culture, sentiment, history and language do count for something. In the case of the US-UK Special Relationship they arguably set the stage for at least a degree of (primarily elite) cooperation and shared understanding. In 1990, Gregory Treverton, reviewing the prospects for Anglo-American cooperation in the post-Cold War era, wrote that 'bright British diplomats in Washington will continue to feel that Anglo-Saxons can understand each other better than those who do not speak (roughly) the same language' (Treverton, 1990, p. 710). My main point at the start of this chapter, however, is to assert that the Special Relationship actually does exist in concrete structural form. We do not need to appeal to the vague gods of culture and sentiment, although culture and sentiment have their role in forming and sustaining these structures. What I have in mind here are the institutionalised structures of defence and military cooperation.

US military and intelligence cooperation in its current form dates back to World War II. It was rooted for nearly 50 years in the doctrine of anti-Soviet containment. The removal of the Soviet threat in the early 1990s led to a weakening of these ties. The ties remained nevertheless, sustained by inertia, and by the British desire to retain close association with what was now the world's only superpower. For Washington, the alliance was clearly far less important than in the days when US air bases in the UK formed a vital part of anti-Soviet forward defence. Yet the alliance still had its utility to Washington, especially since it seemed unlikely to involve commitments which strayed too far from core American interests (Dumbrell, 2004). The ties, of course, were reinvigorated by the Global War on Terror – or rather, by Prime Minister Tony Blair's response to America's War on Terror. In 2006, Jeffrey McCausland wrote in a publication issued by the US Strategic Studies Institute: 'no other state has the daily involvement in the planning and preparation of operations that the UK has with the US' (McCausland, 2006, p. 191). British intelligence has been intimately involved in post-9/11 intelligence operations, even if Washington's fragmented intelligence structure on occasion interrupted close cooperation. The British Government Communications Headquarters in Cheltenham appears to operate as a kind of default facility for America's National Security Agency, actually taking on the NSA role when American electronic spying systems failed in 2001. US-UK defence cooperation is still organised to a large degree in the Mutual Defence Agreement, last renewed in 2004. There remain around 11,000 US service personnel on British soil. The most celebrated instance of US-UK defence association is the British nuclear programme. Most scenarios for Trident renewal involve some continuation of the American role in the UK nuclear programme which was fashioned by John Kennedy and Harold Macmillan at Nassau in 1962. The UK is a major participant in US Ballistic Missile Defence. London has been a conspicuous supporter of War on Terror operations, probably including support for 'extraordinary rendition' and operations involving CIA Predator Drones. The two governments work together on numerous defence projects, notably the Joint Strike Fighter programme. Unsurprisingly, the Pentagon is by some way the biggest customer for BAE Systems (Archik, 2005).

The defence and intelligence relationships also draw upon complex and close economic ties between the US and the UK. Despite the Europeanisation of British trade and commerce, in 2006 each country was still the biggest single country investor in the other's economy. Obviously, the closeness does not encompass a great degree of 'partnership' in the sense of equal weight and mutuality. There are major interoperability and capability gaps between the US and the UK, as there are between the US and all other nations. There is also a gap in strategic culture – with 'force protection' (US) squaring off against 'low intensity' (UK). However, the structures of US-UK defence and intelligence cooperation clearly do exist. They have been greatly strengthened in recent years and are bound to have a continuing impact on transatlantic relations in the post-Blair, post-Bush eras. The intention now is to consider the issue of structure and agency in the Bush-Blair Special Relationship. How much did the structures of Anglo-American defence and intelligence cooperation incline London to support Bush's conduct of the War on Terror, in particular to participate in the invasion of Iraq?

Blair and Iraq: Structure and agency

A simple point to make about the structure/agency problem in relation to British support for the War on Terror is that the US-UK ties as of September 2001 were actually at a historically relatively weak point. Inertia and shifting patterns of national interest kept them broadly in place during the 1990s, but there were distinct signs of strain. The later Clinton period saw an increased American inclination towards unilateral action. The various Iraq bombing campaigns of the late 1990s and the Kosovo campaign did, it is true, involve close US-UK cooperation, even if the Balkans action in particular revealed tensions. The sharpening of the European integration agenda, and especially Blair's sponsorship of the St. Malo defence coordination programme, seemed nevertheless to point in the direction of transatlantic pulling apart. Blair stood opposed to the Bush administration position on the Kyoto agreement on climate change, on the International Criminal Court and on US withdrawal from various multilateral agreements. Labour MPs seemed set to attack Blair if he agreed to allow Britain to participate in the US anti-missile programme. Downing Street's attempts to square the US-European circle risked a double bind: being seen in Western Europe as a stalking horse for American imperialism and in Washington as being implicated in Franco-German schemes to 'rebalance' against the US.

What transformed all this was, quite simply, Blair's response to the Bush response to 9/11. Was agency or structure at the root of this? It is the contention of this chapter that, despite the degree to which Special Relationship structures *inclined* London to stand squarely behind Washington, agency – primarily Blair's own beliefs about international politics and about the obligations and opportunities of the Special Relationship – was key.

Before developing the argument further, let us take a minute to describe the nature of Blair's beliefs.

Most attempts to analyse Blair's foreign policy beliefs begin with his religious outlook. Will Hutton, for example, puts Blair in 'the same Christian reformist tradition as Lord Shaftesbury'. Tony Blair 'believes in the West of the Christian Enlightenment. Any global initiative, whether it's action against climate change or the fight against terror, requires the West to stand collectively together, even when the US is wrong' (Hutton, 2007). Visibly embarrassed when discussing his religious position, Blair described the background to the 2003 Iraq invasion decision thus: 'Well, I think if you have faith about these things then you realise that judgement is made by other people.' Pushed further, he continued: 'If you believe in God it (the judgement) is made by God as well' (*The Guardian*, 4 March 2006).

My intention here is not to portray Blair as some species of religious fanatic, but merely to underline the centrality of a religious conviction, derived from an Anglo-Catholic muscular, Christian reforming outlook, which clearly did attach itself to the 2003 invasion decision. The Blair Doctrine of liberal interventionism, outlined most famously in the speech he gave to the Economic Club of Chicago during the 1999 Kosovo crisis, is extremely well known. Lawrence Freedman, the author of the first draft of the 1999 Chicago speech, recalls it as actually very restrictive in its commitment to military intervention. However, the speech, with its attendant doctrine of legitimate intervention in a globalised international environment, did 'provide a rationale for later interventions' (Freedman, 2007, p. 625; also Plant, 2008). Blair continued to expound it well into the post-2003 period; before the Australian parliament, for example, and to various American audiences during 2006 and 2007. In these speeches, the post-9/11, 'post-Westphalian', Blair Doctrine adopted a rhetorically all-embracing messianism. On 5 August 2006, in Los Angeles, for example, he described the War on Terror as a 'clash about civilisation' (*The Economist*, 26 March 2006 and 5 August 2006). These beliefs were intense, dynamic and pivotal to Blair's decision making. They shared the moral certainty and some of the policy implications of American neoconservatism, while lacking the latter's preoccupation with American destiny and commitment to untrammelled American military primacy.

When asked to explain his decisions to British audiences, Blair generally shied away from expressions of moral absolutism. His justification for staying close to America appeared rather in the traditional garb of the Special Relationship: the garb of influence and favours as well as of 'hands-across-the-sea-manship'. Former Ambassador Christopher Meyer noted that his declaration (at the Labour Party conference in 2002) that 'we will stay with you to the last was "a great line"', though unfortunately 'Americans tend to hear these things literally' (Hitchens, 2007). Blair's domestic defence of his support for Bush tended, however, to be along the lines of 'get real'. American power was a simple fact of life; any French 'world view built around rival poles of power was crazy' (Campbell and Stott, eds, 2007, p. 688). Asked by Timothy Garton Ash what he had achieved from the Special Relationship over the last ten years, Blair replied 'the relationship itself': essentially the opportunity for influence (Garton Ash, 2007). Alongside his moral sense, Blair committed himself to a 'bandwagoning' strategy: staying close to the hegemonic power, thereby hoping to extract various goods, typically a combination of favours and influence. The danger always was that of over-extension – the drawing of British commitments away from the pursuit of core British interests – as well as the possibility of becoming associated with unpopular, even with failed, policies (Beeson, 2007; Walt, 2005). The decision to 'bandwagon' with the US also threatened to compromise Blair's commitment to European integration: essentially a commitment to retaining multipolarity in Europe (Hyde-Price, 2006). For Blair, the US/European circle was squared by his own, neo-Hegelian, conviction that (to quote Freedman once again) 'Britain was a country that could combine opposites and reconcile the contradictory' (Freedman, 2007, p. 616).

Blair told a joint session of the US Congress in 2003 that 'if Europe and America are together, the others will work with us' (Kennedy-Pipe and Vickers, 2007, p. 215). The UK would perform the familiar role of 'Atlantic bridge'. Blair might have added, in line with 'Greeks and Romans' logic, that America was most dangerous and irresponsible when denied the civilising wisdom of its British ally. London would, in John Bolton's tart words, apply itself to the business of 'smoothing off our regrettable colonial rough edges' (Bolton, 2007, p. 210). British closeness to Washington would be good for Britain and good for the US. According to Alastair Campbell, a cabinet meeting of 23 September 2002 was preoccupied with Blair's putative ability to keep 'a mad America' on 'the straight and narrow' (Campbell and Stott, eds, 2007, p. 640).

Empirical research on the Blair belief system points to the British leader's strong belief in his ability to control events, relatively low conceptual complexity and a high need for power (Dyson, 2006). Blair told an American interviewer that 'it is the job of the British Prime Minister to get on with the American President' (Amis, 2008, p. 176). 'Getting on' with George W. Bush would be a bumpy ride. However, personality traits, religious conviction, personal understanding of the logic of global power, the obligations of the Special Relationship, British interests: all these forces conspired to push Blair in the direction of the Bush administration.

Beliefs and the Iraq invasion

Considerable attention has been given to the question of whether Blair lied over the issue of Weapons of Mass Destruction in Iraq. Though distortion and 'spinning' were evident, the term, 'lying', is rather strong (Bluth, 2004). There was, as Robin Cook argued, some element of 'bad faith' – seeking a diplomatic solution in a situation which was almost bound to involve American military action – in Blair's handling of the crisis (Cook, 2004, p. 311). Yet both Bush and Blair had every reason to be genuinely surprised when no WMD were discovered. My intention so far has been not to deride or ridicule Blair's beliefs, but rather to establish their intensity and their characteristic blending of conviction and pragmatic interest. Why should these beliefs, rather than more fundamental 'structures', be seen as determining the key decisions?

In seeking to answer this question, let us consider the parallel case of Prime Minister Harold Wilson and the Vietnam War. Though pressed by President Lyndon Johnson to commit at least a troop of bagpipers to the conflict – and excoriated by left-wingers in his own Labour Party for offering largely rhetorical support for US policy in Indochina – Wilson refused. The comparison with Iraq is not exact. The fact that the Vietnam conflict was slow in building up gave Wilson more room to manoeuvre. For present purposes, however, it is important to appreciate that the structures of the Special Relationship – defence and intelligence sharing – were actually (if anything) stronger, and therefore presumably harder for Wilson to resist, in 1965 than in 2001–3. By 2003, though they had been reinforced by Blair's response to 9/11, they had just suffered the prolonged effects of the disappearance of the integrating Soviet threat. In 1965, moreover, the US had far greater economic leverage over Britain than it was to have 38 years later. In the mid-1960s, the US was engaged in periodic and costly attempts to rescue the over-exposed pound. Though, no doubt, designed primarily to protect the first line of defence against the dollar, the sterling rescues did give the US huge leverage. Though they balked at a repetition of Suez, Johnson and his advisers were able to contemplate employment of the 'Hessian option', whereby Britain would have been *forced* to commit troops. It is difficult to imagine such an option being available in any realistic sense in 2003 (Dumbrell, 2006, pp. 188–96).

Wilson explained to LBJ in 1965 that his government simply could not survive the commitment of British troops to Vietnam. The 2005 general election arguably illustrated that a prime minister *can* commit troops to an unpopular war and still be re-elected. Again, we have to appreciate the force of important distinctions between 1965 and 2003: the difference in the size of the Wilson and Blair parliamentary majorities, the shifting ideological composition of the parliamentary Labour Party and so on. However, it is manifestly the case that in 2003, Blair (unlike Wilson in 1965) took a huge personal, political risk. The risk involved, among other things, a gamble on the likely behaviour of (then Chancellor of the Exchequer and 'heir apparent' to Blair) Gordon Brown. It is difficult to understand what exactly, beyond intensely held personal belief, would explain such a decision. What is also extremely relevant here is the fact that Washington offered Blair a way out. On the eve of war, Defence Secretary Donald Rumsfeld blurted out at a press conference in Washington that British military involvement was not essential to the invasion. Bob Woodward's account of these matters indicates that Bush and Condoleezza Rice were extremely sympathetic to Blair's domestic predicament – as indeed, when it came to the crunch, LBJ had been sympathetic to Wilson's parallel problems (Woodward, 2004, pp. 204–11). Bush apparently gave Blair the clear option of ducking out of the actual invasion (Seldon, 2005, p. 593; Naughtie, 2004, p. 144). Again, especially in view of the clear steer he was apparently receiving from intelligence advisers to stay away from Iraq (Drumheller and Monaghan, 2006, pp. 55–74), it is difficult to imagine what – apart from complex personal conviction – can explain Blair's decision.

The special relationship after the Iraq invasion

To the extent that Blair was seeking influence and favours from participation in the invasion of Iraq, the current consensus is that he failed. Some attempts have been made to argue the case for Blair's influence. Bush's attempt to achieve a second UN resolution in early 2003 surely did owe something to Blair, though it also reflected the desire of the American public that Washington should spread the cost of invasion by seeking multilateral support. British involvement in the negotiations which secured the Libyan renunciation of nuclear ambitions seemed to indicate that London could indeed participate productively in post-9/11 global diplomacy (Bowen, 2006).

Denis MacShane has put the case for seeing Blair's hand not only in the matter of the second UN resolution, but also in America's re-entry into UNESCO, the development of the Israel-Palestine 'road map', shifts in US stances towards Iran and even in the Israeli military exit from Gaza (MacShane, 2006). Such arguments are not especially convincing. They tend to confuse direct British influence with the desire of the Bush team to repair relations, especially after the administration entered its second term in early 2005, even with those Western European countries which had so spectacularly opposed the invasion. In a radio interview broadcast on 11 May 2007, Condoleezza Rice traced Blair's influence in changing the administration's line on climate change and in promoting aid to Africa. She also described Bush's attitude towards Northern Ireland as being 'whatever Tony Blair needs, Tony Blair should have' (BBC, 2007a). Disagreements over Sinn Fein fundraising in the US, however, did break out in 2006, with Washington in post-9/11 conditions actually being reluctant to recognise the IRA's renunciation of the armed struggle (*The Times*, 22 June 2007). It is fair, however, to point out that US activism on Northern Ireland continued under Bush, despite predictions that it would evaporate with the end of the Clinton presidency. It is also reasonable to point to Blair's stance on Africa and on climate change as having some kind of effect in Washington, though policy in such areas reflects infinitely more than simple pressure from London. Tensions between London and Washington were still clearly evident in the final months of the Blair government in the first half of 2007: in the initial coolness of the official British response to the US military 'surge' in Iraq and also in some American reactions to British conduct during the naval hostage-taking by Iran and to the timetable for UK troop withdrawal from Basra. In February 2006, the US scrapped a major defence deal with Rolls-Royce, despite Blair's reported personal intervention (Coughlin, 2006, p. 353). There were some compensatory signs of movement on long-standing British complaints about denial of access to US defence technology. In June 2007 Blair and Bush signed a treaty which went at least some way to answering these complaints (*The Times*, 22 June 2007).

In assessing Blair's influence, it is worth mentioning that there clearly were elements of the Bush administration – especially Rice, Colin Powell and indeed Bush himself – who took Blair very seriously, and were prepared to acknowledge his courage and wisdom in making unpopular decisions. By the same token, there were elements – most obviously in the Pentagon and in the circles around Vice President Cheney – to whom Blair seems to have been little more than a rather sanctimonious nuisance. At the very least, Blair displayed a severe lack of appreciation of the extent and nature of intra-administration divisions under Bush (Kampfner, 2007).

An important strand in the controversy about the transatlantic influence exerted by Blair relates to lost opportunities. Both Christopher Meyer and former president Jimmy Carter have argued that Blair could have used his Washington status to push more forcefully for the policy lines being promoted by Secretary of State Colin Powell: for a new commitment to the Israel-Palestine negotiations, and for the shutting down of Guantanamo (Meyer, 2005, p. 57; *The Observer*, 27 May 2007). This viewpoint is worth recording, and it is even possible that the process of document release may increase its persuasiveness over time. Looked at from the perspective of our current knowledge, however, this argument seems both to attach an unrealistic potency to Blair and to underplay the power of warring factions in Washington. Extending the argument slightly, it is evident that Blair failed to make any impact on the issue of post-invasion planning. The prime minister was certainly advised by Ambassador David Manning in March 2002 that Washington was seriously underestimating the difficulties of Iraqi democratic reconstruction. Blair was kept informed of the deteriorating situation immediately after the invasion in a series of detailed memos from John Sawers, his envoy in Baghdad. Recognition of the post-invasion mess, and arguably of his own failure to press the issue of post-invasion realism, seems to have led Blair to the brink of resignation in the spring of 2004 (Rawnsley, 2007). The story of all this is most likely a familiar one: good-faith efforts by Blair to promote his case in Washington being greeted positively by sympathetic parts of the administration, only subsequently to be undermined by the Pentagon and by Cheney's office. It is also important to acknowledge, as former Defence Secretary Geoff Hoon did in a 2007 interview, that the political leadership in London, almost as much as in Washington, was swept up in naïve optimism, especially following the initial taking of Baghdad (*The Guardian*, 2 May 2007).

By 2004, the conventional wisdom in the UK was that some kind of drawing apart between London and Washington was inevitable. The new Conservative Party leader, David Cameron, even took the opportunity of the fourth anniversary of 9/11 to criticise 'unrealistic and simplistic' world views in Washington (*The Times*, 12 September 2006). The 2006 firing of Jack Straw from his job as foreign secretary was traced even by conservative commentators, notably William Rees-Mogg, to US displeasure at Straw's opposition to US military action in Iran (Rees-Mogg, 2006). The 'Yo Blair' incident at the St Petersburg summit of July 2006 further damaged Blair's public reputation. (In an accidentally recorded conversation, Blair was heard, in tones which seemed to mix desperation with obsequiousness, offering his good offices in connection with the conflict taking place in Lebanon). His position on the Lebanon conflict was additionally undermined by the leaking of a critical memo from David Manning and by the publication of criticism by former adviser Stephen Wall. Wall urged Blair to think 'less about private influence and more about public advocacy'; it was time to 'unhitch' the UK 'from the Bush chariot' (Wall, 2006).

Beyond Blair

Blair's experience with the Special Relationship in the era of the War on Terror was a miserable one. It is exceedingly difficult to imagine any future British leader wishing to tread a similar path. It surely is the case that Iraq 2003 will cast a similar pall over the Special Relationship to that experienced after Suez 1956. No British prime minister will contemplate action which might plausibly be compared to the Blair war decision of 2003 (Niblett, 2007).

Some post-Blair commentators were happy to celebrate the possibility of ending all talks of 'special' US-UK relations (Wheatcroft, 2007). At the least, the opportunity should be taken to re-evaluate the Special Relationship in the light of shifting British interests (Gamble and Kearns, 2007). What actually occurred upon Brown's elevation was a symbolic and rhetorical distancing from an unpopular US leader who had just experienced a huge rebuff in the 2006 mid-term elections. The new government also demonstrated an understandable desire to distance its transatlantic style from that of its predecessor. Early appointments included those of David Miliband as foreign secretary and (former United Nations Deputy Secretary-General) Mark Malloch Brown as minister for Africa, Asia and the UN, with a right to attend cabinet meetings. The former had criticised Israeli conduct in the

Lebanese conflict of 2006, while the latter's 'anti-American' conduct at the UN apparently attracted the anger of Bush himself (Bolton 2007, p. 289). The choreography of Brown's first meeting with Bush was in stark contrast to the practices and symbolism of the Blair era. The *New York Times* offered a helpful translation from 'Brownspeak' into 'Americanspeak': Gordon Brown's formal body language and unwillingness to use the US president's first name came down to: 'It's the United States we love, not George Bush' (Stelzer, 2007). Malloch Brown opined that it was 'very unlikely that the Bush-Brown relationship is going to go through the baptism of fire and therefore be joined together at the hip like the Blair-Bush relationship' (BBC 2007b). A July 2007 address by International Development Secretary Douglas Alexander embodied a stout condemnation of unilateralism, and was widely interpreted as an attack on the Bush foreign policy (Quinn, 2007). The new team seemed strangely reluctant to use traditional British Special Relationship language, preferring to describe the US-UK relationship as 'our single most important bilateral partnership' (Miliband, 2007). Mature distancing, stopping well short of 'abandonment of an ally for domestic political gain', seemed to sum up the initial Brown approach (Kearns, 2007).

It is important to put these rhetorical and symbolic flourishes into context. The Brown government showed no inclination to dismantle the *structures* of the Special Relationship. In terms of defence collaboration – at least beyond Iraq – these structures continued firmly in place. Brown confirmed that London would allow the US to use the air base at Menwith Hill in Yorkshire as an integral part of its Ballistic Missile Defence programme. He announced that Britain would construct two new aircraft carriers, providing platforms for Joint Strike Fighters and American Chinook helicopters. In his early months as prime minister, Brown strongly backed Washington's call for tough sanctions on Iran. As chancellor, Brown had also committed himself to Trident renewal, with its almost inevitable reliance on American technology (*The Economist*, 17 November 2007). It should also be realised that both British political leaders of the immediate post-Blair era – Brown and Conservative leader David Cameron – embraced the traditionally positive elite view of Britain's American connection. Of post-1945 British premiers, only Edward Heath can plausibly be regarded as rejecting the view that closeness to the US – not closeness at any price, but as much closeness as might reasonably be reconciled with domestic harmony and the pursuit of core national interests – is desirable. Brown, in fact, is extremely well versed in American affairs. His contacts are primarily with Democrats, though he has links with Alan Greenspan; he is also a strong admirer of various US social thinkers, including the conservative writers James Q. Wilson and Gertrude Himmelfarb (Lloyd 2007; Himmelfarb, 2008). As Brown's biographer Tom Bowyer put it, 'America inspired Brown'. President Bill Clinton's 'social inclusion', welfare and economic policies were models for the New Labour approach to economic and social management, an approach which

Brown nurtured in the mid-1990s even more conspicuously than Blair himself did (Bowyer, 2007, pp. 232–3). For his part, David Cameron rapidly moved to repair the damage done to Conservative-Republican relations in the Blair years, and to reverse the impression made by his own remarks on the occasion of the fourth anniversary of 9/11. His visit to Washington in November 2007 was the first time that a Conservative leader had set foot in the city since Iain Duncan Smith's 2002 trip (*The Times*, 30 November 2007). The Conservative leader has also made various speeches praising, among other things, America's 'real sense of common identity' and its traditions of anti-centralization (guardian.co.uk, 2007; Google Zeitgeist, 2007).

Clear US-UK tensions persisted through 2008. The deteriorating security situation in southern Iraq caused Brown to reconsider his troop withdrawal timetable. However, the clear British preference for fighting in Afghanistan over Iraq was not welcomed in Washington. Frederick Kagan, the originator of the idea of 'surging' in Iraq in 2007, actually accused the British of irresponsibly abandoning Basra (BBC, 2008). Even regarding Afghanistan, the US and UK clashed publicly over the issue of poppy eradication, with the latter regarding eradication programmes as tending to increase support for the Taliban. However, the Brown government's belief structures are by no means inconsistent with a revivified US-UK Special Relationship. Indeed, Brown's visit to Washington in April 2008 embodied a symbolism which stood in marked contrast to his previous encounter with Bush. The two leaders happily reverted to Stephen Potteresque vocabulary, with the British PM affirming his position 'shoulder to shoulder' with the US. Brown's espousal of 'hard-headed internationalism' linked neatly into the doctrine of 'tough love multilateralism' – essentially a new American commitment to sharing power against a background of reformed transnational institutions – as espoused by some American liberals in the context of the 2008 elections (Jentleson, 2007). In his speech at the Kennedy Library in Boston, Brown even presented his own version of Blair's 1999 Chicago declaration: reaffirming 'the special relationship between America and Britain', and calling for strong, reformed international institutions fit for a 'global society' as well as for a new era of transatlantic cooperation (Brown, G., 2008).

Some commentators urged Brown to take the opportunity of the waning of the Bush administration to assert leadership in a way which redefined US-UK relations: by developing, for example, a clear agenda for the future of EU-NATO relations; by using the process of Trident renewal to promote a new internationalised regime of nuclear inspection; even by floating plans for a strategic 'grand bargain' between the US and Iran (Kaletsky, 2007). Such invocations risk missing one essential truth of the Special Relationship: the fact that it is indeed lop-sided, and indeed almost invisible to many of those viewing from the US side. When Brown visited the US in April 2008, he did so primarily in the context of the global financial crisis, rather than as anything approaching the status of a partner in American international strategy. The Special Relationship figured in the 2008 presidential primary elections only very tangentially and spasmodically: for example, in relation to Hillary Clinton's efforts to argue that she had been an important force in the Northern Irish peace process. British leaders lose sight of this lop-sidedness at their peril. The story of Blair's involvement in the Iraq invasion decisions is the story of a British prime minister who did just that.

If the preceding discussion is correct, leader understandings and beliefs regarding the nature and obligations of the Special Relationship really do matter. The US-UK relationship may be described as having three layers. First, there is the geopolitical and cultural underpinning. This was the underpinning which was eroding in the immediate post-Cold War period: eroding geopolitically with the extinction of the Soviet Union, as well as to some degree culturally, with the increased Europeanisation of British insti-tutions and with changing demographic patterns in the US. Second, there is the routinised bureaucratic interweaving, whose inertia did so much to sus-tain the relationship in the 1990s. Third, we have the top level: the tier of leader beliefs and interactions, sometimes unpredictable, but generally reflec-tive of the instinctive pro-Americanism of British political elites. Following Blair, it is possible to hold that the erosion of the geopolitical/cultural underpinnings will gain fresh momentum. There is some recent evidence that cultural differences between the US and the UK are increasing ('Anglo-American Attitudes', 2008). Geopolitical realities may be pushing the US towards greater Pacific and less European engagement. It should be remem-bered, however, that such predictions were also common fare in the early 1990s. The 2008 US presidential election campaign showed no sign of can-didates wishing to abandon American globalism. The middle tier of the Special Relationship – the mid-level interweaving – will continue to influ-ence and sustain bilateral relations between London and Washington. Elite beliefs on the British side are unlikely to embrace the messianism of a Tony Blair; they are likely to remain wedded to a pragmatic understanding of the need to continue a US-UK Special Relationship rooted in close defence and intelligence cooperation.

20
Blair and the European Union

Scott James and Kai Oppermann

Introduction

The perception of British 'awkwardness' in European affairs can be explained in part by the antipathy of successive governments to supranational forms of integration, by a certain 'style' of negotiation which is a product of the European Union (EU) policy-making process within government, and by the failure to construct a supportive domestic consensus (Allen, 2005, p. 131–2). The aim of this chapter is to address each of these explanatory variables in turn, exploring the extent to which the Blair government has sought to challenge them and so define a new direction for British European policy. It does so by analysing and assessing Labour's record in office under Blair across three core legacies, each of which corresponds to the three variables identified above: the policy legacy, structural legacy, and political legacy.

The chapter begins by placing Blair's European policy within its proper historical context by outlining the inheritance bequeathed by the Thatcher and Major governments in 1997. Rather than provide a historical narrative of Labour's European policy, the second section adopts an analytical approach that focuses on three particular case studies: European security and defence policy, economic and monetary union, and the Constitutional Treaty. We suggest that these not only represent the three most significant aspects of Blair's policy legacy, but also neatly encapsulate the government's inconsistent record of engagement and leadership in Europe. The third and fourth sections attempt to explore the wider structural and political legacies that have been framed and shaped by the policy context. We do so by analysing the strategy pursued for reforming the UK's European policy-making process, and for managing the public salience of European policy. The chapter concludes by considering to what extent the Blair government has charted a new and distinctive European policy trajectory.

The Blair inheritance – Ever the 'Awkward partner'

Rather than rehearse the development of the UK's relations with Europe since accession in 1973 (see in particular George 1998; Gowland and Turner, 2000), we here outline the inheritance bequeathed by Labour's predecessors across the three dimensions that structure this chapter: policy, structural, and political.

With respect to substantive European policy, the Conservatives left behind an ambiguous legacy of semi-detachment. On the one hand the UK remained at the forefront of those members pushing for the completion of the single market and for eastern enlargement, and was generally support-ive of greater intergovernmental cooperation in the areas of foreign and security policy and justice and home affairs. On the other hand the Major government successfully negotiated 'opt-outs' from both economic and monetary union and the Social Chapter in 1992, and opposed proposals at the 1996 IGC to incorporate the Schengen agreements into the EU. In appearing to advocate an agenda of Europe *a la carte*, many member states continued to question the UK's commitment to European integration. Moreover, by committing the Conservatives to a referendum on any deci-sion to join the single currency, Major established a powerful precedent that Blair was forced to emulate in the run-up to the 1997 election.

By contrast, the UK's European policy-making structures were widely admired as one of the most efficient and effective in the EU. Whitehall's rel-atively centralised and highly institutionalised system of interdepartmental coordination on the whole ensured that officials in Brussels were well-prepared and able to 'sing from the same hymn sheet' (see Bulmer and Burch, 1998). Over time, however, the gradual extension of qualified majority voting in the Council placed an increasing strain upon a system designed to project inflexible negotiating positions, and so risked further damaging the UK's relations in Brussels (James, forthcoming).

Finally, the political legacy inherited by Labour in 1997 was characterised by two notable features. First, the Major government presided over a clear reversal of the pro-European trend characteristic of UK public opinion since the late 1980s. The government's increasingly strident Eurosceptic postur-ing, which came to a head with the 1996 policy of 'non-cooperation', con-tributed to a 22 per cent decline in support for EU membership between 1991 and 1997 (Evans 1998, p. 174). Second, the Major government's high profile travails on Europe (including the Maastricht Treaty ratification deba-cle, the ERM crisis, and the Commission-imposed British beef export ban), compounded by growing intra-party divisions, meant that by 1997 Europe had become one of the most salient issues among the electorate (Oppermann, 2008a, pp. 143–4).

Across all three dimensions we see that the Blair government faced a num-ber of profound challenges to its stated desire to assert a more positive approach to Europe. Taking each of these in turn, the following sections explore the extent to which Labour has successfully charted a new European trajectory.

The policy legacy – A record of inconsistency

The new Labour government was elected with a manifesto commitment to a more constructive European policy which aimed to bring about a 'step change' in the UK's relationship with its EU partners. In order to evaluate the government's European policy balance sheet, we here analyse three principal policy legacies. The selection of these case studies permits us to explore the nature of developments in greater detail and provides a valuable snapshot of the Blair government's most significant policy successes and failures.

European security and defence policy – A legacy of leadership

The policy field in which the Blair government was the most successful in establishing itself as a leading partner in Europe was in European Security and Defence Policy (ESDP). By adopting a positive approach towards strengthening the EU's role in this area, Labour positioned itself at the centre of the debate and exerted significant influence on the shape of the future policy. This influence was at its most noteworthy with respect to the 1998 St. Malo declaration. At its core, the declaration enshrined an Anglo-French agreement that the EU should be able to respond with self-contained military operations to international crises in which NATO would not be engaged. Together with the Amsterdam Treaty, St. Malo was the most conspicuous manifestation of the 'Eurohoneymoon' (*The Economist*, 14 June 1997, p. 14) which Labour enjoyed during its early period in office at both the European and domestic levels. The agreement at St. Malo stemmed in large part from the Blair government's initiative and laid the foundation for the UK's role as an agenda-setter in security and defence policy.

The starting point for the process was a fundamental change in British European policy. In contrast to all previous British post-war governments, Labour relinquished the UK's reservations towards an autonomous European defence capacity outside of NATO. At the informal European summit at Pörtschach in October 1998, Blair for the first time articulated the need for the EU to construct an independent defence dimension, thereby placing the issue on the European agenda.

Blair's initiative was based upon three interconnected arguments. First, it was the government's response to the 1998 escalation of the Kosovo crisis which revealed both the inadequacy of the EU's existing political and military instruments and Europe's dependency on the US to deal with large-scale international crises. Second, the initiative reflected the government's re-evaluation of the relationship between a military role for the EU and the durability of NATO. The former was no longer perceived as a threat to the latter, but rather as contributing to the viability of the transatlantic alliance and as a cornerstone of Labour's broader strategy for the UK to act as a 'bridge' between Europe and the US (Kramer, 2003, pp. 90–6). Third, the Blair government sought to exploit its defence initiative as a means to enhance its influence on the future shape of the EU in a significant area of European policy. The initiative followed up on the advice of an extensive European policy review within Whitehall during the first half of 1998 which identified security and defence policy as an auspicious field for the British government in which to set the European agenda and compensate for its absence from monetary union (Holden, 2002, pp. 162–6).

Labour's defence initiative did indeed establish a legacy of British leadership in the field. St. Malo unleashed a sustained integration dynamic towards ESDP, which the Blair government successfully shaped according to British interests (Howorth, 2007). Most notably it wrested from the French government an explicit commitment to NATO's central role in the European security architecture and ensured that the ESDP was constructed in close coordination with NATO. In addition, the intergovernmental character of ESDP and its emphasis on building up military capabilities rather than institutional structures corresponded closely to the Blair government's preferences (Roper, 2000, pp. 11–16).

Labour's ability to set the European agenda in security and defence affairs can be accounted for by the interplay of its strong bargaining position at the European level and its political autonomy to develop a constructive approach to ESDP at the domestic level. At the European level, the Blair government's bargaining power stemmed from the high priority that its European partners attached to their longstanding aspiration of establishing a meaningful ESDP to which Britain's military and diplomatic resources were indispensable. By agreeing to participate in such an endeavour, the Blair government accrued strong bargaining leverage to shape its specific design.

At the domestic level, Labour did not face significant political costs in adopting a proactive stance on European defence. In fact St. Malo received rather scant attention from the Conservative opposition and eurosceptic media. Although both were opposed to Labour's policy on ESDP, the issue was not at the forefront of their attacks on the government, which instead focused on monetary union. Neither did the issue provoke controversy within the Labour Party itself. Consequently the government's stance on European defence did not rank among the public's principal concerns. Insofar as the issue came to the general public's attention at all, Labour could act on the assumption that a majority of the public would support the initiative despite their overall scepticism towards Europe (Oppermann, 2008a, pp. 184–207). Crucially then, Labour's positive legacy of leadership on

ESDP derived in large part from favourable European and domestic-level opportunity structures that were notably absent in other policy fields.

Economic and monetary union – A legacy of deferral

No European policy came to define the Blair government's period in office more than Economic and Monetary Union (EMU). How can we explain Labour's failure to join given its early commitment 'in principle' to doing so and the host of domestic opportunity structures in its favour – not least a solid parliamentary majority, an ineffective opposition, and majority support from business and unions (Gamble and Kelly, 2002, p. 116)? We argue that in pursuing a strategy aimed at de-politicising the issue, the government paradoxically constrained its autonomy to make a decision. This stemmed from the nature of three key informal veto points.

The first veto point originated from Major's pledge in 1995 to hold a referendum on any decision to enter the single currency. Although Blair's emulation of this commitment helped to de-politicise such a sensitive issue in the run-up to the election, the longer term impact of promising without delivering a referendum has been to prevent the issue from being settled through the parliamentary process. The government also undermined its capacity to set the terms of the European debate as its entire policy became framed around the referendum, as well as exposing the timing of any decision to variables beyond its control. Hence over time the prospects for a referendum receded as public support declined after 1999 (Gamble and Kelly, 2002, p. 97), in the wake of failed referenda in Denmark and Ireland in 2000/1, as a consequence of the political time and energy devoted to the Afghan and Iraq wars, and because its marginalisation by the 2004 Constitutional Treaty referendum pledge. In this respect short-term political expediency arguably proved to be a longer term strategic blunder that restricted the government's room for manoeuvre.

The second veto relates to Labour's hastily formulated policy on EMU set out in October 1997. Ruling out entry for the rest of the parliament, the chancellor stated that in the absence of constitutional obstacles the UK should join if the benefits were 'clear and unambiguous' based on a positive assessment of five economic tests: sustainable convergence between the UK and the Eurozone, sufficient flexibility in the UK economy to cope with membership, improving conditions for UK investment, a positive impact on the UK's financial services sector, and the promotion of sustained employment growth. This strategy served two principal political functions, the logic behind which contained inherent flaws.

Firstly, it sought to de-politicise the issue further by framing the debate in terms of narrow, economic benefits. The ambiguity of the tests ensured that the government was able to determine the timing of any referendum (Clark, 2001), while helping to legitimate any decision. Yet it also contributed to a vacuum of debate by constraining the government's ability to openly campaign in favour of entry. To have done so on economic grounds would have under-mined the legitimacy of the assessment process, while engaging in a political debate would wreck the strategy of restricting it to economic terms.

Secondly, in formulating the five tests the Treasury ensured that it would retain an effective veto over any decision to join, restricting the role of the Cabinet Office and Foreign Office to the handling and tone of policy. Predictably the 2003 assessment presented No.10 with a *fait accompli*, wreck-ing Blair's hopes for a route map and timetable for entry, and preventing pro-European ministers from putting their case (Richards, 2005). Blair's fail-ure was therefore to fatally underestimate Brown's scepticism towards mon-etary union.

Intra-party division constituted a third and final veto over the govern-ment's EMU policy. At cabinet level divisions were manifest during Labour's first term as pro-European ministers (notably Cook, Byers, and Mandelson) publicly championed euro entry in open defiance of Brown (see Rawnsley, 2001, pp. 507–8). This incoherence contributed to Blair's decision after the 2001 election to remove Cook and Byers from their positions, and to enhance the Cabinet Office's European machinery in an effort to strengthen No.10's control of EMU policy. By 2003 Blair was expending all his political capital on persuading his own parliamentary colleagues of the case for war with Iraq, leaving little appetite for a further bruising battle over the euro. Given that a hard core of 10–20 per cent of Labour MPs remained deeply hos-tile to the single currency, Blair could never be certain how much opposition a precipitate rush to join would generate (Gamble and Kelly, 2000, p. 19).

Although the Blair government's constant deferral encouraged it to engage more constructively in other areas of EU policy to compensate for the potential loss of influence, this cannot disguise the fact that the prospects for UK membership of the single currency are significantly less favourable than they were in 1997. The Constitutional Treaty debacle not only threatens to turn any future euro referendum into a wider political debate over European integration, but the Brown government now faces a revived Conservative opposition that is more united on EMU than it has been for two decades. The irony is that the present incumbent of No.10 is as much the architect of this problematic legacy as his predecessor.

The European constitutional treaty – A legacy of obfuscation

The European Constitutional Treaty stands out as the issue which came to dominate the Blair government's European policy agenda during the second half of its tenure. The issue also provides an exemplar case of obfuscation by the government in response to a range of domestic political constraints. On the one hand, Labour initially adopted a conciliatory approach to the nego-tiations on the Constitutional Treaty and was in many ways successful in shaping its content. The Blair government's influence was perhaps most consequential regarding the new office of a fixed-term president of the

European Council, and with respect to giving national parliaments a role in monitoring the EU's adherence to the principle of subsidiarity. On the other hand, Labour's stance towards the treaty became increasingly negative as the European-level negotiations wore on, and at the 2004 Intergovernmental Conference its 'red-line' posturing appeared to evoke memories of previous Conservative administrations.

The shift in the Blair government's approach to the Constitutional Treaty mirrors a distinct narrowing of its domestic decision making autonomy. The early deliberations on the treaty went almost unnoticed in British domestic politics, providing the government with considerable autonomy to negotiate within the Convention process. This situation began to shift from 2003 for a number of reasons. First, the Conservative Party increasingly singled out its opposition to the Constitutional Treaty as a major plank of its eurosceptic attacks against the government. In particular, the issue took centre stage in the Conservative's 2004 European parliamentary election campaign. Second, the issue moved to the top of the media's agenda around the time of the publication of the draft Constitutional Treaty in May 2003. The domestic controversy was fuelled by a belligerent campaign led by *The Sun* and *Daily Mail* in favour of a referendum on the issue (Baker and Sherrington, 2005, p. 307). Third, the government's constructive role in the negotiations began to draw criticism from within the trade unions and the Labour Party, and thus weakened the cohesion of Labour's domestic support coalition. The potential for the issue to seriously threaten party discipline became evident in July 2003 when 15 Labour MPs engaged in a parliamentary rebellion against the government and opposed a motion welcoming the draft treaty (Cowley, 2005, p. 267).

In order to deflect mounting domestic pressure, in April 2004 the Blair government committed itself to a referendum on the Constitutional Treaty. In doing so, Labour not only addressed the foremost demand of the Conservative opposition, the eurosceptic press, and intra-party critics, but also accorded to the wishes of a broad majority of public opinion. In the short term the referendum pledge took the treaty off the political agenda and provided Labour with a breathing space at a time when the conclusion of the negotiations was imminent.

In the longer term, however, the prospect of having to ratify the Constitutional Treaty by referendum further constrained Labour's autonomy by establishing an additional veto over UK ratification, thus reinforcing its hard-line bargaining strategy at the European level. Since winning a referendum was in any case going to be an uphill battle in view of the public's overall scepticism (Gill, Atkinson and Mortimore, 2004, pp. 4–9), the Blair government was all the more determined not to compromise on its self-proclaimed 'red lines' at the negotiations.

Against this background the outcome of the French and Dutch referendums in May and June 2005 provided the Blair government with an unexpected escape from its self-imposed domestic constraint. In response to those rejections of the treaty, Labour became the leading advocate of a 'period of reflection' in the ratification process and was quick to stall any plans for a future referendum in the UK. During its presidency of the European Council in the second half of 2005, the Blair government sought to use its position at the helm of the EU to set the European agenda in such a way as to sideline discussions to revive the treaty. Rather than to resubmit a redrafted text for ratification, the Blair government was instrumental in replacing the Constitutional Treaty with a significantly more modest 'Reform Treaty' (Whitman, 2005, pp. 679–87).

Due to increasingly restrictive domestic constraints, the Blair government's erstwhile constructive role in the negotiations on the Constitutional Treaty had, by the end of Blair's tenure, come to resemble the minimalist approach to European treaty revisions of previous British governments. When Gordon Brown took office in June 2007, that legacy of obfuscation was the most immediate European policy legacy to preoccupy the new government. Thus it was Brown – on record for being a longstanding sceptic of the constitutional project (Peston, 2006) – to conclude the negotiations on the substitute for the original treaty. True to the pattern set by its predecessor, the Brown government's stance towards the Lisbon Treaty was strongly driven by domestic political considerations. Its primary objective was to ensure that the treaty maintained a low profile in the domestic debate and to circumvent the Blair government's referendum pledge by portraying the treaty as too insignificant to warrant a popular vote. In this respect, Blair's European policy bequeathed something of a poisoned chalice to the incoming Brown government with respect to European affairs.

These three case studies reveal an inconsistent pattern of engagement in Europe under Blair. Although Labour's policy record has avoided the damaging public rows and token euroscepticism that characterised the Major government in its final years, the potential influence or diplomatic 'credit' that derived from positive strategic initiatives in areas like security and defence policy have been spent defending the government's self-imposed absence from the Eurozone, and its continued 'red line' negotiating issues, to EU counterparts. Hence although it has successfully 'normalised' the UK's relationship, it has not been able to translate its significant achievements into a coherent vision or effective leadership role within Europe.

The structural legacy – Taming the 'Awkward state'

In order to underpin the projection of a more constructive European policy, the Blair government sought to reform the European policy-making process within government. Here we detail the nature of these significant changes with respect to their impact on vertical and horizontal interdepartmental coordination.

As soon as Blair entered office he set about enhancing the vertical coordination of EU policy from No.10 by strengthening the European machinery located within the Cabinet Office. Rather than rely primarily on a Foreign and Commonwealth Office (FCO) private secretary for European policy advice as Major had done, Blair instead turned to Brian Bender, the then head of the Cabinet Office European Secretariat (COES), for policy guidance, appointed Roger Liddle as a No.10 special advisor on Europe, and appointed Peter Mandelson as a 'roving European ambassador' based in the Cabinet Office. His ambitions were somewhat limited, however, by opposition from a number of senior FCO officials who negotiated an informal concordat with the COES in order to limit Bender's role, and from ministerial colleagues who resented Mandelson's *de facto* role as cabinet rank minister for Europe and rejected proposals for a separate European ministry (official quoted in James, forthcoming).

In the run-up to the 2001 election two factors led Blair to conclude that formal reform was necessary: relations with Bender's successor, David Bostock, were not as effective; and with a referendum on EMU a real possibility, Blair wanted a trusted advisor close at hand. With the appointment of Sir Stephen Wall as head of the COES in 2000, the position was upgraded to the level of permanent secretary, re-located to the Prime Minister's Office, and was given the title of Prime Minister's Advisor on European Policy (see Bulmer and Burch, 2005). To support the increased demands placed upon it, staffing levels within the COES were also increased significantly. These reforms were retained after Wall's departure in 2004, not least because of the Constitutional Treaty process and the 2005 UK Presidency.

As a consequence of these changes, the strategic role of the Cabinet Office was greatly enhanced, with around two-thirds of its workload devoted to driving forward the prime minister's priorities on Europe. Its European expertise was such that by the time of Blair's departure, No.10 was 'pretty close' to the point at which it could bypass the FCO altogether for policy advice and strategic thinking on Europe (official quoted in James, forthcoming). By integrating the Cabinet Office and No.10, the reforms provided the institutional capacity to keep Europe foremost on the prime minister's agenda, encourage more constructive engagement with EU counterparts, and offer clearer strategic direction about the negotiating outcomes that Blair desired.

With respect to horizontal coordination, the Blair government set out to reconfigure interdepartmental structures for EU policymaking. Since accession these have been characterized by a three-tier standing committee system at ministerial, senior official, and official level (see Bulmer and Burch 1998), supplemented by a weekly Friday meeting chaired by the head of the COES.

Since 1997 Labour has accelerated a longer-term trend away from the use of formal structures. At ministerial level the role of the formal cabinet sub-committee (the European Policy Committee) has effectively been usurped by a larger and more informal Joint Ministerial Committee (Europe) (see Table 20.1). In addition, there have also been other innovative (albeit short lived) attempts at strengthening strategic thinking and presentation – through the EU Strategy committee and the Ministerial Group for European Coordination (MINECOR). These trends are mirrored at official level as standing committees have been replaced with a system of ad hoc meetings convened by the COES when required (James, 2007). Consequently by 2007 the Friday meeting had evolved from its original incarnation as a 'clearing house' for EU negotiations to being the only standing forum for interdepartmental coordination at official level.

The increasing informality of horizontal coordination was driven in part by a desire to enhance the UK's influence through greater strategic networking, as part of the 1998 'Step Change' initiative (see Bulmer and Burch 2005, p. 862). By making domestic coordinating structures more fluid, the Cabinet Office sought to enhance the effectiveness of EU policymaking in two key respects. First, it would facilitate the delegation of routine coordination downwards to departments, thereby reducing the risk of 'overload' at the centre stemming from the increasing pace and complexity of developments in Brussels. Second, informal structures would permit more efficient decision making at home, allowing policymakers to respond more effectively and constructively in EU-level negotiations. Greater flexibility in both Whitehall and Brussels would therefore be mutually reinforcing.

Prior to 1997 the UK EU policy process was orientated towards formulating rigid negotiating positions, with little longer-term strategic capacity. By strengthening vertical strategic oversight of European policy from the centre, while accelerating the shift towards more flexible horizontal coordination

Table 20.1   Ministerial Committee Structures for EU policy since 1997

Committee	Role
Cabinet	Met rarely to discuss EU policy
European Union Strategy committee (EUS) – Established 2003	Chaired by the prime minister to provide medium-term strategy. Met only three times
Ministerial Committee on European Policy (EP)	Formally agrees EU policy (through written correspondence only since 2003)
Joint Ministerial Committee (Europe) (JMC[E]) – Established 1998	Chaired by the foreign secretary and including representatives from the devolved administrations and European parliament
Ministerial Group for European Coordination (MINECOR) – Established 1999, Disbanded 2004	Chaired by the minister for Europe to improve EU policy presentation and bilateral contacts

Source: James (forthcoming)

structures across government, Labour enhanced the capacity of the system to underpin policy change. The strategy therefore represented a tacit acknowledgement that British awkwardness stemmed in part from the particular 'style' of European policymaking. Despite this, however, the reforms remained a hostage to the vagaries of ministerial willingness to exploit them effectively. To adapt Bulmer and Burch (1998, p. 607), although the Rolls Royce of the Whitehall machinery never worked better, it still relied on the driver having a clear sense of direction.

The political legacy – Containing the salience of European policy

In the political arena, the principal European policy legacy of the Blair era pertains to the issue's 'public salience' – that is, the significance that the general public ascribes to European policy in relation to other political issues (Wlezien, 2005, pp. 556–61). The concept of public issue salience captures a major dimension of electoral politics in that it points to a cognitive precondition for issue voting. Election outcomes will only be shaped by issues which are among the most salient concerns of the public on voting day (Aldrich et al., 1989, pp. 125–7). The higher the public salience of European issues, the more attentive an electorate will be to a government's policies on Europe and the more significant these policies become as a determinant of the electorate's voting behaviour.

Given the entrenched euroscepticism of the British public (Geddes, 2004, pp. 212–6), European policy is likely to become an electoral liability for any British government with a pro-European agenda as soon as the issue is sufficiently salient to become a significant source of issue voting. Thus Labour's desire to adopt a positive approach to Europe was always in danger of harming the government's electoral prospects with the eurosceptic Conservative opposition. The higher the salience of European issues, the greater the potential of this policy field to act against the Blair government's electoral interests.

Against this background, Labour faced strong incentives to contain the salience of European issues. The empirical record reveals a pronounced downward trend in the public salience of European integration during the Blair premiership: European policy was transformed from a decidedly high-salience issue at the beginning of the Blair government's tenure into a downright low-salience issue at the end of Blair's period in office.

Broadly speaking the Blair premiership can be divided into two phases (see Figure 20.1). The first phase covers Labour's first term between May 1997 and June 2001 and is marked by a very high level of the issue's public salience. On average in this period, 24.5 per cent of respondents included European policy on their list of the most important political issues. Furthermore, European policy was among the foremost concerns of voters both at the 1997 and the

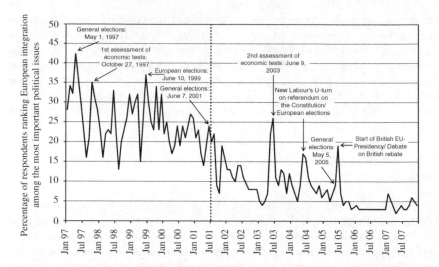

Figure 20.1   The salience of European integration, 1997–2007
Source: Ipsos MORI (2007a); unprompted, combined answers to the questions: 'What would you say is the most important issue facing Britain today?' and 'What do you see as other important issues facing Britain today?'

2001 general elections. In 1997, only health policy and education policy were assigned higher priorities by the electorate. In 2001 the importance attached to European issues was second only to health policy (Denver, 2003, p. 102; Clarke et al., 2004, p. 90).

The second phase spans the second and third terms of the Blair government and features a significantly lower level in the public salience of European policy. Between July 2001 and June 2007, the average level of European issues' salience corresponds to only about one third of the average level during the first phase. In terms of electoral politics, European policy was almost a non-issue in the 2005 general election campaign (Whiteley et al., 2005, p. 154). Moreover, since Labour's third election victory the public salience of European issues did not display any distinct upswings. On the contrary, during its first and – to a lesser extent – second term, the salience of European policy was highly volatile. In that period exceptional European integration-related events (notably with respect to EMU) often induced abrupt upswings in the public salience of European affairs.

The decline in the level and volatility of European policy's salience supported the Blair government's electoral interests and was in part precipitated by the government itself. In this respect Labour devised four governing strategies which attempted to provide as few focal points as possible for political attacks by the Conservative party and eurosceptic press (see Oppermann, 2008b, pp. 170–7). First, it sought to *defuse* the cleavage between its own European policy stance and those of the Conservative party. Second, the Blair government aimed to *depoliticise* its European policy decision-making – in other words, to depict it as a rule-based rather than a discretion-based exercise (Burnham, 2001). This strategy was most notable with respect to Labour's five economic tests on the single currency. Third, the Blair government resorted to referendum pledges to *delegate* responsibility for ratifying any decision on EMU and the Constitutional Treaty to the public, thereby mitigating their potential to become significant sources of issue voting. Finally, Labour *deferred* controversial European policy decisions and thus denied the domestic debate adequate points of reference. This policy of 'delayism' (Aspinwall, 2003, p. 363) again pertained principally to EMU and the Constitutional Treaty.

In combination Labour's governing strategies reduced the prominence of European affairs in the arena of inter-party competition, and so are among the principal explanatory factors for the decline in the public salience of European policy over Blair's decade in office. In contrast with its somewhat inconsistent policy legacy, the Blair government left an unambiguous political legacy that has contained the salience of European integration within the wider electorate. Whether this legacy becomes a permanent feature of British politics remains to be seen.

Conclusion – Still 'Punching below its weight'

The Blair government was elected with a commitment to placing Britain 'at the centre of Europe' (Blair, 1999b, p. 4). How then does Labour's balance sheet compare against its own stated aims and that of its predecessors? Here we take each core legacy of Blair's European policy in turn.

At the level of day-to-day EU policymaking, the structural reforms within Whitehall certainly helped to 'normalise' relations between UK policymakers and their European counterparts. By providing the necessary flexibility and efficiency at home to underpin a more constructive European diplomacy abroad, the changes were important in providing the institutional capacity for the Blair government to shed its image as an increasingly semi-detached state.

In one clear policy arena, security and defence policy, the UK government has demonstrated a willingness to exploit this capacity effectively to articulate a coherent vision and shape the European policy agenda. Yet it has conspicuously failed to translate this into other policy areas. Where the government has been pragmatic in its support of other initiatives – notably in relation to the Lisbon strategy, environmental policy, and justice and home affairs – this has often been in spite of, not because of, Europe. The government's support has therefore remained conditional and often covert (Bulmer, 2008).

This wider failure to articulate a clear European vision reached its zenith over the Constitutional Treaty. Lacking a coherent strategy to sell to either a European or domestic audience, the government lurched from initial hostility to reluctant support while downplaying its wider constitutional implications as a 'tidying up' exercise. This had the effect of satisfying neither their European counterparts nor the wider public. Finally, Labour's constant deferral of a decision over EMU stemmed from both Blair's failure to challenge the domestic political constraints in its way, compounded by Brown's principled doubts over the project (Peston, 2006).

On this basis we argue that the default position for the Blair government was to avoid challenging the strict instrumentalism that has guided UK European policy since accession. Hence although Labour's European policy constitutes a significant break from the recent past, like so much of its legacy in the domestic arena it has remained non-ideological, non-idealistic, and largely pragmatic. However, by pursuing a strategy aimed at decreasing the salience of the European issue among the wider electorate, it has not only left awkward questions of sovereignty and democracy for others to exploit, but has also undermined its own ability to engage the British public on the merits of a more constructive policy. It has consequently been ineffective at shifting public opinion and building the domestic consensus necessary in order for the UK to play the leading role in Europe that its weight and status deserves. The Blair government has therefore contributed directly to the widening of the central paradox at the heart of UK European policy: why public support for EU membership has declined over the past decade while the integration process has gradually aligned with UK policy preferences? Unless and until this paradox is resolved, the UK will continue to punch below its weight.

Conclusion: The Legacy of Tony Blair

Jonathan Tonge

Introduction

Assessing the legacy of Tony Blair is a complex task. A successful Labour Party leader from 1994, Blair became prime minister in 1997 amid an electoral landslide. By 2001, that landslide had become more apathetic and in 2005, Blair's third election victory was accompanied by unease, a notable triumph accompanied by a perception that he was now 'damaged goods'. This concluding chapter explores the legacy of Blair using four key tests. The first test is whether 'Blairism' amounted to a coherent ideology offering a prolonged set of intellectual ideas governing the framing of decisions. A second examination is whether the Blair governments yielded a distinctive, novel set of durable policies. The third exploration is whether the 'Blair settlement' was of sufficient calibre and popularity as to entirely reshape the policies of the Conservative opposition. Finally, the chapter applies a fourth legacy test in exploring whether the Labour party was converted into a 'Blairite' organisation. This concluding chapter begins, however, with an overview of academic interpretations of Blair's performance in office.

Political scientists versus historians on Blair and New Labour

Perceptions of Blair vary markedly among the public and among academic scholars of his era.[1] There remains substantial disagreement among academics over whether Blair can be considered a major or minor political figure. Perhaps the most authoritative (and to date the largest) academic ranking of twentieth-century British prime ministers was undertaken by MORI and the University of Leeds in 2004 (Theakston and Gill 2006). The study surveyed the views of 258 academics in universities across the UK. Among political scientists, Blair was rated a lofty fifth-best of the 20 prime ministers over the period, bettered only by, in order, Attlee, Churchill, Lloyd George and Thatcher, who formed also the top four choices (again in that order) of historians. However, the same historians ranked Blair a modest tenth, with Baldwin, Macmillan, Asquith, Wilson and Salisbury also rated above Blair. Accepting that the historian–political scientist distinction is itself non-absolute, why should historians rate Blair so lowly in comparison to political scientists, below even Wilson, commonly regarded as an under-achiever in terms of political and party reform? The division in terms of ranking is acute, far more significant than that produced when the party allegiances of political scientists and historians are taken into account.

Part of the explanation may lie in the greater emphasis upon electoral pol-itics within political science, attaching major significance to the uniqueness of Blair's achievement in securing a third consecutive term. A deeper reason for the variability of assessment may lie in the rejection of the Old Labour versus New Labour dichotomy by several historians. As examples, Morgan (1999) dismisses the distinctions as overlooking a variety of Labour ideolog-ical and political commitments during the twentieth century, variations which would have allowed the term 'New Labour' to be utilised in several previous decades. Labour's ideological and political outlook had embraced, variously, common ownership, revisionism, socialism through scientific effi-ciency, Keynesianism and even embryonic monetarism. Given this, the por-trayal of Blairism as the start of a new era or as an ideological repudiation of Labour's past appears erroneous. Warming to this theme, Fielding (2000, 2002) suggests that the Labour Party's convoluted history and longstanding internal debates make redundant the Old and New typologies. A more real-istic view is to see the label of New Labour as primarily an electoral market-ing device, designed to re-brand a party accustomed to electoral failure for much of the twentieth century, during which the party governed alone for a mere 18 years.

The scepticism of historians over the novelty of the Blair project is a nec-essary but insufficient explanation of why political scientists are more favourably disposed to the former Labour leader. A further explanation lies in the thesis that political science was indeed influential upon the Blair gov-ernment. This was reflected not merely in the greater use of academic pol-icy advisors by the Labour administration than had been common in British government, but more crucially, it is claimed that the Blair government relied heavily upon a positivist, new institutionalist approach to governance (Rhodes and Bevir 2003; Bevir and Rhodes 2004a, 2004b; Bevir 2005). Labour's belief in top-down, institution-led change was grounded in a rational, scientific approach to government in which if the government adjusted the workings of an institution, it could produce a positive outcome for the 'consumer' of that institution's activities. Bevir and Rhodes are them-selves ill-disposed to such beliefs, arguing strongly for a more critical, inter-pretivist approach to decision making, more cognisant of the role of human agents in determining, interpreting and implementing policy. As an expla-nation of the conduct of the Blair government, with its institutional obses-sions, the thesis nonetheless has much to offer. Indeed it is confirmed in other empirical studies of the period, which report Blair's frustration when levers supposedly controlling institutions were pulled to little discernible effect (e.g. Ludlam and Smith 2000; Seldon 2007).

While operating within a positivist, institutionalist framework, the Blair government also implemented less evidence-based change of considerable interest to political scientists (McAnulla 2007). Most significantly, the establishment of devolved institutions in Scotland, Wales and Northern Ireland emphasised that the rules-based positivism of New Labour did not inhibit radicalism and novelty. The creation of such institutions offered an attractive (to political scientists anyway) fusion of ideational, evidential and electoral reasoning in terms of the restructuring of the state. That historians appear less ready to accept the lasting significance of the most fundamental alteration of the UK for centuries, as undertaken by Prime Minister Blair, might be seen as extraordinary.

Third way or no clear way? Blairism as a non-ideological construct

Given the debates between political scientists and historians outlined above, can a distinctive Blairite ideology be identified? The former prime minister rejected the idea of Blairism as a rigid ideology, preferring to see his political approach as a repudiation of the dogma which he perceived as having scarred British political debate. A pragmatic 'what's best is what works', based upon good practice, formed the core of Blairite 'non-ideology'. Neither unfettered markets nor state domination were seen as ideal. Instead, a multiplicity of policy deliverers, embracing the private sector, state bodies and quangos were utilised. Blair's valedictory speech (10 May 2007) in his Sedgefield constituency on leaving office outlined his bafflement with traditional politics and highlighted his rejection of rigid sets of ideas:

> You stood for individual aspiration and getting on in life, or social compassion and helping others. You were liberal in your values, or conservative. You believed in the power of the state, or the efforts of the individual. Spending more money on the public realm was the answer, or it was the problem. None of it made sense to me.

For some, Blair's rejection of the traditional twin blocks of state-oriented socialism or undiluted economic liberalism constituted a distinctive 'Third Way' (Giddens 1998). Less was heard of the concept in the latter years in office, partly because of Blair's radical favouring of the private sector in most of the economy and much of the arena of welfare delivery, but more evidently because of the difficulty in constructing a coherent definition of the 'Third Way'. Insofar as it offered ideological distinction, the 'Third Way' offered an obvious repudiation of socialism and the undiluted economic liberalism of the New Right. Its critique of these polarities remains stronger than does its precision in charting a clear guide to political activity. For Blair, the Third Way amounted to an ideological framework in which social solidarity (Blair's belief in communitarianism) would be reconciled with continuing economic progress and diminished concern with the redistribution of the wealth generated. Blair's criticism of Old Labour lay not in its social values, but in its apparent determination to redistribute wealth which had not yet been generated.

The debate over whether Blairism represented merely Thatcherism with a more conciliatory face exercised academics and commentators throughout the Blair premiership. Blair offered a ready acceptance of the settlement bequeathed in 1997 and was anxious to promote New Labour as a break with the party's 'tax-and-spend' redistributive history. The extent of dilution or adaptation of Thatcherism was disputed, but some organic link was accepted by a variety of analysts. For Heffernan (2001) 'the Blair project' was largely indistinguishable from the 18 years of Conservative government which preceded its arrival, while for Shaw (2007), the degree of Thatcherite ideology infusing Blairism was obfuscated only by the theoretical vacuity and ambiguity which shrouded New Labour. A neoliberal basis to Blairism was identified by Crouch (2006), one which conditioned its economic reasoning, even if Blairism was obliged to make social democratic gestures for the sake of the Labour Party and also due to the contempt for the rawness of the Thatcher years. Crouch's argument is supported by Driver and Martell (1998, 2002, 2006b), who suggest that economic similarities between Thatcher and Blair were tempered by diminished stridency and communitarian sentiment. Perhaps the strongest academic defence of Blairism was offered by Fielding's (2000; 2002) contentions that the post-1997 Labour government was more redistributive in terms of fiscal and social policy than was commonly assumed, but that such policies were played down due to constant image concerns within a New Labour party anxious not to frighten hard-won middle class voters.

Blair's policy legacy

Many of Blair's domestic achievements were overshadowed by his prosecution of the war in Iraq, arguably the most ill-judged British foreign intervention since Suez. As the claims of Iraqi weapons of mass destruction expired, the credibility of 'intelligence' documents evaporated and the distortion of 'evidence' was exposed. British intervention, which hitherto had fairly evenly divided the British public in terms of perceptions of legitimacy, became increasingly unpopular. Upon his vacating office, it was claimed that only 15 per cent of the public 'spoke well of Blair's foreign policy' (Coates 2007: 429). Blair could claim moral justification, highlighting the removal of the tyrannical regime of Saddam Hussein. However, the perceptions among many British citizens were that the war had not been fully justified (why was this *particular* despot being removed, among many others?); that Blair had been economical with the truth when the decision to go to war had been taken; that evidence had been slanted or doctored to justify the case for participation and that the strong risk of sectarian violence post-Saddam had been blithely overlooked.

Domestically, however, Blair's record bore close scrutiny. It was true that the post-1997 Labour government had enjoyed 'considerable luck in terms of its economic policy' due to favourable global factors and a fair inheritance from the Conservative government in terms of a reformed labour market and growing economy (Smith 2007: 424). Moreover, the prime minister and his chancellor stuck determinedly to Conservative expenditure plans during the first two years of Labour's opening term. Nonetheless, Labour's fortuitous circumstances did not diminish the successes of increasing GDP annually, reducing unemployment and controlling inflation. Blair's legacy was to remove from his party the stigma of economic mismanagement and present Labour credibly as the natural party of proper economic management. The slogan of 'boom not bust' summarised Labour's determination to sustain a defendable economic record. Alongside the introduction of the minimum wage and his peace-building role in Northern Ireland, Blair's economic performance was listed as one of his top three achievements at the conclusion of his time in office (YouGov/*Daily Telegraph*, 2007a). Tactical, if temporary, advantage accrued from Labour's decision not to adopt the Single European Currency. Transient economic benefits and, more saliently, fear of a referendum defeat conditioned Labour's policy far more than the supposed 'five economic tests' for entry posed by the government. Had such tests been applied to other countries within the Eurozone, few would have been permitted to adopt the Euro.

Blair handed over control of the economy to Gordon Brown as part of the 1994 leadership deal and important factors in the construction of economic success, such as Bank of England independence and the decision not to join the Euro, were ideas developed by Brown's largely autonomous team (Smith 2005a). The Brown-Blair economic record withstood inspection. Inflation averaged a mere 2 per cent; average household incomes rose by 2.5 per cent per annum after tax and unemployment fell by over 300,000 during the ten years of the Blair premiership, averaging 1.6 million, less than half the figure presided over by the Conservatives during the 1980s (Smith 2005c; Brewer 2007). Nonetheless, it was possible to pick holes in the economic record. Rates of growth averaged less than those under the often-derided Conservative government of 1992–7. House price inflation was rampant, averaging 28 per cent per annum during the Blair years. Most ominous, in terms of Brown's self-bestowed inheritance as prime minister, were the indicators in terms of taxation and borrowing. The tax burden on average incomes rose by approximately 2 pence from 1997 to 2007 while the balance of payments grew steadily worse, from an even inheritance in 1997 to a record £57 billion trade deficit by 2004 (Smith 2005b). Brown's image as a cautious, prudent chancellor was more myth than reality; by Labour's second term he was doubling public borrowing to a figure approaching £20 billion annually.

What of Blair's seemingly two most substantial achievements, peace in Northern Ireland and devolution for that region, Scotland, and Wales? In considering Northern Ireland, there is a need to disaggregate the peace and political processes. It is possible that any semi-competent prime minister could have presided over peace in the region. The IRA was looking for an exit from an unwinnable war, a position evidenced by its 1994 ceasefire (Moloney 2003; Tonge 2006). The breakdown of that ceasefire in 1996 was due to the continued exclusion of Sinn Fein from multi-party peace negotiations and was not a re-assertion of absolutist Irish republican demands for British withdrawal and a united Ireland. Hampered by a disappearing parliamentary majority, reliance upon Unionist votes and an unwise concern with early decommissioning of IRA weapons, John Major's Conservative government was unable to consolidate the embryonic peace. Unencumbered by any of these difficulties, Blair was soon the beneficiary of a restored IRA cessation. Crucially, Blair was informed by the Sinn Fein leaders Gerry Adams and Martin McGuinness that, regardless of what happened from hereon, they had no intention of returning to violence.[2] Blair's legacy is thus less *peace per se* than an unlikely *political* deal. He displayed considerable diplomatic skills and persistence in facilitating a, far-reaching deal between the Democratic Unionist Party (DUP) under Ian Paisley and Sinn Fein in the 2006 St. Andrews Agreement, a modification to the 1998 Good Friday Agreement which reflected the intra-ethnic bloc realignment which had taken place in favour of Paisley's and Adams's party. Blair's earlier pragmatism concerning the decommissioning of weapons and acceptance of the inevitability of paramilitary prisoner releases and policing changes did much to clear the way to an eventual deal, even though this required difficult compromises (see Aughey 2005; Powell 2008).

Devolution for Scotland and Wales can hardly be seen as a Blairite innovation. Dating from the 1970s, it remained the only Old Labour policy to survive the party upheavals of the following two decades. Blair was evidently nervous of the policy, a concern evidenced by the decision to introduce a separate referendum question on tax-varying powers for the Scottish parliament. Yet retreat from devolution as policy was unthinkable given the views of Labour's supporters in Scotland and the devolved institutions enjoy popular legitimacy. Incremental growth in the powers of the Scottish government and Welsh executive appears certain, but, even in Scotland where considerable autonomy exists, the fiscal dominance of Westminster remains. As Mitchell (2005, p. 110) observes, 'big decisions on health and education, for example, are determined by the funding available and that is decided in London'. Although devolution was introduced as a response to the avowedly settled will of the Scottish and Welsh electorates (although a mere 25 per cent expressed support for devolution in the Welsh case in 1997), the two main controversies associated with greater autonomy remain unresolved. The West Lothian question, concerning the non-reciprocal rights of all Scottish MPs at Westminster to affect English legislation, is unanswered, while the ultimate constitutional direction of devolution – status quo, federalism or independence, is unclear.

All Blairites now? How the Conservative Party responded

Arguably the biggest legacy test of any party leader is the extent to which his rival leader, as head of the Opposition, is obliged to accept the political arrangements that are bequeathed in the event of a change of government. Even prior to the election of David Cameron as party leader in 2005, the Conservatives had been obliged to concede much ground. The independence of the Bank of England, one of Labour's first policies in office, was accepted by the Conservatives. Having claimed that the introduction of the minimum wage would be economically damaging, the Conservatives quietly dropped their opposition during Blair's second term. Opposition to university tuition fees, a policy for which the Conservatives were sometimes criticised even by their own supporters, did not survive the first few months of David Cameron's arrival as leader.

Most strikingly, if inevitably, Labour's introduction of devolved government for Scotland and Wales, described by the Conservative leader from 1990 until 1997, John Major, as the most dangerous proposal ever put before a British electorate, was readily accepted. Although, in Wales the Conservatives continued for a time to moot the possibility of a multi-option referendum which would include the abolition of the Assembly, few saw this as a serious policy. Instead the Conservatives used the proportional voting (Additional Member) system in Wales and Scotland as a means of achieving representation within devolved institutions and reviving party fortunes in those countries.

For the Conservatives, Blair's lack of dogma and Labour's economic success meant that it was difficult to sustain a credible attack. The ill-judged 1997 campaign, portraying Blair as a full-blooded socialist hiding behind the respectable veneer of New Labour, lacked credibility. Insofar as a plausible critique could be developed, it emerged around Labour's statism, no longer concerned with public ownership, but now operationalised through the micro-management of the delivery of public services. Blair's government oversaw the growth of a plethora of delivery agencies, planning and targets. The Conservatives continue to attack such statism during the Brown premiership and promote conservatism as less meddlesome and interventionist, as the party's repudiation of the Blair-Brown approach to government. As chairman of the Conservative Party's Research

Department and Policy Review, Oliver Letwin, attempted to outline the
Conservatives' ideological and policy approach in 2007:

> Cameronian Conservatism ... has a specific theoretical agenda. It aims to
> achieve two significant paradigm shifts. First, a shift from an econocen-
> tric paradigm to a sociocentric paradigm. Secondly, a shift in the theory
> of the state from a provision-based paradigm to a framework-based para-
> digm. The provision-theory of the modern state ... is the essence of
> Gordon Brown's version of New Labour. The provision-theory accepts the
> free market as the engine of economic growth. But ... the provision the-
> orists of Brownian New Labour see the central state not only as the fun-
> der but also as the provider of public services. They also see the state as
> the only possible guarantor of wellbeing through direction and control.
> The Cameronian Conservative framework-theory of the state is funda-
> mentally different. [It] sees government as having two basic roles: to
> guarantee the stability and security upon which ... the free market and
> wellbeing depend and ... to establish a framework of support and incen-
> tive that enables and induces individuals and organisations to act in ways
> that fulfil not merely their self-interested ambitions but also their wider
> social responsibilities. It is in emphasising the second duty of govern-
> ment that Cameronian Conservatism distinguishes itself from Brownian
> New Labour. Cameronian Conservatism puts no faith in central direction
> and control.
>
> (*The Times*, 8 May 2007)

Letwin's arguments concerning Labour's desire for 'direction and control'
were valid and his concerns that a 'sociocentric paradigm' was needed
reflected Conservative anxiety that the party had to be seen as a credible
developer of public services. The argument that New Labour saw the state as
the provider of public services, however, overlooked Blair's determination –
accepted by Brown on all issues except foundation hospitals – not to reverse
the break-up of local state monopolies of service delivery undertaken by
Conservative governments between 1979 and 1997. New Labour's 'Best
Value' policy was less demanding in this area than the rapid contracting out
of services undertaken by the Conservatives, but could not be interpreted as
a strong policy of support for state delivery of services. Many of Letwin's
other articulations, concerning the balance between individual ambition
and broader responsibility, were indistinguishable from Blair's (and
Brownian New Labour's) beliefs in the fusion of individual and collective
responsibility. That Blair's beliefs in this respect were emphasised via state
policies was inevitable given that much social provision was regulated by
the state, a situation unlikely to be reversed by a Conservative government,
whatever the avowed lack of faith in central direction and control.

Is the Labour Party now Blairite?

The final big test for Blair was to ensure that his party came to accept 'Blairism' and its explicit acceptance of the legitimacy of market forces. A teleology of Blair's ascendancy within the party might assume his rise as a moderate re-brander of the party was inevitable, given Labour's dismal electoral performances from 1979 onwards. Such an approach would underplay the extent of internal scepticism to Blair's changes, even if Labour's transformation from 'Militant Tendency' to 'Millbank Tendency' was smoothly completed shortly after his arrival as leader (Fielding 1997). Even Blair's election as party leader, although inevitable after the infamous deal with the only serious potential rival, Gordon Brown, did not amount to an overwhelming endorsement, only 57 per cent of the party choosing him as leader. A similarly modest percentage backed Blair's first clear outline of future Labour policies, the 1996 draft manifesto, which like the actual version, confirmed the end of the advocacy of 'traditional' policies of state control. A £5 billion New Deal welfare-to-work package, funded by a one-off windfall tax on public utilities, reassured the party faithful (Fielding and Tonge 1999).

The most important symbolic change, the revision of Clause 4's commitment to public commitment to an embracing of the 'vigour of the market' did receive fairly substantial support, nearly two-thirds of members backing the change. Nonetheless, Seyd and Whiteley's (2002) extensive re-examination of Labour Party members at the end of the 1990s revealed only modest ideological change, with party members continuing to advocate higher taxation rates and redistributive policies. At the time of Blair's exit, 45 per cent of Labour Party members described themselves as either 'very' or 'fairly' left-wing, with only eight per cent claiming to be centrists (YouGov/*Daily Telegraph*, 2007b).

For Blair, the Labour Party was seen as a structural agent, existing to deliver the policies developed elsewhere. The party could not operate as the primary ideological vehicle of change. Blair's ability to rise without trace to become a Labour MP indicated the sorry state of the party during the early 1980s, demonstrated his personal skills, but, above all, highlighted his lack of commitment to a party in which he had never held even local office and whose annual conference he had yet to attend (Seldon 2007). Blair's suspicion of his party's ordinary members may indeed have been well founded. It has long been evident that party members tend to hold more strident views than those found among ordinary electors (e.g. Blondel 1974; Miller, Timpson and Lessnoff 1996; Seyd and Whiteley 1992; Whiteley, Seyd and Richardson 1994). In terms of moving his party to the centre, Blair was thus obliged to restructure party decision-making mechanisms to centralise control, albeit while maintaining ostensibly democratic structures. Ultimately,

Blair remained tolerated, even admired, by Labour's grassroots, but was still rarely seen as 'of' his party. Insofar as there was adulation, it extended only to the electoral humiliations inflicted by Blair's Labour upon the Conservatives.

Blair-Brown political and ideological continuities and discontinuities

Given that Brown was the architect of New Labour's economic approach, it was unwise to expect radical economic departures on his accession to the prime ministership. However, whereas Brown-Blair inherited an excellent economic position in 1997, Brown-Darling were not bequeathed such bounty. With public sector borrowing already high, Brown's chancellor, Alastair Darling was obliged to seek ways of raising income. His opening gambit, of abandoning the 10 pence tax rate for those on low incomes, proved disastrous, enraging many Labour backbench MPs and contributing to Labour's worst set of local election results for 40 years in 2008.

Aside from the fiscal constraints upon Brown's Labour government, there was little evidence of ideological or policy departure from the Blair years. The biggest problem for Brown, aside from the unpromising economic inheritance, was the apparent absence of big ideas, a problem exacerbated by his assuming the helm in mid-term, when ideological or policy reorientation is more difficult (Hickson 2008). In economic terms, continuity from Blair to Brown was unsurprising because Brown had been responsible for maintaining much of the economic approach of the Thatcher and Major years, in terms of the control of inflation, maintenance of a strong currency, removal of labour market rigidities and greater use of the private sector. As these norms have conditioned successive government approaches, economic policy has become less ideological, a process of depoliticisation which establishes a 'rules-based economic policy that leaves little room for political discretion' (Grant 2003, p. 267). Ideological competition may have been more rhetorical than actual; 'Butskellism' was evident during the 1950s and 1960s as 'Browneronism' (or 'Darborneism') was from 2007.[3] Brown was equally New Labour as Blair in endorsing Labour's economic inheritance, but infused this with measures of social justice (minimum wage and windfall tax) or policy radicalism (Bank of England independence).

By the time Brown became prime minister, it was unclear where Labour's big new ideas lay. Given Brown's lack of oratorical skills so capably deployed by Blair, it was also far from apparent how any bold new initiative would be adequately 'sold' to an increasingly sceptic public. Moreover, those hoping for a revival of collective cabinet government were likely to be disappointed. Blair's style was to eschew collegiate cabinet analysis, collective government and formal decision making, in favour of ad hocery and single-minded or 'court' decisions (Cook 2004; Rhodes 2005). Brown's tendency is to surround himself with a small team of trusted advisers. Blair held the advantage of being able to combine economic orthodoxy with constitutional radicalism (devolution and parliamentary reform) and an apparent reforming zeal (public service delivery) creating the impression of a modern and ambitious government re-shaping Britain. Brown has inherited the tricky, unfinished business associated with these changes, in terms of uncertainty over the future of the UK and a lack of consensus over the extent of the marketisation of public service reform. Brown has also inherited a fractious parliamentary Labour party whose rebelliousness has been evident ever since the expiry of Blair's 'honeymoon' at the end of his first term (Cowley 2005). The big Brown idea has appeared to be the promotion of British values and citizenship (HM Government 2007a; Goldsmith 2008), potentially tricky and unrewarding areas given population diversity and, more significantly, the apparent gradual ebbing of Britishness in favour of country-based identities within Scotland, Wales and England (Bryant 2005).

Summary

Blair's legacy can thus be seen as substantial, less in ideological terms than in the practical policy decisions of his Labour governments. Most of these policy enactments were accepted by the Conservative Party following temporary rhetorical opposition. In ideological terms, the acceptance by Blair of the free market as the generator of wealth is acknowledged by the Conservatives. However, the Conservatives argue that Labour's preference for state control at the expense of private sector delivery of services and the promotion of individual choice has been largely undiminished by Blairism. A combination of party constraints, ideological barriers and ineffective policy development prevented Blair from fundamentally reforming the delivery of public goods in the way he desired. Given that Brown's greater interest was in economic stability than in public service reform, it is difficult to envisage the post-2007 Labour government achieving where Blair partly failed.

Blair's 1997 election victory is generally not considered a watershed election in the way in which 1945 and 1979 are regarded.[4] Aspects of good fortune and sound management by Labour, in respect of a generally impressive economic record, are palpably reversible and the party's hard-won reputation as a party of economic competence can easily disappear, risks accentuated by global economic problems. Brown's inheritance (but also his legacy, for the two cannot be distinguished given his ubiquitous presence under Blair) was an economy in poorer shape than in 1997 and an electorally unpromising landscape. The lasting significance of the Blair government, in two areas, matches the importance of the fundamental changes of the welfare state and labour market reform introduced by the Attlee and Thatcher victories respectively. Firstly, the seemingly irreversible restructuring of the UK via devolution, a process whose endpoint may yet be the fracturing of that Kingdom, was a change which places the signifi-cance of the Blair government – in constitutional terms – way beyond any predecessor government since Britain withdrew from most of Ireland in 1922. Secondly, Blair's role in facilitating the political process in Northern Ireland was important in bringing to a final conclusion the worst and most enduring conflict in western Europe since the Second World War. It appears unlikely that many future British prime ministers will offer a legacy as dis-tinctive or important.

Notes

1. As indications of public opinion, a Populus poll published in May 2007 found the following rankings of Blair: Great PM: 2 per cent; Good PM: 31 per cent; Average PM: 43 per cent; Bad PM: 20 per cent. A You Gov/*Daily Telegraph* poll in April 2007 found fairly similar ratings: Great PM: 4 per cent; Good: 28 per cent; Mediocre: 32 per cent; Pretty bad: 17 per cent; Disastrously bad: 13 per cent.
2. Interview with Tony Blair, *Hearts and Minds*, BBC Northern Ireland, 10 April 2008.
3. Alistair Darling being Brown's Chancellor of the Exchequer and George Osborne being David Cameron's first Conservative Shadow Chancellor.
4. A survey of 416 Political Studies Association members by YouGov in 2006 found the following: 49 per cent of members believed Labour's 1945 election victory to have been the most important British general election since the Second World War; 36 per cent believed that 1979 was the most important election. The 1997 election, although ranked the third most important since the War, trailed well behind, only 5 per cent viewing it as the most important.

References

Primary Sources

Adams, J., Clark, M., Ezrow, L. and Glasgow, G. (2004) 'Understanding Change and Stability in Party Ideologies: Do Parties Respond to Public Opinion or to Past Election Results?'*British Journal of Political Science*, 34:4, pp. 589–610.

Adler, M. (2004) 'Combining Welfare-to-Work Measures with Tax Credits: A New Hybrid Approach to Social Security in the United Kingdom', *International Social Security Review*, LVII, pp. 87–106.

Aldrich, J. H., Sullivan, J. L. and Bordiga, E. (1989) 'Foreign Affairs and Issue Voting: Do Presidential Candidates "Waltz Before a Blind Audience?"', *American Political Science Review*, 8:1, pp. 123–41.

Allawi, A. (2007) *The Occupation of Iraq: Winning the War, Losing the Peace* (New Haven: Yale University Press).

Allen, D. (2005) 'The United Kingdom: A Europeanized Government in a non-Europeanized Polity', in S. Bulmer and C. Lequesne (eds), *The Member States of the European Union* (Oxford: Oxford University Press), pp. 119–41.

Amable, B. (2003) *The Diversity of Modern Capitalism* (Oxford, UK: Oxford University Press).

Amis, M. (2008) *The Second Plane: September 11: 2001–2007* (London: Jonathan Cape).

Andeweg, R. (1997) 'Collegiality and Collectivity: Cabinets, Cabinet Committees and Cabinet Ministers', in P. Weller, H. Bakvis and R. A. W. Rhodes eds, *The Hollow Crown: Countervailing Trends in Core Executives* (Basingstoke: Macmillan).

Archik, K. (2005) *The United Kingdom: Issues For The United States* (Washington DC: Congressional Research Service).

Ashcroft, M. (2005) *Smell the Coffee: A Wakeup Call for the Conservative Party* (London: Politico's).

Ashdown, P. (2000) *The Ashdown Diaries: Volume One 1988–1997* (London: Allen Lane).

Ashdown, P. (2001) *The Ashdown Diaries: Volume Two 1997–1999* (London: Allen Lane).

Aspinwall, M. (2003) 'Odd Man Out: Rethinking British Policy on European Monetary Integration', *Review of International Studies*, 29:3, pp. 341–64.

Atkinson, R. (2007) 'Boosting European Prosperity through the Widespread Use of ICT', Report of the Information Technology and Innovation Foundation.

Audit Commission (2007) *CPA – The Harder Test: Scores and Analysis of Performance in Single Tier and County Councils 2006* (London: Audit Commission).

Aughey, A. (2005) *The Politics of Northern Ireland: Beyond the Belfast Agreement* (London: Routledge).

Bagehot, W. (1963) *The English Constitution* (London: Oxford University Press).

Baggott, R., Allsop, J. and Jones, K. (2005) *Speaking for Patients and Carers: Health Consumer Groups and the Policy Process* (Basingstoke: Palgrave Macmillan).

Baker, D. and Sherrington, P. (2005) 'Britain and Europe: The Dog that Didn't Bark', *Parliamentary Affairs*, 58:2, pp. 303–17.

Baker, D., Gamble, A. and Ludlam, S. (1994) 'The Parliamentary Siege of Maastricht 1993: Conservative Divisions and British Ratification', *Parliamentary Affairs*, 47, pp. 37–60.

Bakvis, H. and Wolinetz, S. B. (2005) 'Canada: Executive Dominance and Presidentialization', in T. Poguntke and P. Webb, eds (2005).

Bale, T. (1999) 'The "Logic of No Alternative"? Political Scientists, Historians and The Politics of Labour's Past', *British Journal of Politics and International Relations*, 1:2, pp. 192–204.

Bale, T. (2006) 'Between a Soft and a Hard Place? The Conservative Party, Valence Politics, and the Need for a New "Eurorealism"', *Parliamentary Affairs*, 59:3, pp. 385–400.

Bale, T. (2008) '"A Bit Less Bunny-Hugging and a Bit More Bunny-Boiling"? Qualifying Conservative Party Change under David Cameron,' *British Politics*, 3:3, pp. 270–299.

Ball, S. (2003) 'The Conservatives in opposition, 1906–1979: A comparative analysis', in Mark Garnett and Philip Lynch (eds), *The Conservatives in Crisis* (Manchester: Manchester University Press), pp. 7–28.

Ball, S. and Seldon, A. (2005) *Recovering Power: The Conservatives in Opposition since 1867* (Basingstoke: Palgrave Macmillan).

Bank of England (2007), 'Inflation Report, November 2007', (London: Bank of England) (http://www.bankofengland.co.uk/publications/inflationreport/2007.htm), accessed 15 April 2008.

Barber, M. (2007) *Instruction to Deliver: Tony Blair, Public Services and the Challenge of Achieving Targets* (London: Politico's, Methuen).

Bauer, H. and Rudorf, C. (2006) *Local Finance in Europe: An Overview 2000/2005* (Innsbruck, Austria: Centre for Public Administration Research).

Bayliss, F. (1962) *British Wages Councils* (Oxford: Basil Blackwell).

BBC (2007a) 'Global Reaction to Blair's Exit', BBC website 11 May, accessed 11 May 2007.

BBC (2007b) 'US and UK "No Longer Inseparable"', BBC website 14 July, accessed 17 July 2007.

BBC (2008) 'Beleaguered Brown Seeks US Filip', BBC website 16 April, accessed 16 April 2008.

BBC News (2008) *Brown and Bush Reignite the Special Relationship*, 18 April.

BCC (2007) 'UK Transport Infrastructure Needs Investment' Press Notice, February 15 2007, (London: British Chambers of Commerce).

BCC (2008) 'The Cost of Regulation on British Business Rises to £65.99 billion', Press Notice, 17 Feb 2008, (London: British Chambers of Commerce).

Beech, M. and Lee, S. (2008) *Ten Years of New Labour* (Basingstoke: Palgrave Macmillan).

Beer, S. (1969) *Modern British Politics* (London: Faber and Faber).

Beer, S. (1982) *Britain Against Itself: the Political Contradictions of Collectivism* (London: Faber and Faber).

Beeson, M. (2007) 'The Declining Utility of "Bandwagoning": American Hegemony in the Age of Terror', *British Journal of Politics and International Relations*, 9, pp. 618–35.

Bellamy, R. (2007) *Political Constitutionalism: A Republican Defense of the Constitutionality of Democracy* (Cambridge: Cambridge University Press).

Benedetto, G. and Hix, S. (2007) 'The Rejected, the Ejected, and the Dejected: Explaining Government Rebels in the 2001–2005 British House of Commons', *Comparative Political Studies*, 40, pp. 755–81.

Benn, T (2003), *Free At Last: Diaries 1991–2001* (London: Arrow).

Bennister, M. (2007) 'Tony Blair and John Howard: Comparative Predominance and Institutional Stretch in Britain and Australia', *British Journal of Politics and International Relations*, 9:3, pp. 327–45.

Bennister M. (2008) 'Blair and Howard: Predominant Prime Ministers Compared', *Parliamentary Affairs*, 61:2, pp. 334–55.

Bernstein, E. (1961) *Evolutionary Socialism*, 2nd edition (New York: Schocken).

Berrington, H. (2007) *Parliament, Past and Future: Exploring Backbench Dissent and Executive Dominance*, British Academy Seminar, London.

Bevir, M. (2005) *New Labour: A Critique* (London: Routledge).

Bevir, M. and Rhodes, R. (2004a) 'Interpreting British governance', in Finlayson, A., Bevir, M., Rhodes, R., Dowding, K. and Hay, C. 'The Interpretive approach in Political Science: A Symposium', *The British Journal of Politics and International Relations*, 6, pp. 130–6.

Bevir, M. and Rhodes, R. (2004b) 'Interpretation as Method, Explanation and Critique: A Reply', in Finlayson, A., Bevir, M., Rhodes, R., Dowding, K. and Hay, C. 'The Interpretive approach in Political Science: A Symposium', *The British Journal of Politics and International Relations*, 6, pp. 156–64.

Birch, A. H. (1964), *Representative and Responsible Government: An Essay on the British Constitution,* (London: George Allen and Unwin).

Blackburn, R. and Plant, R., eds (1997) *Constitutional Reform: The Labour Government's Constitutional Reform Agenda,* (London: Longman).

Blair, C. (2008) *Speaking for Myself* (London: Little Brown).

Blair, T. (1994), 'New Labour's Vision', Annual party conference, Blackpool.

Blair, T. (1996) *New Britain: My Vision of a Young Country* (London: Fourth Estate).

Blair, T. (1998) *The Third Way: New Politics for the New Century* (London: Fabian Society).

Blair, T. (2002) *The Courage of Our Convictions: Why Reform of the Public Services is the Route to Social Justice* (London: Fabian Society).

Blair, T. and Schröder, G. (1999) 'Europe: The Third Way/die Neue Mitte', in B. Hombach (ed.) (2000) *The Politics of the New Centre* (Oxford: Blackwell).

Blick, A. and Jones, G. W. (2007) *The 'Department of the Prime Minister' – Should It Continue?* History and Politics, Policy Paper 58, June 2007.

Blondel, J. (1974) *Voters, Parties and Leaders: The Social Fabric of British Politics* (London: Penguin).

Blundell, R. (2004) 'Evaluating the Employment Impact of a Mandatory Job Search Assistance Program', *Journal of the European Economics Association*, II, pp. 569–606.

Bluth, C. (2004) 'The British Road to War: Bush, Blair and the Decision to Invade Iraq', *International Affairs*, 80, pp. 871–92.

Bogdanor, V. (1999) *Devolution in the United Kingdom* (Oxford: Oxford University Press).

Bogdanor, V. (2003) *The British Constitution in the Twentieth Century* (Oxford: Oxford University Press).

Bogdanor, V. (2007) 'The Historic Legacy of Tony Blair', *Current History*, 106, pp. 99–105.

Bolton, J. (2007) *Surrender Is Not An Option: Defending America at the United Nations and Abroad* (New York: Threshold Editions).

Bowen, W. Q. (2006) *Libya and Nuclear Proliferation*, Adelphi Paper 380 (London: Institute for Strategic Studies).

Bowlby, R. (1957) 'Union Policy toward Minimum Wage Legislation in Postwar Britain', *Industrial and Labour Relations Review*, XI, pp. 72–84.

Bowyer, T. (2007) *Gordon Brown: Prime Minister* (London: Harper Perennial).

Bradbury, J. (2006) 'Territory and Power Revisited: Theorising Territorial Politics in the United Kingdom After Devolution' *Political Studies*, 54:3, pp. 559–82.

Bradbury, J., (ed.) (2008) *Devolution, Regionalism and Regional Development: The UK Experience* (London: Taylor Francis).

Bradbury, J. and Mawson, J. (1997) *British Regionalism and Devolution, the Challenges of State Reform and European Integration* (London: Jessica Kingsley).

Brewer, M. (2007) *Welfare Reform in the UK: 1997–2007* (London: Institute for Fiscal Studies), WP20/07.

Brewer, M., Goodman, A., Muriel, A. and Sibieta, L. (2007) *Poverty and Inequality in the UK* (London: Institute for Fiscal Studies).

Brewer, M., Sibieta, L. and Wren-Lewis, L. (2008) *Racing Away? Income Inequality and the Evolution of High Incomes*. (London: Institute for Fiscal Studies).

Bromund, T. R. (13 March 2008) 'Boot, Pollak, and Power', *Commentary*, (http://www.commentarymagazine.com/viewarticle.cfm/Boot—Pollak—and-Power-11264), accessed on 29 May 2008.

Brown, G. (1992), *Making Mass Membership Work* (London: Fabian Society).

Brown, G. (2006), *Chancellor of the Exchequer's Budget Statement*, HM Treasury Website, 22 March 2006, (http://www.hm-treasury.gov.uk/budget/budget_06/bud_bud06_speech.cfm).

Brown, G. (2008) 'Keynote Foreign Policy Speech', Downing Street website 18 April, accessed 21 April 2008.

Brown, M. (2008) 'The John W. Holmes Lecture: Can the UN Be Reformed?' *Global Governance*, 14:1, pp. 1–12.

Bryan, M. and Taylor, M. (2004) *An Analysis of the Household Characteristics of Minimum Wage Recipients* (London: Low Pay Commission).

Bryant, C. (2005) *The Nations of Britain* (Oxford: Oxford University Press).

Bryant, C. (ed.) (2007) *Towards a New Constitutional Settlement* (London: Smith Institute).

Budge, I. (1994) 'A New Spatial Theory of Party Competition: Uncertainty, Ideology and Policy Equilibria Viewed Comparatively and Temporally', *British Journal of Political Science*, 24:4, pp. 443–67.

Bull, B. (October 2007) 'Mission Accomplished', *Prospect Magazine*, Issue 139, (http://www.prospect-magazine.co.uk/printarticle.php?id=9804), accessed on 22 May 2008.

Bulmer, S. (2008) 'New Labour, New European Policy? Blair, Brown, and Utilitarian Supranationalism', *Parliamentary Affairs*, 61:4, pp. 597–620.

Bulmer, S. and Burch, M. (1998) 'Organising for Europe – Whitehall, the British State and the European Union', *Public Administration*, 76:4, pp. 601–28.

Bulmer, S. and Burch, M. (2005) 'The Europeanization of UK Government: From Quiet Revolution to Explicit Step-Change?' *Public Administration*, 83:4, pp. 861–90.

Bulpitt, J. G. (1983) *Territory and Power in the United Kingdom, an Interpretation* (Manchester: Manchester University Press).

Burch, M. and Holliday, I. (2004) 'The Blair Government and the Core Executive', *Government and Opposition*, 39:1, pp. 1–21.

Burnham, P. (2001) 'New Labour and the Politics of Depoliticisation', *British Journal of Politics and International Relations* 3:2, pp. 127–49.

Butler, Lord (2004) *Review of Intelligence on Weapons of Mass Destruction, Report of a Committee of Privy Counsellors*, HC 898 (London: HMSO).

Butler, R. (Lord) (2005) *Report of Inquiry* (London: The Stationery Office).

Cabinet Office (2000) 'Code of Practice on Written Consultation', www.cabinet-office.gov.uk/servicefirst/index/consultation.htm.

Callinicos, A. (2001) *Against the Third Way* (Cambridge: Polity).

Campbell, A. (1998), 'Testimony to House of Commons' Select Committee on Public Administration', available at http://www.publications.parliament.uk/pa/cm199798/cmselect/cmpubadm/770/8062307.htm.

Campbell, A. (2002), 'Time to Bury Spin', *British Journalism Review*, 13:4, pp. 15–23.

Campbell, A (2007) *The Blair Years: The Alistair Campbell Diaries* (New York: Knopf).

Campbell, A. and Stott, R. (2007) (eds) *The Blair Years, Extracts from the Alastair Campbell Diaries* (London: Hutchinson).

Casey, T. (2009) 'Mapping Stability and Change in Advance Capitalisms', *Comparative European Politics*, (Forthcoming).

Castro, F. and Ramonet, I. (2007) *Fidel Castro: My Life* (London: Allen Lane).

Childs, S. (2004) *New Labour's Women MPs: Women Representing Women* (London: Routledge).

Childs, S., Lovenduski, J. and Campbell, R. (2005) *Women at the Top 2005: Changing Numbers, Changing Politics* (London: Hansard Society).

Clarke, H., Sanders, D., Stewart, M. and Whiteley, P. (2004) *Political Choice in Britain* (Oxford University Press, Oxford).

Clarke, H., Sanders, D., Stewart, M. and Whiteley, P. (2006) 'Taking the Bloom off New Labour's Rose: Party Choice and Voter Turnout in Britain, 2005', *Journal of Elections, Public Opinion and Parties*, 16:1, pp. 3–36.

Clayton, T. (2005) 'IT Investment, ICT Use and UK Firm Productivity' *Office of National Statistics Report* (London: ONS).

Clift, B. (2001) 'The Jospin Way', *Political Quarterly*, 72:2, pp. 170–9.

Coates, D. (2002) 'Strategic Choices in the Study of New Labour', *British Journal of Politics and International Relations*, 4:3, pp. 479–86.

Coates, D. (2005) *Prolonged Labour: The Slow Birth of New Labour in Britain.* (New York: Palgrave Macmillan).

Coates, D. (2007) 'Life After Blair', *British Politics*, 2:3, pp. 428–34.

Coates, D. (2008) '"Darling, It Is Entirely My Fault!" Gordon Brown's Legacy to Alastair and Himself', *British Politics*, 3:1, pp. 3–21.

Coates, D. and Krieger, J. (with Rhiannon Vickers) (2004) *Blair's War* (Cambridge: Polity Press).

Cohen, M., March, J. and Olsen, J. (1972), 'A Garbage Can Model of Rational Choice', *Administrative Science Quarterly*, 1, pp. 1–25.

Coleman, N., Wapshott, J. and Carpenter, H. (2004) *Destinations of Leavers from NDYP and ND 25 Plus* (London: BMRB).

Collini, S., Winch, D. and Burrow, J. (1983) *That Noble Science of Politics: A Study in Nineteenth Century Intellectual History* (Cambridge: Cambridge University Press).

Commons Treasury Committee (2007) *Financial Stability and Transparency: Sixth Report of 2007/08*, (London: The Stationery Office), HC371, p. 12.

Conservative Party (Social Justice Policy Group) (2006) *Breakdown Britain.*

Conservative Party (Social Justice Policy Group) (2007) *Breakthrough Britain: Ending the Costs of Social Breakdown.*

Cook, C. (1989) *A Short History of the Liberal Party, 1900–88* (Basingstoke: Macmillan).

Cook, R. (2001–02) *Modernisation of the House of Commons: A Reform Programme for Consultation*, Memorandum submitted by the Leader of the House of Commons, HC 440 (Cook Memorandum).

Cook, R. (2004) *The Point of Departure: Diaries from the Front Bench* (London: Pocket).

Cook, R. (2007) *The Point of Departure: Why One of Britain's Leading Politicians Resigned over Tony Blair's Decision to Go to War in Iraq* (New York: Simon and Schuster).

Coughlin, Con (2006) *American Ally: Tony Blair and the War on Terror* (New York: Ecco).

Cowley, P. (2002) *Revolts and Rebellions: Parliamentary Voting under Blair* (London: Politico's).

Cowley, P. (2005) *The Rebels: How Blair Mislaid His Majority* (London: Politico's).

Cowley, P. (2007) 'Parliament', in A. Seldon, (ed.), pp. 16–34.

Cowley, P. and Childs, S. (2003) 'Too Spineless to Rebel? New Labour's Women MPs', *British Journal of Political Science*, 33, pp. 345–65.

Cowley, P. and Stuart, M. (2003) 'Parliament: More Revolts, More Reform', *Parliamentary Affairs*, 56:2, pp. 188–204.

Cowley, P. and Stuart, M. (2005) 'Parliament', A. Seldon and D. Kavanagh, (eds) pp. 20–42.

Cox, G. (1997) *Making Votes Count: Strategic Coordination in the World's Electoral Systems* (Cambridge: Cambridge University Press).

Crafts, N. (2007) 'Industrial Policy' in A. Seldon (ed.) (2007).

Crewe, I. (2006) 'New Labour's Hegemony: Erosion or Extension?' in J. Bartle and A. King (eds) *Britain at the Polls 2005* (Washington, DC: CQ Press), pp. 200–20.

Crewe, I. and King, A. (1995) *SDP: The Birth, Life and Death of the Social Democratic Party* (Oxford: Oxford University Press).

Crouch, C. (2006a). 'Neo-Corporatism and Democracy' in C. Crouch and W. Streeck (eds) *The Diversity of Democracy: Corporatism, Social Order and Political Conflict* (Cheltenham: Edward Elgar), pp. 46–70.

Crouch, C. (2006b) 'New Labour and the Problem of Democracy', in G. Hassan, (ed.) *After Blair: Politics after the New Labour Decade* (London: Lawrence and Wishart).

Crozier, M. (1979) *On ne change pas la société par décret* (Paris: Grasset).

Cunliffe, J. and Shepherd, A. (2007) *Home Office Statistical Bulletin. Re-offending of Adults: Results from the 2004 Cohort* (London: Home Office).

Curtice, J. (2007a) 'Elections and Public Opinion', in A. Seldon (ed.) (2007).

Curtice, J. (2007b) 'New Labour, New Protest? How the Liberal Democrats Profited from Blair's Mistakes' *Political Quarterly* 78, pp. 117–27.

Cutts, D. (2006), 'Where We Work We Win: A Case Study of Local Liberal Democrat Campaigning', *Journal of Elections, Public Opinion and Parties*, 16, pp. 221–42.

Cutts, D. and Shrayne, N. (2006) 'Did Local Activism Really Matter? Liberal Democrat Campaigning and the 2001 British General Election', *British Journal of Politics and International Relations*, 8, pp. 427–44.

Cyr, A. (1977) *Liberal Party Politics in Britain* (London: John Calder).

Danchev, A (2007a) 'I'm with you: Tony Blair and the Obligations of Alliance: Anglo-American relations in historical perspective', in *Iraq and the Lessons of Vietnam*, in L. C. Gardner and M. B. Young (eds) (New York: The New Press).

Danchev, A. (2007b) 'Tony Blair's Vietnam: The Iraq War and the "Special Relationship" in Historical Perspective', *Review of International Studies*, 33, pp. 189–204.

Davis, K. (1961) 'The Future of Judge-made Public Law in England: A Problem of Practical Jurisprudence', *Columbia Law Review* 61, pp. 201–20.

De Giorgi, G. (2005) *Long-Term Effects of a Mandatory Multistage Program: The New Deal for Young People in the UK* (London: Institute for Fiscal Studies).

Denham, A. and Dorey, P. (2007) 'The Caretaker Cleans Up: The Liberal Democrat Leadership Contest of 2006', *Parliamentary Affairs*, 60, pp. 26–45.

Denver, D. (1998) 'The Government That Could Do No Right', in A. King (ed.) *New Labour Triumphs: Britain At The Polls* (Chatham, New Jersey: Chatham House) pp. 15–48.

Denver, D. (2003) *Elections and Voters in Britain* (Basingstoke: Palgrave Macmillan).

Department for Children, Schools and Families (2007) *Schools and Pupils in England, January 2007* (London: Department for Children, Schools and Families).

Department for Communities and Local Government (DCLG) *Long-term Evaluation of the Local Government Modernisation Agenda (LGMA)*, (http://www.communities.gov.uk/localgovernment/localregional/crosscuttingissues/longtermevaluation).

Department for Work and Pensions (2006a) *The Abstract of Statistics for Benefits, National Insurance Contributions, and Indices of Prices and Earnings 2005 Edition* (London: Department for Work and Pensions).

Department for Work and Pensions (DWP) (2006b) *A New Deal for Welfare: Empowering People to Work* (London: The Stationery Office).

Department for Work and Pensions (2007) *Households Below Average Income 1994/5–2005/6* (London: Department for Work and Pensions).

Department for Work and Pensions (2008a) *Households Below Average Incomes* (London: DWP).

Department for Work and Pensions (2008b) *Transforming Britain's Labour Market: Ten Years of the New Deal* (London: The Stationery Office).

Department for Work and Pensions (2008c) *Ready for Work, Skilled for Work: Unlocking Britain's Talent* (London: The Stationery Office).

Department of Health (2000) *The NHS Plan: A Plan for Investment, A Plan for Reform*, (London: The Stationery Office).

Department of Health (2001) *Shifting the Balance of Power in the NHS*, (London: The Stationery Office).

Department of Health (2002) *The NHS Plan: Next Steps for Investment, Next Steps for Reform* (London: The Stationery Office).

Department of Health (2006) *Our Health, Our Care, Our Say* (London: The Stationery Office).

Department of Health (2007) *Departmental Report 2007* (London: The Stationery Office).

Department of Health and Social Security (DHSS) (1983) *Letter to the Secretary of State* (the Griffiths Report), October 6 (London: The Stationery Office).

Department of Social Security (1998) *New Ambitions for Our Country: A New Contract for Welfare* (London: The Stationery Office).

Department of the Environment, Transport and the Regions (DETR) (1998a) *Modernising Local Government: Local Democracy and Community Leadership* (London: DETR).

Department of the Environment, Transport and the Regions (DETR) (1998b) *Modern Local Government: In Touch with the People* (London: DETR).

Dicey, A. (1902) *Introduction to the Study of the Law of the Constitution* (London: Macmillan).

Dicey, A. V. (1915) *Introduction to the Study of the Law and the Constitution*, 8th edition (London: Macmillan).

Dolowitz, D. (2004) 'Prosperity and Fairness? Can New Labour Bring Fairness to the 21st Century by Following the Dictates of Endogenous Growth?' *British Journal of Politics and International Relations*. 6:2, pp. 213–30.

Dorey, P. (ed.) (1999) *The Major Premiership: Politics and Policies Under John Major, 1990–97* (Basingstoke: Palgrave Macmillan).

Dorling, D., Rigby, J., Wheeler, B., Ballas, D., Thomas, B., Fahmy, E., Gordon, D. and Lupton, R. (2007). *Poverty, Wealth and Place in Britain, 1968 to 2005* (Bristol: Policy Press).

Draca, M., Machin, S. and Van Reenen, J. (2005) *The Impact of the National Minimum Wage on Profits and Prices* (London: Low Pay Commission).

Driver, S. and Martell, L. (1998) *New Labour: Politics after Thatcherism* (Cambridge: Polity).

Driver, S. and Martell, L. (2002) *Blair's Britain* (Cambridge: Polity).

Driver, S. and Martell, L. (2006) *New Labour* (Cambridge: Polity).

Drucker, H. M. (1979) *Doctrine and Ethos in the Labour Party* (London: George Allen and Unwin).

Drumheller, T. and Monaghan, E. (2006) *On The Brink: An Insider's Account of How the White House Compromised American Intelligence* (New York: Carroll and Graf).

Duelfer Report (30 September 2004) 'Comprehensive Report of the Special Adviser to the DCI on Iraq's WMDs', (http://www.globalsecurity.org/wmd/library/report/2004/isg-final-report/), accessed on 29 May 2008.

Dumbrell, J. (2004) 'The US-UK "Special Relationship" in a World Twice Transformed', *Cambridge Review of International Affairs*, 17, pp. 437–50.

Dumbrell, J. (2006) *A Special Relationship: Anglo-American Relations from the Cold War to Iraq* (Basingstoke and New York: Palgrave Macmillan).

Dunleavy, P. (2003) 'Analysing Political Power,' in P. Dunleavy, A. Gamble, R. Heffernan and G. Peele (eds), *Developments in British Politics 7* (Basingstoke: Palgrave Macmillan).

Dunleavy, Patrick (2006), 'The "Westminster Model" and the Distinctiveness of British Politics', in P. Dunleavy, R. Heffernan, P. Cowley, and C. Hay, (eds) *Developments in British Politics 8* (Basingstoke: Palgrave Macmillan), pp. 315–41.

Duverger, M. (1954) *Political Parties: Their Organization and Activity in the Modern State* (New York: Wiley).

Dyson, S. B. (2006) 'Personality and Foreign Policy: Tony Blair's Iraq Decisions', *Foreign Policy Analysis*, 2, pp. 289–306.

Dyson, S. B. (2007) 'Alliances, Domestic Politics, and Leader Psychology: Why Did Britain Stay out of Vietnam and go Into Iraq?' *Political Psychology*, 28, pp. 647–66.

Economic and Social Research Council (2004) *The UK's Productivity Gap: What Research Tells Us and What We Need to Find Out* (London: ESRC).

Edwards, G. (2004) *Cabinet Government* (London: Politico's).

Elgie, R. (1995) *Political Leadership in Liberal Democracies* (Basingstoke: Macmillan).

Enthoven, A. (1985) *Reflections on the Management of the NHS* (London: Nuffield Trust).

European Innovation Scoreboard (2006), (http://trendchart.cordis.lu/tc_innovation_scoreboard.cfm), accessed on 17 August 2007.

Evans, G. (1998) 'How Britain Views the EU', in R. Jowell, J. Curtice, A. Park, L. Brook, K. Thomson and C. Bryson (eds), *British and European Social Attitudes. The 15th Report: How Britain Differs* (Aldershot: Ashgate), pp. 173–89.

Evans, G. and Andersen, R. (2005) 'The Impact of Party Leaders: How Blair Lost Labour votes' in P. Norris and C. Wlezien (eds) *Britain Votes 2005* (Oxford: Oxford University Press), pp. 162–80.

Farrell, D. and Webb, P. (2000), 'Political Parties as Campaign Organizations', in R. Dalton and M. Wattenberg, (eds), *Parties Without Partisans: Political Change in Advanced Industrial Democracies* (Oxford: Oxford University Press), pp. 102–28.

Faucher-King, F. (2005), *Parties: Anthropology of British Political Party Conferences* (Houndmills: Palgrave Macmillan).

Faucher-King, F. (2008), 'La modernisation du parti travailliste, 1994–2007', *Politix*, 21:81, pp. 125–49.

Faucher-King, F. and Le Galès, P. (2007) *Tony Blair 1997–2007: Le bilan des réformes* (Paris: Presses de Sciences Po).

Fawcett, P. and Rhodes, R. A. W. (2007) 'Central Government,' in A. Seldon (ed.) (2007).

Fieldhouse, E., Cutts, D. and Russell, A. (2006) 'Neither North nor South: The Liberal Democrat Performance in the 2005 General Election' *Journal of Elections, Public Opinion and Parties*, 16, pp. 77–92.

Fielding, S. (1997) 'Labour's Path to Power' in A. Geddes and J. Tonge, (eds) *Labour's Landslide: The British General Election 1997* (Manchester: Manchester University Press), pp. 23–35.

Fielding, S. (2000) *Labour: Decline and Renewal* (Tisbury: Baseline).

Fielding, S. (2002) *The Labour Party: Continuity and Change in the Making of New Labour* (Basingstoke: Palgrave Macmillan).

Fielding, S. and Tonge, J. (1999) 'Economic and Industrial Policy', in R. Kelly, (ed.) *Changing Party Policy in Britain* (Oxford: Blackwell).

Finlayson, A. (2002) 'Elements of the Blairite Image of Leadership', *Parliamentary Affairs*, 55:3, pp. 586–99.

Finlayson, A. (2003), *Making Sense of New Labour* (London: Lawrence and Wishart).

Fisher, J. (2006) 'The General Election in the UK, May 2005', *Electoral Studies*, 25:4, pp. 814–20.

Flinders, M. (2006) 'The Half-Hearted Constitutional Revolution', in P. Dunleavy, R. Heffernan, P. Cowley and C. Hay, (eds) *Developments in British Politics 8* (Basingstoke: Palgrave Macmillan).

Foley, M. (2000) *The Blair Presidency* (Manchester: Manchester University Press).

Food and Drink Federation, *The Next Five Years*, (http://www.fdf.org.uk/economics_report_next_five.aspx), accessed 18 April 2008.

Francis, M. and Morrow, J. (1994) *A History of English Political Thought in the 19th Century* (London: Duckworth).

Freedman, L. (2007) 'Defense' in A. Seldon (ed.) *Blair's Britain: 1997–2007* (Cambridge: Cambridge University Press).

Gaddis, J. L. (2005) *Strategies of Containment: A Critical Appraisal of American National Security Policy During the Cold War* (New York: Oxford University Press).

Galbraith, J. (1992) *The Culture of Contentment* (London: Sinclair-Stevenson).

Gamble, A. (2007) 'Blair's Legacy', *British Politics*, 2:1, pp. 123–8.

Gamble, A. and Kearns, I. (2007) 'Recasting the Special Relationship' in D. Held and D. Mepham (eds) *Progressive Foreign Policy* (London: Wiley).

Gamble, A. and Kelly, G. (2000) 'The British Labour Party and Monetary Union', *West European Politics*, 23:1, pp. 1–25.

Gamble, A. and Kelly, G. (2002) 'Britain and EMU', in K. Dyson (ed.) *European States and the Euro: Europeanization, Variation and Convergence* (Oxford: Oxford University Press), pp. 97–119.

Game, C. (2003) 'Elected Mayors: More Distraction Than Attraction?' *Public Policy and Administration*, 18:1, pp. 13–28.

Game, C. (2007) 'Mayors, Monitors and Measurers: Blair's Legacy to Local Democracy', paper delivered at the British Politics Group conference, 'Britain After Blair', Chicago, IL.

Gardiner, N. (15 April 2008) 'The Bush-Brown White House Meeting: A Chill in the Special Relationship?', (http://www.heritage.org/Research/Europe/wm1892.cfm), accessed on 29 May 2008.

Garner, R. (2008) 'The Politics of Animal Rights', *British Politics*, 3:1, pp. 110–19.

Garnett, M. and Lynch, P. (2003) *The Conservatives in Crisis* (Manchester: Manchester University Press).

Gearty, C. (2006) *Can Human Rights Survive? The Hamlyn Lectures 2005* (Cambridge: Cambridge University Press).

Geddes, A. (2004) *The European Union and British Politics* (Basingstoke: Palgrave Macmillan).

George, S. (1998) *An Awkward Partner: Britain in the European Community*, 3rd edition (Oxford: Oxford University Press).

Giddens, A. (1998) *The Third Way: Renewal of Social Democracy* (Cambridge: Polity).

Giddens, A. (2007) 'New Labour: Tony Blair and After,' *British Politics*, 2:1, pp. 106–10.

Gill, M., Atkinson, S. and Mortimore, R. (2004) *The Referendum Battle* (London: The Foreign Policy Centre).

Goldsmith, Lord (2008) *Citizenship: Our Common Bond* (London: Ministry of Justice).

Google Zeitgeist (2007) 'Cameron: San Francisco Speech', www.conservatives.com, 12 October, accessed 16 April 2008.

Gordon, R. (2004) 'Why was Europe Left at the Station When America's Productivity Locomotive Departed?', CEPR Working Paper.

Gould, P. (1998), *The Unfinished Revolution: How the Modernisers Saved the Labour Party* (London: Abacus).

Gowland, D. and Turner, A. (2000) *Reluctant Europeans: Britain and European Integration 1945–1998* (Edinburgh: Pearson Education Limited).

Grant, W. (2000) *Pressure Groups and British Politics* (Basingstoke: Macmillan).

Grant, W. (2003) 'Economic Policy', in P. Dunleavy, A. Gamble, R. Heffernan and G. Peele, (eds) *Developments in British Politics 7* (Basingstoke: Palgrave Macmillan). pp. 261–81.

Grant, W. (2008) 'The Changing Pattern of Pressure Group Politics in Britain', *British Politics*, 3:2, pp. 204–222.

Greaves, J. (2004) 'The Reform of Business Representation in Britain, 1970–97', PhD thesis, University of Warwick.

Greaves, J. (2008) 'Continuity or Change in Business Representation in Britain? An Assessment of the Heseltine Initiatives of the 1990s', *Environment and Planning C: Government and Policy*, published online 3 April.

Green, J. (2005) 'Conservative Party Rationality: Learning the Lessons from the Last Election for the Next?' *Journal of Elections, Public Opinion and Parties*, 15:1, pp. 111–27.

Greenstein, F. I. (1998) 'The Impact of Personality on the End of the Cold War: A Counterfactual Analysis', *Political Psychology*, 19:1, pp. 1–16.

Greer, S. (2004) *Territorial Politics and Health Policy*, (Manchester: Manchester University Press).

Griffith, J. A. G. (1979) 'The Political Constitution', *The Modern Law Review* 42, 1, pp. 1–21.

Griffith, J. A. G. (1997) *The Politics of the Judiciary*, 5th ed. (London: Fontana Press).

Griffith, J. A. G. (2000) 'The Brave New World of Sir John Laws', *The Modern Law Review* 63, p. 159.

Groningen Growth and Development Centre (GGDC) Total Economy Database (January 2008) www.ggdc.net

Guardian.co.uk (2007) 'Cameron: UK Should Follow US Example', 5 June, (guardian.co.uk), , accessed 16 April 2008.

Gudgin, G. and Taylor, P. (1978) *Seats, Votes and the Spatial Organization of Elections* (London: Pion).

Hall, M, 'Unions Win Concessions from Ministers on Employment Law Agenda', EIROnline, UK0409102N, 06-09-2004, (http://www.eurofound.europa.eu/eiro/2004/09/inbrief/uk0409102n.htm), accessed 15 April 2008.

Hall, P. and Soskice, D. eds (2001) *Varieties of Capitalism: The Institutional Foundations of Comparative Advantage.* (New York: Oxford University Press).

Hall, S. (2007) 'Will Life After Blair Be Different?' *British Politics*, 2:1, pp. 118–22.

Harden, I. and Lewis, N. (1986) *The Noble Lie: The British Constitution and the Rule of Law* (London: Hutchinson).

Hargrove, E. and Owens, J. E. (2002) 'Leadership in Context,' *Politics & Policy*, 30:2, pp. 199–205.

Harlow, C. and Rawlings, R. (1997) *Law and Administration* (London: Butterworths).

Harmel, R. (2002), 'Party Organizational Change: Competing Explanations?' in K. Luther and F. Müller-Rommel, *Political Parties in the New Europe: Political and Analytical Changes* (Oxford: Oxford University Press), pp. 119–42.

Harmel, R. and Janda, K. (1994), 'An Integrated Theory of Party Goals and Party Change', *Journal of Theoretical Politics*, 6:3, pp. 259–87.

Harmel, R., Heo, U., Tan, A. and Janda, K. (1995), 'Performance, Leadership, Factions and Party Change: An Empirical Analysis', *West European Politics*, 18:1, pp. 1–33.

Harper, K. (2006) *NHS Reform: Getting Back on Track*, (London: King's Fund).

Harris Poll (21 August 2006) 'The *Financial Times*/Harris Poll', (http://www. harrisinteractive.com/news/allnewsbydate.asp?NewsID=1081), accessed on 29 May 2008.

Harris, P. and Lock, L. (2002), 'Sleaze or Clear blue Water: The evolution of corporate and pressure group representation at the major UK party conferences', *Journal of Public Affairs*, 2:3, pp. 136–51.

Hart, H. L. A. (1961) *The Concept of Law*, (Oxford: Clarendon Press).

Hay, C. (1999) *The Political Economy of New Labour: Labouring under False Pretences?* (Manchester, UK: Manchester University Press).

Hay, C. (2001) 'The Invocation of External Economic Constraint: A Genealogy of the Concept of Globalization in the Political Economy of the British Labour Party, 1973–2000,' *The European Legacy*. 6:2, pp. 233–49.

Hazell, R., (ed.) (1999) *Constitutional Futures: A History of the Next Ten Years* (Oxford: Oxford University Press).

Hazell, R., (ed.) (2006) *The English Question* (Manchester: Manchester University Press).

Heath, A., Jowell, R. and Curtice, J. (1994) *Labour's Last Chance: The 1992 Election and Beyond* (Aldershot: Dartmouth).

Heath, A., Jowell, R. and Curtice, J. (2001) *The Rise of New Labour* (Oxford University Press).

Heffernan, R. (2001) *New Labour and Thatcherism: Political Change in Britain* (Basingstoke: Palgrave Macmillan).

Heffernan, R. (2003) 'Prime Ministerial Predominance? Core Executive Politics in the UK', *British Journal of Politics and International Relations*, 5:3, pp. 347–72.

Heffernan, R. (2006a) 'The Prime Minister and the News Media: Political Communication as a Leadership Resource,' *Parliamentary Affairs* 59(4) 582–98.

Heffernan, R. (2006b) 'The Blair Style of Central Government', in P. Dunleavy, R. Heffernan, P. Cowley and C. Hay, eds, *Developments in British Politics 8*, (Basingstoke: Palgrave Macmillan).

Heffernan, R. and Webb, P. (2005) 'The British Prime Minister: More Than First Among Equals', in T. Poguntke and P. Webb (eds) (2005).

Hennessy P. (2000) *The Prime Minister: The Office and Its Holders Since 1945*, (London: Penguin).

Hennessy P. (2005) 'Rules and Servants of State: The Blair Style of Government 1997–2004' *Parliamentary Affairs* 58 (1) pp. 6–16.

Héritier, A. (2005) 'Managing Regulatory Developments in Rail: Compliance and Access Regulation in Germany and the UK' in D. Coen and A. Héritier (eds) *Refining Regulatory Regimes* (Cheltenham, Edward Elgar), pp. 120–44.

Hickson, K. (2008) 'Three of a Kind?' *The Parliamentary Monitor*, 9 April 2008.

Hill, A. and Whichelow, A. (1964) *What's Wrong with Parliament?* (Harmondsworth: Penguin).

Himmelfarb, G. (2008) *The Roads to Modernity* (London: Vintage) (Introduction by G. Brown).

Hindmoor, A. (2004) *New Labour at the Centre: Constructing Political Space* (Oxford: Oxford University Press).

HM Government (1975) *The Attack on Inflation*, Cmnd. 6151 (London: Her Majesty's Stationery Office).

HM Government (2001) *The House of Lords: Completing the Reform*, Cm. 5291 (London: The Stationary Office).

HM Government (2005) *Higher Standards, Better Schools for All*, Cm. 6677 (London: The Stationary Office).

HM Government (2006) *A New Deal for Welfare: Empowering People to Work*, Cm. 6730 (London: The Stationary Office).

HM Government (2007a) *The Governance of Britain*, London: HMSO, Cm. 7170.

HM Government (2007b) *The House of Lords: Reform*, Cm. 7027 (London: The Stationery Office).

HM Revenue and Customs (2006) *Child Tax Credit and Working Tax Credit: Take Up Rates 2003–04.*

HM Revenue and Customs (2007) *Child Tax Credit and Working Tax Credit: Statistics.*

HM Treasury (1998) *The Modernization of Britain's Tax System, Number Two: Work Incentives.*

HM Treasury (2001) *Productivity in the UK: Enterprise and the Productivity Challenge* (London: The Stationery Office).

HM Treasury (2002) *The Child and Working Tax Credits: The Modernization of Britain's Tax and Benefit System.*

HM Treasury (2004) *Skills in the Global Economy* (London: The Stationery Office).

HM Treasury (2006) *The Eddington Transport Study* (London: The Stationery Office).

HM Treasury (2007) *Public Expenditure Statistical Analyses 2007*, HM Treasury Website (http://www.hm-treasury.gov.uk/media/E/B/pesa07_complete.pdf).

Holden, R. (2002) *The Making of New Labour's European Policy* (Basingstoke: Palgrave Macmillan).

Hollis, C. (1949) *Can Parliament Survive?* (London: Hollis & Carter).

Hombach, B. (2000) *The Politics of the New Centre* (Oxford: Blackwell).

Hopkin, J. and Wincott, D. (2006) 'New Labour, Economic Reform and the European Social Model', *British Journal of Politics and International Relations* 8:1, pp. 50–68.

House of Commons (2008c) *Hansard*, 22 February, Column 1119W.

House of Commons Committee of Public Accounts (2007) *Update on PFI debt Refinancing and the PFI Equity Market*, House of Commons Website, (http://www.publications.parliament.uk/pa/cm200607/cmselect/cmpubacc/158/158.pdf).

House of Commons Committee of Public Accounts (2008) *Helping People from Workless Households into Work: Ninth Report of Session 2007–08* (London: The Stationery Office).

House of Commons Information Office (2006) *Women in the House of Commons* Factsheet M4.

House of Commons Public Accounts Committee (2008a) *Tax Credits and PAYE*, Eighth Report of Session 2007–08.

House of Commons Public Accounts Committee (2008b) *Sustainable Employment: Supporting People to Stay in Work and Advance*, Thirteenth Report, Session 2007–08.

House of Lords Select Committee on the Constitution 6th Report of Session 2006–07, 'Relations between the Executive, the Judiciary and Parliament' (26 July 2007).

Howorth, J. (2007) *Security and Defense Policy in the European Union* (Basingstoke: Palgrave Macmillan).

Hurst, G. (2006) *Charles Kennedy: A Tragic Flaw* (London: Politico's).

Hutton Inquiry (28 January 2004) 'Report of the Inquiry into the Circumstances Surrounding the Death of Dr David Kelly C.M.G.', (http://www.the-hutton-inquiry.org.uk/content/rulings.htm), accessed on 30 May 2008.

Hyde-Price, A. (2006) *European Security in the Twenty-first Century: The Challenge of Multipolarity* (London: Routledge).

Independent Inquiry Committee into the United Nations Oil-for-Food Programme (8 August 2005), 'Third Interim Report', (http://www.iic-offp.org/documents.htm), accessed on 29 May 2008.

Institute for Fiscal Studies (2007) 'Poverty and Inequality in the UK', Briefing Note 73, (London: IFS).

Ipsos MORI (2007a) 'The Most Important Issues Facing Britain Today', (http://www.ipsos-mori.com/polls/trends/issues.html), accessed on 12 February 2008.

Ipsos MORI (2007b) *Ten Years of Blair: How Did He Do?*, Slide pack available at (www.ipsos-mori.com), accessed on 10 June 2008.

Iraqi Perspectives Project (24 March 2006), Kevin M. Woods, with Michael R. Pease, Mark E. Stout, Williamson Murray, and James G. Lacey, 'Iraqi Perspectives Project: A View of Operation Iraqi Freedom from Saddam's Senior Leadership', (http://www.foreignaffairs.org/special/iraq/ipp.pdf), accessed on 29 May 2008.

Irvine, A. (2003) *Human Rights, Constitutional Law and the Development of the English Legal System* (Oxford: Hart Publishing).

ITV News (2007) *Gordon Brown backs President Bush*, 30 July 2007.

Jackson, G. and Deeg, R. (2006) 'How Many Varieties of Capitalism? Comparing the Comparative Institutional Analyses of Capitalist Diversity', Discussion Paper 06/2 Max Planck Institute for the Study of Societies.

James, S. (2007) 'Taming the Awkward State? Europeanisation and the Changing Face of UK EU Policy Making under Blair', paper presented at the British Politics Group 'Britain after Blair' Conference, Chicago, 29 August 2007.

James, S. (forthcoming) 'Taming the Awkward State? The Changing Face of European Policy Making under Blair', *Public Administration*.

Jeffery, C. (2007) 'The Unfinished Business of Devolution: Seven Open Questions' *Public Policy and Administration*, 22:1, pp. 92–108.

Jeffery, C. and Wincott, D. (2006) 'Devolution in the United Kingdom: Statehood and Citizenship in Transition' *Publius*, 36:2, pp. 3–18.

Jenkins, S. (1995) *Accountable to None: The Tory Nationalisation of Britain* (London: Hamish Hamilton).

Jenkins, R. (2002) *Churchill: A Biography* (London: Pan Macmillan).

Jenkins, S. (2006) *Thatcher and Sons: A Revolution in Three Acts* (London: Penguin).

Jennings, I. (1936) *Cabinet Government* (Cambridge: Cambridge University Press).

Jennings, I. (1939) *Parliament* (Cambridge: Cambridge University Press).

Jentleson, B. (2007) 'America's Global Role After Bush', *Survival*, 49, pp. 179–200.

Jessop, B. (2002) The *Future of the Capitalist State*, (Cambridge: Polity).

Johnston, R. and Pattie, C. (2006) *Putting Voters in their Place* (Oxford: Oxford University Press).

Johnston, R., Cowley, P., Pattie, C. and Stuart, M. (2002) 'Voting in the House or Wooing the Voters at Home: Labour MPs and the 2001 General Election Campaign', *Journal of Legislative Studies*, 8, pp. 9–22.

Jospin, L. (2002) *Je m'engage* (presidential programme), (www.psinfo.net).

Jowell R., Curtice, J. and Heath, A. (1994), *Labour's Last Chance? The 1992 Election and Beyond* (Aldershot: Dartmouth).

Kaiser versus the NHS' (15 January 2002) Special edition of the *British Medical Journal*.

Kampfner, J. (2003) *Blair's Wars* (London: The Free Press).

Kampfner, J. (2004) *Blair's Wars* (London: Simon & Schuster).

Kavanagh, D. and Seldon, A. (2000) *The Powers Behind the Prime Minister* (London: Harper Collins).

Kavanagh, D. and Butler, D. (2005) *The British General Election of 2005* (Basingstoke: Palgrave Macmillan).

Kearns, I. (2007) 'Special Relationship Needs More Space', Institute for Public Policy Research website 20 August, accessed 16 April 2008.

Keating, M. (1998) *The New Regionalism in Western Europe: Territorial Restructuring and Political Change* (Cheltenham: Edward Elgar).

Keating, M. (2005) *The Government of Scotland: Public Policy making after Devolution* (Edinburgh: Edinburgh University Press).

Kennedy-Pipe, C. and Vickers, R. (2007) '"Blowback" for Britain? Blair, Bush and the War in Iraq', *Review of International Studies*, 33, pp. 205–22.

Kettell, S. (2006) *Dirty Politics* (London: Zed Books).

King, A. (ed.) (1993) *Britain at the Polls 1992* (Chatham NJ: Chatham House).

King, A. (ed.) (1998) *New Labour Triumphs: Britain at the Polls* (Chatham NJ: Chatham House).

King, A. (2007) *The British Constitution*, (Oxford: Oxford University Press).

Kingdon, J. (1984) *Agendas, Alternatives and Public Policies*, (Boston: Little Brown).

Kirchheimer, O. (1966) 'The Transformation of the Western European Party Systems' in J. LaPalombara and M. Weiner, (eds) *Political Parties and Political Development* (Princeton, NJ: Princeton University Press).

Klingemann, H-D., Hofferbert, R. and Budge, I. (1994) *Parties, Policies and Democracy* (Boulder, CO: Westview).

Knapp, A. and Wright, V. (2001) *The Government and Politics of France* 4th edition (Oxford: Routledge).

Kramer, S. P. (2003) 'Blair's Britain after Iraq', *Foreign Affairs*, 82 (4), 90–104.

Labour Party (1997) *New Labour – Because Britain Deserves Better* (London: The Labour Party).

Labour Party (2001) *Ambitions for Britain* (London: Labour Party).

Labour Party (2005) *Britain Forward not Back* (London: Labour Party).

Laws, J. (1995), 'Law and Democracy', *Public Law*, 72, p. 92.

Lea, R. (2007) *The Chancellor's Record: An Audit of the Last 10 Years* (London: Centre for Policy Studies).

Leaman, A. (1998) 'Ending Equidistance' *Political Quarterly*, 69, pp. 160–9.

Lees-Marshment, J. (2001), *Political Marketing and British Political Parties* (Manchester: Manchester University Press).

Le Grand, J. (2007) *The Other Invisible Hand* (London: Princeton University Press).

Liaison Committee (1999–00) *Shifting the Balance: Select Committees and the Executive*, HC 300.

Liaison Committee (2001–02) *Evidence from the Prime Minister: First Special Report*, HC 984.

Liaison Committee (2002) *Oral Evidence Presented by Rt. Hon Tony Blair MP, Prime Minister on 16 July 2002*, HC1095, published 26 July 2002.

Lindbeck, A. (1997) 'Incentives and Social Norms in Household Behavior', *American Economic Review*, LXXXVII, pp. 370–7.

Lloyd, J. (2007) 'An Intellectual in Power', *Prospect*, July, 24–28.

Lovenduski, J. (1997) 'Gender Politics: A Breakthrough for Women?' P. Norris and T. Gavin, (eds) *Britain Votes 1997* (Oxford: Oxford University Press).

Lovenduski, J. (2005) *Feminizing Politics* (Cambridge: Polity).

Low Pay Commission (2007) *National Minimum Wage: Low Pay Commission Report* (London: The Stationery Office).

Ludlam, S. and Smith, M. (2000) New *Labour in Government* (London: Palgrave Macmillan).

Lyons, Sir M. (2007) *Lyons Inquiry into Local Government – Final Report. Place-Shaping: A Shared Ambition for the Future of Local Government* (London: The Stationery Office).

MacAllister, I., Fieldhouse, E. and Russell, A. (2002) 'Yellow Fever? The Political Geography of Liberal Support' *Political Geography*, 21, pp. 421–47.

Macmillan, H. (1972) *Pointing the Way: 1959–1961* (London: Macmillan).

MacShane, D. (2006) 'No, Ambassador', *Prospect,* January, pp. 64–5.

Mair, P. (2000) 'Partyless Democracy: Solving the Paradox of New Labour?', *New Left Review,* 2 (2), 21–35.

Maher, M. and Wise, M. (2005) 'Product Market Competition and Economic Performance in the United Kingdom', Economics Department Working Paper # 433, OECD.

Mandelson, P. and Liddle, R. (1996) *The Blair Revolution: Can Labour Deliver?* (London: Faber and Faber).

March, J. and Olsen, J. (1989), *Rediscovering Institutions: the Organizational Basis of Politics* (New York: Free Press).

Marshall, T. H. (1950) *Citizenship and Social Class.* (Cambridge: Cambridge University Press).

Martin, S. and Bovaird, T. (2005) *Meta-evaluation of the Local Government Modernisation Agenda: Progress Report on Service Improvement* (London: ODPM).

May, J. D. (1973), 'Opinion Structure of Political Parties: the Special Law of Curvilinear Disparity', *Political Studies,* 21:2, pp. 135–51.

McAllister, I. (2007) 'The Personalization of Politics', in R. J. Dalton and H. Klingemann eds, *Oxford Handbook of Political Behavior* (Oxford: Oxford University Press).

McAnulla, S. (2007) 'New Labour, Old Epistemology? Reflections on Political Science, New Institutionalism and the Blair Government', *Parliamentary Affairs,* 60.2, pp. 313–31.

McCausland, J. (2006) 'When You Come to a Fork in the Road, Take it – Defense Policy and the Special Relationship' in J. McCausland and D. Stuart (eds) *US-UK Relations at the Start of the 21st Century* (Carlisle PA: Strategic Studies Institute).

McGarvey, N. and Cairney, P. (2008) *Scottish Politics* (Basingstoke: Palgrave Macmillan).

McLean, I. and McMillan, A. (2007) 'Professor Dicey's Contradictions,' *Public Law,* Autumn, pp. 435–43.

McLean, I., Spirling, A. and Russell, M. (2003) 'None of the Above: The UK House of Commons Votes on Reforming the House of Lords, February 2003', *The Political Quarterly* 74, pp. 298–310.

Merkel, W. (2000) *The Third Ways of Social Democracy into the 21st Century,* FES, (http://www.fes.or.kr/Publications/pub/The%20Third%20Ways/Third%20Ways-Merkel.doc#_Toc484422195).

Metcalf, D. (2007) *Why Has the British Minimum Wage Had Little or No Impact on Employment?* (London: London School of Economics Centre for Economic Performance).

Meyer, C. (2005) *DC Confidential* (London: Weidenfeld and Nicolson).

Meyer, J. and Rowan, B. (1977) 'Institutionalized Organizations: Formal Structure as Myth and Ceremony,' *American Journal of Sociology,* 83:2, pp. 340–63.

Milken Institute, *Capital Access Index 2006* (Santa Monica: Miliken Institute) (http://www.milkeninstitute.org/pdf/CAI2006.pdf), accessed on 12 May 2008.

Mill, J. S. (1963–91) 'Considerations on Representative Government', in *The Collected Works of John Stuart Mill,* Vol. 19 (Toronto: University of Toronto Press).

Miller, D. and Dinan, W. (2000), 'The Rise of the PR Industry in Britain, 1979–98', *European Journal of Communication,* 15:1, 5–35.

Miller, W., Timpson, A. and Lessnoff, M. (1996) *Political Culture in Contemporary Britain* (Oxford: Clarendon).

Ministry of Justice (2007) *The Governance of Britain,* CM 7170.

Ministry of Justice (2008) *The Governance of Britain – Constitutional Renewal,* CM 7342 (London: The Stationery Office).

Mitchell, J. 'Scotland', in A. Geddes and J. Tonge, (eds) (2005) *Britain Decides: The UK General Election 2005* (Basingstoke: Palgrave Macmillan), pp. 98–111.

Mitchell, J. and Bradbury, J. (2004) 'Devolution: Comparative Development and Policy Roles', *Parliamentary Affairs*, 57, pp. 329–46.

Moloney, E. (2003) *A Secret History of the IRA* (London: Allen Lane).

Moran, M. (1999) *Governing the Healthcare State* (Manchester: Manchester University Press).

Moran, M. (2005) *Politics and Governance in the UK* (Basingstoke: Palgrave Macmillan).

Morgan, K. (1999) *The 'People's Peace': British History since 1945* (Oxford: Oxford Paperbacks).

MORI (2007) 'Blair vs. Thatcher: Public Perceptions Following Resignation Announcements', (available at www.ipsos-mori.com).

Morris, J. (1986) *Women Workers and the Sweated Trades: The Origins of Minimum Wage Legislation* (Aldershot: Gower).

Morris, J. (2007) 'From the Polls: Blair's Legacy', *Public Policy Research*, 14:2, pp. 151–3.

Mortimore, R. (1994) 'Great Britain', *Electoral Studies*, 13 (3), 341–3.

Mulgan, G. (1994), *Politics in the Antipolitical Age* (Cambridge: Polity).

Nairn, T. (2000) *After Britain, New Labour and the Return of Scotland* (London: Granta).

National Audit Office (2007) *Helping People from Workless Households into Work* (London: The Stationery Office).

Naughtie, J. (2001) *The Rivals, The Intimate Story of a Political Marriage* (London: Fourth Estate).

Naughtie, J (2004). *The Accidental American: Tony Blair and the Presidency* (New York: Public Affairs).

Neill, (Lord) P. (1998), *Report of the Committee on Standards in Public Life on the Funding of Political Parties in the UK* (London: Stationery Office, vol 1, Cm. 4057-1).

Newman, J. (2001), *Modernising Governance: New Labour, Policy and Society* (London: Sage).

Niblett, R. (2007) 'Choosing Between America and Europe: A New Context for British Foreign Policy', *International Affairs*, 83, pp. 627–41.

Nickell, S. (2003) 'Poverty and Worklessness in Britain', Royal Economic Society Presidential Address.

Nicol, D. (2001) *EC Membership and the Judicialization of British Politics* (Oxford: Oxford University Press).

Norris, P. and Lovenduski, J. (2004) 'Why Parties Fail to Learn: Electoral Defeat, Selective Perception and British Party Politics', *Party Politics*, 10:1, pp. 85–104.

Norton, P. (1975) *Dissension in the House of Commons, 1945–1974* (London: Macmillan).

Norton, P. (1980) *Dissension in the House of Commons, 1974–1979* (Oxford: Clarendon Press).

Norton, P. (2005) *Parliament in British Politics* (London: Palgrave Macmillan).

Norton, P. (2007) 'The Constitution', in A. Seldon (ed.) (2007).

OECD Tax Database (www.oecd.org/ctp/taxdatabase).

OECD (2002) *OECD Reviews of Regulatory Reform: United Kingdom*, (Paris: OECD).

OECD (2003) *From Red Tape to Smart Tape*, (Paris: OECD).

OECD (2005) *Economic Survey of the United Kingdom [OECD Observer Policy Brief]*. (Paris: OECD).

OECD (2007a) *OECD Economic Outlook No. 81 – Statistical Annex Tables*, OECD, (http://www.oecd.org/document/61/0,3343,en_2649_34113_2483901_1_1_1_1,00.html).

OECD (2007b) *Revenue Statistics for OECD Member Countries, 1965–2006* (Paris: OECD).

Ofcom (2008) *Initial Assessments of When to Adopt Self- or Co-Regulation: Consultation* (London, Office of Communications).

ONS (2007) 'First Release: Profitability of UK Companies, 1st Quarter 2007', (London: Office for National Statistics).

ONS (2008) *Social Trends 38* (London: Office for National Statistics).

ONS Office for National Statistics Series D7G7, (http://www.statistics.gov.uk/statbase/tsdintro.asp).

Oppermann, K. (2008a) *Prinzipale und Agenten in Zwei-Ebenen-Spielen: Die inner-staatlichen Restriktionen der Europapolitik Großbritanniens unter Tony Blair* (Wiesbaden: VS Verlag für Sozialwissenschaften).

Oppermann, K. (2008b) 'The Blair Government and Europe: The Policy of Containing the Salience of European Integration', *British Politics*, 3:2, pp. 156–82.

Owen, G. (2001) 'Industry', in A. Seldon (ed.) (2001).

Page, E.C. (1999) 'The Insider/Outsider Distinction: An Empirical Investigation', *The British Journal of Politics and International Relations* 1:2, pp. 205–214.

Pain, N. (2001) 'Inward Investment: Closing the Productivity Gap in the UK', *New Economy*, 8:3, pp. 151–6.

Paterson, W. and Sloam, J. (2006) 'Is the Left Alright? The SPD and the Renewal of European Social Democracy', *German Politics* 15:3, pp. 233–48.

Paton, C. (2006) *New Labour's State of Health: Political Economy, Public Policy and the NHS* (Aldershot: Ashgate).

Paton, C (2007), 'He Who Rides a Tiger Can Never Dismount: Six Myths About NHS Reform In England', *International Journal of Health Planning and Management*, 22(2), pp. 97–111.

Paton, C (2008), 'The NHS After Ten Yeas of New Labour: In Better Shape then New Labour after Ten Years of the NHS?', in Powell, M (ed.), *Modernising the Welfare State: The Blair Legacy* (Bristol: Policy Press).

Pearce, N. (2005) 'For "Liberal" Now Read "Anglo-Social"', *Parliamentary Brief*, 1 September 2005.

Perraton, J. and Clift, B. (2004) *Where are National Capitalisms Now?* (Basingstoke: Palgrave Macmillan).

Peston, R. (2006) *Brown's Britain* (London: Short Books).

Pharr, S. and Putnam, R. (2000) *Disaffected Democracies: What's Troubling the Trilateral Countries?* (Princeton, NJ: Princeton University Press).

Plant, R. (2008) 'Blair's Liberal Interventionism' in M. Beech and S. Lee (eds) *Ten Years of New Labour* (Basingstoke: Palgrave Macmillan).

Plows, A. (2008) 'Towards an Analysis of the "Success" of UK Green Protests', *British Politics*, 3:1, pp. 92–109.

Poguntke T. (2005) 'A Presidentializing Party State? The Federal Republic of Germany' in T. Poguntke and P. Webb (eds) (2005).

Poguntke, T. and Webb, P., (eds), (2005) *The Presidentialization of Politics: A Comparative Study of Modern Democracies* (Oxford: Oxford University Press).

Political Studies Association (2007) *Failing Politics? A Response to The Governance of Britain Green Paper* (Newcastle Upon Tyne, Political Studies Association).

Potter, S. (1970) *The Complete Upmanship* (London: Hart-Davis).

Powell, E. (1991) 'Parliamentary Sovereignty in the 1990s,' in P. Norton (ed.) *New Directions in British Politics* (Aldershot: Edward Elgar).

Powell, J. (2008) *Great Hatred, Little Room: Making Peace in Northern Ireland* (London: Bodley Head).

Powell, J. E. (1977) *Joseph Chamberlain* (London: Thames and Hudson).

Powell, M. (2002) 'The Hidden History of Social Citizenship', *Citizenship Studies*, VI, pp. 229–44.

Powell, W. W. and DiMaggio, P. J., (eds) (1991), *The New Institutionalism in Organizational Analysis* (Chicago, IL: University of Chicago Press).

Power Inquiry (2006) *Power to the People: An Independent Inquiry into Britain's Democracy* (London: Power Inquiry).

Prescott, J. (2008) *Prezza: My Story: Pulling No Punches* (London: Headline Review).

Program on Program for International Student Assessment (PISA), (http://pisacountry. acer.edu.au/), accessed on 20 August 2007.

PS (1999) *Reform Paper of the French Socialist Party: For a Fairer World* (Contribution to the Socialist International Congress), Socialist International Website (www. socialistinternational.org).

Public Broadcasting System (2001) Transcript of Interview with Gordon Brown.

Putnam, R. (2003) *Bowling Alone: The Collapse and Revival of American Community* (New York: Simon and Schuster).

Quinn, A. (2007) 'Gordon's Game', *Argentia* (newsletter of the BISA US Foreign Policy Working Group), 1, 2, p. 8.

Rallings, C. and Thrasher, M. (2000) British Electoral Facts 1832–1999 (Aldershot: Ashgate).

Rallings, C. and Thrasher, M. (2001) *Election 2001: The Official Results* (London: Electoral Commission).

Rallings, C. and Thrasher, M. (2005) Election 2005: *The Official Results* (London: Electoral Commission).

Rallings, C. and Thrasher, M. (2006) *Local Elections Handbook 2006* (Plymouth: LGC Elections Centre).

Rallings, C. and Thrasher, M. (2007) *Local Elections Handbook 2007* (Plymouth: LGC Elections Centre).

Rawlings, R. (2003) *Delineating Wales, Constitutional, Legal and Administrative Aspects of National Devolution* (Cardiff, University of Wales Press).

Rawnsley, A. (2001) *Servants of the People: The Inside Story of New Labour* (London: Penguin).

Rhodes, R. (2005) 'The Court Politics of the Blair Presidency', Department of the Senate Occasional Lecture, Canberra Australia, 27 June 2005.

Rhodes, R. and Bevir, M. (2003) *Interpreting British Governance* (London: Routledge).

Riddell, P. (1996) 'Introduction: Pressure Groups, Media and Government', in Social Market Foundation (ed.) *Pressure Group Politics in Modern Britain* (London: Social Market Foundation).

Riddell, P. (2000) *Parliament under Blair* (London: Politico's).

Riddell, P. (2004), *Hug Them Close* (London: Politico's).

Riddell, P. (2006) *The Unfulfilled Prime Minister: Tony Blair's Quest for a Legacy* (London: Politico's).

Riley, R. and Young, G. (2001) 'Does Welfare-to Work Policy Increase Employment? Evidence from the UK New Deal for Young People', National Institute for Economic and Social Research, Discussion Paper #183.

Roper, J. (2000) 'Keynote Article: Two Cheers for Mr. Blair? The Political Realities of European Defense Co-operation', *Journal of Common Market Studies*, 38 (Annual Review), pp. 7–23.

Rosenblatt, G. (2006) *A Year in the Life: From Member of Public to Member of Parliament* (London: Hansard Society).

Royal Commission on Reform of the House of Lords (Wakeham Commission) (2000) *A House for the Future*, Cm. 4534 (London: The Stationery Office).

Royal, S. (2007) *Désirs d'avenir*, Royal Candidacy Website, (www.desirsdavenir.org).

Runciman, D. (2006), *The Politics of Good Intentions* (Princeton: Princeton University Press).

Russell, A. (2005) 'The Liberal Democrat Campaign' *Parliamentary Affairs*, 58, pp. 743–56.

Russell, M. (2005), *Building New Labour: The Politics of Party Organisation* (Basingstoke: Palgrave Macmillan).

Russell, A. and Fieldhouse, E. (2005) *Neither Left nor Right? The Liberal Democrats and the Electorate* (Manchester: Manchester University Press).

Russell, A., Fieldhouse, E. and Cutts, D. (2007) 'De Facto Veto? The Parliamentary Liberal Democrats', *Political Quarterly*, 78, pp. 89–98.

Russell, M. and Scaria, M. (2007) 'The Policy Impact of Defeats in the House of Lords', paper presented to the Political Studies Association Conference (University of Bath).

Russell, M. and Sciara, M. (2006) 'Parliament: The House of Lords – A More Representative and Assertive Chamber?' in M. Rush and P. Giddings, (eds) *The Palgrave Review of British Politics 2005* (London: Palgrave Macmillan, 2006) pp. 122–36.

Sandbrook, D. (1997) *White Heat: A History of Britain in the Swinging Sixties* (London: Abacus).

Sanders, D. (2005) 'Popularity Function Forecasts for the 2005 UK General Election', *British Journal of Politics and International Relations*, 7:2, pp. 174–90.

Scarman, L. (1974) *English Law – the New Dimension* (London: Stevens & Sons).

Schafer, M. (2000) 'Issues in Assessing Psychological Characteristics at a Distance: Symposium Lessons and Future Research Directions', *Political Psychology*, 21, pp. 511–27.

Schmidt, V. (2002) *The Futures of European Capitalism* (New York: Oxford University Press).

Sefton, T. (2004) 'What We Want from the Welfare State', in A. Park, J. Curtice, K. Thomson, L. Jarvis and C. Bromley (eds) *British Social Attitudes: The 20th Report* (London: Sage).

Seldon, A., (ed.), (2001) *The Blair Effect*. (London: Little, Brown and Company).

Seldon, A (2005) *Blair* (New York: Free Press).

Seldon, A., (ed.) (2007) *Blair's Britain, 1997–2007*. (Cambridge, UK: Cambridge University Press).

Seldon, A. (2008) *Blair Unbound* (London: Simon and Schuster).

Seldon, A. and Snowden, P. (2005), 'The Barren Years: 1997–2005', in Ball and Seldon (2005).

Seldon, A. and Kavanagh, D., (eds) (2005) *The Blair Effect, 2001–05* (Cambridge: Cambridge University Press).

Select Committee on Health of the House of Commons (2006) *Inquiry into NHS Deficits* (London: The Stationery Office).

Self, A. and Zealey, L. (2007) *Social Trends No.37* (Houndmills: Palgrave Macmillan).

Seyd, P. and Whiteley, P. (1992) *Labour's Grass Roots: The Politics of Party Membership* (Oxford: Clarendon Press).

Seyd, P. and Whiteley, P. (2002) *New Labour's Grassroots: The Transformation of the Labour Party Membership* (Basingstoke: Palgrave Macmillan).

Shaw, E. (1994) *The Labour Party Since 1979: Crisis and Transformation* (London: Routledge).

Shaw, E. (2000) 'The Wilderness Years, 1979–1994', in B. Brivati and R. Heffernan (eds), *The Labour Party: A Centenary History* (Basingstoke: Palgrave Macmillan).

Shaw, E. (2007) *Losing Labour's Soul? New Labour and the Blair Government 1997–2007* (London: Routledge).

Shaw, E. (2008) 'New Labour and the Unions: the Death of Tigmoo?' in M. Beech and S. Lee (eds) *Ten Years of New Labour* (Basingstoke: Palgrave Macmillan), pp. 120–35.

Short, C. (2004) *New Labour: An Honourable Deception?* (London: Simon & Schuster).

Simms, B. (2001) *Unfinest Hour: Britain and the Destruction of Bosnia* (London: Allen Lane).

Slaughter, A-M., Sweet, A. and Weiler, J. (2000) *The European Court and National Courts – Doctrine and Jurisprudence: Legal Change in its Social Context* (Oxford: Hart Publishing).

Sloam, J. (2004) *The European Policy of the German Social Democrats: Interpreting a Changing World* (Basingstoke: Palgrave Macmillan).

Smith, B. (1964) *Regionalism in England* (London: Acton Society Trust).

Smith, D. (2005a) 'The Treasury and Economic Policy' in Seldon and Kavanagh (2005).

Smith, D. (2005b) 'The Treasury and Economic Policy', in A. Seldon and D. Kavanagh, (eds) (2005) *The Blair Effect* (Cambridge: Cambridge University Press), pp. 159–83.

Smith, D. (2005c) *Labour's Record under a Cloud*, www.economics.com, 3 April 2005.

Smith, M. (2007) 'Tony Blair: The First Prime Minister of the Global Era', *British Politics*, 2:3, pp. 420–7.

Smith, M. J. (2003) 'The Core Executive and the Modernisation of Central Government', in P. Dunleavy, A. Gamble, R. Heffernan and G. Peele, (eds) *Developements in British Politics 7* (Basingstoke: Palgrave Macmillan).

Smookler, J. (2006) 'Making a Difference? The Effectiveness of Pre-Legislative Scrutiny', *Parliamentary Affairs*, 59, pp. 522–35.

SPD (2002) *Erneuerung und Zusammenhalt – Wir in Deutschland* (election manifesto), (http://juni2002.spd-parteitag.de/servlet/PB/show/1076197/spd-regierungsprogramm_1.pdf).

SPD (2005) *Vertrauen in Deutschland*, Election Manifesto, (http://kampagne.spd.de/040705_Wahlmanifest.pdf).

SPD (2007) *Sozial Demokratie im 21: Jahrhundert*, SPD Website, (http://programmdebatte.spd.de/servlet/PB/show/1700699/bremer_entwurf_navigierbar.pdf).

Stelzer, I. (2007) 'Now We Know: Brown is a European, not an Atlanticist', *The Spectator*, 11 August 2007.

Stephens, P. (2001) 'The Treasury Under Labour,' in A. Seldon (ed.) (2001).

Stephens, P. (2004) *Blair: The Price of Leadership* (London: Politico's).

Stoker, G. (2006) *Why Politics Matters* (Basingstoke: Palgrave Macmillan).

Stothard, P. (2003) *Thirty Days: An Inside Account of Tony Blair at War* (New York: Harper Collins).

Straw, J. (2007) *The Governance of Britain*, available at (http://www.pm.gov.uk/files/pdf/TGoB_print.pdf), accessed on 14 April 2008.

Streeck, W. and Trampusch, C. (2005) 'Economic Reform and the Political Economy of the German Welfare State', *German Politics*, 14:2, pp. 174–95.

Studlar, D. (2007) 'From Collectivist Consensus to 21st Century Neoliberalism: Orders and Eras in Postwar Britain,' *The Forum* 5:3, Article 3. Available at (http://www.bepress.com/forum/vol5/iss3/art3).

Taylor-Gooby, P (2005) 'The Work-Centered Welfare State', in A. Park, J. Curtice, K. Thomson, L. Jarvis and C. Bromley (eds) *British Social Attitudes: The 21st Report* (London: Sage).

Tetlock, P. E. and Belkin, A. (1996) 'Counterfactual Thought Experiments in World Politics: Logical, Methodological, and Psychological Perspectives', in P. E. Tetlock and A. Belkin, (eds) *Counterfactual Thought Experiments in World Politics* (Princeton, NJ: Princeton University Press), pp. 1–38.

Theakston, K. (2002) 'Political Skills and Context In Prime Ministerial Leadership in Britain', *Politics and Policy*, 30:2, pp. 283–323.

Theakston K. (2007) 'What Makes for an Effective British Prime Minister?' *Quaderni di scienza politica*, 14. pp. 227–49.

Theakston, K. and Gill, M. (2006) 'Rating 20th Century British Prime Ministers', *British Journal of Politics and International Relations*, 8:2, pp. 193–213.

Tiernan, A. (2007) *Power Without Responsibility* (Sydney: UNSW Press).

Tonge, J. (2006) *Northern Ireland* (Cambridge: Polity).

Total Economy Database, http://www.ggdc.net, accessed March 2008.

Toynbee, P. and Walker, D. (2005) *Better or Worse? Has Labour Delivered?* (London: Bloomsbury).

Trade Association Forum (2008) 'The Voices of British Business: Ensuring Representation for Enterprise at the Heart of Government' (London: Trade Association Forum).

Travers, T. (2007) 'Memories of Tony', *Local Government Chronicle*, 26 April, p. 20.

Trench, A. (2004) 'The More Things Change the More They Stay the Same: Intergovernmental Relations Four Years On' in A. Trench (ed.) *Has Devolution Made a Difference? The State of the Nations 2004* (Thorverton: Imprint Academic).

Trench, A, (ed.) (2007) *Devolution and Power in the United Kingdom* (Manchester: Manchester University Press).

Treverton, G. (1990) 'Britain's Role in the 1990s: An American View', *International Affairs*, 72, 703–10.

Tsebelis, G. and Money, J. (1997) *Bicameralism* (Cambridge: Cambridge University Press).

Tuohy, C. (1999) *Accidental Logics,* (New York: Oxford University Press).

Turnbull, A. (2007) 'The Machinery of Government: Intelligent Design or Brownian Motion?', *Briefing Paper*, Booz Allen Hamilton, November 2007.

United Nations Security Council Resolution 707 (15 August 1991), (http://www.un.org/Docs/scres/1991/scres91.htm), accessed on 29 May 2008.

United Nations Security Council Resolution 1194 (9 September 1998), (http://www.un.org/Docs/scres/1998/scres98.htm), accessed on 22 October 2008.

United Nations Security Council Resolution 1205 (5 November 1998), (http://www.un.org/Docs/scres/1998/scres98.htm), accessed on 22 October 2008.

United Nations Security Council Resolution 1441 (8 November 2002), (http://www.un.org/Docs/scres/2002/sc2002.htm), accessed on 29 May 2008.

Vincent-Jones, P. (1994) 'The Limits of Near Contractual Governance: Local Authority Internal Trading Under CCT', *Journal of Law and Society* 21, pp. 214–37.

Wadsworth, J. (2007) *Did the Minimum Wage Change Consumption Patterns?* (London: Low Pay Commission).

Walt, S. (2005) *Taming American Power: The Global Response to US Primacy* (New York: Norton).

Waltman, J. (2008) *Minimum Wage Policy in Great Britain and the United States* (New York: Algora).

Waltz, K. N. (1979) *Theory of International Politics,* (New York: McGraw-Hill).

Wanless, D. (2002) *Securing our Future Health* (London: HM Treasury).

Wanless, D. (2007) *Our Future Health Secured?* (London: King's Fund).

Watson, M. and Hay, C. (2003) 'The Discourse Of Globalisation and the Logic of No Alternative: Rendering the Contingent Necessary in the Political Economy of New Labour', *Policy and Politics*, 31:3, pp. 289–305.

Webb, P. (2002), 'Political Parties: Adapting to the Electoral Market', P. Dunleavy, R. Heffernan, I. Holiday and G. Peele (eds), *Developments in British Politics 6* (Basingstoke: Palgrave Macmillan), pp. 151–68.

Webb, P. and Fisher, J. (2003), 'Professionalism and the Milbank Tendency: The Political Sociology of New Labour Employees', *Politics*, 23, pp. 10–20.

Weller, P. (2003) 'Cabinet Government: An Elusive Ideal' *Public Administration*, 81:4, pp. 701–22.

Wheatcroft, G. (2005) *The Strange Death of Tory England* (Harmondsworth: Penguin).

Wheatcroft, G. (2007) *Yo, Blair! Tony Blair's Disastrous Premiership* (London: Politico's).

Whitaker, R. (2006) 'Ping-Pong and Policy Influence: Relations between the Lords and Commons, 2005–06', *Parliamentary Affairs*, 59, pp. 536–45.

Whiteley, P. and Seyd, P. (2002), *High Intensity Participation: The Dynamics of Party Activism in Britain* (Ann Arbor: University of Michigan Press).

Whiteley, P., Seyd, P. and Billinghurst, A. (2006) *Third Force Politics: Liberal Democrats at the Grassroots* (Oxford: Oxford University Press).

Whiteley, P., Seyd, P. and Richardson, J. (1994) *True Blues: The Politics of Conservative Party Membership* (Oxford: Oxford University Press).

Whiteley, P., Stewart, M. C., Sanders, D. and Clarke, H. D. (2005) 'The Issue Agenda and Voting in 2005', in P. Norris and C. Wlezien (eds), *Britain Votes 2005* (Oxford: Oxford University Press).

Whitman, R. (2005) 'No and After: Options for Europe', *International Affairs*, 81:4, pp. 673–87.

Wiliams, H. (1998) *Guilty Men: Conservative Government, 1992–97* (London: Aurum Press).

Wilson, D. and Game, C. (2006) *Local Government in the United Kingdom*, 4th edition (Basingstoke: Palgrave Macmillan).

Wilson, F. (1994), 'The Sources of Party Change: The Social Democratic Parties of Britain, France, Germany, and Spain', in K. Lawson (ed.), *How Political Parties Work. Perspective from Within*, (London: Praeger), pp. 263–84.

Wilson, G. (2007) 'A Blair Era? The Political Order of Modern Britain', *The Forum* 5:3, Article 2 available at: http://www.bepress.com/forum/vol5/iss3/art2.

Wlezien, C. (2005) 'On the Salience of Political Issues: The Problem with "Most Important Problem"', *Electoral Studies*, 24:4, pp. 555–79.

Woodward, B. (2004) *Plan of Attack* (New York: Simon and Schuster).

Worcester, R. and Mortimore, R. (1999) *Explaining Labour's Landslide* (London: Politico's).

YouGov/*Daily Telegraph* (2007a) *Ten Years of Tony Blair survey*, 30 April.

YouGov/*Daily Telegraph* (2007b) *Survey on Labour leadership*, 3 May.

Young, H. (1989) *One of Us* (Basingstoke: Macmillan).

Newspapers

'Anglo-American Attitudes', *The Economist*, 29 March 2008, pp. 35–7.

'Blair: The Poll', *The Observer*, 8 April 2007, (http://www.guardian.co.uk/politics/2007/apr/08/tonyblair.labour3), accessed on 3 April 2008.

'Chirac lashes out at "new Europe"', CNN, 18 February 2003, (http://www.cnn.com/2003/WORLD/europe/02/18/sprj.irq.chirac/), accessed on 29 May 2008.

'Eurohoneymoon', *The Economist*, 14 June1997, pp. 27–8.

'Fighting Low Pay: Has Britain's Minimum Wage Made a Maximum Difference?' *The Observer*, 20 November 2005.

'Help or Hindrance?' *The Economist*, 7 April 2005.

'On Hypochondria,' *The Economist*, 8 April 2007.

'Pressure Groups Could Exploit Party Funding Limits, Warns Straw', *The Guardian*, 5 September 2006, (http://www.guardian.co.uk/politics/2006/sep/05/partyfunding.uk). Accessed 29 June 2007.

'Tony Blair: "I wanted war – it was the right thing to do"', Times Online, 17 November 2007, (http://www.timesonline.co.uk/tol/news/politics/the_blair_years/article2886547.ece). Accessed on 11 December 2007.

'Top Exporters,' *The Economist*, 26 April 2008.

'The Cameron Interview', *The Observer*, 18 December 2005.

Baldwin, T. and Charter, D. (2003) 'Cabinet united over Iraq war, Blair insists', *The Times*, January 9, p. 14.

Branigan, T. (2006) 'Intervention in Iraq "pretty much of a disaster" admits Blair, as minister calls it his "big mistake"', *The Guardian*, 18 November 2006, p. 7.

Brittan, S. (2008) 'Pressure on Living Standards', *Financial Times*, 29 February, p. 9.

Clark, D. (2001) 'Tell Gordon to Stop Playing Games', *The Guardian*, 12 June 2001.

Fidler, S. (2007) 'Run out of Town: How the British Army lost Basra', *The Financial Times*, 21 August, p. 9.

Garton Ash, T. (2007) 'Like It or Loath It' (interview with Blair), *The Guardian*, 26 April 2007.

Hitchens, C. (2007) 'A Friend In Need', *The Observer*, 8 April 2007.

Hoge, W. (2003) 'Blair Doubted Iraq had Arms, Ex-Aide Says', *New York Times*, 6 October.

Hoggart, S. (2007) 'From Stalin to Mr. Bean, in Just a Few Weeks', *The Guardian*, 29 November 2007.

Hutton, W. (2007) 'The Private Man I Knew Who Drove the Public Revolution', *The Observer*, 13 May 2007.

Kaletsky, A. (2007) 'Four Ways for Britain to Shape a Better World', *The Times*, 1 February 2007.

Kampfner, J. (2007) 'Stitch-up' (interview with David Manning), *New Statesman*, 13 September 2007.

Letwin, O. (2007) 'Cameron raises his standard in the battle of ideas', *The Times*, 8 May 2007.

Mahmoud, M., O'Kane, M. and Black, I. (2007) 'UK has left behind murder and chaos, says Basra police chief', *The Guardian*, 17 December, p. 1.

Miliband, D. (2007) 'Waking up to the New World Order', *New Statesman*, 19 July.

Mulholland, H. (2008) 'Labour's funding crisis', *The Guardian*, 29 May 2008.

Perkins, A. (1999) 'Women: So Far, So What?' *The Guardian*, 29 April 1999.

Preston, P. (2007) 'Let's Just Suppose', *The Guardian*, 7 May 2007, (http:// politics. guardian.co.uk/iraq/comment/0,,2073939,00.html.), accessed 19 July 2007.

Prince, R. (2007) 'No mercy for Ming' *The New Statesman* 16 August 2007.

Rawnsley, A. (2007) 'Gordon and George Spend Their First Night Together', *The Observer*, 29 July 2007.

Rees-Mogg, W. (2006) 'How the US Fired Jack Straw', *The Times*, 7 August 2006.

Richards, S. (2005) 'The Truth about Blair's Downing Street', *The Independent*, 2 September, p.31.

Rycroft, M. (2005) Memorandum from Matthew Rycroft to Sir David Manning, Iraq: Prime Minister's Meeting, 6/23/2002, Times Online, (http://www.timesonline.co.U.K./ newspaper/0,,176-1593607,00.html), accessed 2 May 2005.

Schröder, G. (2003) 'Modernise or Die', *The Guardian*, 8 July, (http://www.guardian. co.uk/comment/story/0,3604,993464,00.html).

Travis, A. (2005) 'Don't Try to Push Us Around, Lord Chief Justice Tells Labour', *The Guardian*, 12 October 2005.

Wall, S. (2006) 'Unhitch Us', *New Statesman*, 31 July.

Speeches

Blair, T. (1995) 'The Rights We Enjoy Reflect the Duties We Owe', *The Spectator Lecture* (22 March 2005), London.

Blair, T. (1997a) Speech to the Parliamentary Labour Party (London: Church House).

Blair, T. (10 October 1997b) Speech at the Council of Europe Summit, available at (http://www.number-10.gov.uk/output/Page1062.asp), accessed on 14 April 2008.

Blair, T. (24 April 1999a) 'Doctrine of the International Community', (http://www.number-10.gov.uk/output/Page1297.asp), accessed on 29 May 2008.

Blair, T. (1999b) *Making the case for Britain in Europe*, Speech by the Prime Minister at the London Business School, 27 July 1999, (http://www.bmdf.co.uk/blaireurope.pdf), accessed on 15 January 2007.

Blair, T. (1999c) Speech to Labour Party Conference, October.

Blair, T. (30 June 2000) 'Value and Community', Speech delivered at Tübingen University, Germany.

Blair, T. (2 October 2001) 'Blair: Surrender Terrorist or Surrender Power', (http://archives.cnn.com/2001/WORLD/europe/10/02/ret.blair.address/), accessed on 29 May 2008.

Blair, T. (17 July 2003) Transcript of Blair's Speech to Congress, available at (http://www.cnn.com/2003/US/07/17/blair.transcript/), accessed 30 May 2008.

Blair, T. (2007) 'Reflections on 21st Century Security,' Speech delivered on 12 January 2007.

Bush, G. W. (1 June 2002) 'President Bush Delivers Graduation Speech at West Point', (http://www.whitehouse.gov/news/releases/2002/06/20020601-3.html), accessed on 29 May 2008.

Clinton, H. R. (10 October 2002) 'Floor Speech of Senator Hillary Rodham Clinton on S.J. Res. 45', (http://clinton.senate.gov/speeches/iraq_101002.html), accessed on 29 May 2008.

Cook, R. (12 May 1997) 'Speech on the Government's Ethical Foreign Policy', (http://www.guardian.co.uk/world/1997/may/12/indonesia.ethicalforeignpolicy), accessed on 29 May 2008.

Falconer, Lord (2006) Speech to the ESRC Devolution and Constitutional Change programme final conference, London, 10 March 2006.

Index